More praise fo
THE CHILE PR(

"*The Chile Project* is an eye-opener. I lived through the
Chicago end of the story, but Sebastian Edwards illuminates
the whole episode. I knew all the actors but didn't know the play
until I read the book. It is an excellent book."

—JAMES J. HECKMAN, Nobel Prize–
winning economist

"*The Chile Project* is a gripping account by a fine writer and
economist of how economists and their ideas have influenced,
or tried to influence, political and economic arrangements in Chile
starting in the early 1970s, continuing until today. Tensions between
liberalism and authority, and between equalities and efficiencies,
run through the story. I couldn't put this book down.
The story fascinates and bothers me."

—THOMAS J. SARGENT, Nobel Prize–
winning economist

"An excellent book. . . . This is the only book on this topic where
I feel I am finally getting to the bottom of what happened. . . . Strongly
recommended, one of the must-reads of the year."

—TYLER COWEN, *Marginal Revolution*

"[Edwards] is one of those rare economists who can explain
economic policy in simple and understandable language.
He is a good writer and has an eye for a telling anecdote. . . . *The Chile
Project* offers a cautionary tale for policymakers of all political
and ideological stripes about the perils of unintended consequences."

—BRUCE CALDWELL, *Literary Review*

"[An] absorbing, mystifying tale of how neoliberal economics took
root in the Southern Hemisphere only to be uprooted."

—MICHAEL M. ROSEN, *National Review*

"Meticulous. . . . Marked by Edwards's firm grasp of regional
politics and lucid explanations of economic theory,
this is a valuable primer on a complex subject."

—*Publishers Weekly*

THE CHILE PROJECT

The Chile Project

THE STORY OF THE CHICAGO BOYS AND
THE DOWNFALL OF NEOLIBERALISM

SEBASTIAN EDWARDS

With a new preface by the author

PRINCETON UNIVERSITY PRESS

PRINCETON & OXFORD

Published by Princeton University Press
41 William Street, Princeton, New Jersey 08540
99 Banbury Road, Oxford OX2 6JX

press.princeton.edu

GPSR Authorized Representative: Easy Access System Europe - Mustamäe tee 50,
10621 Tallinn, Estonia, gpsr.requests@easproject.com

All Rights Reserved

First published in 2023
First paperback edition, with a new preface by the author, 2025
Paperback ISBN 978-0-691-24937-7
ISBN (e-book): 978-0-691-27078-4
LCCN: 2024951284

British Library Cataloging-in-Publication Data is available

Editorial: Joe Jackson, Josh Drake, Whitney Rauenhorst
Jacket/Cover Design: Karl Spurzem
Production: Erin Suydam
Publicity: James Schneider, Kate Farquhar-Thomson
Copyeditor: Brian Bendelin

Jacket/Cover images: (*top*) Courtesy of Carlos Massad; (*bottom*) Brastock /
Shutterstock

THIS book has been composed in Arno Pro

This book is for
Alejandra Cox,
Adrian Wainwright,
and
Al Harberger

CONTENTS

ILLUSTRATIONS

TABLES

TABLES

TIMELINE

August 1938. The Colloque Lippmann is inaugurated in Paris. A group of intellectuals meet to discuss the principles of what will become neoliberalism.

July 1946. Milton Friedman joins the Department of Economics at the University of Chicago.

April 1947. The first meeting of the Mont Pèlerin Society takes place in Vaud, Switzerland. Friedrich von Hayek is appointed the first president of the society.

June 27, 1955. University of Chicago professors Earl Hamilton, Arnold "Al" Harberger, Simon Rottenberg, and Theodore Schultz travel to Chile to negotiate an agreement with the Pontificia Universidad Católica de Chile (Pontifical Catholic University of Chile, commonly known as Católica).

April 1956. The official agreement between the University of Chicago and Católica is signed.

September 1956. The first group of Chilean students arrives in Chicago to study economics under the agreement.

June 1958. The first Chilean graduates of the University of Chicago, known as the Chicago Boys, join Católica as full-time economics faculty.

September 1964. Eduardo Frei Montalva of the Partido Demócrata Cristiano (Christian Democratic Party) is elected president of Chile. The economic program draws on the US Alliance for Progress, and agrarian reform is a key component.

November 1969. The Chicago Boys draft an economic program for Jorge Alessandri's presidential campaign. The candidate says, "Take these crazy guys away!"

November 3, 1970. Salvador Allende is inaugurated as president of Chile.

December 1970. Some Chicago Boys leave Chile and take positions in international organizations.

March 1973. Eleven of the Chicago Boys begin working on an economic program for the post-Allende period. The report is known as El Ladrillo (The Brick).

September 11, 1973. Armed forces led by the commander in chief of the Chilean Army, General Augusto Pinochet, stage a coup d'état and depose President Salvador Allende. After resisting the insurgents, Allende commits suicide at the Palacio de La Moneda.

July 11, 1974. Jorge Cauas, an "honorary" Chicago Boy, is the first civilian to hold the post of Chilean minister of finance during Pinochet's dictatorship.

March 1975. Milton Friedman travels to Chile and on March 21 meets for an hour with General Pinochet. Friedman recommends "shock treatment" for the economy.

April 12, 1975. The Plan de Recuperación Económica (Plan for Economic Recovery) is announced, following Friedman's anti-inflationary recommendations. Shock treatment starts.

October 1976. Milton Friedman is awarded the Nobel Prize in Economics.

December 31, 1976. Chicago Boy Sergio de Castro replaces Jorge Cauas as Chilean minister of finance.

1978. Chile's gross domestic product surpasses its previous peak (in 1971).

June 1979. Chile fixes the peso to the US dollar as a means of reducing inflation to international levels.

September 11, 1979. Pinochet gives a speech announcing a new social program called the Siete Modernizaciones (Seven Modernizations), and a Chilean neoliberal model is born.

October 1979. Theodore Schultz, a signatory of the University of Chicago–Católica agreement, is awarded the Nobel Prize in Economics.

September 11, 1980. A new constitution drafted by the Comisión Constitucional (Constitutional Commission) appointed by the military is approved in referendum.

November 1981. The Mont Pèlerin Society holds a regional meeting in Viña del Mar, Chile. Milton Friedman makes his second visit to Chile.

April 1982. Chicago Boy Sergio de la Cuadra replaces Sergio de Castro as Chilean minister of finance.

June 14, 1982. The peso is devalued, and Chile suffers the worst currency and banking crisis in its history.

August 30, 1982. Chicago Boy Rolf Lüders replaces Sergio de la Cuadra as Chilean minister of finance.

February 1983. Mont Pèlerin Society member Carlos Cáceres, an economist, replaces Rolf Lüders as Chilean minister of finance.

April 1984. Luis Escobar Cerda, the former chair of the Department of Economics at the Universidad de Chile (University of Chile), and a rival of the Chicago Boys, is appointed Chilean minister of finance.

1984. Al Harberger becomes a professor of economics at the University of California–Los Angeles.

February 12, 1985. Hernán Büchi, an honorary Chicago Boy, replaces Luis Escobar Cerda as Chilean minister of finance, with a focus on growth, rather than inflation, as a priority.

October 5, 1988. A referendum is proposed to decide the continuity of the dictatorship. The "no" option wins. Presidential elections are scheduled for late 1989.

October 1989. The junta passes a law granting independence to the Banco Central de Chile (Central Bank of Chile), a novel idea in Latin America.

December 14, 1989. Patricio Aylwin of the Christian Democratic Party is elected Chilean president over Hernán Büchi. Aylwin maintains (most of) the Chicago Boys' policies.

February 8, 1991. The Comisión Nacional de Verdad y Reconciliación (National Truth and Reconciliation Commission) releases its report, which documents in detail more than two thousand cases of violations of human rights, including assassination, torture, and imprisonment.

June 1992. The Brick is officially published by the Centro de Estudios Públicos (Center of Public Studies), almost twenty years after it was first presented by the Chicago Boys to a senior officer of the Chilean Navy.

October 1992. Gary Becker is awarded the Nobel Prize in Economics.

December 11, 1993. Eduardo Frei Ruiz-Tagle of the Christian Democratic Party is elected Chilean president over Arturo Alessandri Besa. José Piñera wins 6 percent of the vote.

June 1998. Milton Friedman and his wife, Rose, publish their memoirs, *Two Lucky People.* A full chapter and a lengthy appendix are dedicated to Friedman's relationship with Chile and Pinochet.

September 1998. Capital controls are eliminated. Chile joins the small group of countries with full international capital mobility.

September 1999. A freely floating exchange rate system is adopted in Chile.

January 16, 2000. Socialist Ricardo Lagos is elected Chilean president over Joaquín Lavín, a Chicago Boy. Lagos is the first socialist to make it to the presidency since Salvador Allende in 1970.

2001. Fiscal rule starts, resulting in an automatic countercyclical fiscal policy.

2002. Chile becomes the Latin American country with the highest income per capita.

August 16, 2005. Constitutional reform brings major amendments that eliminate many (but not all) of the authoritarian enclaves from the 1980 Pinochet constitution.

January 15, 2006. Socialist Michelle Bachelet is elected Chilean president over Sebastián Piñera.

2008. The Consejo Asesor Presidencial Para la Reforma Previsional (Presidential Advisory Council for Pension Reform) releases its report. The private pensions system is supplemented by a public "solidarity-based pillar."

January 17, 2010. Sebastián Piñera, a conservative economist who studied at Harvard University and is close to the Chicago Boys, is elected Chilean president over Eduardo Frei Ruiz-Tagle, bringing about the end of the Concertación governments.

May 2011. Massive student demonstrations begin. Student activists will become members of the Congreso Nacional de Chile (National Congress of Chile) and government in the coming years.

December 15, 2013. Socialist Michelle Bachelet is elected Chilean president for the second time, with the support of the Partido Comunista de Chile (Communist Party of Chile).

2013. For the first time, the number of those living below the poverty line drops below 10 percent.

June 2017. The United Nations Development Programme releases the report *Desiguales: Orígenes, cambios y desafíos de la brecha social en Chile* (Unequal: Origins, changes and challenges in Chile's social divide). Its authors argue that inequality in Chile is multidimensional and rooted in racism, segregation, and classism.

December 17, 2017. The Center-Right economist Sebastián Piñera is elected Chilean president for the second time. Second- and third-generation Chicago Boys are appointed to the cabinet.

October 18, 2019. The Chilean "revolt" erupts. Several metro stations are set on fire, and there is looting of supermarkets, office buildings, pharmacies, and banks. During the weeks that follow, massive demonstrations take place.

November 15, 2019. Most traditional political parties reach an agreement that calls for the election of a Constitutional Convention to write a new constitution. The Communist Party and most of the Far-Left parties do not participate in the accord.

December 19, 2021. Gabriel Boric, a thirty-five-year-old former student activist and a member of the leftist coalition Apruebo Dignidad (Approval and Dignity), is elected Chilean president. It is the beginning of the end of neoliberalism in Chile.

July 4, 2022. The Constitutional Convention finishes its work. The proposed text is feminist in nature and provides the longest list of social rights of any charter in the world.

September 4, 2022. A referendum is held to determine if the new constitution will be adopted. The referendum is won by the *rechazo* (rejection) option by 62 percent, versus 38 percent for the *apruebo* (approval) option. The results are considered to be a "political earthquake."

September 7, 2022. Political forces of all persuasions begin negotiations for putting in place a new constitutional process. There is (almost) universal agreement that Chile needs a new constitutional charter. Many argue that it should be adopted before September 11, 2023, the fiftieth anniversary of the coup d'état and President Salvador Allende's death.

DRAMATIS PERSONAE

The University of Chicago Professors

Gary Becker. Winner of the Nobel Prize in Economics, 1992. The French philosopher Michel Foucault called him the most prominent representative of American neoliberalism.

Milton Friedman. Winner of the Nobel Prize in Economics in 1976 and one of the most influential economists of the twentieth century. A supporter of free markets and deep reforms, he suggested a "shock treatment" in Chile.

Arnold Harberger. Known as the father of the Chicago Boys. He visited Chile for the first time in 1955. He was considered more pragmatic and less doctrinaire than Gary Becker or Milton Friedman.

Theodore Schultz. Winner of the Nobel Prize in Economics, 1979. He led the team of University of Chicago faculty that initiated the Chile Project in 1955, and was considered an eminence in agricultural economics.

The Chicago Boys

Pablo Baraona. Agricultural economist. He served as a governor of the Banco Central de Chile (Central Bank of Chile) and as minister of economics during the dictatorship of Augusto Pinochet.

Sergio de Castro. Undisputed leader of the group, he arrived in Chicago as a student in 1956. He later became dean of the faculty of economics at the Pontificia Universidad Católica de Chile (Pontifical Catholic University of Chile, commonly known as Católica), and served as minister of economics and finance during the Pinochet dictatorship.

Sergio de la Cuadra. A student of Harry Johnson at the University of Chicago who later became president of the Central Bank and minister of finance during the Pinochet dictatorship.

Ernesto Fontaine. Senior Chicago Boy who trained hundreds of students at the Católica. He did not have an official position during the Pinochet dictatorship.

Miguel Kast. Minister of planning during the Pinochet dictatorship, and one of the great advocates of using the market system to allocate social services. He championed antipoverty measures and targeted social programs.

Rolf Lüders. A student of Milton Friedman. He later became minister of economics and finance during the Pinochet dictatorship, and an upper executive in the BHC Group, a highly diversified conglomerate.

Emilio Sanfuentes. Liaison between the Chicago Boys and the Chilean Navy before the coup d'état. He was one of the authors of the Chicago Boys' blueprint for market-oriented reform, a document colloquially known as El Ladrillo (The Brick).

The "Honorary" Chicago Boys

Hernán Büchi. Columbia University graduate, and leader of the second-generation Chicago Boys, who served as minister of finance between 1984 and 1989. He became a presidential candidate in 1989, but was defeated by Patricio Aylwin of the Partido Demócrata Cristiano (Christian Democratic Party).

Carlos Cáceres. Cornell University graduate. He became minister of finance in February 1983 and minister of the interior at the end of the Pinochet dictatorship. He was the only member of Pinochet's cabinet who belonged to the Mont Pèlerin Society.

Jorge Cauas. Columbia University graduate, and the first civilian to hold the post of minister of finance during the Pinochet dictatorship. He implemented the shock treatment policies of 1975.

José Piñera. Harvard graduate and eminence grise behind the adoption of market policies in the social sectors. He served as minister of labor and mining during the Pinochet dictatorship, implemented pensions reform, and was in charge of writing the labor and mining laws.

The Military

Manuel Contreras. Chilean Army general and chief of the secret police who was involved in the assassination of several opponents to the junta, including former ambassador and cabinet member Orlando Letelier in Washington, DC.

Gustavo Leigh. Chilean Air Force general and early plotter to depose President Salvador Allende. General Leigh got into several clashes with Pinochet. He was dismissed from the military junta in 1978.

César Mendoza. General of the militarized police force, the Carabineros, and a member of the military junta.

Toribio Merino. Chilean Navy admiral and early plotter. He was a member of the military junta, and it was he who received the Chicago Boys' blueprint for market reforms in 1973.

Augusto Pinochet. Army general who led the coup d'état that deposed President Salvador Allende, resulting in Pinochet holding a dictatorship for almost seventeen years. He was detained in London in 1998, accused of being an accomplice in the torture and forced disappearance of several Spanish citizens. He spent over a year in detention until he was released due to health problems.

The Politicians

Salvador Allende. Socialist president elected in 1970 and deposed by Pinochet in the 1973 coup d'état. He committed suicide instead of going into exile.

Patricio Aylwin. First president elected after the return to democracy in 1990, serving from 1990 through 1994. His government maintained the Chicago Boys' policies.

Michelle Bachelet. Socialist president for two distinct terms, 2006–10 and 2014–18. During her first term, market reforms were deepened and social programs were expanded. During her second term, the Partido Comunista de Chile (Communist Party of Chile) joined the coalition and an effort was made to introduce reforms to the market system; emphasis was placed on education and pensions.

Gabriel Boric. A former student activist from the Far-Left coalition Frente Amplio (Broad Front), he was elected president in December 2021 by a landslide. His election signaled the end of the neoliberal era in Chile.

Eduardo Frei Ruiz-Tagle. President from 1994 to 2000. He deepened market reforms.

Jaime Guzmán. A Catholic and anticommunist scholar close to the Chicago Boys. He was a leader of the Comisión Constitucional (Constitutional Commission) in charge of giving political and doctrinal support to the Chilean Constitution of 1980. A Far-Left group murdered him in 1990.

Ricardo Lagos. First socialist president (2000–2006) since Salvador Allende, and an economist with a PhD from Duke University. During his administration the 1980 Chilean Constitution, which was passed under Pinochet, was reformed. His administration's motto was "Growth with equity."

Sebastián Piñera. President during two terms, 2010–14 and 2018–22, and a Harvard University graduate with conservative promarket views. He was president when the 2019 revolt erupted, and the Constitutional Convention started during his second term.

Other Economists

Luis Escobar Cerda. Chairman of the Departmento de Economía (Department of Economics) at the national Universidad de Chile (University of Chile), Católica's main rival. He was named minister of finance by Pinochet in April 1984.

Alejandro Foxley. First minister of finance after the return of democracy in 1990. He was the founder of the Corporación de Estudios para Latinoamérica (Corporation of Studies for Latin America), an independent research center that became the most severe critic of the Chicago Boys during the dictatorship.

Aníbal Pinto. Development economist at the United Nations Economic Commission for Latin America and the Caribbean. During the 1950s and 1960s, he was one of the most severe critics of the Chicago Boys. He was a believer in protectionism and import substitution.

The Leopard, by Giuseppe Tomasi di Lampedusa, is one of those rare works where the film adaptation (directed by Luchino Visconti and released in 1963) is almost as good as the novel. In the most famous scene, the Prince of Salina, Fabrizio Cobrera, is shaving in front of a small mirror. He holds the razor in his right hand, a white towel draped over his shoulders. Through the window, the rugged Sicilian landscape is visible. The actor is Burt Lancaster—tall and handsome, with intense blue eyes. His nephew, Tancredi Falconeri, played by Alain Delon, stands beside him. He, too, has blue eyes and is elegantly dressed. They talk about the revolutionary events in Italy in 1860 and how they will impact the Salina family. Tancredi announces that he will join the rebels. His uncle scolds him, and the young man replies, "If we want things to stay as they are, everything must change." This is the essence of what is known as *gatopardismo*.

In many ways, *gatopardismo* captures what happened—or did not happen—in Chile during the past few years. Everything appeared to be changing, but has mostly stayed the same.

I began working on this book in October 2019, after I visited Chile to see with my own eyes the massive and violent protests that had engulfed the most prosperous country in Latin America. In little more than one generation Chile had risen from the lower half of the region's income rankings to the very top. What I saw both impressed and confused me. Chile had become a paradox: it was the wealthiest country south of the Rio Grande, yet millions of people were rejecting the "neoliberal" economic model that had brought them this prosperity. *The Chile Project* was published in June 2023, when the country was still facing political turmoil and was embarking on a second effort to write a new constitution.

On November 15, 2019, after weeks of massive and largely violent protests, politicians recognized that the time had come for a national dialogue about the country's future. The best course of action was to elect a body to draft from scratch a new constitution, one that would replace the charter originally enacted under Pinochet's dictatorship in 1980 and amended multiple times following the country's return to democracy in 1990.

In September 2022, citizens were asked whether they "approved" or "rejected" the charter written by a Constitutional Convention largely composed of left-wing and Far-Left activists, many influenced by identity politics. The proposed text aimed to transform Chile into a plurinational state, establishing several semiautonomous Indigenous nations. It also sought to end "neoliberalism," abolish the Senate, reduce protections for property rights, limit the independence of key institutions—including the Supreme Court—and enshrine over a hundred new social rights, including rights for animals and nature. The draft was widely viewed as too radical and was soundly rejected by 62 percent of voters.

In 2023, a second attempt was made, under different rules. This time the Constitutional Council—note the change in name, from Convention to Council—was dominated by conservatives. Although the Council put forward a more traditional text, once again the people said no— 56 percent. According to the *New York Times*, Chile's double failure was rare—only twelve other nations have rejected a full constitutional referendum in 181 such votes since 1789.

In this book I tell the story of how Chile, the most successful country in Latin America, has become trapped in a political struggle between two irreconcilable worlds. On one side are those advocating for deep reforms to Chile's market-oriented model. They want a system based on solidarity, social justice, environmental protection, Indigenous rights. On the other side are those who view the market-driven model as a success, arguing that thanks to it Chile moved from poverty to middle-class status in just one generation. They acknowledge that social services need improvement but believe that the engine of growth—the market system—should not be dismantled.

The narrative begins in 1955, when the U.S. Department of State launched the Chile Project, a program to train Chilean economists at the University of Chicago. Chile was transformed from a heavily regulated, protectionist, and inflation-prone economy into one where markets were allowed to operate freely in nearly every sector, including health care, education, pensions, culture, and the arts. The reforms worked and propelled Chile to the top position in terms of income and most social indicators in Latin America. In 2015, however, the model began to fizzle, and the rate of economic growth gradually declined. With the economic slowdown came frustration, grievances, unhappiness, and social turmoil. Chile's neoliberal dream began to show some deep fissures that ended up in the massive protests of 2019.

The book concludes with an analysis and deconstruction of the first constitutional convention and the rejection of its proposal by 62 percent of voters on September 4, 2022. When the book went to print the second assembly had not yet been convened. That would occur in the months to follow, and by the time of the book's release the members of the new Constitutional Council had just been elected.

I write this preface during the week marking the fifth anniversary of the 2019 revolt. Most people in Chile have reflected somberly on the events of October 18, 2019, and the weeks that followed. There is now a widespread recognition that despite the violence, the constitutional debates, the massive marches, the speeches and harangues, the fistfights, and the police's human rights violations, very little has truly changed. Chile remains trapped in *gatopardismo*.

Five years after the social uprising, there is broad agreement that the country faces three questions: After two failed attempts, will there be another effort to draft a new constitution? Will the country experience another violent uprising, with rioting, looting, and arson, as in 2019? And what kind of economic and social model will guide Chile in the years to come?

Answering the first question is easy. The country is tired of constitutional fights. Two intense battles, in 2022 and 2023, tore families and friends apart. Five years after the unrest of 2019, most Chileans want to avoid another convention. During the next decade we will see amendments and some constitutional changes, but the basic legal scaffolding of the country will remain as it is today.

Nonetheless, in its 2024 report on Chile, the United Nations Development Programme (UNDP) noted that the core demands of the people remained unmet. According to the report, due to this and the elites' continued neglect of the plight of the poor, another conflict similar to the social unrest of October 2019 cannot be ruled out. The UNDP's warnings should be taken seriously. Back in 1998, it pointed to growing discontent among the marginalized, the disadvantaged, and even the emerging middle class, but those warnings were largely ignored. The political Right would later claim they "didn't see the revolt coming." Reflecting on the future, I can't help but paraphrase Marx: history sometimes repeats itself—first as tragedy, then as farce.

As for what model will guide Chile, neoliberalism is effectively dead. The fall began with free university education under President Michelle Bachelet, then with the enactment of a government-paid universal pension scheme under President Sebastian Piñera in early 2022. Several of President Gabriel Boric's policies after 2023 have driven further nails into neoliberalism's coffin. To borrow from the Munchkins in *The Wizard of Oz*, neoliberalism in Chile is now "morally, ethically, spiritually, physically, positively, absolutely, undeniably, and reliably dead."

Chile is navigating toward an undefined economic model, with a myriad of possibilities ahead. On one end lies a statist vision—characterized by controls, restrictions, and strict social rights. On the other end lies a nostalgic push for free markets and minimal regulation. I believe neither extreme will prevail. After much negotiation and hesitation, Chile will likely settle on a European-style social democracy. It will retain the core principles (though not the excesses) of the Chicago school model—open markets, fiscal discipline, a floating exchange rate, a strong central bank, and competition laws—but with significant adjustments: new social policies, improved pensions, and stricter environmental regulations. Chile won't abandon but will reshape capitalism.

The lessons that emerge from Chile's experience with neoliberal policies are important for countries from across the world. They demonstrate the power of unleashing competitive forces that encourage innovation, competition, investment, productivity, the rule of law, price stability, and fiscal prudence. If applied in the right doses and in the correct order, market-oriented reforms may indeed propel a country forward toward prosperity. But there are dangers. An efficiency-based revolution is likely to generate social dislocation. Many people will be left behind, jobs will be lost, and many will face significant reductions in their incomes. For the reform program to work and be sustained, these people need to be compensated, retrained, taught new skills, and helped to transition from old to new jobs. If social imbalances—including inequality—are not corrected, the disaffected will join forces with Far-Left activists and may put the whole transformation at risk. For deep market reforms to succeed, they must be accompanied by a sturdy and efficient social safety net and by an effective regulatory system that protects consumers from potential abuses. Chile's historical experience suggests that coldhearted capitalist reforms may not generate lasting and sustainable changes. A more promising route is a combination of Chicago school policies and measures that promote fairness and reduce inequality. Chile's saga also has lessons about the "war of ideas" in the public policy domain. Contrary to what the Chicago Boys thought in the earlier part of the twenty-first century, these ideological wars are never over. Those who lose a particular battle regroup, go to school, and prepare themselves for new scrimmages. When that happened in Chile, the Chicago Boys and their supporters had already abandoned the battlefield, under the assumption that their triumph was eternal. But they were wrong. The battle of ideas is never-ending, and those engage will benefit from understanding how it evolved in Chile.

Los Angeles, November 2024

THE CHILE PROJECT

Introduction

IN 1955, as the Cold War reached a new peak, the US Department of State launched the Chile Project. The purpose of this program was to train Chilean economists at the University of Chicago, the bastion of capitalist thought and Milton Friedman's academic home. Once they returned to Chile, the young graduates were supposed to tout the principles of free markets in the increasingly ferocious war of ideas that raged in Latin America. Their adversaries in these intellectual battles were leftist economists who believed that the only way to defeat poverty and backwardation was by increasing the role of the state through nationalization, planning, and socialism. In 1961, after Fidel Castro declared that he was a Marxist-Leninist, the Chile Project became an integral part of the US strategy to contain the spread of communism in Latin America.[1]

For more than a decade the Chicago Boys—this was the name the media gave to the young graduates—had very little influence in policy design in Chile. They toiled in academia, trained other economists, wrote newspaper columns and insipid academic papers, and consulted for large banks and firms. But they were not taken seriously. In fact, the establishment looked at them with a combination of derision and amusement.

Things changed dramatically on September 11, 1973, when General Augusto Pinochet led a coup d'état that deposed socialist president Salvador Allende. The military's accession to power gave the Chicago Boys a unique opportunity to apply the theories they had learned from Milton Friedman and his colleagues. For the next seventeen years they had a free hand with which to experiment on the Chilean economy. They freed prices and interest rates, lowered import tariffs, privatized hundreds of state-owned enterprises, instituted school vouchers, created individual savings pension accounts, deregulated businesses and banks, and furthered markets everywhere. They applied a "shock treatment" to balance the budget and to reduce inflation, reformed labor legislation, contained the power of unions, attracted foreign investors, and strengthened the rule of law.

When democracy was reinstated in 1990, the country looked very different from how it had looked in 1973, when President Allende was overthrown by the military. In less than two decades the Chicago Boys had created a modern capitalist economy that, after some sputtering and a deep currency crisis in 1982, produced an acceleration in efficiency, productivity, and growth. In financial and economic circles there was talk of a budding "Chilean miracle."[2]

The miracle, however, had an original sin: it was put in place by a dictatorship, a regime that violated human rights and systematically persecuted, imprisoned, tortured, and assassinated its opponents. It was precisely for this reason that most observers were surprised when after the return to democracy in 1990 the model put together by the Chicago Boys was not scrapped by the country's new leaders, many of whom had been persecuted by Pinochet. Instead of undoing the free-market policies, successive left-of-center governments deepened the reforms. To be sure, the new democratic administrations expanded social programs, but the main building blocks of the so-called neoliberal model—a small state, very light regulations, full openness to the rest of the world, restrictions on union activities, very low corporate taxes, voucher-based education and health systems, narrowly targeted social programs, a pension system based on individual savings accounts, and the reliance on markets at every level—were expanded. Contrary to what many uninformed critics have proclaimed, the Chicago Boys model was not supported exclusively by the military. It was continued by members of the Partido Demócrata Cristiano (Christian Democratic Party), Partido por la Democracia (Party for Democracy), and Partido Socialista de Chile (Socialist Party of Chile) for over thirty years.[3]

After more than a century of mediocre performance, in the early 2000s Chile became, by a wide margin, the wealthiest nation in Latin America. Around that time it also attained the best social indicator levels in the region for health, education, and life expectancy. As a result, people living below the poverty line declined from 53 percent of the population in the mid-1980s to merely 6 percent in 2017.[4] In terms of income and other economic statistics, by 2020 Chile looked more like a southern European country, such as Portugal or Spain, than a Latin American nation. Notably, when Chile's reforms were first launched, most analysts were skeptical. They considered the market policies championed by the Chicago Boys to be extreme and thought that they would not work in a small and poor Latin American nation. On April 16, 1975, two weeks after Milton Friedman met with General Pinochet in Santiago, the *Guardian* reported that the military was considering embracing some *"lunatic schemes* dreamt up by the Chicago economists."[5]

Figures I.1 and I.2 summarize some of the most important economic aspects of Chile's story with neoliberalism. Figure I.1 presents the evolution of gross domestic product per capita, between 1980 and 2019, for a group of Latin American nations. As can be seen, in the first half of the 1980s Chile was at the bottom of the pack, jointly with Colombia, Costa Rica, Ecuador, and Peru. By 2003, and largely as a result of the market reforms initiated by the Chicago Boys and continued by the left-of-center governments, Chile had become the country with the highest income per capita in the region; it maintained the leading position until 2019, when it was surpassed by Panama.[6] Figure I.2 shows that the poverty head count declined from 53 percent of the population in 1987 to merely 6 percent in 2017, the lowest in Latin America by a significant margin. As a point of comparison, in 2017 the poverty head count in Costa Rica was 22.5 percent and 21.5 percent in Ecuador.[7]

After the return of democracy in 1990 Chile was frequently hailed as an example of how to conduct public policy in an emerging or transitional economy. Analysts from around the world and from every political persuasion used adjectives like *sensational* and *inspiring* to refer to Chile's development experience. Politicians from countries in the former Soviet sphere traveled to Chile to learn firsthand how to put in place a

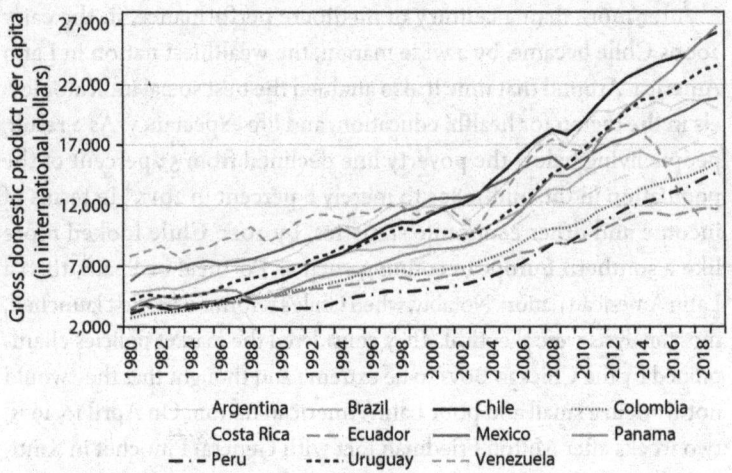

FIGURE I.1. Gross domestic product per capita, 1980–2019, in international dollars (purchasing power parity), selected Latin American countries
Source: International Monetary Fund (n.d.)

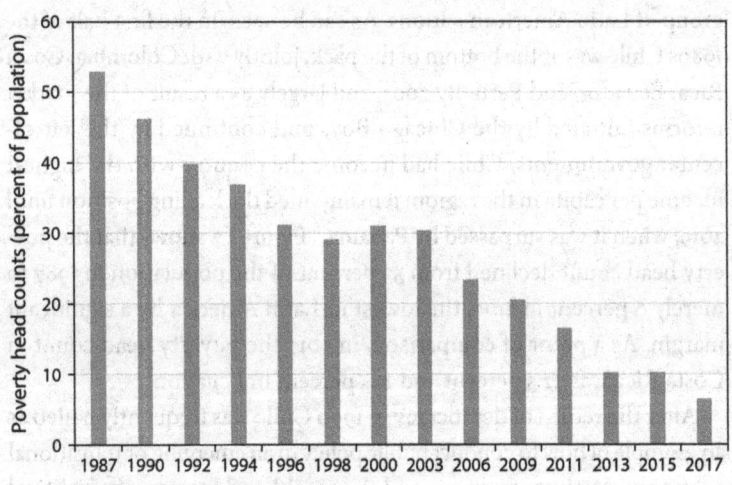

FIGURE I.2. Percentage of the population living below the poverty line in Chile, 1987–2017, measured as anyone living with less than $5.50 a day (2011 purchasing power parity). *Source*: World Bank (n.d.)

successful promarket program, how to open the economy, and how to privatize a massive number of state-owned enterprises.

Notwithstanding the rapid rate of growth and the drastic reduction in poverty, inequality remained high throughout the period. In 2022 Chile had the third highest degree of income disparity among the members of the Organisation for Economic Co-operation and Development, a group of high-income countries that Chile joined in 2010. Between 2000 and 2020 progress was made in reducing income differences, but they continued to be very high. Persistent inequality was Chile's Achilles heel, a serious weakness that was mostly ignored by the architects of the model and that would come to haunt them. The struggle for income and wealth distribution is a recurrent theme in the chapters that follow.

From the Chilean "Miracle" to the Popular Revolt of 2019 and the Constitutional Convention

On October 18, 2019, and to the surprise of most observers, massive protests erupted throughout the country. Demonstrations were triggered by a small increase in metro fares—thirty pesos, or the equivalent of four cents of a US dollar. But the rallies were about much more than the fare increase. Hundreds of thousands of people marched in several cities and demonstrated against the elites, corporate abuse, greed, for-profit schools, low pensions, segregation, and the neoliberal model. Demonstrators asked for debt forgiveness for students and free universal health services. Protesters carried Mapuche flags and demanded the return of lands taken from Indigenous peoples in the nineteenth century. Although most of the demonstrations were peaceful, some turned violent. There was arson, destruction of public and private property, and looting; more than twenty metro stations were set on fire during the first few days of the protests. The police responded with unjustified force and were accused of multiple human rights violations.

After weeks of massive demonstrations, rioting, looting, and arson, on November 15, 2019, the leaders of most political parties—with the important exception of the Partido Comunista de Chile (Communist Party of Chile) and the Far-Left Frente Amplio (Broad Front)—concluded that the only way of controlling violence was by initiating a national conversation on a new "social pact." A referendum was called to determine if a new constitution was to be written to replace the 1980 charter adopted during the Pinochet regime and amended during different democratic administrations. A year later (the process was delayed because of the COVID-19 pandemic), the option of rewriting the Chilean Constitution won the referendum by a landslide, and in mid-May 2021 a 155-member Constitutional Convention was elected. Seventeen out of the 155 seats were reserved for representatives of the Indigenous peoples. According to the rules, for a norm to be included in the new constitutional text it had to be supported by at least two-thirds of the delegates.

Most elected members of the new body belonged to the Far Left, and many supported specific causes related to social and reproductive rights and environmental protection; they declared that the convention's goal was to write an "anti-neoliberal constitution," one that put an end to the Chicago Boys' model. They wanted a constitutional charter that granted broad social rights to everyone, recognized and provided compensation to the Indigenous peoples for lands taken during the nineteenth century, and protected sexual minorities and the environment. The conservative forces (the Right and Center Right) elected 27 percent of the convention's delegates and, thus, could not garner the one-third required to exercise veto power. In a front-page story published on December 29, 2021, the *New York Times* noted, "In Chile . . . a national reinvention is underway. After months of protests over social and environmental grievances, 155 Chileans have been elected to write a new constitution amid what they have declared a 'climate and ecological emergency.'"[8]

On December 19, 2021, Gabriel Boric, a thirty-five-year-old congressman, former student activist, and member of the coalition Apruebo Dignidad (Approval and Dignity) was elected president by an ample margin. He was supported by the Communist Party and by the Frente Amplio (Broad Front), a coalition of smaller and Far-Left parties and political movements with names such as Comunes (Commons), Convergencia Social (Social Convergence), Fuerza Común (Common Force), and Revolución Democrática (Democratic Revolution). Most of these "collectives," as they liked to call themselves, were born in the early 2010s during major student demonstrations and protests.

In speech after speech during the campaign, Gabriel Boric called for eradicating "the neoliberal model," including some of its most distinctive accomplishments, such as the pension system based on private saving accounts.

Three months after Boric was inaugurated as president, the Constitutional Convention finished its work. With great fanfare a draft was presented to the population on July 4, 2022. A referendum to be held on September 4 would determine, by simple majority, whether the new charter was adopted. There would be two months for campaigning for one of two options: *apruebo* (approval) of the future text, or *rechazo* (rejection) of the constitutional draft.

The proposed new constitution went well beyond reforming the neoliberal model that had prevailed for forty years. The text made major changes to the country's political system. It declared that Chile was a "plurinational" state that consisted of several Indigenous nations. It weakened fiscal responsibility and the protection of property rights, and provided ample territorial autonomy to Indigenous peoples. The proposal eliminated the senate and defined a wide range of social rights (103 in total), including the right of glaciers not to be disturbed. It created several justice systems, one for each of the eleven officially recognized Indigenous peoples and one for the rest of the population. It established that the Indigenous peoples would have reserved seats in Congress and directed the government to focus foreign policy on the Latin American region instead of on the Pacific, as all governments had done since the end of the twentieth century.

As the referendum date approached, several left-of-center politicians, including former presidents Eduardo Frei Ruiz-Tagle and Ricardo Lagos, criticized the proposed text. The issue, they pointed out, was that the draft did not address the real needs and aspirations of the people; it was an overly partisan proposal largely inspired by "identity politics." The draft did not explain how the provision of social rights would be financed, and there was a danger that the text would become a multitude of unfulfilled promises. A new constitution was needed, they affirmed, but the one drafted by the convention was not adequate. Their position was to reject the proposal and start a new constitutional process all over again.

On September 4, after a fierce and bitter campaign, the *rechazo* option won by a substantial margin: it got 62 percent of the votes, while *apruebo* garnered only 38 percent. The vote was a major blow for President Boric, who had campaigned for approving the new text. According to a *New York Times* article published on September 6, "The transformational vision laid out by a constitutional convention of 154 elected members, many of them political outsiders, proved too drastic an overhaul."[9] On September 5, the *Economist* wrote, "Much of the blame for the defeat lies with the convention itself. . . . More than two-thirds of those elected were outside mainstream political parties. They included many political newbies and activists from the hard left. . . . They quickly alienated the average [voter]."[10]

At the time of this writing, in late September 2022, politicians of all persuasions are discussing the next steps in Chile's constitutional saga. Although the timing and details of the new process are not yet known, three things are certain: First, Chile will replace the old constitution with a new one that will enshrine and guarantee many social rights that will be provided for free by the state. It is unlikely that there will be as many as in the rejected draft, but the number will be substantial. Second, the new constitutional text will be written by an elected body, with the assistance of "experts"—constitutional scholars, sociologists, economists, and anthropologists. However, this time the process will be guided by the political parties and will avoid the excesses and bureaucracy of the original convention. And third, the neoliberal era will not be revived; most of the economic system built by the Chicago Boys will be replaced by a social democratic system like the one that prevails in the European and, especially, Nordic nations. Whether this deep change will help move the country toward social harmony, inclusiveness, greater equality, and prosperity is still an open question.

Living the 2019 Revolt

On November 3, 2019, merely two weeks after the explosion of what Chileans call "the revolt," I traveled to Chile. As soon as I arrived, I sensed a dramatic change relative to the last time I had visited, just three months earlier. Tension and anxiety were in the air. For ten days I mingled with protesters and marched with them; I listened to their chants and had several one-on-one conversations with demonstrators of all ages. On several occasions I had to run away from the police, who in full antiriot gear charged against the crowds. To minimize the effects of tear gas, I covered my mouth and nose with a wet scarf. I tried to avoid the police water cannons, but I was not successful: one afternoon I was soaked from head to toe, and my (rather) fancy clothes were ruined forever. When the police advanced, most demonstrators retreated as fast as they could. But a handful of members of the so-called front line stood their ground; they protected themselves with homemade shields, hurled Molotov cocktails, and used slings to throw rocks at the militarized police force, the Carabineros. As night fell, they used laser beams to disorient the antiriot cops. Many of these tactics were learned from demonstrators in Hong Kong. I saw young people being arrested and police beating up protesters. I saw looters running away from department stores and other businesses with TV sets, fancy sneakers, and even refrigerators. I saw burned metro stations and destroyed pharmacies and banks. To my surprise, many demonstrators chanted the fight songs of the most popular soccer teams in the country, Colo Colo and La U (Club Universidad de Chile). One night I had trouble finding my hotel. As it turned out, the entrance had been boarded up, and guests, including a group of stunned Chinese tourists, had to come in through a garage at the side.

There were graffiti everywhere:

Neoliberalism was born and will die in Chile!

No more Chicago Boys!

Chile woke up!

It's not thirty pesos [in reference to the metro fare hike], *it's thirty years of neoliberalism!*

The mood among the young protesters was extremely optimistic. Every demonstrator I talked to was convinced that the revolt would end the neoliberal model. To them, the future looked bright; life would be much better under a system based on "solidarity" and equal opportunities. The revolt, including its violent manifestations, would result in the end of individualism, greed, and the profit motive. The patriarchal model would be replaced by a feminist perspective, and everyone would be treated with dignity. Neoliberal obsessions such as competition, efficiency, punctuality, and "hyperproductivism" would be replaced by nobler goals, including the pursuit of a "better life." The rich would pay more taxes, education would be free and of high quality, there would be universal and free health services, everyone would enjoy the culture and the arts, Indigenous peoples would recover their ancestral lands, and the environment would be protected. The idea of a trade-off between economic growth and equality did not cross the protesters' minds.

I also talked to business leaders and politicians, both conservative and left-of-center. They were stunned. They talked about a great paradox: while every traditional indicator showed that Chile was a major success and was steadily moving toward the ranks of the advanced nations, substantial portions of society were deeply unhappy and demanded major changes. The elites did not comprehend the reasons behind the revolt. Even those who had been critical of the model were surprised by the massiveness and violence of the protests. As it turned out, and as I discuss in chapter 12, there had been plenty of warnings that economic success rested on a social powder keg of sorts. A small number of sociologists and political analysts pointed out in the early 2000s that a growing malaise was spreading through the population. This was referred to as the *malestar* (malaise, discomfort) hypothesis. But those warnings were systematically ignored, and those who made them were treated as lunatics. Many conservatives were convinced that foreign militants were behind the revolt. They assured me that Venezuelan president Nicolás Maduro and the Cuban government had sent thousands of activists to incite local anarchists and antifa gangs. Conservatives could not accept that this was a homegrown protest movement. The fact that billionaire Sebastián Piñera, an economist by training and a strong supporter of the Chicago Boys, had been elected president less than two years earlier (in December 2017) with 53 percent of the vote added to the elite's incredulity.

The day I left Santiago I almost missed my flight. The main avenues and highways were blocked by protesters, barricades, and debris. The Uber driver tried different routes, only to run into more demonstrations. He was scared. At some point he suggested that I go back to my hotel. "You are witnessing an insurrection," he said. He then added, "The insurrection that will end the neoliberal model." I could not tell if he was against or in favor of the revolt, and I didn't ask. He told me that the car he was driving was his only asset, and he was afraid that it would be damaged by a rock or a Molotov cocktail. After I promised him a substantial tip—one commensurate with a neoliberal regime—he agreed to deliver me to the airport.

That night, as the plane flew north over the Pacific Ocean, I decided to write an essay on the rise and fall of neoliberalism, using Chile's experience as an illustration. While in Santiago I had taken copious notes, and I had written down a tentative outline. Once I was back in Los Angeles, I penned three short articles, which were published in *VoxEU*, *ProMarket*, and the *Milken Review*. Although the pieces were well received, I had mixed feelings about them. They were too short and did not capture all the granularity of the story. They did not explain in sufficient detail how the US State Department's version of Chile was conceived in the 1950s, nor did they delve into how the thinking of specific University of Chicago faculty—Milton Friedman, Gary Becker, Arnold "Al" Harberger, and George Stigler, among others—had influenced the economic revolution put in place by their former students. One of the main points I made in those pieces was that to understand Chile's story—and, thus, the story of the rise and fall of neoliberalism—it was essential to go beyond income distribution and income inequities. It was also necessary, I argued, to focus on "horizontal inequality," or what philosopher Elizabeth Anderson has called "relational inequality."[11] It is not only about monetary income but also about social interactions, segregation, racism, and the provision of amenities and public goods; and it is also about the way common people are treated by the elites. As it turned out, Chile did poorly in most of those areas. Many of the protesters I talked to mentioned achieving "dignity" as a key goal. Plaza Baquedano, the main square in Santiago where protests began every afternoon in the final months of 2019 and occurred every Friday in 2020–21, was unofficially renamed Plaza de la Dignidad (Dignity Square) by the demonstrators.

What Is Neoliberalism?

One of my greatest challenges in writing this book has been dealing with the terms *neoliberal* and *neoliberalism*. It is not because they are particularly difficult philosophical categories, but because with time they have become bastardized terms, derogatory labels tossed around by politicians, pundits of various types, and academics to diminish their adversaries and enemies. Nowadays, most of the media uses *neoliberalism* lightly, without trying to explain what is meant by it. This trend became particularly acute with the eruption of social media. Twitter is replete with short statements blaming neoliberals for almost every social, economic, environmental, and sanitary ill. A reader of the popular press or social media would not be at fault in concluding that almost every Western political leader in the last half century was a "neoliberal" and that most forms of capitalism and market-based economics systems are a manifestation of neoliberalism. Benjamin Wallace-Wells of the *New Yorker* has asserted that Larry Summers is a neoliberal, and according to a June 21, 2021, article by Gary Gerstle in the *Guardian,* "the neoliberal order . . . dominated American politics for 40 years."[12]

The term *neoliberal* had its origins in the 1920s and 1930s, and gained some currency after the Colloque Lippmann, a meeting organized by French philosopher Louis Rougier and held in Paris in August 1938 to discuss the policy implications of Walter Lippmann's book *The Good Society.*[13] In this work Lippmann argued that in order to preserve democracy and defeat authoritarian and collectivist regimes it was necessary to rescue liberalism from the jaws of laissez-faire economic theory, a system that had created social distress, poverty, and acute inequality. The only way to defeat the likes of Adolf Hitler and Joseph Stalin was by reforming capitalism and by adding social concerns to the profit motive. He argued that doing this did not constitute a betrayal of classical liberal principles. On the contrary, it meant going back to the views of thinkers such as Adam Smith and Jeremy Bentham.[14] The participants in the colloquium debated on what name to give the new movement, this renewed perspective about liberalism, this approach that incorporated social goals to the market system. After much discussion, during the last day of the meeting it was decided that *neoliberalism* was a succinct term that captured the concerns of the majority (but not all) of the participants. And so, the neoliberal movement was born on a summer day in 1938. (For further details, see the appendix.)

For many years the term *neoliberalism* was confined to academic discussions and writings. In the period immediately following World War II, it was mostly used to refer to German ordoliberalism, or the ideas behind the policies of Konrad Adenauer and Ludwig Erhard, the founders of the Federal Republic of Germany and the men behind its economic "miracle." In 1951 Milton Friedman wrote a short piece titled "Neo-liberalism and Its Prospects," but as far as I have been able to ascertain—and I have looked everywhere and talked to most Friedman experts—he did not use the term again in his writings. In it, Friedman argued, along the lines of Walter Lippmann, that there was a need to move away from nineteenth-century laissez-faire economics and to develop institutions to "protect consumers from exploitation [by monopolies]." In addition, the state "would have the function of relieving misery and distress."[15]

It was not until the early 1990s that neoliberalism was used, mostly in the popular press and in nonacademic policy writings, to denote "market fundamentalism," or a doctrine that puts markets and individuals above everything else and is based on the belief that human behavior and social interactions are guided by greed, profits, and economic considerations. In the late 1990s, and especially in the United Kingdom and United States, the term *neoliberalism* came to be associated with a readiness to rely primarily on markets rather than on the state to achieve certain policy objectives, including improving social conditions. Several catchwords became associated with *neoliberalism*, including *globalization, competition, balanced budgets, low inflation, deregulation, privatization,* and *Homo œconomicus.*[16]

In writing this book I had to decide whether to use the term *neoliberalism* loosely, as it is currently used in the popular media, or to offer a narrow and precise definition, a characterization devoid of value content. Naturally, I opted for the latter.

I define *neoliberalism* as a set of beliefs and policy recommendations that emphasize the use of market mechanisms to solve most of society's problems and needs, including the provision and allocation of social services such as education, old-age pensions, health, support for the arts, and public transportation. Neoliberals believe that a "purer" form of capitalism, where markets are allowed to function in most spheres, is better for society than hybrid versions of capitalism, with regulated markets controlled by government functionaries. Of course, for neoliberals this purer form of capitalism is vastly superior to a system based on planning of any sort, a point emphasized by Friedrich Hayek throughout most of his career.[17] In a neoliberal system everything has a price—either implicitly or explicitly—and those prices are seen as providing useful information to consumers, producers, citizens of all ages, and policy makers.

Philosopher Michael Sandel, a severe critic of the neoliberal view, got it almost right when he related neoliberalism to the "marketization of everything."[18] The reason why he didn't get it completely right is that in his book *What Money Can't Buy* (Sandel, 2012) he painted a caricature that helped him score easy points in his crusade against Gary Becker, the economist that French philosopher Michel Foucault considered to be the key figure of American neoliberalism. A better and more useful definition would be that "neoliberalism is the marketization of *almost* everything." Of course, *almost* is just one word, but it makes a huge difference, as it moves the discussion from an attempt at ridiculing the concept into serious terrain. If one accepts this alternative definition, one immediately must dig into what is meant by *almost*. What type of decisions should be excluded from market solutions? Are there different intensities in the use of markets? What are the moral limits captured by *almost*? As will be seen in this book, in Chile the extent of the market was very large. Market mechanisms and principles were used extensively to allocate social services and to guide day-to-day life. The Chicago Boys did not use the term *neoliberalism* to describe their own economic model. They preferred the term *subsidiarity*, in the sense that the state should only be involved in those areas where the private sector, broadly defined as including civil society and not-for-profit organizations, could not operate efficiently.

In 2018, Sandel expressed his views on the consequences of neoliberalism, noting that "the neo-liberal [model] . . . benefits those at the top but leaves ordinary citizens feeling disempowered. . . . For those left behind . . . the problem is not only wage stagnation and the loss of jobs; it is also the loss of social esteem. It is not only about unfairness; it is also about *humiliation*."[19] This emphasis on "humiliation" resonates with the demands of the protesters in Chile—and in other countries, for that matter—for respect and dignity; it resonates with Anderson's concept of "relational equality," an area where despite its enormous material progress, and as noted, Chile did particularly poorly, even in the late 2010s (see chapter 13).

The definition of *neoliberalism* used in this book overlaps, in some respects, with definitions offered by other academics who have resisted the temptation of expanding the meaning of the term until it becomes useless. In his 2005 book *A Brief History of Neoliberalism*, David Harvey, an often-cited Marxist, defines neoliberalism as "a theory of political economic practices that proposes that *human well-being can best be advanced by liberating individual entrepreneurial freedoms* and skills within an institutional framework characterized by strong private property rights, free markets, and free trade."[20] My definition is also consistent with that of Geoffrey Gertz and Homi Kharas, who emphasize that neoliberals use "the logic of market competition to allocate resources wherever possible, including in areas such as education and health policy."[21]

Certainly the fact that neoliberals believe that the market provides the most efficient way of delivering social services does not mean that they ignore social conditions or the plight of the poor. On the contrary; as I have noted, it was precisely the concern for the social consequences of the free market and laissez-faire that prompted Walter Lippmann to write his book and that convinced Louis Rougier to assemble the Colloque Lippmann in 1938. What is true, however, is that for neoliberals the main goal of social policies is reducing (eliminating) poverty through targeted programs rather than reducing inequality. Income distribution—either vertical or horizontal—is not a priority. George Stigler, the University of Chicago professor who won the Nobel Prize in Economics in 1982, made this point succinctly when he wrote in his famous textbook *The Theory of Price* that "good income distribution" was an absurd policy goal in a complex modern economy.[22]

After considering my definition of neoliberalism, some readers may think that the adjective *purer*—as in "a purer form of capitalism"—is too weak and may prefer to characterize neoliberalism as an *extreme, fundamentalist,* or *radical* form of capitalism. Although in the book I try not to use those terms, any of them is fine with me. To repeat, what I strongly reject is fishing in the ocean of ideas with a very wide net that will label as *neoliberal* most any variant of capitalism, without distinguishing different shades of gray. In the appendix, I discuss, in some details, the historical origins of neoliberalism and the evolution of the term through the years—from the Colloque Lippmann in 1938 to the present.

The War of Ideas

This, of course, is not the first work that tackles Chicago economics, neoliberalism, and Chile. There have been many articles, essays, and books on the subject. Yet many of them have taken what I consider to be an overly partisan perspective, either praising or criticizing the reforms from a rather ideologized perspective. This is true of works both in English and Spanish.

The most important work on neoliberalism and Chile is Juan Gabriel Valdés's *Pinochet's Economists*, a book that analyzes several archives to trace how, starting in the 1950s, Chicago economics gained a foothold among Latin American economists. Valdés's book is a very fine piece of work, but by now it is somewhat dated. Its original version, in Spanish, is from 1989, before Chile returned to democratic rule, before the incoming democratic government of President Patricio Aylwin adopted (most of) the Chicago Boys' policies, and before Chile's success transformed the country into an example for other emerging and transitional nations trying to modernize their economies. In addition, since 1989 significant material has been added to different archives—including Milton Friedman's archive at the Hoover Institution, the archives at the Pontificia Universidad Católica de Chile (Pontifical Catholic University of Chile), and the Universidad Finis Terrae's oral history on economic policy in Chile. Moreover, since 1989 many of the original Chicago Boys have published memoirs, Al Harberger's oral history became available in 2016, and Milton and Rose Friedman's own memoirs, which include abundant material on Chile, were published.[23] Additionally, after all these years, many of the actors of this story are willing to talk more openly about how they lived the events that transpired during that time. For this book I interviewed many of them. Most of the interviews were on the record; in a few cases, the individuals in question preferred to keep their remarks off the record. (See the acknowledgments at the end of this book.)

For Valdés the Chile Project was a deliberate effort by the United States to *impose a foreign ideology* on a poor developing country. According to Valdés, the ideas and policies advocated by the Chicago Boys were not only foreign to Chile's reality and culture but also didn't work. They generated increased poverty and destitution, and it was only possible to implement them because of the Pinochet dictatorship. In 1989—and in 1995, when the English translation of the book was released—Valdés intimated that once Chile returned to democratic rule, the Chicago Boys' policies would be abandoned rapidly, and a more appropriate model, one that made sense for a country like Chile, would be put in place by successive democratic governments.[24] This more appropriate model would rely on structuralist views and would implement protectionist policies, controls, and regulations. The new model would be based on a strong role for the state and aggressive distributive policies. Of course, and as is narrated in detail in this book, none of this occurred.

My own view differs from Valdés's. I believe that the best way to understand what happened in Chile is within the context of the competition for ideas on economic policy and the effort by thinkers with different views of the world to persuade policy makers that their perspective was superior and more adequate than the alternatives. In some of my previous work I have argued that in the four decades spanning from 1950 to 1990 the two main camps in the global "war of ideas" were those advocating a planning approach and those advocating a market perspective. This war was fought all over the world. In Africa, it was Julius Nyerere's African Socialism versus the World Bank's and Elliot Berg's market incentives approach; in Asia, it was P. C. Mahalanobis's plan versus Jagdish Bhagwati's liberal model; in Latin America, it was the structuralist school versus the market perspective of the Chicago Boys. To be sure, there were peculiarities in each region, and variants and gradations within each of these views, and in many cases policies combined elements of planning with those of markets. But from a "big picture" perspective, those were the two camps.

There are (at least) two ways to determine which viewpoint triumphed in this competition of ideas. The simplest one is to compare the performance of (similar) economies that have followed different economic models. For instance, one could compare Chile, Costa Rica, and Ecuador, three countries that had an almost identical income per capita in the late 1980s but followed very different policy paths. Chile followed the Chicago Boys' model, Costa Rica chose a traditional middle-of-the-road Latin American regime that combined elements of control with market incentives, and Ecuador followed a populist model under the leadership of several politicians, including President Rafael Correa. In that comparison, Chile comes up on top by a very wide margin. In 2022 its income per capita was 50 percent higher than Costa Rica's and 100 percent higher than Ecuador's. If instead of income per capita one were to use the United Nation's Human Development Index, the results would be very similar, with Chile progressing much faster than Costa Rica and Ecuador.

But comparing numbers and indexes is not the only way of judging the success of economic ideas. An alternative—or maybe I should say *complementary*—approach is to analyze whether representatives of one school are able to persuade their adversaries about the merits of their ideas. This is the "persuasion approach" to determining who won in the ideas' tournament. And when that method is used, and in contrast to what Valdés intimated in 1989, the Chicago Boys did very well in Chile. As I have noted, and as I explain in greater detail in the rest of this book, the bases of the model they built were maintained, improved, and deepened by precisely those who for many years had lambasted and ridiculed their views and policy proposals.

If the market perspective won the war of ideas in Chile, and the policies it inspired produced so much fruit, how can one explain the October 2019 revolt and the election of a Far-Left president (Gabriel Boric) who promised to end neoliberalism? How can we explain that, even after the new constitution was rejected in September 2022, there was generalized talk about ending the policies that catapulted Chile to the first position in the region? How can we account for this paradox? This is, precisely, the main question addressed in this book: an inquiry that will take the reader from the mid-1950s to the current time, from policy to policy, from grievance to grievance, from mistakes to policy blunders.

This book also contributes to the vast—and, I must say, uneven—literature on "Chicago economics."[25] Many of these works have focused on the thoughts developed by people such as Gary Becker, Milton Friedman, Frank Knight, Henry Simons, George Stigler, and Jacob Viner. Yet there is almost no work on how prominent Chicago economists affected policy and thinking in the developing and emerging markets. Moreover, there has been no effort to distinguish between two strands within the second Chicago school: the "purer neoliberals" (Gary Becker, Milton Friedman, and George Stigler, to mention just a few) and the "pragmatist neoliberals" (Al Harberger, Harry Johnson, and Ted Schultz), and how their views and advice often differed and, on occasion, even clashed. In this book, I make a distinction between different strands within the Chicago school. Milton Friedman was, of course, the best-known member of the faculty, but he was not the most influential in Chile or in the rest of Latin America. The most salient and persuasive figure in those countries—and in other developing nations, for that matter—was Al Harberger, a more pragmatic and more flexible thinker than Friedman (see chapter 9).

Chile as a Neoliberal Laboratory

Not a single Chicago Boy that I interviewed for this book acknowledged that the edifice they built was based on a neoliberal model. Every time I brought up the subject, I got the same reaction: "We, neoliberals? Of course not. Those who say it are trying to ruin our reputation; we favored a social market economic system, like the one put together by Ludwig Erhard in West Germany after World War II." This reaction is, to some extent, understandable given the bad reputation currently associated with the term *neoliberal*. Yet in order to analyze seriously and in detail the evolution of economic thinking and policy making, it is fundamental to go beyond labels and examine carefully the nature of the economic models implemented. It is also necessary to explore the doctrines behind those policies and the results they produced. That is what I do in this book.

Juan Andrés Fontaine, a second-generation Chicago Boy and a member of the cabinet in both post-1990 conservative administrations, told me that throughout this period Chile had a number of state-owned companies—including Codelco, the largest copper company in the world—contradicting the notion of extreme capitalism. He noted that for many years the government controlled cross-border capital mobility, and that many sectors (including banking) were firmly regulated. All of this, he declared, showed that the regime was far from fundamentalist and that, despite the vast literature that claimed that Chile was the poster child for neoliberalism, this was not true. Other Chicago Boys, including Rolf Lüders and Sergio Undurraga, two important figures who helped shape policy during the Pinochet years, made similar points when I talked to them about Chile and neoliberalism. In a January 2022 interview, Lüders denied that Chile ever implemented neoliberal policies, stating that "the idea of a neoliberal model is a slogan, both in Chile and in the rest of the world."[26] Economists associated with the postdictatorship left-of-center governments were even more adamant in rejecting any relation between the policies they put in place and neoliberalism. For them those statements were, simply, slander.

Certainly the model was not static. Like the characters in a good novel, it greatly evolved through time. Emphases changed and priorities shifted as different issues became pressing and new individuals took over the most important cabinet positions. Indeed, it is possible to differentiate among three distinct phases in Chile's neoliberal experience: Between 1973 and 1982, we can talk about *incipient neoliberalism*. During these years the original Chicago Boys were in charge. Prices were freed, the economy was opened to the rest of the world, a "shock treatment" policy was implemented to defeat a stubborn three-digit inflation, there was massive deregulation, and many state-owned enterprises were privatized. In 1979, Pinochet decided to expand the model to social services such as education, health, and pensions. His goal was to transform institutions that had existed since the early years of the republic and to change Chile's culture. He presumptuously called this program the Siete Modernizaciones (Seven Modernizations). This period ended with a major and very costly currency and banking crisis in June 1982. As I point out in chapter 10, economic performance during this period was poor; income barely grew, inequality was very high, and inflation was stubborn. These years (1973–82) are covered in chapters 4–8.

In 1984, after the military briefly flirted with a nationalistic and protectionist approach, a new team made up of second-generation Chicago Boys took over the key cabinet posts. Their trademark was *pragmatic neoliberalism*. The main goal of this era was to further liberalization, introduce market mechanisms at most levels in society, expand the privatization process, attract foreign investment, and maintain competitiveness in the export sector. In contrast with the first generation of Chicago Boys, eliminating inflation was not the main objective of this younger team; they were willing to live with an inflation in the order of 20 percent per annum that declined gradually. This period lasted until the return to democracy in March 1990. Developments during this phase are covered in chapters 8 and 9, where I discuss the relationship between the Chicago economists and the military and ask whether the Chicago Boys knew about the systematic violation of human rights during the dictatorship.

The third phase, which I call *inclusive neoliberalism*, was inaugurated with the return to democracy and the accession to power of the Center Left with President Patricio Aylwin in 1990. He was followed in the presidency by Eduardo Frei Ruiz-Tagle, Ricardo Lagos, and Michelle Bachelet, all Center-Left leaders; Frei was a Christian Democrat and the son of iconic president Eduardo Frei Montalva (1964–70), and Lagos and Bachelet were members of the Socialist Party, the party of Salvador Allende.

Throughout these administrations social programs were expanded, but they continued to be delivered through market mechanisms, as was the case during the dictatorship. The economy was further opened to international trade, a market-determined exchange rate regime was adopted, international capital flows were freed, competition laws were passed, a loan system for college education was put in place, a fiscal rule that kept public expenditures under tight control was adopted, and more state-owned firms were privatized. At the same time, social expenditures increased, and several programs aimed at reducing poverty and increasing access to education and health were implemented. Most of the admired "Chilean miracle" took place during the early years of this time. These were also the years when the malaise grew and generalized. The reference to "thirty years of neoliberalism" repeatedly made by the demonstrators in 2019, and by supporters of Gabriel Boric during the 2021 presidential campaign, correspond to this period. Different aspects of this phase, including the dynamics of the social movement, are analyzed in chapters 10 through 15.

I premise my discussion with a word or two on methodology. Throughout the book I rely on the "analytical narrative" approach that I used in some of my previous works on Africa, Latin America, and the Great Depression in the United States. That is, I combine information from archives, data analysis, graphs, and statistical inquiry. I have tried to keep the main text free of jargon. Figures and tables are used to summarize ideas and to provide information in a succinct way.

At times—and if I think that it helps the story—I interject my personal experiences into the narrative. After all, I was born in Chile—although I emigrated to the United States when I was very young, more than forty years ago—and I have done extensive research on its economy. I was trained at the University of Chicago, and I am a colleague, coauthor, and close friend of Al Harberger, who is the intellectual father of the Chicago Boys. In many ways I became an accidental and atypical Chicago graduate, one who opposed the dictatorship and fled the country in 1977 because of it. For this, and for other reasons, I was never considered a member of the Chicago Boys' tribe.

Before plunging into the story of the rise and fall of neoliberalism, the Chile Project, and the Chicago Boys, a word about Pinochet's human rights record is merited.[27] After the military takeover, thousands of people were put in prison and tortured, vast numbers were executed, and some opponents were assassinated by agents of the junta on foreign soil. In 1990, the Comisión Nacional de Verdad y Reconciliación (National Truth and Reconciliation Commission) determined that during the almost seventeen-year dictatorship, 2,279 people were murdered by the military, with many of them "disappearing" from the face of the earth. Years later it was determined that many of the "disappeared" were killed while in custody and their bodies tossed into the Pacific Ocean from helicopters.[28] In 2011 a new inquiry commission concluded that the total number of victims of the dictatorship—including those executed, tortured, kidnapped, harassed, and fired from their jobs—surpassed forty thousand people. In addition, almost a quarter of a million people, out of a population of eleven million, were forced into exile.[29] An important question, and one that has haunted many scholars who have analyzed the Chilean experiment with markets is whether the reforms that generated the so-called Chilean model and its miracle would have been possible under democratic rule. I address this issue throughout the book, and I conclude that, given the timeframe and the historical moment—a decade and a half before the fall of the Berlin Wall—a neoliberal economic revolution of this magnitude could not have been possible under a democratic regime. This makes the adoption of the reforms by the post-1990 democratic governments even more extraordinary.

Joseph Brodsky, the Russian poet and winner of the 1987 Nobel Prize in Literature, has said that what makes a narrative good is not the story line itself, but the order in which the story is told, "what follows what." In deciding how to tell the story of the Chile Project, neoliberalism, Chicago economics, and the Chicago Boys, I faced two alternatives: to tell it thematically, covering one topic at the time—say, shock treatment, privatization, trade openness, pensions, and so on—or to tell the story chronologically, advancing through time, one year at the time. After much thought and consultation with several colleagues, and after trying my hand at a thematically organized narrative, I decided to tackle the story from a chronological perspective. In some sense this is a less exciting approach, but I think that it is a cleaner strategy, one that allows the reader to keep closer track of a complex and often surprising story that covers several decades, and has many characters—including, of course, Milton Friedman and the other notable Chicago economists who dazzled the world by winning one Nobel Prize after another.

PART I

The Early Years

1

Exporting Capitalism

THE ORIGINS OF THE CHICAGO BOYS

ON JUNE 27, 1955, Theodore Schultz, the chairman of the Department of Economics at the University of Chicago and a future Nobel Prize laureate, landed at Santiago's old Los Cerrillos Airport. He was accompanied by three of his colleagues who were fluent in Spanish: Earl Hamilton, Arnold Harberger, and Simon Rottenberg. The purpose of the trip was to negotiate an agreement between the University of Chicago and the Pontificia Universidad Católica de Chile (Pontifical Catholic University of Chile), commonly known as just Católica, aimed at modernizing the teaching of economics in Chile and Latin America. At the airport, the Chicagoans were greeted by fifth-year students Sergio de Castro and Ernesto Fontaine, who would be their chaperones during the two-week visit. A year later, De Castro and Fontaine were among the first Chileans enrolled in the Chicago graduate program in economics. Little did they know that they would eventually change the course of economic policy not only in Chile but also in the rest of Latin America and in many emerging and Eastern European nations. During the late 1990s and early 2000s, they traveled the world explaining how the Chicago Boys' policies had transformed a country that for decades had had a mediocre performance into the most vibrant and advanced nation in Latin America. In most of their travels they had to confront demonstrators who denounced the model's "original sin," the fact that it had been launched during a dictatorship led by Augusto Pinochet, one of the most reviled strongmen in modern history. In dealing with those accusations De Castro and Fontaine pointed out that the left-of-center democratic governments elected since 1990 had not only maintained the model, but, in fact, had expanded it and deepened it.

The so-called Chile Project was part of a US government initiative launched during the administration of President Harry Truman to confront communism during the early years of the Cold War. In his inaugural address on January 20, 1949—the Four Point Speech—Truman stated that aid to poor nations had to be an important component of US foreign policy. He noted that "more than half the people of the world are living in conditions approaching misery. . . . For the first time in history, humanity possesses the knowledge and the skill to relieve the suffering of these people." He added that one of the goals of his administration was to foster "growth of underdeveloped areas."[1]

Ted Schultz was the main force behind the launching of the Chile Project. For years he had worked on agricultural issues in Latin America, under the auspices of the US government's International Cooperation Administration (ICA). His contact point at the ICA was Albion "Pat" Patterson, a Princeton University graduate and Nelson Rockefeller protégé who had lived in Paraguay and Chile. In the early 1950s, Patterson and Schultz concluded that a serious problem in Latin America was the lack of economists with the analytical abilities to understand the role of markets, prices, investment in people, and innovation.[2] Peasants and farmers could learn better planting techniques and how to use fertilizer efficiently, but there would be no deep or lasting changes in Latin America as long as there were no economists who understood the big picture.[3] Schultz's general views about the agricultural sector and economic development were aptly summarized in his 1964 book *Transforming Traditional Agriculture*, in which he wrote, "Whatever the reason, it is much easier for a poor country to acquire a modern steel mill than a modern agriculture."[4]

For Patterson and Schultz the most effective way of achieving their goal was through local universities. There was, however, a serious problem: there were no universities with a faculty that could introduce a state-of-the-art economics curriculum. In most Latin American nations, including

Chile, the economic profession was in an embryonic stage and was dominated by Keynesians, Marxists, and structuralists.[5] For Patterson and Schultz the answer to this challenge was to train a handful of economists at top American research universities, such as the University of Chicago, and, after graduation, have them join local schools as full-time faculty. With time, students trained locally would help design the economic policies of the future, a future that, in the midst of the Cold War, Patterson and his colleagues at the ICA hoped would be democratic and market friendly.

The Chile Project

During 1953 Patterson discussed a possible partnership with the authorities of the national university, the Universidad de Chile (University of Chile). Its economics research arm, the Centro de Investigación Económica (Center of Economic Investigation), was directed by Joseph Grunewald, a respected American economist with an ample network of international contacts and a strong reputation in the region. After negotiations that lasted most of 1954, the chairman of its department of economics, Luis Escobar Cerda, told Patterson that the faculty was reluctant to enter into a partnership with an American school, and particularly with the University of Chicago, with its reputation of being a white knight for monetarism, free trade, deregulation, and free markets.[6] The dominant view among progressive intellectuals in Chile, and in other Third World countries, for that matter, was that economics training in France, the United Kingdom, and the United States did not prepare students to deal with the unique problems of underdevelopment.

Pat Patterson did not feel scorned by the Universidad de Chile's rejection. He immediately turned around and approached Católica with an identical proposal. For Católica the timing could not have been better. For some time, students had complained about the old-fashioned economics curriculum and demanded a modernizing reform.[7] They were particularly unhappy at the fact that readings were confined to old notes from a commercial law course developed by a long deceased lawyer. They were also dissatisfied with the capstone course, Mercería (Haberdashery), where

blindfolded students had to recognize different types of textiles by touch-
ing them. Since, at the time, every kind of fabric had a different import
tariff—ranging from 0 percent to 150 percent—this skill was considered
essential for anyone involved in international trade.

In October 1954 an informal agreement was reached between Católica
and the ICA, to launch a program with an American university, possibly
with the University of Chicago. However, there were some concerns
about the partnership on both ends of the deal. Some faculty in Chicago
worried about the religious affiliation of Católica, and some members of
the Chilean Catholic hierarchy worried that Chicago economists would
oppose the social teachings of the church. After several meetings, where
Schultz's charm was in full display, a preliminary agreement was reached
in late 1954. There would be three contracts: one between Católica and
the ICA, one involving Católica and the University of Chicago, and a
third between the ICA and the University of Chicago.

At a formal level the process was initiated with a letter, dated January 27, 1955, from Católica's dean Julio Chaná Cariola to Patterson: "Our
desire is to sign an agreement between our university and an institution
in the United States, such as the University of Chicago, or the Massa-
chusetts Institute of Technology."[8] The first contract, between Católica and
the ICA, was signed three months later, on April 28, 1955. The language
was very general and stated that there would be an agreement between
Católica and "a University in the United States," without stating that the
decision had already been made that that the latter would be the University of Chicago.[9]

The contract between Católica and the University of Chicago was
signed almost a year later, on March 30, 1956.[10] This time the language
was very specific and detailed. The contract had six main clauses: (1) the
program would last for three years (it was eventually renewed until
1961); (2) a number of Chilean students—both from Católica and
the national university—would enroll in Chicago's graduate program,
and expenses and tuition were to be paid by the US government and
American foundations; (3) fellowships were, in principle, for one year,
renewable for a second year if grades and progress were satisfactory;
(4) Católica made a commitment to hire at least four of the newly trained
economists as full-time faculty, and would pay them competitive market

salaries; (5) Chicago professors involved in the program were to be paid by the University of Chicago, which in turn was to get a $350,000 grant from the ICA; and (6) the University of Chicago would appoint a director of the program, who would live in Chile. But that individual would not do any teaching; he would only make sure that resources were used appropriately, do research, help select new students who would enroll at the university, and provide general guidance to his Chilean colleagues.[11] The first director in situ was Simon Rottenberg, who had accompanied Schultz during the first visit in June 1955. The overall program was directed from Chicago by Arnold Harberger and H. Gregg Lewis, each of whom had the title of project coordinator.[12] Both became very close to Chilean and other Latin American students, but it was Harberger— "Al" to his American friends and "Alito" to his Latin American *amigos*— who became a true inspiration and mentor to many generations of Latin Americans, first at the University of Chicago and later at the University of California–Los Angeles, at which he took a position in 1984.[13]

In 1957 James Bray and Tom Davis joined Simon Rottenberg, taking up residence in Santiago as senior economists in the new research center at Católica. Bray was an agricultural economist who wrote extensively about productivity and mechanization in Chile's farms, and Davis was a macroeconomist who eventually published an influential study on eight decades of Chile's high and persistent inflation.[14] During 1956 and 1957, Martin Bailey and Harberger also spent long stays in Chile. While Harberger did significant research on the Chilean economy and published some important papers that used the country as an example—including his celebrated *American Economic Review* article "The Measurement of Waste"—only two of Bailey's papers published around that time touched tangentially on Chile.[15]

In 2020, in one of his last public appearances, former secretary of state George Shultz, who at the time was a professor at the University of Chicago's Booth School of Business and was soon to be named its dean, remembered the early years of the Chile program:

And here is Chile, I remember so well they gave a program to us when I was at the University of Chicago and said the Chilean economy was in a mess. They said, "Would you run an aid program in

Chile?" We said, "We don't know how to run an aid program. We know how to teach economics." So they developed a scholarship program. We sent one of our best teachers down to Chile to identify students and professors who would give us honest evaluations. And we had a stream of Chilean economists come to the University of Chicago. And then Chile changed, and Allende was thrown out and Pinochet became the head. And he didn't know what to do either. Does anybody around here know how to [run the] economy? And our Chicago boys put up a hand and said, "We know how to do it." And so, he let them do it. And they produced the only really good economy in Latin America in the 1980s, it was sensational."[16]

The Boys in Chicago

In September 1955, even before the bilateral universities' contract was signed, the first group of three Chilean students enrolled at the University of Chicago. Another three arrived between September and October 1956. Two students came in the winter quarter of 1957, and one arrived in June of 1957. Five out of the original nine students were graduates from Católica, and four were from the Universidad de Chile.[17] Only one of them was a woman—Herta Castro. Two out of these nine students would eventually become Chilean cabinet ministers: Sergio de Castro, during the Pinochet regime; and Carlos Massad, after the return to democracy, during the administration of President Patricio Aylwin. Massad was also governor of the central bank on two occasions: from 1967 to 1970 and from 1996 to 2003.[18]

At the University of Chicago, the Chileans quickly discovered that their undergraduate training was deficient; they had trouble following graduate-level courses.[19] Lewis suggested that they enroll in undergraduate classes during the first two quarters, paying particular attention to Intermediate Economic Theory, Economics 209.[20] Even though this was not a PhD course, readings were difficult, and included eight chapters of the first volume of Alfred Marshall's *Principles of Economics*, Jacob Viner's 1932 article "Cost Curves and Supply Curves," and chapter 2 of Joan Robinson's *The Economics of Imperfect Competition*.[21] In addition to Economics 209, the Chileans took History of Economic Thought, Economics 302, taught by Frank Knight; it was a course with a massive reading list, including several books and articles in German. Knight described the course as a "very brief survey of economic thought prior to the 'classical school' with chief attention devoted to the latter, especially to the price and distribution theory of Smith, Ricardo, Senior and Mill."[22]

The Chileans were shocked by the exams' questions. Many were in the traditional University of Chicago style, where a statement was provided, and the students had to comment or evaluate it. What made these questions particularly difficult was that at that time most prices in Chile were controlled by the government and did not adjust freely to reflect changes in market conditions. Thus, before arriving in the Chicago neighborhood of Hyde Park, where the university was located, the students had not experienced in person what a market economy was really like. One can only imagine how puzzled they were by the following statement in one of the exams: "Some of the gasoline companies are reputed to sell gasoline to their own filling stations, who market it as a branded gas, at a higher price than they sell the same gasoline to independent filling stations who market it as an unbranded gas. This is equivalent to charging a higher internal than external price." In Chile, gasoline prices were set by the government, and were the same in every gas station, in every city, and in every province.[23]

At the graduate level, the Chileans took courses from Martin J. Bailey (in macroeconomics), Lloyd Metzler (in international trade), Gregg Lewis (in labor), Al Harberger (in public finance), and Ted Schultz (in agriculture). The early members of the group also took a course on monetary theory from Gary Becker, who had just obtained his PhD and had not yet left for Columbia University, where he stayed until 1968, at which time he returned to Chicago.[24]

But, without any doubt, their greatest learning experience was from Milton Friedman's sequence of courses on price theory (Economics 301 and 302). Although not many took the courses for a grade, they all sat in and listened carefully to what transpired in that classroom in the old Social Sciences building. They were enthralled by Friedman's charisma, by the ease with which he presented and dissected difficult problems, and by his total commitment to free-market economics. In his memoirs, Dominique Hachette, a Chicago Boy who was born in France and migrated to Chile with his family in the mid-1940s, remembers that they were fascinated by the force with which Friedman rejected Keynesianism and anything related to planning and dirigisme.[25] Ernesto Fontaine recalls that they were very impressed by Friedman's commitment to the superiority of monetary rules.[26] Hachette also noted that the students quickly realized that Harberger "was not a monetarist in the Friedman sense. He was the most intellectually balanced professor that I have known. As he did more consulting work for governments around the world, his way of seeing economics became closer to us and our [Chilean] reality."[27]

The early students missed, by a few years, some of the University of Chicago's luminaries, including George Stigler, who joined the Department of Economics in 1958, and Harry Jonson, who arrived in Hyde Park in 1959. The first group of Chileans did, however, interact with Robert Mundell, who in 1956–57 was a postdoctoral fellow. Mundell would return to Hyde Park as a member of the faculty in 1965. As noted earlier, they also encountered Gary Becker, who was a young assistant professor. Surprisingly, however, Becker taught money and banking and not the type of microeconomics theory that would make him famous and that would make French philosopher Michel Foucault, an icon of the Left, fall in love with his way of thinking.[28]

As De Castro, Fontaine, and Hachette have acknowledged in their reminiscences, during their stay in Chicago, Chilean students had no interaction with Friedrich Hayek, who at the time was a professor on the Committee on Social Thought. Fontaine remembers that they often ran into an older gentleman in the elevator of the Social Sciences building. The man looked frail, had small blue eyes, a neatly cropped mustache, and thinning hair. He always carried books in his hands, and sometimes was accompanied by another man with whom he spoke in German. Since he did not get off the elevator on the fourth floor, where the Department of Economics was located, they assumed that he was a sociologist or maybe a political scientist. It was only eventually that they realized that he was the famed Austrian economist. In later years Fontaine regretted not having interacted with Hayek, as he regretted not getting to know Ronald Coase, who taught at the University of Chicago School of Law. After the military coup, Friedrich Hayek became very interested in Chile and the Chilean experiment. He visited the country several times, met with Pinochet and other authorities, and became the honorary chairman of the promarket think tank Centro de Estudios Públicos (Center of Public Studies).[29] In 1982 Hayek wrote a letter to Prime Minister Margaret Thatcher suggesting that the United Kingdom follow Chile's path in implementing deep market-oriented reforms. The prime minister's reply was polite but very clear in making a distinction between the United Kingdom and Chile: "I am sure you will agree that, in Britain with our democratic institutions and the need for a high degree of consent, some of the measures adopted in Chile are quite unacceptable."[30]

During the early period, the vast majority of the Chilean graduates stayed in Hyde Park for two years and earned master's degrees. Only a handful—Sergio de Castro, Ernesto Fontaine, Ricardo Ffrench-Davis, and Rolf Lüders—went back for a second stay and finished their doctorates. Many critics of the Chicago Boys maintained that with a mere two-year residence, the training was deficient, and mostly based on ideology. Structuralist economist Aníbal Pinto, one of the Chicago Boys' fiercest detractors during the 1950s and 1960s, wrote that the graduates had "esoteric" and "dogmatic" ideas and reached conclusions "based on premises or facts imagined by the analyst."[31] Harberger disagreed strongly with the idea that obtaining a master's degree was insufficient, and argued that in contrast with other top American universities, at the University of Chicago the MA was an earned and useful degree for professional economists who would work in government or in the private sector. It was not a consolation prize for those who did not pass the first-year core exam. That was true of every student—American, Latin American, or from any other part of the world. Harberger said, "[At Chicago] we made a bit of fun of Harvard and Yale because they practically guaranteed that every entrant would get a Ph.D. And we thought that that was for the birds! On the other hand, I think that two-thirds of the people who entered Chicago had the capacity to get the Ph.D., and two-thirds of them actually got the Ph.D."[32]

Al Harberger and Gregg Lewis wrote periodic reports to the ICA in which they commented on how much progress the Chileans were making. Between 1956 and 1964, a total of fourteen reports were written. In 1957 Lewis wrote that Carlos Massad had "a performance record today on a par with the very best students in our department. Massad's capacity obviously is superior."[33] Massad would go on to have a number of influential roles in the conduct of economic policy in Chile. As a member of the Partido Demócrata Cristiano (Christian Democratic Party), he opposed the Pinochet dictatorship, and in 1990, after the return to democracy, he was appointed to the cabinet of President Patricio Aylwin. In some ways, he was a bridge between the Chicago Boys who worked for Pinochet and the economists who replaced them in key positions. Al Harberger also thought highly of Ffrench-Davis, a Católica graduate who was active in the leftmost wing of the Christian Democratic Party and was never quite comfortable in Chicago. Fifty years later, in the documentary Chicago Boys, Ffrench-Davis said that from early on he thought that the training was highly ideological. In 2021 he became a member of a high-level advisory board appointed by presidential candidate Gabriel Boric to help him draft the development program that would replace the Chicago Boys' neoliberal model.

2

The Chicago Boys in
the Ivory Tower

THE FIRST GROUP of Chicago Boys returned to Santiago in mid-1958, and immediately revolutionized the teaching of economics at Católica.[1] Reading lists, lecturing style, and math requirements changed overnight. Courses that until then were based on anecdotal evidence were replaced by classes that developed critical and analytical thinking. A course on statistical inference became required and was taught by Sergio de Castro. Problem sets were instituted, and a well-stocked library with over two thousand volumes on every modern economic subject was built in a matter of months. As Dominique Hachette has pointed out in his memoirs, from a methodological point of view, the approach was strongly flavored by Milton Friedman's *Price Theory* and Alfred Marshall's *Principles of Economics*, a treatise covered extensively in the Economics 209 course at the University of Chicago; it was, asserts Hachette, a decisively partial equilibrium perspective.[2]

The young professors were extremely demanding, and during the first two years after their return they flunked hordes of students. They also challenged the authorities. In his memoirs, Ernesto Fontaine remembers that the first clash with the university hierarchy was when the admissions office turned down a qualified applicant because he was Jewish. De Castro and Fontaine protested until the decision was reversed and the promising prospect enrolled in the program.[3]

Following the University of Chicago's tradition, a weekly seminar was instituted. Initially, there was a discussion on whether it should be tailored after Friedman's or Arnold "Al" Harberger's workshops. The former was rigid and guided by Friedman with an iron fist. Papers were discussed line by line, and comments had to be confined to the papers; veering off topic was never allowed. Harberger's workshop, in contrast, was more flexible and covered a wide variety of issues.[4] Harberger recalls that his workshop went well beyond Latin American students and economic development. Some members of his seminar who eventually left a mark in the economics profession include Gregory Chow, Robert Lucas, and Richard Muth.[5] Years later, James Lothian remembered that the Latino students were always ten to fifteen minutes late to the seminar, and that efforts by Harberger to change that practice were fruitless.[6] After some debate at Católica, the Harberger style of workshop (including the fifteen minutes late start) was adopted.

The War of Ideas

Suddenly, there were two distinct economic camps and a nascent war of ideas in Chile, a competition for influence that would slowly spread to other countries in the region. One camp was represented by the Universidad de Chile, with its (mostly) structuralist, Keynesian, and Marxist faculty, and the other was represented by Católica and the newly minted Chicago Boys.

Everything taught at Católica by the recently arrived Chicago Boys challenged the models and beliefs of the "planning approach" dominant at the Universidad de Chile. The young professors followed Theodore "Ted" Schultz in arguing that peasants' behavior, everywhere in the world, including in Chile, responded to incentives. Students read *Penny Capitalism*, the book by Sol Tax that showed that Guatemalan peasants were extremely rational and that, as other economic agents in more advanced countries, optimized subject to constraints.[7] Regarding Chile's perennial trade deficits, they argued that, as Harberger had shown in an influential *Journal of Political Economy* article, trade elasticities were rather high when properly measured.[8] Thus, currency devaluations—or, more generally, exchange rate fluctuations—were a very effective tool to deal with trade imbalances.[9] Contrary to the conventional wisdom in the region, which ascribed inflation to supply rigidities, lack of competition, and other structural factors, the young economists at Católica taught that inflation was the result of monetary largesse, which was often driven by major fiscal imbalances. They pointed out that Friedman and Harberger had provided ample evidence on the stability of the demand for money in countries of different stages of development.[10] In contradiction to the ideas of Aníbal Pinto and Raul Prebisch on import substitution industrialization, the Chicago Boys argued that protectionism generated serious inefficiencies and that trade liberalization characterized by massive reduction of import tariffs would greatly benefit poorer countries. They also pointed out that there was abundant evidence—much of it amassed by H. Gregg Lewis—that regulations in the labor market, including minimum wages, distorted the economy and often had negative effects on social conditions, income distribution, and economic growth. This topic was particularly close to the heart of Sergio de Castro, the man who would lead the Chicago Boys' revolution during the years of Augusto Pinochet's dictatorship; he was writing (rather slowly) a PhD dissertation on wage rate differentials across industries in Chile. Most of the ideas touted by the Chicago Boys were considered "esoteric" in Chile at the time.[11] The fact that they pushed them without much regard to the accepted views paved the impression among their detractors that they lived in an ivory tower.

The spat between the two economists' factions was also affected by the different personalities. Some of those involved in the policy debates, simply, did not like each other. This was particularly the case of Sergio de Castro, Ernesto Fontaine, and Aníbal Pinto. In the early 1990s, I interviewed Pinto in his Santiago home for a project on the 1950s Chilean stabilization program of the Klein-Saks Mission, and we ended talking about the history of economics in Chile and Latin America. His personal dislike for the Chicago Boys was evident, and he did not mince words about it; he did not like Sergio de Castro, and he truly disliked Simon Rottenberg, with whom he engaged in a heated debate in the pages of the journal *Panorama económico*. The same was true on the other side. Ernesto Fontaine, a colorful and engaging man with a contagious laugh, often referred to the structuralists, including Aníbal Pinto and Osvaldo Sunkel, as "ignorant" and as "populists" who knew very little about economics.

No one knows for sure who coined the name Chicago Boys. Initially it was used mockingly. "Boys" had two connotations: first, that these were very young individuals who did not know much about practical economics, and second, that they were imbued with a foreign ideology. They were always referred to as Boys, in English, and not *Niños*, in Spanish. Worse yet, they came from Chicago, the land of Milton Friedman and the defenders of "extreme capitalism."[12]

In April 1958 the agreement between the University of Chicago and Católica was renewed for three years, until 1961. Now Católica made a commitment to fund research assistants, selected among senior undergraduates and potential candidates to travel to Chicago. The renewed contract reiterated that Católica would fund at least four full-time professorships in economics, hired among those students who were trained under the program.[13] Implicit in the new agreement was the idea that once it was over, in 1961, Católica would continue to engage in the war of ideas and send students to Chicago, with financing from various foundations. Even before the initial Chicago Boys came back to Chile, Albion Patterson made sure that Católica got sufficient funding for several research projects. Through the years, monies were obtained from the Atlas, Bradley, Ford, Guggenheim, and Rockefeller Foundations and the US Foreign Office Administration. The Organization of American States and the World Bank financed agriculture and international trade projects.[14]

To Devalue or Not to Devalue, That Is the Question

In August 1962 a major controversy erupted between Sergio de Castro, who had emerged as the leader of the Chicago Boys, and the administration of conservative president Jorge Alessandri. In a research paper, De Castro argued that the government's attempt to control inflation by fixing the exchange rate was doomed.[15] His calculations, based on the purchasing power parity methodology that compares accumulated inflation in the home country and in its trading partners, indicated that the currency—the escudo, at the time—had to be devalued by at least 50 percent to reestablish external balance. De Castro pointed out that an overvalued exchange rate fueled speculation, resulted in huge increases in external debt, discouraged exports, and amplified other distortions. He argued that the best policy was to devalue the escudo and, simultaneously, reduce import tariffs and other trade controls in order to improve efficiency and resource allocation. His views were clearly influenced by research done by some members of the faculty at the University of Chicago, including Milton Friedman, Al Harberger, and Harry Johnson. De Castro's analysis was summarized in a two-page article in the August 15, 1962, issue of the weekly magazine *Ercilla*. Reporter Rubén Corvalán wrote that according to the young professor it was necessary to "permanently maintain a realistic [devalued] exchange rate policy."[16]

The government authorities were incensed by what they considered to be "friendly fire." After all, Católica was supposed to be in favor of pro-business policies, and that was exactly what the Alessandri administration was trying to do. The minister of finance approached Monsignor Alfredo Silva Santiago, the rector of Católica, and asked him to keep his economists on a short leash. The Left was also critical of the report, but for a different reason. Aníbal Pinto argued (once again) that the Chicago Boys didn't understand Chile or Latin America, and that freeing trade would impede industrialization and import substitution, the two most important policies that would take Chile out of underdevelopment. On this issue, Pinto followed Swedish economist Gunnar Myrdal and other progressive development experts who believed that devaluations were ineffective under most circumstances due to very low-price elasticities of imports and exports (the "elasticity pessimism" hypothesis).[17]

Dean Chaná Cariola was also furious. He had taken leave from the university to serve in Alessandri's cabinet and took the criticism as a personal affront. After meeting with the monsignor, he decided that, in the future, research papers had to be cleared by him before they were circulated to the public. The faculty immediately cried censorship and stated that academic freedom was of the essence. After heated discussions, H. Gregg Lewis, Al Harberger, and Ted Schultz were called in to mediate between the professors and the university administration. For Schultz this was a particularly serious issue, since in 1943 he and a group of colleagues had left Iowa State College because the authorities had tried to censor a paper where they argued that, during the war, it was recommendable to substitute margarine for butter. At the end, and after a long mediation by the Chicago professors, an agreement of sorts was reached at Católica. An internal peer review committee would determine whether papers were ready for circulation to the outside world. This, however, was not fully satisfactory to either side, and the conflict dragged on until 1965, when Julio Chaná Cariola was replaced as dean by none other than Sergio de Castro.

What makes the 1962 exchange rate / devaluation controversy particularly ironic is that fifteen years later, as Pinochet's minister of finance, Sergio de Castro implemented a fixed exchange rate stabilization program very similar to Alessandri's 1959 plan—a plan that he had savaged in his controversial report. Both programs ended up in severe crises; at some point, the external imbalances generated by the overvalued exchange rate became unsustainable, and the currency had to be devalued massively and abruptly. In the earlier episode (during the Alessandri administration) the price of the dollar jumped by 75 percent in one year. In the later episode (during the Pinochet dictatorship), a year after the crisis, the price of the dollar had increased by 92 percent. (On the currency crisis of 1982, see chapter 8.)

Research and Doctrine

In September 1963 the first issue of *Cuadernos de economía* (Notebooks on economy), an academic journal housed at Católica, was published. The initial editors were Pablo Baraona, who years later would be appointed governor of the Banco Central de Chile (Central Bank of Chile) and minister of economics by Pinochet, and Ricardo Ffrench-Davis, the University of Chicago graduate who was critical of markets,

FIGURE 2.1. *From left to right*: Sergio de Castro, Arnold Harberger, and Carlos Massad in 2008, fifty-two years after the first Chicago Boys enrolled at the University of Chicago. *Source*: Rolf Lüders's personal collection

globalization, and monetarism. The idea of launching the journal came from Lewis, who had been a member of Ffrench-Davis's and De Castro's dissertation committees in Chicago. In figure 2.1. we can see Sergio de Castro, Al Harberger, and Carlos Massad in 2008, fifty-two years after the first Chicago Boys enrolled at the University of Chicago. The occasion was a celebration of Harberger's contributions to the teaching of economics at Católica.

In the maiden issue of the journal, Dean Chaná Cariola noted that the only criterion for publication was that articles reflected "scientific research . . . [A]ll other purposes are foreign to our review." This was a veiled criticism of *Panorama económico*, the dominant economics journal at the time, which was edited by Aníbal Pinto, the prolific economist who, with his colleague Osvaldo Sunkel, were the major forces behind the structuralism approach to inflation and two of the most severe critics of the Chicago Boys.

Between 1963 and 1970—the year socialist Salvador Allende was elected president—*Cuadernos de economía* published seventy-four articles. Four future Pinochet cabinet members were frequent authors—Jorge Cauas, Sergio de Castro, Sergio de la Cuadra, and Rolf Lüders—as were some members of the Chicago faculty with close connections to Chile: Harberger, Lewis, Johnson, and Schultz. The articles in the early issues were mostly pedagogical and included topics such as how to interpret regression coefficients or how to set up a simple linear programming model. With time, however, several detailed and in-depth empirical studies on the Chilean economy were published. Many dealt with the agricultural sector and showed Schultz's enormous influence among Católica's faculty.

In his reminiscences, Pablo Baraona, the first editor of *Cuadernos de economía*, points out that despite the importance of the agricultural sector—both politically and economically—no one in Chile really knew how to analyze it from a rigorous and market-oriented perspective. Since he had taken the agricultural economic sequence—taught by Ted Schultz, D. Gale Johnson, and later by George Tolley at the University of Chicago—he was considered an expert on the subject, and was asked by politicians from the Right to lead a number of research projects.[18] The most prominent agricultural expert on the other side of the academic divide was Jorge Ahumada, a development specialist who in 1958 published a very influential book titled *En vez de la miseria* (Instead of misery), where he argued that productivity in the agricultural sector could only be increased if there was deep agrarian reform through which large holdings of land—the so-called *latifundios*—were expropriated, divided into smaller plots, and distributed to peasants. This was not the main tack taken by Católica's experts. Although they recognized that absentee ownership was detrimental to growth in productivity, they believed that the main impediment for rapid improvements in efficiency was the lack of investment in people, a theme that was at the heart of Schultz's research. At the time, the differences in educational attainment between rural and urban workers were abysmal—indeed, a large proportion of farm workers (known as *inquilinos*) were illiterate.[19] Católica economists also thought that the perennially overvalued currency contributed negatively to agriculture by discouraging exports. Other impediments for the growth of agriculture were the absence of a market for water rights and high import tariffs on key inputs, including machinery and fertilizers. Agrarian reform would become a major political issue in the years to come, generating deep political conflicts during the Frei and Allende administrations.[20]

During the first decade of *Cuadernos de economía* several detailed articles on inflation, one of Chile's most serious problems since the 1940s, were published. Although the studies differed in methodology and details, they all emphasized the monetary source of inflation, and related it to the perennial fiscal imbalance in the country. Rolf Lüders published a thorough analysis of the failed stabilization programs since the mid-1950s, as well as an investigation on how inflation eroded tax receipts. Ricardo Morán discussed the merits of abrupt stabilization programs, and Ernesto Fontaine tackled the connection between devaluations and inflation, or what came to be known as the pass-through problem in international economics.[21]

This research was not well received outside Católica. Critics, including representatives of the private sector, argued that the Chicago Boys ignored the realities of the country. Flavián Levine, the CEO of the largest steel mill, Compañía de Aceros del Pacífico (Pacific Steel Company), engaged in a lively debate with Martin J. Bailey on the causes and dynamics of inflation, which had averaged 40 percent per annum for the years 1953–57. Levine, who had been an early supporter of Keynesian views and a personal friend of politicians from the Right and the Left, did not deny that money growth played a role, but argued that it was a secondary one, much less important than some structural supply considerations.[22] When it came to inflation, Levine and other captains of industry sided with the structuralist approach and thought that the Chicago Boys completely missed the boat by overemphasizing the role of money growth.

Between 1963 and 1973 Sergio de Castro published four articles in *Cuadernos de economía*. In the January 1965 issue of the journal he published a paper titled "Política cambiaria: ¿Libertad o controles?" (Exchange rate policy: Freedom or controls?), in which he used many of the ideas presented by Milton Friedman in his famous essay "The Case for Flexible Exchange Rates" to argue in favor of a market-determined currency value in Chile.[23] In those years, most development economists took the position that exchange rate adjustments did not work in poor nations. This idea had been pushed by Swedish economist and future Nobel Prize laureate Gunnar Myrdal, who in his *Asian Drama* wrote, "*Devaluation is not an alternative to import controls. . . .* [I]t should be frankly recognized that the concept [devaluation] is not applicable to these countries."[24] This was exactly the opposite of what Friedman had asserted in his essay and in a short book that summarized a series of lectures he gave in India in 1963.[25] Surprisingly, Friedman's work on flexible exchange rates was not cited by Sergio de Castro in his article.

In the April 1969 issue of the journal, Sergio de Castro published an extensive essay on "price policy" in which he made two points that at the time were highly controversial and that would become central to the policies of the military regime after the 1973 coup d'état: price controls were not an effective tool for redistributing income, and freeing interest rates and allowing them to find their equilibrium would have a positive overall effect on economic efficiency and economic growth. At the time this message sounded like a Chilean version of Friedman's *Capitalism and Freedom*. De Castro's last journal article as an academic was published in December 1972. He examined Chile's experience in 1961, when automatic wage adjustments according to past inflation were suspended. Most analysts believed that the pause in wage indexation would result in a decline in real wages and salaries. But a careful analysis of the data showed that in several industries real salaries rose significantly. In De Castro's view, this showed, clearly, that when there was no government intervention, markets functioned properly, and relative wages adjusted according to supply and demand forces. The main message from this piece also made it to the menu of policies implemented during the Pinochet regime.

A Think Tank and the Press

In 1965, a group of business leaders founded one of Chile's first pro-free-markets think tanks, the Centro de Estudios Sociales y Económicos (CESEC; Center of Social and Economic Studies). Originally directed by sociologist Guillermo Chadwick, its role was to work on the intersection between politics and economics, and issue reports to help private-sector firms make investment decisions. CESEC's main promoter was Agustín Edwards, the owner of the most important newspaper—*El Mercurio*—and the heir to one of Chile's largest fortunes, with interests in banking, insurance, agriculture, and manufacturing. Edwards, who was educated at Princeton University and had a vast network of friends and associates in the United States, was convinced that Latin America's greatest danger was the spreading of the Cuban Revolution.[26]

The CESEC economics branch was led by Emilio Sanfuentes, a Chicago Boy who also had a degree in sociology and worked as a consultant for the Edwards Group. Sanfuentes hired other University of Chicago graduates and worked with trade groups to promote the principles of market economics. What made Emilio Sanfuentes a key piece in the machinery that eventually propelled the Chicago Boys to the center of political power was his vast network of relations with retired Chilean Navy officers, including Hernán Cubillos and Roberto Kelly, both of whom would become members of Pinochet's cabinet. It was through them that, during the Allende administration, a group of Chicago Boys got in touch with active navy officers, including Admiral José Toribio Merino, one of the leaders of the coup, and provided them with the blueprint for a new economic model (see chapter 4 for details).

In 1967 *El Mercurio* inaugurated a new business and economics section—initially, it was just one page—where economic trends and doctrinaire issues were explained to the general public. Adelio Pipino, a Chicago Boy who would become a senior International Monetary Fund official, was initially in charge of the section. Most of those who wrote in it were either University of Chicago or Católica graduates. The first article was published on April 17, 1967, and was titled "Fluctuaciones cíclicas en la producción industrial, 1957–1966" (Cyclical fluctuations in

Chile's industrial output, 1957–1966). The last article in this series was published on October 10, 1970, only five weeks after the presidential election where candidate Salvador Allende of the Partido Socialista de Chile (Socialist Party of Chile) got a plurality of votes; on October 24 he was confirmed as president-elect by a joint session of the Congreso Nacional de Chile (National Congress of Chile). The article was simply titled "El programa económico de la Unidad Popular" (The economic program of Popular Unity) and presaged many of the challenges that Chile would face during the socialist experiment (see chapter 3 for a detailed analysis). All in all, between 1967 and 1970, the Chicago Boys and their friends and associates published 170 articles in *El Mercurio*. Some of them were celebrated by the business elite, and some— especially those arguing for free trade, market-determined interest rates, and flexible exchange rates—were derided and criticized for being completely disconnected from reality.[27]

A Failed Foray into Politics

During the 1970 presidential election—an election that, as noted, was eventually won by Salvador Allende—Sergio de Castro, Ernesto Fontaine, and Pablo Baraona were asked by industrialists Pierre Lehmann and Sergio Silva Bascuñán to draft an economic program for conservative candidate (and former president) Jorge Alessandri. The idea was to develop a plan that emphasized the role of private investment and the private sector and, at the same time, reduced inflation, from around 25 percent to a single-digit level.

The program had several innovations relative to previous conservative platforms and included many of the policies the Chicago Boys had been promoting for a dozen years: lowering import tariffs, freeing up most prices, deregulating industry, creating a capital market with market-determined interest rates, allowing the exchange rate to move in response to supply and demand forces, and eliminating the fiscal deficit in order to reduce inflation.[28]

The proposal was not well received by the Alessandri campaign; the candidate's senior advisers immediately said that it was excessively audacious. It was not possible, they noted, to end inflation rapidly, nor was it possible to free prices, deregulate the financial sector, allow for free capital mobility, or abolish exchange controls. But the most contentious issue by far was lowering import tariffs and ending the process of import substitution launched in the mid-1940s. At the time, Chile's business elite—and elites in other emerging countries, for that matter—believed that the only way for a poor nation to make progress was by industrializing and creating a robust manufacturing sector. This required government assistance in several areas: subsidized credit, import protection to key industries, and regulations of various kinds in order to limit "excessive and harmful foreign competition."

In the 2015 documentary *Chicago Boys*, Sergio de Castro tells the interviewer that when the candidate Alessandri—an austere man who had been the CEO of one of the largest companies in the country—heard their proposals he told his aides, "Get these crazy men out of here; and make sure that they never come back!"[29]

As it turned out, preparing Alessandri's economic platform had not been a complete waste of time for the Chicago Boys. Three years later, it became the basis for the broad-based and ambitious program they prepared for the military—a program that revolutionized economic policy in Chile and greatly influenced the thinking about economics in the rest of the emerging world. That document became known colloquially as El Ladrillo (The Brick); its genesis, contents, and the story behind it are detailed in chapter 4.

3

Salvador Allende's Thousand Days of Socialism and the Chicago Boys, 1970–1973

ON SEPTEMBER 6, 1970, the *New York Times* reported, in a front-page article, the results of Chile's presidential election. The story was titled "Allende, Chilean Marxist, Wins Vote for Presidency." Veteran reporter Juan de Onis explained that getting a plurality did not make Allende the president automatically. According to the Chilean Constitution, if no candidate obtained more than 50 percent of the votes, a joint session of the Chilean Congress would elect the head of state among the two candidates with the highest number of votes. Salvador Allende, a physician who had been in politics for decades and had unsuccessfully run for the presidency three times, obtained 36.6 percent of the votes. Former president Jorge Alessandri—a conservative supported by most of the Chicago Boys—came in second with 35.3 percent; the two top candidates were separated by merely forty thousand votes. Third place went to Christian Democrat Radomiro Tomic, with 28 percent support. Allende's coalition, Unidad Popular (Popular Unity) included the two largest Marxist parties in the country—the Partido Comunista de Chile (Communist Party of Chile) and the Partido Socialista de Chile (Socialist Party of Chile)—as well as smaller groups, including the Movimiento de Acción Popular Unitaria (Popular Unitary Action Movement), a new party formed by former Christian Democrats who followed the social doctrine of the Catholic Church.[1] The *New York Times* story ended by stating that Allende "would like to see Chile follow the road of revolutionary Cuba."[2]

The Right was utterly shocked by the election's result. Most of the conservative elite was convinced that Alessandri would win by a comfortable margin. In fact, not a single major poll taken between May and late August—eight in total—predicted a Unidad Popular win.[3]

Merely two days after the election, Jorge Alessandri declared that if the Congress opted for him, he would resign immediately after inauguration. This opened the possibility of an anti-Left gambit: the Congress would elect Alessandri, who would resign, and a new election would take place right away. The outgoing president, Christian Democrat Eduardo Frei Montalva, would run as the sole anticommunist candidate, and with a high degree of probability would defeat Allende.[4] The conservative wing of the Christian Democratic Party pushed for the gambit, while the leftist wing—including former candidate Radomiro Tomic—argued that the party had to support Allende, whose progressive political platform and socialist economic program were similar to their own. At most, they contended, they should demand that Unidad Popular made a series of commitments regarding the protection of the democratic system, religious freedom, and the independence of the judiciary. These pledges were to be enshrined in the constitution through an amendment known as the Estatuto de Garantías Constitucionales (Statute of Democratic Guarantees). At a raucous and massive meeting of its National Committee, the Christian Democratic Party decided, by a wide margin, to support Allende if he was willing to go along with the constitutional reform, which he did.

During the next two months, the international press published hundreds of articles on Chile. Many of them noted that immediately after the election the economy went into a tailspin. There were bank runs, the currency sank to historical lows, and the stock market collapsed. Many wealthy families feared that Allende would indeed try to emulate Cuba, and they were leaving the country as quickly as they could.[5] On October 3, less than a month after the election, *El Siglo*, the Communist Party's newspaper, reported that because of massive capital flight the exchange rate in the black market had jumped to 65 escudos per US dollar, implying a 260 percent premium over the official rate of 18 escudos per dollar.

One day after the election, Edward Korry, the US ambassador to Chile, sent a somber cable to the US Department of State in which he analyzed the results:

> Chile voted calmly to have a Marxist-Leninist state, the first nation in the world to make that choice freely and knowingly. . . . [Allende's] margin is only about one percent but it is large enough to nail down his triumph as final. There is no reason to believe that the Chilean armed forces will unleash a civil war. . . . It is a sad fact that Chile has taken the path to Communism with little more than a third (36pct) of the nation approving this choice, but it is an immutable fact. It will have the most profound effect on Latin America and beyond.[6]

On September 15, President Richard Nixon met in the White House with Central Intelligence Agency (CIA) director Richard Helms, National Security Adviser Henry Kissinger, and Attorney General John Mitchell to discuss the events in Chile. It was decided to launch a plan—eventually code-named Operation FUBELT—coordinated by Thomas Karamessines, the CIA's deputy director for plans, to impede Allende's accession to power. Helms took notes at the meeting and wrote that one of the goals of the strategy was to "make the [Chilean] economy scream."[7]

As part of the strategy, the CIA contemplated supporting a coup led by retired general Roberto Viaux. After interviewing scores of Chileans, including retired and active armed forces' officers, the agency concluded that "a Viaux coup attempt carried out by him alone with the forces at his disposal would fail."[8] In spite of rejecting Viaux's plot, the CIA provided arms—submachine guns and pistols—to a group of civilians that, on October 23, tried to kidnap General René Schneider, the commander in chief of the Chilean Army and a loyalist officer who was firmly committed to maintaining democratic rule. The attempt failed, and the general was seriously wounded as he tried to repel the kidnappers using his Walther service pistol. On October 24, 1970, a day after Schneider's failed kidnapping attempt, the Chilean Congress, in a joint session, elected Salvador Allende as president by a 153–35 vote. A day later, General Schneider died, becoming an instant hero of the Left.[9]

The *New York Times* carried the news of Salvador Allende's accession to the presidency on its front page, with a headline that emphasized the fact that he was a Marxist: "Allende, Marxist Leader, Elected Chile's President." Reporter Joseph Novitski summarized the new government's economic goals, writing, "The president elect and his coalition have promised to nationalize Chile's mines and basic industry, its banking and insurance system, and foreign trade. They have also pledged to plan the country's economic and social development and to expropriate privately owned farming land as part of an expanded agrarian reform program."[10]

Although the reference to an economic "plan" was buried in the middle of a sentence, the idea of moving from a market to a planned economy was at the center of Unidad Popular's economic strategy. The first chapter of its economic platform stated, "The main goal of the popular political forces is to replace the current economic structure, putting an end to the power of national and international monopolistic capital and latifundia, and to initiate the construction of socialism. *In the new economy, planning will play a fundamental role.* . . . The economic policy of the state will be implemented through a *system of national economic planning and control mechanism.*"[11]

After being confirmed as president-elect, Allende told reporters that his government would not implement blanket nationalization of industry. He assured them that his administration would only target large, monopolistic, and strategic firms in key sectors. He pointed out that the nationalized sector would include "all banks, nitrate, the telephone company, coal . . . foreign trade companies, insurance companies, and liquefied gas producers," as well as a number of manufacturing firms considered to have monopolistic power.[12]

The fact that Salvador Allende was a member of the Socialist Party, and not the Communist Party, has led to confusion among many uninformed authors. At that time—in the 1950s, 1960s, and early 1970s—there were two Marxist-Leninist political parties in Chile. The Communist Party followed the political line developed in the USSR and favored building broad electoral alliances with "petit bourgeois" parties; this was the so-called Frente Popular (Popular Front) strategy, based on a gradual, incremental implementation of socialism. The Socialist Party—the one Allende belonged to—was significantly to the Left, had close ties with Cuba and North Korea, and believed that the move to socialism had to be fast and based on "workers' power," a strategy that excluded social democratic and Center-Left parties. Before Allende's election in 1970, the dominant faction within the Socialist Party—a faction Allende did not belong to—became disappointed with electoral politics and began to consider the guerilla warfare option. During the Unidad Popular government, moderates and extremists within the Socialist Party clashed constantly. After the coup, left-leaning analysts blamed the Socialist Party, and in particular its secretary-general, Carlos Altamirano, for pushing revolutionary changes too fast and too hard. According to this view, those policies and violent rhetoric alienated the middle class and ultimately contributed to the armed forces' decision to stage the 1973 coup.[13]

On November 4, 1970, Salvador Allende was inaugurated as president. His cabinet included communists, socialists, union leaders, and followers of the social doctrine of the Catholic Church. The minister of economics was Pedro Vuskovic, a Marxist economist and expert on planning, who had served as head of the economics faculty at the Universidad de Chile, Católica's longtime rival. The title of minister of finance went to Américo Zorrilla, a linotype union leader and a member of the Communist Party who had no college education.

On November 9, 1970, five days after Allende's inauguration, Henry Kissinger sent a top secret memorandum to senior officials in the CIA, the US Department of Defense, and the US Department of State in which he stated that "the public posture of the United States will be correct but cool. . . . [We will] seek to maximize pressures on the Allende government to prevent its consolidation and limit its ability

TABLE 3.1. Chile's Comparative Performance, 1945–1970

	Chile	Latin America 6[a]	Latin America[b]
Average GDP growth (% per year, 1945–72)	4.1%	5.6%	5.3%
Average growth manufacturing (% per year, 1945–72)	5.2%	6.7%	6.8%
Average inflation (% per year, 1950–70)	33%	18%	12%
Gini coefficient (closest year to 1970)	0.50	—	0.48
Historical living standard index in 1970 (1950 = 100)	136	147	145

Source: Thorp (1998).

[a] Average of the six largest countries in the region: Argentina, Brazil, Chile, Colombia, Mexico, and Venezuela.
[b] Average of all countries with data (usually between thirteen and nineteen).

to implement policies contrary to U.S. and hemisphere interests."[14] During the next three years Chile and the United States went through a series of diplomatic confrontations, with the most serious one taking place in July 1971, when the Chilean government expropriated large copper mines that belonged to US corporations without paying any compensation.

Table 3.1 presents the data on a series of economic and social indicators that summarize the state of the Chilean economy in 1970, when Allende reached the presidency. These data are also helpful to put the Chicago Boys' reforms program (discussed in the chapters that follow) in the proper context. For comparative purposes, I include information on two groups of Latin American countries. As may be seen, between 1945 and 1970, Chile underperformed its peers in every dimension. Growth was lower, inflation was much higher, inequality (as measured by the Gini coefficient) was higher, and overall living conditions were poorer in Chile than in the average Latin American nation. To be sure, in 1970 Chile was not the poorest of the countries south of the Rio Grande—those were Bolivia, Honduras, and Nicaragua—but it was being left behind steadily by many other nations on the continent.[15]

Expansive Macroeconomic Policies with Price Controls: Modern Monetary Theory in the 1970s

Allende's short-term economic policy was based on a major surge in aggregate demand. The idea, developed by Pedro Vuskovic, was that in an economy dominated by monopolies there was ample unutilized capacity that could accommodate a substantial increase in demand. The strategy was built around "the simultaneous control of prices, wage increases, and increase in the public sector deficit . . . financed by money and credit creation."[16] The Unidad Popular economists believed that substantial increases in government expenditures could be financed by Chile's Central Bank without generating a spike in inflation or an external crisis. Of course, they realized that Chile's currency was not convertible and that the availability of foreign exchange provided a hard constraint. But, according to them, that potential obstacle could be handled by imposing price and exchange control. Foreign exchange could only be used for "productive purposes," including the importation of intermediate inputs, spare parts, and capital equipment. Chileans traveling abroad on business or vacation were given a small stipend of twenty US dollars per day at the official rate; if they needed more, they had to get it in the parallel market. Since inflation was considered to be the result of monopolistic practices and structural bottlenecks, price controls at the retail level were a key component of the short-term economic strategy. In many ways, what the Allende government engaged in, decades before it got its name, were policies very similar to those touted by the supporters of Modern Monetary Theory.[17]

Initially the new policies appeared to work. During 1971, average real wages increased by 21 percent, real gross domestic product (GDP) growth shot up to 8 percent, and inflation was contained at 22 percent. Yet, behind these figures, major imbalances were mounting. Investment in equipment and machinery (especially in the nationalized manufacturing sector) all but disappeared, agricultural output collapsed, and a substantial trade deficit developed. As a result of an increasingly large fiscal deficit financed with money printing by the Central Bank, pressures on prices intensified rapidly, and by the third year of the Allende government "open inflation" was almost 700 percent.

Expropriation, Nationalization, and "Intervention"

Unidad Popular's longer-term strategy was based on the nationalization of copper mines, the banking sector, large trading companies, insurance companies, and a number of large firms with monopoly power. In addition, millions of acres of farmland were to be expropriated and transformed into cooperatives or state-owned farms. Nationalized companies would form the core of the new state-owned means of production and would lead the way to a society in which only small- and medium-size enterprises would be in the hands of the private sector. In figure 3.1 we can see, seated, from left to right, Minister of Planning Gonzalo Martner, Minister of Economics Pedro Vuskovic, President Salvador Allende, and Minister of Finance Américo Zorrilla, accompanied by two military aides.

On July 15, 1971, the large copper mines owned by US multinationals were nationalized through a constitutional amendment approved unanimously by the Congress. The novelty of the initiative was that compensation to the American companies was calculated as book value minus "excessive profits" accrued since 1964.[18] The amendment and related legislation established that the Oficina de la Contraloría General de la República (Office of Comptroller General of the Republic) would determine appropriate book value, and that the Oficina del Presidente (Office of the President) would estimate historical "excessive profits." These were defined as any net income in excess of 10 percent of book value. The result of these calculations was that the mining companies owed Chile some US$400 million.[19]

Banks were nationalized through massive tender offers—*poder comprador* (buying power)—where the state holding company, the Corporación de Fomento de la Producción (Corporation for Production Development) paid handsome prices for shares, independent of the size of the blocks sold to the government. On average, the offers

FIGURE 3.1. President Salvador Allende (*third from left*), with his
economic team and military aides in 1971
Source: La Tercera photo archive

carried premiums of 100 percent. These purchases were financed by
loans from the Central Bank to the government, or pure money printing. As a result, in 1971 the money supply grew by almost 150 percent
(see table 3.2). Expropriated farmland was paid for with long-term government bonds issued in nominal local currency, whose real value was
eroded by galloping inflation.[20]

Manufacturing companies were nationalized through a highly controversial mechanism, whose legal bases emanated from an executive
order dating from the Great Depression.[21] According to the 1932 executive order, if certain goods became in short supply due to a factory stoppage, the government could "intervene" in the company in question and
take over its facilities for an undetermined period; such intervention
could, in principle, last for years, even decades.[22] By 1973, hundreds of
companies—some of them quite small—had been taken over by the
government through this procedure. Frequently, unions staged takeovers

TABLE 3.2. Chile and the Unidad Popular Government

	Public-sector balance (% of GDP)	Consolidated public-sector balance (% of GDP)	Rate of growth of money supply (base; %)	Inflation % per annum (average)	Current account balance (% of GDP)	Real GDP growth % per year
1968	-2.4	NA	36.80	27.94	-2.16	3.60
1969	-1.5	NA	43.61	29.34	-0.08	3.71
1970	-2.9	-6.69	66.15	34.93	-1.27	2.05
1971	-11.2	-15.28	135.88	22.13	-2.36	8.96
1972	-13.5	-24.53	178.25	163.43	-4.31	-1.21
1973	-24.6	-30.40	365.03	508.05	-8.81	-5.57
1974	-10.5	NA	319.58	375.88	-3.71	0.97

Sources: "Public-sector balance (% of GDP)" from Edwards and Edwards (1991); "Consolidated public-sector balance (% of GDP)" from Larraín and Meller (1991); "Rate of growth of money supply (base; %)," "Inflation % per annum (average)," "Current account balance (% of GDP)," and "Real GDP growth % per year" from Banco Central de Chile (2001).

in order to force operations to stop, creating artificial shortages. The unavailability of the goods produced by the firms—for example, cooking pots, cement, textiles, garments, or shoes—was then used as a legal justification to "intervene" in the company, de facto nationalizing it. In some cases a negotiation between the government and the shareholders ensued, and if an agreement was reached, the company was officially purchased by the state and owners were compensated using Central Bank credits.

Price Controls and Shortages

One of the most damaging aspects of Unidad Popular's economics program was the surrealistic system of price controls. Maximum prices for over three thousand goods were determined by the Dirección de Industria y Comercio (DIRINCO; Directorate of Industry and Commerce), under the assumption that in every one of those industries there was monopolistic power and companies abused their clients.

I personally know how bad, arbitrary, and harmful the system was, because I was there. As a nineteen-year-old college student at the Universidad de Chile, I was offered the position of assistant to the director of costs and prices at DIRINCO. The unit oversaw every controlled price in the country and had the legal authority to determine whether a price increase was authorized. The position gave me unusual power, as I assigned price adjustment requests to the different accountants who worked in the office, and I kept the director's appointment book. On more than one occasion I was told to misplace a file, or to move it to the top of the pile, or to assign it to a given employee who was sympathetic to one view or another. In 1973, with inflation moving toward the 700 percent mark, prices authorized by the directorate became outdated within a week or so. New requests were immediately submitted, and the directorate promptly denied them. Any first-year student would have predicted the results of this viciously circular process: massive shortages and a thriving black market for all sorts of goods, including such essentials as sugar, rice, coffee, cooking oil, and toilet paper. But the political authorities believed that a strong hand was needed to deal with price gouging promoted by the "enemies of the revolutionary process." An army of inspectors roamed the city looking for "specula-tors," for shop owners who refused to sell at the official price, and for traitors and "antipatriots." If they found merchandise in a warehouse, the store was closed, the goods were confiscated, a huge fine was imposed, and, sometimes, the owner was sent to jail.

Some of the economists in the political leadership realized that mas-sive shortages and rationing through neighborhood committees were negatively affecting the support for President Allende and tried to find a solution to the increasingly fragile and chaotic economic conditions. In mid-1971 Fernando Flores, who would eventually become minister of finance, convinced management guru and mathematical superstar Staf-ford Beer to travel to Chile and work with the government on a techni-cal, computer-based planning system that would find the correct prices for most goods in the country. The secret project was called Cybersyn.

I remember the one meeting I attended with the famous British sci-entist, held at the Ministerio de Economía (Ministry of Economics) on Teatinos Street in Santiago. There was a great sense of anticipation, especially among the cadre of young progressive economists who worked in the government. Stafford Beer arrived with Fernando Flores and other functionaries from the planning office. He sat at the head of the table, but instead of making a presentation, he asked questions of those in attendance. He wanted to know what was done in the different departments and what the most pressing problems were according to those who were doing the actual work. He was also interested in finding out what type of models were being used so as to determine "appropri-ate" prices for different products. A senior member of the directorate explained our artisanal modus operandi: when a company made a re-quest for a price increase, it provided information on all its costs and added a "profit margin" that ranged from 7 percent to 15 percent. Once the request was received, an army of accountants reviewed the figures. In most cases, they slashed the cost estimates, halved the margin, and approved a much smaller price increase than the one requested. Com-pany executives, of course, knew that this was going to happen, and systematically inflated the cost figures. Beer asked for spillover effects, or what economists would call general equilibrium consequences of the different decisions made by the directorate. The answer was that they were largely ignored. He smiled and muttered to himself something like "Oh my!" Then, someone in the audience—a young theoretician who had degrees in both economics and mathematics—said that there was a computer program that estimated cross-sector supply requirements and generated "true accounting or shadow prices as the dual of the optimization process," to which Beer replied, "Interesting." The young mathematician continued, explaining some technical aspects of the model. When he finished, Beer asked how many sectors, industries, and goods were included in the analysis. The young man hesitated for a few seconds and finally answered, "Fifteen." Beer appeared confused and asked the translator if the number was fifteen or fifty. When it was clarified that the model considered only fifteen industries, he just said, "But, my friend, you really want to determine true, social, equilibrium prices for over three thousand goods, with a fifteen-sector input-output matrix?"[23]

I never saw Stafford Beer again. But I do remember that as the year advanced and the economic conditions worsened, we often wondered where he was, and we asked ourselves when he would produce the magical computer program that would solve every economic problem in Chile and thus would help avoid the coup d'état that we saw looming on the horizon.

Stagnation and Runaway Inflation

In 1972 economic growth stagnated, official inflation climbed to 260 percent, and real wages fell below their 1970 levels. Shortages became more acute, and a generalized black market for goods and foreign exchange developed. An important factor behind the collapse of the economy was the increase in labor unrest, a succession of national strikes called by the opposition parties, and stoppage in many factories that would eventually be taken over by the government. Particularly disruptive was a national strike organized by the trucking industry in October 1972, a strike that was partially financed by the CIA.[24] As a result of the strike, there was no gasoline, and public transportation became spotty and infrequent. Lines formed in front of every supermarket and neighborhood grocery store. In light of these developments the government decided to ration food through neighborhood committees called Juntas de Abastecimientos y Precios (Committees on Supplies and Prices). The opposition pointed out that, as they had warned, Chile was following Cuba's step toward rationing, dictatorship, and collapse.

In spite of the crisis, no efforts were made to introduce changes to fiscal or monetary policy. With a mixture of naïveté and stubbornness, government officials insisted that their program was a recipe for income expansion, redistribution, growth, and the construction of a fair and egalitarian socialist society. At the end of 1972 the consolidated fiscal deficit—a metric that includes the losses of state-owned firms—surpassed 20 percent of GDP, and the money supply continued to expand at an increasingly rapid pace (see table 3.2).

A Failed Coup

Politics became highly toxic, and the possibility of agreement and dialogue between the government and the opposition diminished by the day. On June 29, 1973, the officers of the Regimiento Blindado No. 2 (Armored Regiment No. 2) led an insurrection, with the hope that the rest of the armed forces would join. Early that morning, six tanks and several trucks carrying a group of about 150 soldiers moved toward the presidential palace, El Palacio de la Moneda.[25] By midmorning a loyal unit of the army, led by none other than General Augusto Pinochet, number two in the army command, put an end to the insurrection. The coup attempt failed for two key reasons. First, the leaders were rather junior officers, and the plan had no support from anyone with the rank of general or admiral. Second, the tanks were barely operational; they had no ability to fire their guns and had very little fuel. According to one story, when retreating from downtown after the assault had failed, one of the tanks had to be refueled at a commercial gas station, from which it left without paying a substantial bill. Although the coup did not succeed and those involved were arrested, the episode made it clear that the political situation had deteriorated rapidly. From that day onward, Unidad Popular supporters lived expecting another coup attempt.

Many senior government officials developed contingency plans, including how to reach certain embassies to seek asylum in case they needed to go into exile.

In September 1973 the Chilean economy was in shambles: inflation exceeded 700 percent, and there were pervasive shortages. Black markets were widespread, the trade deficit was gigantic, and the country had no international reserves. Inflation-adjusted wages had declined by 35 percent relative to the pre-Allende period. According to Paul Rosenstein-Rodan, a progressive economist and one of the world authorities on economic development, the collapse of the Chilean economy during 1970–73 was the result of Allende's socialist policies. As Rosenstein-Rodan noted, "After [Allende] took office, he accomplished a major redistribution of income that dramatically increased demand, but he did nothing to increase production to satisfy that demand. Instead, he printed money. A breakdown was inevitable, and the resulting inflation not only destroyed the income redistribution that had taken place, but lowered real wages below the level of 1970."[26]

Rosenstein-Rodan also expressed his critical views in private correspondence. In a June 26, 1975, letter to German econometrician Gerhard Tintner, a scholar who would be extremely critical of Friedman's involvement with the junta, Rosenstein-Rodan wrote, "I view with concern those who compromise the great idea of socialism. That is fundamentally true of Allende . . . who was a populist rather than a socialist, and compromised the idea."[27] French philosopher Michel Foucault also had harsh words for the Unidad Popular government and its plan for implementing socialist policies. When, in 1975, Chilean sociologist and left-wing activist Antonio Sánchez met with him in his Parisian apartment, Foucault told him, "Chile's tragedy [the coup and its aftermath] is not the result of the Chilean people's failure, but the result of the serious mistakes and the monstrous responsibility of you, Marxists."[28]

Table 3.2 summarizes the state of the economy in 1973. As can be seen, there was galloping inflation (500 percent), runaway fiscal deficits (30 percent of GDP), and falling national income (−5.6 percent). But the most damaging figure was that during the Allende administration, and mostly due to runaway inflation, real wages declined by almost 40 percent.

The Chicago Boys during the Allende Period

Shortly after Allende was elected president by the Congress, several Chicago Boys left the country and joined the ranks of international institutions such as the International Monetary Fund, the Organization of American States, and the World Bank. Sergio de la Cuadra, Ernesto Fontaine, Rolf Lüders, Adelio Pipino, Marcelo Selowsky, Alberto Valdés, and "honorary" Chicago Boy Jorge Cauas took senior posts in Washington, DC.

Those who remained in Chile after Allende's election, including Sergio de Castro, became active in the opposition to the government. They wrote reports scrutinizing the socialist administration's policies and criticized every misstep, including the reliance on money creation to finance a rapidly growing fiscal deficit. They questioned price controls, nationalization, and massive regulations. They also advised opposition politicians (including former president Eduardo Frei Montalva), helped members of Congress refute the claims made by Allende and his team, and met with increasing frequency with senior officers of the armed forces. A key figure in this process was economist Sergio Undurraga, one of the early Católica students of Sergio de Castro and Ernesto Fontaine and, thus, a Chicago Boy "by proximity." Undurraga worked as an analyst in the private sector and maintained a vast data set that he and Chicago Boy Alvaro Bardón used to forecast inflation, exchange rates, unemployment, and economic activity. In early 1972, when inflation was still contained at approximately 35 percent per year, they used a simple Chicago-style monetarist model to forecast an inflation of 180 percent for that year. Many analysts thought that they were (deliberately) exaggerating, and government officials talked of a "campaign of terror" to frighten the population and reduce the support to the government. As it turned out, their forecast fell short: official inflation in 1972 was 260 percent.[29]

The archives show that during this period there was limited research done at Católica, either by the Chicago Boys who remained in Chile or by their students. Only a handful of working papers were released between 1971 and 1973. Among them, the most intriguing one was penned by Sergio de Castro in March 1972 and titled "Programa de Desarrollo

Económico y Social" (Program for economic and social development).[30] In it De Castro provides a scathing criticism of the redistribution policies followed by the Unidad Popular government. The main problem, he argues, is that the combination of mandated wage increases, controlled prices, a fixed exchange rate at an artificial level, and de facto expropriation through the "intervention" mechanism created huge distortions that lowered the rate of growth to almost zero. He states that if redistribution is the goal, there are better ways of approaching it. More specifically, he proposed the creation, by law, of a "Social Property Fund" that would own "33.33% (1/3) of capital (assets minus liabilities) of all companies in Chile, both private and public." The fund would, in turn, belong to all Chilean workers, who would receive dividends from the complete portfolio. Controls, prohibitions, quotas, and licenses would then be eliminated, and the free market would be allowed to provide the signals to these hybrid firms and to consumers. Needless to say, this scheme was never put to work, neither during the time of Unidad Popular nor during Pinochet's dictatorship.

The most interesting and lasting work undertaken by the Chicago Boys who stayed in Chile was preparing a broad blueprint for economic reform. The document became known colloquially as El Ladrillo (The Brick) and listed a series of policies that became the basis for Pinochet's economic revolution (for a detailed analysis, see chapter 4). With time, and as Chile's "economic miracle" unfolded, The Brick became a cultlike document, consulted by finance ministers who were in a bind and by would-be reformers from around the world.

The Path to the Coup and the US Role in It

On September 11, 1973, General Augusto Pinochet led a coup d'état that deposed president Salvador Allende. In Chile's collective memory, the date 9/11 always refers to that event. Of course, Chileans are aware of the terrorist attacks on the United States in 2001, but a simple reference to September 11 takes them straight back to that fateful day when democracy was trounced in their country. What made that episode particularly traumatizing, both for Allende's supporters and for his detractors, was that Chile had been a country with a long tradition of constitutional rule; during the twentieth century, and in contrast with most countries in Latin America, authoritarian governments had been few and short-lived. (For details of the coup, see chapter 4.)

In many ways, the machinery that led to the uprising began moving the day Allende was elected president. Important events in this slow-motion tragedy included Roberto Viaux's attempted coup and the assassination of commander in chief René Schneider a few weeks later in 1970, the impeachment of several members of the cabinet, the CIA-financed truckers' strike that paralyzed the economy in 1972, and the failed insurgency by Armored Regiment Number 2 in June 1973. But the most important event, the one that gave the armed forces a justification for staging the September 11, 1973, coup, was a resolution passed by the lower house of the Congress, the Cámara de Diputados (Chamber of Deputies) on August 22, 1973. The majority of members accused the Allende government of violating the Chilean Constitution by trying to impose a totalitarian political regime and by systematically ignoring the rulings of the courts. The congressional declaration ended with a call to the armed forces to put an end to the "illegitimate" Allende government. In the years that followed, Pinochet and his allies would repeatedly argue that, from a legal point of view, the resolution by the Chamber of Deputies gave them the green light to depose the constitutionally elected president.[31]

Ever since the September 11, 1973, putsch that brought Pinochet to power, analysts, scholars, and the media have asked to what extent the United States was involved in the coup d'état and in the subsequent implementation of the Chicago Boys' reforms. There is little doubt that Allende's election was not welcomed by the Nixon administration. In his memoirs, Henry Kissinger wrote, "Allende's election was a challenge to our national interest. . . . We were persuaded that it would soon be . . . making common cause with Cuba, and sooner or later establishing close relations with the Soviet Union."[32] According to information since declassified by the U.S. government, Washington provided financial assistance to Chile's opposition political parties and organizations after Allende's election. For example, a CIA secret memorandum sent from

Santiago and dated March 14, 1973, states that while the Christian
Democratic Party was using US financial support effectively, the conservative Partido Nacional (National Party) was not very well organized
and was wasting the CIA's assistance.[33] A report by the US Senate's
Select Committee to Study Governmental Operations with Respect to
Intelligence Activities (commonly known as the Church Committee,
after its chairman, Senator Frank Church) concluded that the CIA was
involved in an early attempt to keep Allende from becoming president
(General Roberto Viaux's 1970 plot). After reviewing thousands of confidential documents and cables, however, the committee determined
that there was no evidence supporting the view that the CIA was directly behind the September 11 coup d'état. Even if doubts remain on
the extent of the CIA's support to Pinochet and his coconspirators, it is
clear that, as Foucault and Rosenstein-Rodan, among others, have
noted, Allende's economic policies were a failure.

The Chicago Boys and the Pinochet Dictatorship, 1973–1990

PART II

4

Augusto Pinochet's Coup and the Chicago Boys' Reform Program

IN THE EARLY HOURS of September 11, 1973, the Chilean fleet returned to port from a naval exercise earlier than anticipated. The battleships moved slowly, in complete radio silence and with their lights turned off. As soon as the battleships docked in Valparaíso, marine commandos disembarked and took control of government buildings and critical infrastructure, including power plants, the phone company, and TV and radio stations. The military coup that many supporters of the Unidad Popular coalition had feared for a long time was underway.[1]

At 6:00 a.m., President Salvador Allende was informed about the events at Valparaíso and other major ports.[2] His initial reaction was that the Chilean Navy was acting on its own, and that the Chilean Army, led by General Augusto Pinochet, would defend the constitutional government. The president tried to reach Pinochet, but the general was nowhere to be found. Nor could he get through to the commanders in chief of the other branches of the armed forces. At 7:35 a.m., protected by a handful of bodyguards, the Grupo de Amigos Personales (GAP; Group of Personal Friends),[3] Allende arrived at the Palacio de La Moneda, where he was relieved to see that the militarized police force, the famed Carabineros, were defending the presidential palace and the main government buildings in downtown Santiago. Allende was joined by cabinet members and other aides, including philosopher Fernando Flores. The president once again tried to contact Pinochet, but to no avail. He feared that the insurgents had taken the commander in chief prisoner; at some point he told one of his companions, "Poor Augusto, he must be under arrest." In the meantime, the minister of defense, Orlando Letelier—an urbane and charming lawyer who three years later would be assassinated in Washington, DC, by agents of the junta—was detained by his own aide-de-camp and placed in custody.[4]

By 8:20 a.m. it became clear that Pinochet, the general who had repeatedly pledged his support to the Chilean Constitution, had betrayed the president and was leading the putsch. The government was isolated. It was only supported by the twenty-five-thousand-strong Carabineros, and maybe not even all of them were on Allende's side. At 8:25 a.m. the president decided to mobilize "the people" in defense of the government. During a short radio speech, he asked workers to gather at their workplaces—especially in the factories that had been taken over by the government—and to be ready to march toward the palace. He also told them to be careful, not to accept provocation, and not to expose themselves to danger unnecessarily.[5]

At 8:42 a.m. an announcement, transmitted over most radio stations, informed the population that the armed forces had taken over the government. The junta compelled the president to give up his post. A plane was at his disposal; he and his family could go into exile in the country of his choice. The announcer added that "workers should rest assured that their social and economic conquests will not be affected" by the coup. Ten minutes later, Allende spoke on the Communist Party station, Radio Magallanes, and stated his "irrevocable decision" to stay in the palace and defend the constitution.[6]

Suddenly, the Carabineros changed sides and joined the insurgency. The green-and-white Mowag light antiriot tanks that were guarding the palace turned around and left the Plaza de la Constitución (Constitution Square) on the north side of La Moneda. The president's loneliness was profound and palpable. Only thirty or so supporters, including his bodyguards and some cabinet members and medical personnel, were with him. He put on a helmet and moved from room to room, holding the AK-47 that Fidel Castro had given him for his birthday.

At 9:15 a.m. Admiral Patricio Carvajal, one of the coup leaders and the future minister of foreign affairs of the junta, called La Moneda to give Allende an ultimatum: if the president didn't step down, fighter jets would bomb the palace at 11:00 a.m. sharp. Allende did not budge; he refused to surrender, and at 10:37 a.m. he gave his last radio speech. In closing, he said, "Workers of my homeland, I have faith in Chile and her destiny. Other men will get over this gray and bitter moment, where treason has imposed itself. You should know that sooner rather than later the wide avenues will open to let a free man walk toward a better and more just society."[7]

At 11:52 a.m. two Hawker Hunter jets bombed the palace, which was already receiving heavy fire from tanks positioned in the Plaza de la Constitución. The palace's thick nineteenth-century walls resisted round after round of heavy shelling. A ferocious fire engulfed most of the building, which filled with a thick, dark smoke; it was difficult to breathe, and some of the walls eventually began to crumble. The president understood that resistance was hopeless and agreed to surrender. Hearing this, Augusto Olivares, his chief media adviser and an old comrade, committed suicide by shooting himself in the head with an Uzi submachine gun.[8] Allende was despondent, but there was no time for mourning. He gathered those who had stayed with him and told them that they had to leave the palace. They should form two lines: the women first, followed by the men. He said that someone should take the original 1810 Declaration of Independence, a sacred document that was on display in the palace. He didn't want it to burn down with the building.

The noise from the gunfire made it difficult for the loyalists to communicate among themselves, and it became almost impossible to breathe. Allende asked one of the GAP bodyguards to use a medical gown as a white flag and to lead the group toward the entrance on the east side of the building, on Morandé Street. He shook hands with some of the men, and hugged others; he kissed the few women in the group on the forehead. After the last aide moved toward the stairs leading down to the side entrance, President Allende sat down on a sofa and committed suicide with his AK-47. There was a plaque on the buttstock that read, "To Salvador Allende, from his comrade in arms, Fidel Castro."

It was 2:34 p.m. on September 11, 1973.

At 3:15 p.m. firemen were allowed to enter the building to put out the raging fire. My friend Alejandro Artigas, a lieutenant from Primera

Compañía de Bomberos (Fire Station Number One), was among the first to climb the stairs and go to the second floor, where the presidential offices were located. Lieutenant Artigas carried a flashlight and went from room to room, making sure that nobody was trapped under a collapsed wall. Because of the smoke and the fire, he moved carefully. When he entered the Salón Blanco (White Room), a small and ornate office on the east side of the building, he saw the dead president on the couch. The AK-47 was on the floor at Allende's feet. The image would haunt Alejandro Artigas for the rest of his life. He does not like to talk about it, and when he does, he speaks slowly, in a gentle cadence with a very soft tone.

The Chicago Boys Join the Military Government

Three days after the coup, Sergio de Castro, the most senior of the Chicago Boys, was called in by Admiral José Toribio Merino, one of the members of the junta. The admiral shook his hand and told De Castro that he was appointing him as senior adviser to General Rodolfo González, the new minister of economics. De Castro immediately realized that this was not a job offer; it was a military order. His first assignment was to devise a plan to get the economy going; the economy had recorded negative growth in 1972, and people needed to go back to work, the admiral explained. De Castro was also to think of ways to reduce inflation, which stood at almost 700 percent. An idea crossed his mind immediately; it was a simple one, and yet counterintuitive to those not initiated in the arcane science of economics. In order to defeat inflation, De Castro thought, it was first necessary to free up the thousands of prices that had been controlled with an iron fist by the Unidad Popular coalition. To be sure, prices would jump in order to find their equilibrium, but that was required for the system of subtle and yet powerful signals to begin working again. Only then could inflation be tackled by reigning in the public-sector deficit and the money supply.[9]

Almost everyone would have been intimidated by the tasks at hand, but not Sergio de Castro. After all, during the previous months, he and a handful of colleagues—most of them Chicago Boys associated with

Católica—had prepared a blueprint for Chile's future, a plan to reform the Chilean economy by introducing market forces, reducing import tariffs, balancing the government accounts, privatizing state-owned firms, eliminating inflation, and strengthening institutions and the rule of law. At some levels the report was similar to the document prepared in 1970 for conservative presidential candidate Jorge Alessandri. The new proposal, however, went deeper into the reform front, as the Chicago Boys had become convinced that the collapse of the economy during the Allende administration called for major surgery.

The formal title of the report was simple and unobtrusive, almost anodyne: *Programa de desarollo económico* (A program for economic development). Nowhere did it say who the authors—or what their affiliations—were. But the handful of people who had read it suspected that it had been written by a group of Chicago Boys associated with Católica. Very few copies were printed, on 8½ × 11-inch paper. It was a massive document, several inches thick, and it was precisely because of its thickness that those who had seen it referred to it colloquially as El Ladrillo (The Brick). The name stuck, and the document has been known as The Brick ever since. In his biography, Sergio de Castro is quoted as saying that when he first met General González, the new minister of economics had a copy of the report in his hands.[10] What the general did not know (yet) was that his new adviser was the main author of the document that, with time, would guide one of the deepest economic revolutions in the developing world, the neoliberal revolution.[11]

During the early years, many stories were woven around The Brick, including that it was financed by the CIA and that Milton Friedman and Arnold "Al" Harberger had helped write it. In 1992, almost twenty years after The Brick was distributed to the junta, the Centro de Estudios Públicos, a promarkets think tank closely associated with Católica and the Chicago Boys, published the document in book form with an introduction by Sergio de Castro. In it the former minister of finance shed some light on how it came to life, how and when it was written, and who contributed to the different chapters.[12]

In December 1972 retired Navy officer Roberto Kelly met in Valparaíso with Admiral José Toribio Merino, who at the time was the second in command of the Chilean Navy and one of the earlier coup conspirators. Kelly, who was an executive in the Edwards Group, asked his friend whether, given the depth of the crisis, the navy was considering toppling Allende. Merino agreed that the economic situation was chaotic, with inflation already at 500 percent, plunging real wages, generalized strikes, and massive black markets. But he said that the dire economic conditions were precisely the reason why the armed forces were reluctant to stage a coup. Generals and admirals feared that the economy would continue to tank, and that they would be blamed for it. Kelly immediately thought of Emilio Sanfuentes and the Centro de Estudios Sociales y Económicos (Center of Social and Economic Studies) think tank and told the admiral that he could ask a group of economists to prepare a confidential program for economic recovery and reform. Not only that, he would have it ready in less than ninety days. The republic, said Kelly, could not wait much longer; it was a sinking ship.

During the next few months, a group of eleven economists led by Sergio de Castro and Emilio Sanfuentes worked on a plan for Chile's future. Their routine was simple: almost every evening they met in the offices of the newsweekly *Qué pasa* (What's happening) to discuss strategy and policies. Then each of them worked on a specific chapter. De Castro took the raw material and wrote a policy proposal in a unified and coherent style. The manuscript was typed in the offices of consulting firm Informatec, which was headed by economist Sergio Undurraga, the Católica graduate who cultivated a low profile and had worked for the private-sector Sociedad de Fomento Fabril (Manufacturing Development Society), a trade association.

Table 4.1 presents the list of the eleven economists directly involved in the writing of The Brick. Nine had graduate degrees from the University of Chicago; seven had undergraduate degrees from Católica, and four from the Universidad de Chile. Eight of them ended up holding executive positions during the dictatorship, including two at the cabinet level—Pablo Baraona and Sergio de Castro. From a political point of view, seven were decisively to the right of the spectrum; four—Alvaro Bardón, Andrés Sanfuentes, Juan Villarzú, and José Luis Zabala—were close to the more centrist Christian Democratic Party, but were strong opponents of the Unidad Popular government. The presence of these

TABLE 4.1. Economists Who Participated in the Drafting of The Brick

Name	Field / education	Area(s) covered in The Brick	Position(s) during the Pinochet dictatorship
Pablo Baraona	Católica economist / University of Chicago MA in economics	Agricultural sector	President of the Central Bank; minister of the economy
Alvaro Bardón	Universidad de Chile economist / University of Chicago MA in economics	Overall, trade	President of the Central Bank; undersecretary of economics
Juan Braun	Católica economist / Harvard University MA in economics	Capital markets	None; private sector
Manuel Cruzat	Católica economist; University of Chicago MA in economics	Capital markets	None; head of a major conglomerate
Sergio de Castro	Católica economist / University of Chicago PhD	Overall responsibility; philosophical approach, stabilization, prices, trade	Minister of the economy; minister of finance
Juan Carlos Méndez	Católica economist; University of Chicago MA in economics	Taxation, fiscal policy	Director of the Office of the Budget
Andrés Sanfuentes	Universidad de Chile economist / University of Chicago MA in economics	Macroeconomics, social sector	None; academic who quickly became a critic of the military
Emilio Sanfuentes	Católica sociologist / University of Chicago MA in economics	Overall coordination, pensions, and social services	Adviser to the minister of planning, Roberto Kelly
Sergio Undurraga	Católica economist	Capital markets, pensions	Director of research, Ministry of Planning; head of the Corporación de Fomento de la Producción's office in New York City
Juan Villarzú	Universidad de Chile economist; University of Chicago MA in economics	State-owned enterprises, privatization, fiscal policies, taxes	Director of the Office of the Budget
José Luis Zabala	Universidad de Chile economist; University of Chicago MA in Economics	Monetary and fiscal policy	Director of research, Central Bank

centrist economists, who followed the social doctrine of the Catholic Church, explains why the chapter on industrial organization in The Brick included the possibility of creating Yugoslavia-style firms, where workers owned the companies and participated actively in their management. As Sergio de Castro was quoted as saying in his official biography, to include that form of ownership was the only way to keep the Christian Democrats actively engaged in the project.[13]

Did the Chicago Boys Know That The Brick Was Intended for the Military?

Most of those who participated in the drafting of The Brick have said that when working on the document they did not know that it was being prepared at the request of a group of senior navy officers who were plotting to depose President Salvador Allende. They thought that it was a program for the next government, although they did not know when a new government would take over, nor did they know whether it would come to power through elections or nondemocratic means. At the time, there were all sorts of rumors, including that Allende would call for a plebiscite to decide the future of his administration. If he lost the referendum, the rumor went, the president would step down and new presidential elections would be called. Under this scenario, the most likely outcome was that former president Eduardo Frei Montalva would be elected to serve another six years at the helm of a new government. As the introduction to the 1992 published version of The Brick noted, "It is important to point out that only one of the members of the academic group [Emilio Sanfuentes] had contact with the high command of the national Navy, something the rest of us did not know about. Thus, [in September 1973,] our surprise was immense when we realized that the Junta had our document and was contemplating the possible implementation [of our suggested policies]."[14]

In the 2015 documentary *Chicago Boys*, Sergio de Castro insists on this point, and states that he had no idea whom the document was created for. He adds that some of the participants thought that maybe senior officers in the armed forces would read it, but they were not sure if that would be the case.[15] In June 2021, I interviewed Sergio Undurraga, in whose office The Brick was typed in 1973. Undurraga made a similar statement, adding that starting in late 1972, he and Alvaro Bardón were constantly writing reports and giving advice to opposition members of the Congress, including the Christian Democratic Party senator José Musalem and former president Eduardo Frei Montalva. "In some ways," Undurraga told me, "We saw 'The Brick' as an extension of those reports, a more encompassing piece, one that covered multiple sectors in one coherent and longer document." He also told me that no one was paid for the effort, and that the costs involved were minimal; basically, the paper used to print the initial 25 copies.[16]

There is, however, a different version of the story. In his 1988 book on Pinochet and the reforms, journalist Arturo Fontaine Aldunate notes that during a weekend in May 1973 most of the economists involved in the writing of The Brick met with retired navy officer and Edwards Group executive Roberto Kelly to discuss the progress being made on the project. Kelly told them that this was an urgent assignment. He stressed that serious political developments could erupt at any minute. Fontaine writes,

> Work on the manuscript was taking longer than expected. Some of the economists did not believe Emilio Sanfuentes when he said that this program was a requirement for the Armed Forces to intervene in the political future of the country. Navy officers put pressure on Kelly, who decided to summon the economists to a meeting in the resort Viña del Mar. They spent the night in the Hotel San Martín. It was there where the program took its final shape. . . . Emilio Sanfuentes summarized the discussion in a five-page memorandum that he handed to Kelly. He, in turn, passed it on to [active duty] Commander [Arturo] Troncoso. It should be erased."[17]

Whether some of the authors of the report—in addition to Emilio Sanfuentes—knew that Roberto Kelly was a mere intermediary for senior navy officers is a mystery that will never be fully resolved.[18] My own conjecture is that Sanfuentes did not keep the information to himself, and that some (if not all) of the participants understood that the final users were active members of the armed forces who were seriously contemplating deposing president Salvador Allende.[19]

The Chicago Boys' Blueprint for Reform:
A Deconstruction

From today's perspective, the policy suggestions in The Brick look mild and quite run-of-the-mill. There is nothing radical about them, and most of the proposed changes—with the possible exception of pension reform—read like a collection of Social Democratic policies. The text lists eight goals for the program: (1) accelerating the economic rate of growth within a democratic political system; (2) eradicating extreme poverty; (3) targeting social programs for the poor, and especially for children and the elderly; (4) ensuring that there is equal opportunity for everyone; (5) working toward full employment, with productive jobs (as opposed to a bloated government bureaucracy); (6) achieving price and political stability; (7) minimizing dependence on foreign assistance through a system that generates enough foreign exchange; and (8) decentralizing the country's political administration.

A careful appraisal of the document does not indicate that it would become the basis for what would come to be called the neoliberal revolution. The more profound policies came later, once the Chicago Boys realized that Pinochet had given them a tremendous amount of power and that that power allowed them to move further with reforms, expanding the use of the markets to many areas where they had never had any role. The sheer length of the dictatorship (almost seventeen years) allowed them to experiment, to make mistakes and correct errors, to try one thing and then another, and to enact markets on an increasing number of fronts.

The Brick covered fourteen specific policy areas, including the price system, trade policy, privatization, deregulation, health care provision, old-age pensions, agriculture, industrialization, and education. Table 4.2 summarizes, with a fair amount of detail, the contents of the document. The first column denotes the fourteen policy areas; the second column describes the specific recommendations made in the original 1973 document; and the third column provides information on how each policy was actually implemented during the Pinochet dictatorship. A comparison between the second and third columns shows that, as time went by, the Chicago Boys felt emboldened to implement bolder and deeper policies. (For a detailed discussion on how the actual policies evolved throughout the dictatorship, see chapters 5–9.)

In presenting the general principles behind the program, De Castro, Sanfuentes, and their colleagues proposed an economic system that combined markets with light and decentralized planning, very much in the style promoted by the Alliance for Progress, the program launched by the administration of President John F. Kennedy in 1961 as an antidote to the Cuban Revolution. The following quote is illustrative of the original spirit of The Brick: "[The proposed] decentralized *planning system* has to assure the correct functioning of markets. This means that there is a necessary active role for the state through global policies aimed at achieving an efficient allocation of resources. . . . This type of system is absolutely and completely different from last century's classical capitalism, which was characterized by passive government policies."[20]

The reference to, and rejection of, nineteenth-century unfettered classical capitalism is consistent with Walter Lippmann's views in *The Good Society* and Milton Friedman's comments in "Neo-liberalism and Its Prospects," in which he wrote that it was necessary to amend "a basic error in 19th century individualist philosophy," which "assigned almost no role to the state."[21] Like Moliere's *bourgeois gentilhomme* (bourgeois gentleman), who spoke prose without knowing it, the Chicago Boys were threading into true and traditional neoliberal terrain without knowing it; they had no inkling that the model they were pushing would receive the label *neoliberal* in the years to come and would become extremely controversial—praised by some and reviled by others.

The trade liberalization proposal is, possibly, the best illustration of the middle-of-the-road nature of The Brick. Sergio de Castro and his colleagues called for eliminating quantitative restrictions (import licenses and quotas) and setting import tariffs at a uniform 30-percent level. Although this was a major change with respect to the import substitution strategy pushed by structuralisms such as Aníbal Pinto and Osvaldo Sunkel, it was a far cry from free trade.[22] As can be seen in table 4.2, the reduction of import tariffs was to be accompanied by a substantial real devaluation of the currency and by the adoption of an exchange rate

TABLE 4.2. Policy Proposals in The Brick (1973) versus Policies Implemented by the Military (1973–1990)

Policy area	Policies proposed in The Brick (1973)	Policies implemented by the military (1973–90)
Decentralization policies	Replace heavy-handed planning with "decentralized" planning Rely on market to allocate resources "Intermediate organizations" to provide social services Reduce red tape Reduce extent of government controls	Markets at (almost) every level are implemented Central planning is discarded in favor of policy coordination "Intermediate organizations" become a key element of social policies, which is enshrined in the Chilean Constitution of 1980
Trade policy and exchange rates	Replace quantitative restrictions and licenses with tariffs Lower import tariffs to uniform tariff close to 30% Reevaluate Chile's membership in regional trade pacts Recognize that the exchange rate plays a key role in trade "Realistic" real exchange rate to encourage exports Frequently devalue the Chilean peso Maintain a dual exchange rate in the short term	Quantitative restrictions are eliminated Import tariffs rapidly reduced to a uniform 10% (15% in 1989) Chile abandons the Andean Pact Mini-devaluations exchange rate regime (1973–78) Fixed exchange rate (1978–82) Crawling peg (1982–90)
Capital controls	Maintain capital controls (on outflows) in the short term Encourage foreign direct investment Central Bank should regulate the foreign exchange market Dual exchange rate system in short term: one rate for capital movements and one for trade transactions	Control on inflows and outflows (1973–82) Capital inflows controlled until 1982 Controls on outflows gradually and selectively relaxed (1982–90)
Price policy	Eliminate price controls if there is foreign competition Control prices for monopolies only Establish a government agency in favor of competition Severely sanction collusion and monopolistic practices	Price controls eliminated for all but thirty "essential goods" (1973) Number of prices controlled reduced to eighteen (1976) Free prices for all goods (1978) Public utility rates determined to yield a certain return to capital Free trade agreement to promote low prices for imports were negotiated

Monetary and fiscal policies (anti-inflation)	Monetary policy to support economic activity, ensure price stability, and ensure adequate employment Fiscal dominance should be avoided Coordinate monetary and fiscal policy Reduce the number of public-sector employees Establish a national commission of remuneration to guide wage increases, especially for the public sector	Fiscal dominance; Central Bank finances deficit (1973–75) Money growth consistent with "shock treatment" (1973–78) Semipassive monetary policy; pegged exchange rate (1978–82) Monetary program aimed at gradual disinflation and rapid growth (after 1982)
Tax policy	Replace sales tax with modern value-added tax Eliminate most loopholes and tax exemptions Establish an income tax main mechanism for redistributing income Encourage savings and investment through the tax code Higher inheritance tax, paid in installments	Value-added tax with 20% rate, then lowered to 18% Tax system indexed to inflation Corporate income tax integrated with personal income tax Corporate income tax reduced from 40% to 0% for retained earnings (1989)
Capital markets	Allow loans indexed to inflation Allow positive real interest rate in short-term operations Encourage new financial institutions, such as finance houses Create a modern regulator Allow domestic institutions to operate internationally Government to issue bonds in the global capital markets	Capital markets encouraged and deregulated; new financial institutions allowed Individual savings pension accounts allowed to invest in securities issued by domestic firms Financial oversight tightened after 1980–82 financial and banking crisis Income tax exemption for low- and middle-income investors
Social policies	Goal should be to eliminate extreme poverty Guaranteed income to families with income bellow "extreme poverty" line Social services should be targeted to poor Once poverty is eliminated, income distribution is not a major concern	Targeted social policies Social register for households' main instruments for targeting Guaranteed income to families is not implemented Progressive tax on personal income tax, with a top marginal tax of 40%

(continued)

TABLE 4.2. (*continued*)

Policy area	Policies proposed in The Brick (1973)	Policies implemented by the military (1973–90)
Pensions	Create a unified system instead of multiple regimes	Individual savings accounts created
	Two-part system: (1) basic pension funded from general taxes; (2) personal savings accounts for retirement	Transitional costs (pensions of existing retirees) paid from general budget
	Basic pension requires twenty-five years of contribution	Contributors not included in management firms' boards
	Pension fund boards include representatives of workers	Vesting period for basic minimal pension after twenty-five years
	Funds invested in (newly developed) capital market	No vesting period for personal savings
	Funds' management companies compete and are tightly regulated	Freelance and informal workers do not contribute to main system and thus do not have a pension
		Voluntary pension savings encouraged
Health care	Decentralize existing inefficient national system	Two-tier system developed
	National health system to cover lower-income families	Public health system covers 80% of the population
	Higher-income families may enroll with paid insurance providers	Individuals may use "health contribution / tax" as a voucher to finance private insurance scheme
	Families freely choose between national or for-pay system (vouchers)	
Education	Emphasis on "human capital"	School vouchers system
	Decentralization: local communities run schools	Three-tiered system: (1) public; (2) subsidized private; (3) private
	Reallocate funding from tertiary to basic education	New private universities allowed (1981)
	Increase funding to preschools and primary schools	Universities required to be not-for-profit
	Charge tuition to university students	Scholarships based on merit for tertiary education
	Provide student loans to those who cannot afford tuition	Loans at slightly subsidized rates to pay tuition

Agricultural sector	Expropriated land distributed to individual farmers; no state-owned farms	Agrarian reform ended; expropriated land distributed to peasants as individual plots
	Eliminate negative "effective protection" in agriculture	Market for land developed; peasants allowed to sell their newly received plots
	Small holders very poor; optimize size of holdings	Market for water rights developed; water rights separated from land ownership
	Launch a modern market for land	Subsidies for forest planting; most takes place in the Araucania region
	Long-term loans to farmers	
	Launch market for water rights	
Privatization and state-owned enterprises	Four areas of property: (1) state-owned; (2) joint management; (3) traditional private; (4) consumers' cooperatives	Massive privatization of banks, insurance companies, and manufacturing firms
	Very few (strategic) firms to be maintained in the hands of the state	Handful of large firms (copper companies, some ports) maintained as public companies
	Joint management may include Yugoslavia-type companies	Banks privatized first
	Compensate owners of nationalized companies that are not returned	After 1982 banking crisis, "people's capitalism" allows the retail public to participate in the reprivatization process
Industrial sector	Import substitution policies to come to an end	No specific policies
	Encourage technological progress and innovation	Export promotion office established
	Industrial policy should be consistent with employment creation	No bailouts for firms that cannot survive due to foreign competition
	Promising sectors: building materials, food	Main support provided through exchange rate and tax policy
	Develop supply chains in agribusiness, fisheries, and mining, all promising export sectors	

Note: According to de Castro (1992, n), there were three chapters (on housing, public works, and mining) that the hadn't yet written by the time the armed forces staged the coup. Juan Andrés Fontaine provided insightful comments to the author in 2002.

regime based on frequent mini-devaluations. The purpose of this policy, which was fully endorsed by Milton Friedman during his first visit to Chile in 1975, was to avoid currency overvaluation and to encourage nontraditional exports. Foreign direct investment was to be stimulated, and Chile's participation in regional trade arrangements, such as the Andean Pact, a trade association with a highly protective bent, was to be reconsidered. According to The Brick, capital movements had to be regulated and restricted in order to avoid "capital flight" and speculation. On this latter topic the Chicago Boys departed significantly from Milton Friedman, who since the 1940s had argued that in a world with free interest rates and free capital mobility, speculators played a key and positive role in stabilizing the financial markets.

Eventually, the move toward free trade was significantly more profound and provided an example of the benefits of liberalizing unilaterally without waiting for successive multilateral rounds and negotiations on the part of the General Agreement on Tariffs and Trade or the World Trade Organization. By 1978 Chile had eliminated all import prohibitions and dismantled licenses, quotas, and prior deposits for 2,872 goods. In 1978, merely five years after the Chicago Boys entered the government, the liberalization effort went well beyond what was suggested in The Brick; import tariffs were slashed to a uniform 10 percent, one-third of their original target of an average import duty of 30 percent. In that sense, Chile contributed to the view, espoused by trade theorist Jagdish Bhagwati, that the best strategy for liberalizing trade was "going alone."[23]

Despite the program's mildness, many business leaders were shocked by what they read. Private-sector firms had operated for so long under a system of controls that executives felt completely disoriented by the idea of economic freedom; they did not know how to operate in a world where machinery, inputs, and spare parts could be imported freely. They were also shocked by the notion that firms could decide what prices to charge for the goods they produced. In his biography, Sergio de Castro tells the story of an early meeting with representatives of the cooking oil industry. The businessmen (indeed, they were all men) presented him with a study justifying a specific price increase. De Castro said that he did not need the thick report and pushed it back to them across the desk. The executives were livid. After a long silence, one of them said that costs of every input had increased, and that he was surprised that the military government would reject their request for a price increase. De Castro smiled and told them that he was not rejecting the request; they were free to set any price they wanted. He warned them, however, that if they decided to set a very high price, someone would import cooking oil at a lower price and undercut them. The men thought that he was kidding; they left in confusion. A week later they came back with a new (and thinner) study and a request for a more moderate price increase. It took them three visits to understand that De Castro was serious and that the government would not intervene in the price-setting process.[24]

Inequality, Education, and Pensions

A distinctive aspect of The Brick was the emphasis on reducing "extreme poverty" through targeted social programs. Reducing inequality was not one of the program's goals. The Chicago Boys believed that if the number of those living below the poverty line declined, it did not really matter what happened to income distribution. This viewpoint was maintained by (most of) the Chicago Boys until recently. For instance, in the 2015 documentary *Chicago Boys*, Rolf Lüders, who was appointed minister of finance and economics by Pinochet in 1982, told the interviewer: "I really don't care about inequality . . . the problem with income distribution is that it's an envy problem. . . . Do you understand me?" In the same film, Ernesto Fontaine—who in 1955 met the original Chicago entourage led by Theodore Schultz at Santiago's Los Cerrillos airport—affirmed, "Yes, there is inequality, but the people at the bottom improved a lot and they are doing super well."[25] (For a discussion on how the persistence of inequality became the model's Achilles' heel, see chapter 13.)

The emphasis on targeted (as opposed to general or universal) social programs was also reflected in the proposals for education reform, which called for providing free and universal public preschool and primary education while charging full tuition at the university level—even at public universities (see the "Education" row in table 4.2). Those who could not afford tuition were eligible for (some) loans, at market interest rates, with government guarantees. As with other policy areas, the extension of the military government in time, and the suppression of dissent, allowed the Chicago Boys to implement educational policies that went further than what was delineated in The Brick. Eventually, a voucher system was put in place for primary and secondary education, and families could use public money to pay for tuition in private and for-profit schools. By the late 1980s, the educational system was characterized by three segments: (1) purely public schools; (2) private schools financed by a combination of voucher money and parents' "copayments" (a group made up of a combination of for-profit and not-for-profit schools, many associated with the Catholic Church); and (3) purely private schools.

The proposal for pension reform was undoubtedly the most daring of all of the recommended policies. The Chicago Boys suggested replacing a highly inefficient, underfunded, and unfair pay-as-you-go regime with one based on individual savings accounts. Workers would make monthly contributions to their individual accounts, and private pension management companies would invest those monies in diversified portfolios. At the end of their working lives, individuals would use the accumulated funds to purchase an annuity to cover their living expenses during retirement. One of the aims of reform was to end the discrimination against blue-collar workers, who were subject to a much longer vesting period than their white-collar counterparts. The Brick also emphasized that a savings-based system would be a great incentive for the takeoff of an efficient and deep capital market. Firms would be able to issue equity and debt, which would be added to workers' savings accounts, helping them build a financial cushion for retirement. In order to establish "ownership" of the new regime, the Chicago Boys suggested that representatives of workers have a seat on the board of the pension management firms.

As will be discussed in greater detail in chapter 7, a pension reform along these lines was launched in late 1981. With time it was lauded by many international analysts and politicians—including US president George W. Bush—as a big success and as an example of how to use a markets approach to deal with the intricate and political issue of retirement and social security. But things did not work out as planned. As I discuss in detail in chapter 14, pensions turned out to be significantly lower than what was expected and promised by the architects of the reforms. By 2015, replacing the individual accounts with a public-run system became a rallying cry of critics of the model. Indeed, during the 2019 uprising and the demonstrations that followed, putting an end to the private pensions system was one of the most important demands made by protesters. In 2021 the number one item in Gabriel Boric's electoral platform was replacing the individual savings system with a hybrid regime with a pay-as-you-go component and a collective savings element run by a public-sector institution.

Land Distribution and a Market for Land

In The Brick, the Chicago Boys proposed ending agrarian reform, a policy that had been launched rather timidly during Jorge Alessandri's conservative administration in 1962, at the behest of the US Alliance for Progress program. The policy of land redistribution was accelerated during the Christian Democratic government (1964–70) and intensified drastically by Salvador Allende.

For Sergio de Castro and his colleagues, the problem was not that there were too many extremely large farms (*latifundios*) that were poorly run by their mostly absentee owners. For them the main issue had to do with the lack of well-functioning markets, and with price distortions introduced by the protectionist policies of the import substitution industrialization strategy pushed by the structuralists. The Chicago Boys postulated that most plots were too small and not financially feasible in the long run; there was a need for consolidation, and that could only happen if there were efficient markets for land, water rights, and agricultural products. It was fundamentally important, they contended, to allow farmers to discover their natural comparative advantages. This meant that subsidies were not to be used to artificially encourage certain crops selected by bureaucrats in an office in the capital city.

The Chicago Boys further argued that in a world with low import tariffs on fertilizers and farm equipment, as well as "competitive" exchange rates, many farmers would shift away from traditional crops and would produce highly valued export products that would be sold to the advanced nations. Chile, they asserted, could produce quality peaches and pears, among others, that would command high prices in Europe and the United States during the off-season. With time this became a reality, and by the early twenty-first century Chile had become one of the most successful exporters of fresh produce (berries, cherries, and avocados) in the world. Critics of the model, however, argued that the export strategy had several limitations. First, they asserted, agricultural exports had a low level of value added; by exporting farm products Chile was not creating a solid manufacturing class. This, of course, was very similar to the argument used in the 1940s and 1950s to launch the import substitution strategy based on heavy protectionism. A second criticism was that fruits' exports—and, more specifically, the exports of avocados and cherries—was nothing more than exporting water, a resource that had become increasingly scarce due to climate change.

Inflation and Macroeconomic Policies

The proposals for monetary and fiscal policies in The Brick were closely related. A first step was to accept that inflation distorted the tax system, creating a costly vicious circle: the fiscal deficit generated inflation, which in turn—and through the erosion of tax collection—contributed to an even higher deficit and thus even higher inflation. According to The Brick, two key tools to deal with this problem were the adoption of a value-added tax and the indexation of tax system. Once the fiscal deficit was contained, the Central Bank would stop financing the government, and could run a monetary policy based on rules like the ones advocated by Milton Friedman.

The key was to put an end to Chile's historical fiscal dominance. In 1963 Albert Hirschman published a detailed analysis of inflation in Chile from the late nineteenth century through 1962. Hirschman's data clearly showed the ratcheting up of inflation in Chile's history. Between 1880 and 1900 inflation averaged 5 percent per year; in the 1950s and 1960s that grew to 36 percent. Hirschman, who was not particularly sympathetic toward Friedman and the Chicago school of economics, recognized the key role of money printing, but added an important twist: the reason the Central Bank ended up printing excess money had to do with distributional struggles. In his analysis, Hirschman went through Chile's recurrent currency crises and failed stabilization attempts and concludes that in every one of those failed attempts there had been a fight, within the elite, for the allocation of the budget. It would be landowners against industrialist; heavy industry against light manufacturing; exporters against importers.[26]

The Brick's discussion on inflation and macroeconomic (fiscal and monetary) policy was also influenced by Al Harberger's work on inflation. In 1963 he published an important piece titled "The Dynamics of Inflation in Chile," which opens, "[Chile's] history of inflation is long, and for practical purposes continuous. Its rate of inflation has varied greatly over time, permitting the testing of theories in which not only the level of prices but also the rate of change plays a role." One of the notable aspects of this study is that it explicitly analyzes what Harberger calls "two extreme hypotheses.... One denying any true explanatory power to wage changes, and the other denying any true explanatory power to money supply changes." Harberger's results suggest that neither of the two extreme hypotheses is supported fully by the data. His findings indicate that in Chile during the period under analysis (1939–58) both monetary changes and wage conditions played a role in fueling and perpetuating inflation in Chile. In his concluding remarks Harberger writes, "These results suggest that one of the major roles of the wage variable was indeed as a 'transmitter' of inflation from one period to the next, responding to the monetary expansion of the past, and inducing monetary expansion in the subsequent."[27]

When, on December 13, 1973, they were called to the government, the Chicago Boys had no idea of how to put the program in The Brick to work. Only a few of them had ever operated in the public sector, and none in an executive or senior position. They would soon find out how different pontificating from the ivory tower was from actually implementing policies aimed at changing decades of entrenched policies.

5

Milton Friedman's 1975 Visit and the Shock Treatment

ON MARCH 21, 1975, Milton Friedman, the most famous and polemical economist in the world, met for one hour with General Augusto Pinochet in Santiago. During the meeting, Friedman told Pinochet that the only way to eradicate inflation in Chile, which at the time was running at almost 350 percent per year, was to apply a "shock treatment" consisting of "an across-the-board reduction of every separate [budget] item by 25 per cent."[1] Friedman noted that Chile's inflation was a textbook case of monetary excesses. The fiscal deficit, which was fully financed by money printing, was 10 percent of gross domestic product (GDP), and the stock of money held by the public was approximately 3 percent of aggregate income. Back-of-the-envelope calculations suggested that the "inflation tax" required to finance such a deficit was approximately 330 percent each year, a figure that was very close to the actual rate of inflation.[2] Friedman warned the general that the shock treatment would entail substantial short-term costs in the form of high unemployment. He anticipated, however, that "the period of severe transitional difficulties would be brief—measured in months—and that subsequent recovery would be rapid."[3]

Friedman also told Pinochet that adopting a free-market system was the only way to achieve sustained growth, poverty reduction, and, eventually, generalized prosperity.[4] The overall reform program, he affirmed, should include opening up the economy to international competition, implementing a vast deregulation program, freeing up interest rates and all prices, privatizing state-owned enterprise, reforming labor legislation in order to make hiring and firing more expeditious, and eliminating subsidies to specific industries in the so-called strategic sectors. Many of these recommendations were already in The Brick, a document that Friedman had not read and possibly did not yet even know existed.

Friedman Lectures the Elite

Two days after meeting with Pinochet, Friedman gave a public talk to several hundred businesspeople. The seminar was organized by Chicago Boy Rolf Lüders, who at the time was an executive vice president of one of the most dynamic and aggressive Chilean conglomerates, the BHC (Banco Hipotecario de Chile) Group.[5] During his presentation, Friedman roughly repeated what he had told the general: Chile's captains of industry were seriously alarmed by what they heard, and they rejected the idea of abandoning gradualism. After decades of heavy government intervention, they were leery of abrupt policies; the prospects of a shock treatment and of rapid trade and financial reforms terrified them. Their concerns about the consequences of rapid changes were shared by a small but powerful cadre of senior officers in the armed forces. In contrast, the Chicago Boys were delighted by Friedman's statements. Finally a world-recognized authority backed their views publicly and explained to the elites that putting the reforms in place, sooner rather than later, would generate employment, growth, and prosperity. The Chicago Boys hoped that Friedman would help tip the balance of power within the military toward their perspective and that Pinochet would finally choose the free-market alternative over the interventionist option peddled by some army and air force generals. (The navy was, early on, behind the market reforms.)

The mood among business leaders was reflected in the questions and answers that followed Friedman's talk. A member of the audience stated that the fiscal shock would generate a major spike in unemployment, a true "earthquake" that Chile would be unable to withstand. Friedman's answer was simple and underlined the difference between productive and unproductive employment: "Let's assume that between 20 and 25 percent of public-sector functionaries are fired. In that case, can anyone explain to me how it would result in a reduction of shoes' production by 25 percent, or that bread production is reduced by one loaf, or that one fewer shirt is produced . . . ? As you can see, the problem is that the people that are employed in those [state] institutions are not productive, they are not adding anything to the amount of goods and services available in Chile."[6]

Another question dealt with financial-sector reforms, usury, and speculation. Friedman replied that speculators played an important and positive role in a market economy: "Speculation is just a word and does not correspond to something bad." He was then asked if the capital market should be completely free or if it should be regulated. Friedman responded that financial markets should be "fully free," with "free people writing contracts with other free people." The only role of the government was to make sure that there was no fraud. Another participant asked Friedman what he thought about interest rates at 15 percent per month, and he replied that the real problem was inflation; if prices increased at a monthly rate of 15 percent, then 15 percent interest rates were not high.[7] Figure 5.1 captures the most senior Chicago Boys in 1978, three years after Friedman met with Pinochet and recommended the "shock treatment."

Regarding the overall costs of his proposed adjustment and reform program, Friedman said, "Chile's fundamental problems are two: inflation and developing a free market [system]. These are different problems, but they are related, because the faster you strengthen the free market, the easier the transition will be. . . . There should be no mistakes: you cannot end inflation without costs. . . . The simple fact is that Chile is 'very sick.' A sick man cannot recover without costs. . . . I must emphasize an extremely important fact: Chile's problems are, without any doubt, 'made in Chile.'"[8]

There were also questions about the trade reform. A participant asked whether in a poor country manufacturing firms could compete internationally. Friedman's answer reflected his uncompromising belief

FIGURE 5.1. *From left to right:* Chicago Boys Sergio de Castro, Sergio de la Cuadra, Pablo Baraona, and Alvaro Bardón, circa 1978
Source: La Tercera photo archive

in the benefits of free trade, and emphasized, with great force, the need for trade reform to be accompanied by the appropriate exchange rate policy (see chapter 9 for a detailed discussion on this issue):

> Of course, Chilean firms can compete internationally, if the exchange rate is an adequate one. . . . The destruction of capital [during the time of Unidad Popular] means that you are a poor country. But poor countries can compete. . . . Isn't it true that Japan was able to develop an incredible international presence in spite of the fact that in 1948, when everything started, most of the industrial plants had been destroyed to a much larger extent than in Chile? . . . I am sorry to say that the notion behind this question is mistaken in a fundamental

way: it does not recognize the crucial role played by the exchange rate in allowing a country to compete with other nations, independently of its relative technological and productive development.[9]

Questions and answers continued for more than an hour. There were twenty-two questions in total, some expressing genuine surprise at what Friedman said, some openly confrontational. Friedman explained, with his legendary pedagogical ability, why in his view the costly adjustment period would be short. He repeated that, in the end, a better country would emerge, a country that could grow in a steady fashion. He used a number of examples from other nations' experiences, mostly from Germany, Japan, and the United States after World War II. At some point Friedman became somewhat exasperated and said that he understood why so many in the audience opposed the reforms' program: "Very few businessmen truly believe in free enterprise, they often are among its worst enemies. Every businessman favors free competition for others, but not for himself."[10]

Friedman also gave a lecture to a group of officers from all branches of the armed forces. About two hundred men assembled in the amphitheater of the Edificio Diego Portales, the building where the junta was housed while the presidential palace, La Moneda, was rebuilt after being bombed during the coup. Friedman noted that they were sitting strictly according to rank: generals and admirals were in the front rows, followed by brigadiers, lieutenant colonels, and majors. In his unpublished reminiscences, he wrote that he had a very hard time extracting a laugh from the military. He wondered if it was because that they had limited command of the English language or if it reflected an across-the-board lack of sense of humor in the Chilean armed forces—or maybe in the Chilean people in general.[11]

Friedman's visit marked a turning point in Chile's economic history: there is a *before Friedman* and an *after Friedman*. Up to that point, Pinochet had not decided whether to support the Chicago Boys' vision or to back the state capitalism model dear to a group of nationalist officers and influential businessmen who had become wealthy thanks to protectionism. Friedman was so vehement and articulate in his multiple talks, presentations, and meetings that Pinochet became convinced that the best strategy included a major fiscal shock coupled with market-oriented reforms. Pinochet's support to the Chicago Boys was conditional, however, as he continued to be suspicious of civilians in general and economists in particular. As a counterbalance to his own economic team, he decided to create a parallel economic advisory council made up exclusively of senior armed forces' officers who looked at the world through national security lenses. The council was simply called the Comité Asesor (Advisory Committee), and its members often clashed with the Chicago Boys on issues related to privatization, labor and pension reforms, the role of unions, and exchange rate policy.

Friedman and the 1975 Shock Treatment

On April 12, 1975, almost one month after Friedman's visit, the government announced a new effort to bring down inflation and to enhance the role of the private sector in the economy. The Plan de Recuperación Económica (Plan for Economic Recovery) followed Friedman's anti-inflationary recommendations at every level. Domestic currency expenditures were cut across the board by 15 percent, and foreign currency outlays were reduced by 25 percent. Pinochet asked his minister of finance, Jorge Cauas, a Columbia University graduate who had been chairman of the economics department at Católica, to lead the implementation of the drastic stabilization plan. Although he had not been trained at the University of Chicago, Cauas was one of the most important "honorary Chicago Boys," a man who wholeheartedly embraced the teachings of Friedman and the Chicago school.[12] Eight days after the recovery plan was announced, Pinochet reshuffled the cabinet and appointed Sergio de Castro as minister of economics. The hour of the Chicago Boys had arrived, and the odds that they could implement their plan increased significantly.

In the months that followed, an increasing number of Chicago Boys joined the government in different capacities and at different levels. Sergio de la Cuadra, who had been a student of Harry Johnson at the University of Chicago, returned from the United States to lead the trade liberalization reform. Juan Villarzú became director of the Dirección de Presupuestos (Budget Office) and was later replaced by Juan Carlos Méndez. In 1975 Pablo Baraona became governor of the Central Bank, and in 1976 he replaced Sergio de Castro as minister of economics when De Castro moved up to the Ministerio de Hacienda (Ministry of Finance). Alvaro Bardón took the helm of the Central Bank in 1976; José Luis Zabala and Sergio Undurraga shepherded the financial reform from the Central Bank and the Oficina de Planificación (Office of Planning). Ernesto Fontaine worked as a consultant and put in place an ambitious system of public investment appraisals; no public-sector investment project, regardless of size, was approved unless it met the strict social rate of return requirements. In designing the system Fontaine relied heavily on the analytical framework developed by Arnold "Al" Harberger at the University of Chicago.[13] A younger crew of Chicago graduates that had just returned to Chile at the time of the coup became fundamentally important in reforming social services. This group included Joaquín Cortez, Álvaro Donoso, Enrique Goldfarb, María Teresa Infante, Miguel Kast, Joaquín Lavín, Jorge Selume, and Ernesto Silva.

During his visit, Friedman was particularly impressed by Miguel Kast, a man who would take the lead in the implementation of antipoverty programs and, a few years later, in reforming the labor and health laws. Although Kast had obtained the best grades in both of Friedman's price theory courses, the professor did not remember him from Hyde Park. As Friedman wrote in his unpublished notes from the trip, "Miguel Kast, who studied at the University of Chicago, is a very bright and able fellow, has just come back to Chile not long since, and is obviously playing a very important role in the new government."[14]

Those involved in policy making at that time have systematically diminished Friedman's influence in the preparation and launching of the April 1975 shock treatment stabilization plan. For example, in his authorized biography, Sergio de Castro does not mention Friedman in connection with the recovery plan; in fact, he does not mention Friedman's 1975 trip at all. Arturo Fontaine Aldunate completely ignores Friedman's visit in his book on the Chicago Boys and Pinochet, and Friedman's visit is not mentioned in any of the Chicago Boys' interviews and conversations taped for Universidad Finis Terrae's oral history project, currently held at the Centro de Investigación y Documentación (Center of Investigation and Documentation).[15] Moreover, in his May 16, 1975, reply to Friedman's shock treatment letter, Pinochet intimated that the government's draconian adjustment policies were developed independently of the professor's recommendations: "The valuable approaches and appraisals drawn from an analysis of the text of your letter coincide for the most part with the National Recovery Plan proposed by the Secretary of the Treasury, Mr. Jorge Cauas. The plan is being fully applied at the present time."[16] More recently, Bruce Caldwell and Leonidas Montes have asserted that the recovery plan was not influenced by Friedman's visit.[17]

Yet a careful, day-to-day analysis of events during February–May 1975, based on newspaper records and interviews with many of those involved in the decision-making process, tells a different story. The evidence suggests that when Friedman met with Pinochet on March 21, the recovery plan had not been drafted or even outlined.[18] Of course, many in the government—including every Chicago Boy—were concerned with the inflationary prospects. It was clear to them that the recurrent deficits of most state-owned enterprises not yet privatized were being financed by the Central Bank. The problem was that these companies were now run by the military, and that generals and admirals refused to make adjustments, fire unneeded personnel, and reduce the companies' losses. Furthermore, many of the senior officers in the armed forces were against privatization. For them there were "national security reasons" for maintaining a strong and diversified group of public-sector companies.

Work on the details of the new adjustment program was only started on April 4, when Minister of Planning Roberto Kelly returned from a trip to Peru. By then, Friedman had left Chile—he departed for Fiji on March 27—and his recommendations were known by Pinochet, his cabinet, the armed forces, those who had attended his public talks, and everyone who had read his interviews. A very preliminary draft for a new stabilization program was presented to Pinochet on April 6. The draft included massive firings of public-sector workers and drastic budget cuts. On April 9, a revised version of the plan was discussed by Pinochet and his closer military and economic advisers at a meeting in the summer presidential residence in Viña del Mar. Among those present was an obscure colonel who did not say a word during the daylong meeting. His name was Manuel Contreras, and he headed the Dirección de Inteligencia Nacional (DINA; Directorate of National Intelligence), the regime's secret police, an outfit that was later found to be responsible for massive violations of human rights, including assassinations, torture, and disappearances.[19] At the time, the members of the economic team did not give a second thought to the fact that the chief of security was at the meeting. What they did not know was that Manuel Contreras and his DINA agents would spy on them and do whatever they could to convince Pinochet that the Chicago Boys were not true patriots and that their only interest was to privatize state-owned enterprises at low prices in order to have private investors (including their friends and associates) own and run key strategic industries.[20]

At the end of the day, and after listening to all sides, including respected sage Raúl Sáez, a man who favored gradual middle-of-the-road policies with a protectionist bent, Pinochet approved the Friedman-inspired program as presented by Jorge Cauas and Sergio de Castro. The final version of the plan was released to the public on April 12. That same day an executive order was published, giving Minister of Finance Jorge Cauas extraordinary powers to make the necessary adjustments to the budget and to implement major economic reforms.

Of course, it is possible that a similar—or, even, identical—program would have been written without Friedman's influence. But the reality of things is that he did visit Santiago, he did meet with Pinochet, he did talk to scores of generals and admirals, and he vehemently touted a drastic program that looked very similar to the shock treatment that was put in place in mid-April 1975.

It is not an exaggeration to say that, in March 1975, Friedman played the role of an umpire. He was seen by Pinochet as an arbitrator who weighted two alternative visions and paths of action: the abrupt program that called for "cold turkey" stabilization, favored by the Chicago Boys, and the gradualist route supported by the air force and some army generals, and intellectually sustained by éminence grise Raúl Sáez. Not surprisingly, Friedman called it for his disciples, the Chicago Boys. With his intellectual approval and backing, the path for drastic measures and (some) reform was open. It is interesting to note that Friedman was not the first foreign expert who played the role of an umpire in deciding what type of adjustment policy to follow. In his essay on Chile's inflation, Albert Hirschman wrote that the team led by Julius Klein and Julian Saks played exactly that role in 1955 when President Carlos Ibañez del Campo embarked on an ambitious anti-inflationary program aimed at reducing a 50 percent annual inflation to single digits. According to Hirschman, "[The Klein-Saks proposal] did not contain any substantial innovation with respect to [stabilization].... The conclusion is therefore inescapable that the [foreign advisers'] mission served principally as an umpire."[21]

The Exchange Rate: To Crawl or Not to Crawl, That Is the Question

In those years, almost every Latin American country experienced a significant shortage of foreign currency and had an active black market or parallel market for dollars. The state of economic conditions and expectations about the future were often gauged by how high the black-market premium was. In early September 1973 Chile had ten official exchange rates, and the black-market premium relative to the lowest official dollar price exceeded 750 percent. A few days after the coup, Admiral Lorenzo Gotuzzo, the junta's first minister of finance, decided to unify the exchange rate and set a unique value of 280 escudos per US dollar, which implied an official devaluation of 90 percent of the national currency.[22] An important question was what to do after the devaluation. With inflation running at almost 1,000 percent, it was clearly unwise to try to rigidly peg the peso once again. If done, the currency would rapidly become overvalued. Following the advice of the Chicago Boys, a mini-devaluations or "crawling peg" exchange rate regime, which had been used sporadically in the past, was adopted; the value of the dollar was increased every day in order for the exchange rate to keep up with inflation.

For a long time, Friedman had been a severe critic of the system of fixed but adjustable exchange rates created at the Bretton Woods Conference in 1944. In 1953 he published a famous essay, "The Case for Flexible Exchange Rates," in which he argued in favor of floating, market-determined exchange rates.[23] Through the years he had tried, with little success, to convince the authorities in many countries to reform their exchange rate regime and to opt for flexibility. By 1975 Friedman had altered his views regarding poor countries. He now favored two possible arrangements: either a flexible exchange rate or an irrevocable fixed exchange rate. The latter option meant that the country had to abolish its Central Bank. (For details, see chapter 8.)

During his 1975 trip to Chile, businessmen and bankers asked Friedman several questions about the exchange rate regime. In his reply to a question on the optimal degree of openness of the economy, he made a point that he had made many times before: a fixed exchange rate was not sustainable in a country with a high rate of inflation, let alone in a country like Chile with inflation in excess of 300 percent per year. He then added that, in his view, the crawling peg regime in place at the time in Chile was adequate.[24] The exchange rate was again brought up in a question regarding indexation.[25] Friedman insisted that the source of Chile's very rapid inflation was massive money printing to finance a fiscal deficit that amounted to 10 percent of GDP. Inflation, he stated, was unrelated to indexation. The third question relating to the exchange rate dealt with the effects of the mini-devaluations on costs and profits. Friedman answered,

Mini devaluations . . . don't result in higher real costs. They are simply a response to price increases. . . . If prices in Chile increase by 10 percent each month, then it is necessary to devalue in 10 percent in order to maintain a stable *real* value of foreign currency. . . . And you already know the story: if you try to maintain a low price for foreign exchange [overvaluation of the peso], there would simply be a need to ration it. What happens then? Everyone would want to buy it [foreign exchange]. How would you decide who is allowed to buy [dollars]?[26]

For the next two years the Chicago Boys maintained a crawling peg regime in which the rate of the mini-devaluations was roughly determined by the differential between domestic and international inflation. The policy was changed in early 1978, when the path of mini-devaluations was deliberately set below the ongoing rate of inflation and preannounced for the next six months. In mid-1979 the policy was again changed, and the value of the dollar was pegged at thirty-nine pesos. As it turned out, and as will be discussed in detail in chapter 8, this was a major policy mistake that led to a gigantic crisis in 1982 and almost resulted in the demise of the Chicago Boys' policies.

Unemployment and the Economic Costs of the Shock Treatment

Friedman's prediction that the shock treatment would produce a major spike in unemployment proved to be correct. Yet he was wrong in assuming that the pain would be short-lived. Unemployment reached 22 percent in 1976, only comparable to the years of the Great Depression, and stayed at extremely high levels until the mid-1980s.[27] The military understood that high and persistent unemployment affected its support among the population and decided to put in place an "emergency employment program" run by local governments, the Programa de Empleo Mínimo (Program of Minimal Employment). Participants were paid minimal amounts—less than half the minimum wage—for menial jobs, including tending to parks and gardens, painting fences, and the like. By 1978 the open rate of unemployment was 14.2 percent, and the emergency employment programs covered 4.4 percent of the labor force, adding up to almost 19 percent. Average real wages were 23 percent lower than what they had been at their peak during Salvador Allende's first year in office, in 1971. Figure 5.2 presents the evolution of total unemployment (open plus emergency programs) between 1970 and 2000. As can be seen, the peak was in 1982–83, at the time of the great currency and banking crisis that, according to some observers, including Nobel Laureate Joseph Stiglitz, was the result of Milton Friedman's advice. (For a detailed account on the crisis, see chapter 8.)

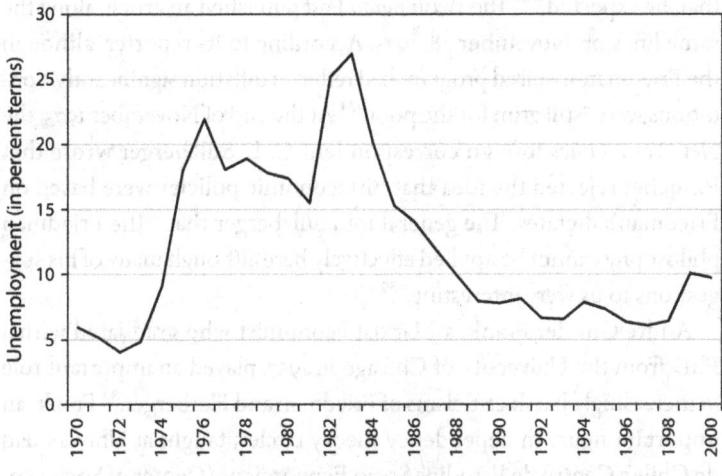

FIGURE 5.2. The unemployment rate, 1970–2000
Source: Díaz, Lüders, and Wagner (2016)

Due to draconian censorship, the local press carried few stories about the plight of the unemployed. The international press, however, maintained an interest in what was happening in Chile. Five months after Friedman's visit, the *New York Times* published a very critical editorial on the junta and its policies, noting, "After many months of applying Prof. Milton Friedman's monetary theories and harsh austerity programs, unemployment hovers around 20 per cent, industrial production fell off sharply for the first half of the year, foreign investment remains at a trickle and a fantastic inflation rate has only recently shown signs of slackening."[28]

Ten days later, Anthony Lewis wrote a column about torture and repression in Chile and related them to Friedman's advice.[29] In the months that followed, *New York Times* reporters continued to cover Chile and to emphasize the costs of the adjustment policies. On November 4, 1975, a front-page article pointed out that in Chile there was generalized "suffering" as a result of the "shock" policies put in place according to "the theories of Prof. Milton Friedman." The story underlined that "even Gen. Augusto Pinochet, president of the military government, concedes that the 'social cost' of his shock treatment is greater than he expected."[30] The *Washington Post* published an article along the same lines on November 28, 1975. According to its reporter, although the Friedman-inspired program had reduced inflation significantly, conditions were "still grim for the poor."[31] At the end of November 1975, the *New York Times* foreign correspondent C. L. Sulzberger wrote that Pinochet rejected the idea that his economic policies were based on Friedman's dictates. The general told Sulzberger that "The Friedman philosophy cannot be applied effectively here although many of his suggestions to us were interesting."[32]

André Gunder Frank, a Marxist economist who graduated with a PhD from the University of Chicago in 1957, played an important role in increasingly harsh criticisms of Friedman and Harberger.[33] Frank, an important figure in dependency theory circles, taught at Universidad de Chile's Centro de Estudios Socio Económicos (Center of Socioeconomic Studies) during the Allende years and was a committed supporter of the Allende government.[34] His work on the "underdevelopment of development" was very influential in radical leftist circles during the 1960s and 1970s. In August 1974 Frank published a long open letter condemning Harberger's involvement with the junta. In April 1976 he wrote a second open letter, but this time it was mainly directed against Friedman. He claimed that "the new policies were implemented by Pinochet as equilibrium on the point of a bayonet" and that "Pinochet gave the Chicago Boys free reign over economic policy."[35]

The Assassination of Orlando Letelier

On September 21, 1976, lawyer Orlando Letelier was assassinated in Washington, DC, by agents of the military junta. Letelier had been Allende's ambassador to the United States and had held three different cabinet positions during the last four months of the Unidad Popular government. At the time of his death, he was one of the most effective activists working against the military regime around the globe. A bomb planted in his car killed him and Ronni Moffitt, his colleague at the Institute for Policy Studies; Moffitt's husband, Michael, was seriously injured. The crime generated worldwide condemnation, especially as the involvement of DINA, Pinochet's secret police, was suspected. Three weeks before his assassination, on August 28, 1976, Letelier had published an essay in the *Nation* entitled "The 'Chicago Boys' in Chile: Economics Freedom's' Awful Toll." The article was widely reproduced and talked about after the assassination. It contained a severe criticism of Pinochet's economic policies and labeled Friedman as "the intellectual architect and unofficial adviser for the team of economists now running the Chilean economy."[36]

It did not take long for the US Federal Bureau of Investigation to find out that Colonel Manuel Contreras, the head of DINA and one of the Chicago Boys' most powerful enemies within the Pinochet government, was involved in the planning of the assassination. Two of his agents had traveled to the United States with fake passports and hired a group of Cuban dissidents and explosive experts to plant a bomb in Letelier's Chevrolet Chevelle. The bomb exploded when the car reached Sheridan Circle, not too far from the Chilean embassy. The US authorities did not take the issue lightly, and they immediately let the Chilean government know that they would follow their intelligence relentlessly, regardless of where it led. This was the first time in a very long time that a political assassination had taken place in the nation's capital. The Chicago Boys were shocked by the news and the atrocity of the act; they became deeply concerned about the consequences of the crime on Chile's external economic relations. After significant efforts, they had just managed to weaken the sanctions imposed by the international community, and all that work was now in jeopardy.[37] Sergio de Castro and his colleagues had already had problems with DINA. In 1975 Colonel Contreras had asked for a significant increase in the budget for his unit, a request that De Castro turned down. From that moment on the already tense relations between the Chicago Boys and the secret police became even more strained.[38]

Friedman's Nobel Prize

Meeting Pinochet proved to be very costly for Friedman. Everywhere he went he was met by demonstrations and picket lines. He was accused of advising the Chilean junta and being complicit with the systematic

violation of human rights. According to a *New York Times* article published in March 1976, "Mr. Friedman has been attacked . . . for identifying himself with a government notorious for its violations of human
rights and for carrying out economic policies that have shifted the
heaviest burden of sacrifice to the poorest Chileans. Two-and-half [*sic*]
years after the coup against the Marxist government, a concerted effort
to apply the Friedman theories in Chile has failed to turn around the
floundering economy that the junta inherited from the late President
Salvador Allende."[39]

Criticism increased significantly after Friedman was awarded the
Nobel Prize in Economics in October 1976. Several former Nobel laure-
ates wrote op-eds criticizing him and the Nobel Prize committee. During the award's ceremony, and at the precise moment Friedman was
being introduced to King Carl XVI Gustaf, a demonstrator dressed in
white tie and seated in the upper balcony blew a whistle and shouted,
in Swedish: "Freedom for Chile! Friedman go home! Long live the
people of Chile! Crush capitalism!"[40]

In the years that followed, Friedman showed a defiant public face
regarding his visit with Pinochet. He pointed out that the purpose of
the meeting was to gather information, he denied advising the military,
and wrote columns accusing his attackers of hypocrisy: they questioned
his visit to Chile, but not his 1980 and 1988 trips to Communist China,
a country with many more human rights violations than the South
American nation.[41]

But deep inside, Friedman was bothered by the Chilean episode.
Through the years, every time I talked to Milton Friedman about
Chile and Pinochet, I noticed some discomfort and uneasiness. In
2004 California governor Arnold Schwarzenegger appointed me to his
Council of Economic Advisers. To me this was a big surprise, since I was
not a Republican and I had never met the governor. One of the great
attractions of the (unpaid) position was that Gary Becker and Milton
Friedman were members of the group, so I accepted immediately.
The council met periodically—once a month or so—in Sacramento.
Meetings were chaired by former secretary of state George Shultz with
great efficiency. We assembled at nine-thirty in the morning—usually

without Schwarzenegger, at first—and Shultz asked us our views on recent developments and on specific issues raised in the preceding meeting. We went around the table, and every member had about two minutes to give a brief commentary. The last one to speak was Milton Friedman, who sat on Shultz's right. By the time Friedman spoke, the governor had joined the meeting. He paid close attention to what Friedman had to say and took detailed notes on a yellow pad. Most times, Friedman spoke at length, exceeding the two minutes' limit imposed on the rest of us. As in his public appearances and in the PBS documentary series *Free to Choose*, his points were logical and persuasive.[42] Whatever the problem at hand, Friedman would dissect it and reduce it to its bare bones, making everything seem simple and almost obvious.

During breaks I would talk to Friedman about several issues, including his experience in Chile. Although I had not been his student at the University of Chicago—he left for the Hoover Institution one year before I enrolled—we had met on several occasions; he knew that I was from Chile and that I had worked with Al Harberger, the putative godfather of the Chicago Boys. Every time I approached the subject of Pinochet, the shock treatment, or any other aspect of the Chilean economy, I noticed some reluctance on Friedman's behalf. It was not that he avoided the issues, but he hesitated—something that was quite unusual for him. He repeated the points that he had made many times in columns, interviews, speeches, and in his memoir. Yes, he had met with Pinochet, as he had met with many other heads of state and government leaders, including Zhao Ziyang, the secretary-general of the Communist Party of China. But meeting with a politician was not the same as being an adviser. He had not advised Pinochet or Zhao, and that was the main point. He also told me that his personal relationship with the Chicago Boys was minimal. Before traveling to Santiago in 1975, he didn't even know their names, with one notable exception—that of Rolf Lüders. With time, he said, he established a personal and friendly relationship with Sergio de Castro and Ernesto Fontaine.

On one occasion I asked Friedman whether he regretted writing a letter to Pinochet and putting the shock treatment recommendation on paper. He said that many of his friends had told him that it had been a mistake. He disagreed, however. After all, he had mentioned the need for shock treatment in many public lectures, including one in Santiago in 1975. He often talked about abrupt and decisive policies when discussing the reconstruction of Germany and Japan after World War II. Many times he had referred to Germany's overnight price liberalization in 1948 as the best example of how a sudden shock treatment was the best solution to economic crises. He mentioned Konrad Adenauer and Ludwig Erhard and explained that prices in West Germany were liberalized during a weekend so the occupying forces could not object or stop the initiative. One time, after talking about the German experience, Friedman looked at me intensely, and with what I thought was some impatience, he said something like, "I was on the record on the subject of the benefits of a shock treatment, and there was no harm putting it in writing to Pinochet. After all, I wrote that letter out of courtesy."[43]

6

Market Reforms and the Struggle for Power, 1975–1981

IN LATE DECEMBER 1976, three months after Orlando Letelier's assassination in Washington, DC, Jorge Cauas stepped down as minister of finance. He was replaced by Sergio de Castro, who became the indisputable leader of the economic reforms. The position of minister of economics was taken by Chicago Boy Pablo Baraona, and at the helm of the Central Bank was University of Chicago graduate Alvaro Bardón. It was a perfect Chicago trifecta. In little more than three years Milton Friedman's disciples had moved from the fringes of the political system to the very center of power.[1]

Yet the Chicago Boys' plan to expand and deepen the reforms faced a serious obstacle: not everyone in the military was happy with the direction the country had taken since Friedman's visit in 1975. The most powerful detractor of the Chicago Boys was air force general Gustavo Leigh, one of the earliest conspirators and a member of the junta. With time, Leigh's relationship with Pinochet had become seriously strained, both because of disagreements regarding economic policy and because of divergent visions about the political future of the country. Leigh led a group of highly nationalist officers who believed that the state should play a central role in economic development by both shepherding investment decisions and by owning and operating a large number of what they called strategic firms. Leigh also believed that power had to be returned to civilians sooner rather than later. The air force general was incensed when, in October 1974, Pinochet appointed himself president of the republic, a significant upgrade from being president of the military junta. Leigh was also unhappy about privatization, the freeing of all prices, and the opening of the economy to foreign competition; he had been particularly opposed to the abrupt devaluation of the peso in the early days of the regime. Leigh was a nationalist, a protectionist, and a gradualist.

The clash between the two high-power generals was resolved on July 24, 1978, when Pinochet staged a "coup-within-the-coup" and convinced the other members of the junta to dismiss Leigh under the argument that he was "incapacitated" to exercise military command. He was replaced by air force general Fernando Matthei, an officer of German descent who was sympathetic to market orientation and who had served as minister of health. With General Leigh out of the way, the Chicago Boys had a freer hand to push for deeper and farther-reaching reforms.

A few months before removing Leigh from the junta, Pinochet decided to collaborate fully with the US inquiry into the assassination of former ambassador Orlando Letelier and his colleague Ronni Moffitt. In early March 1978 the military government acknowledged that the two men accused of planning and carrying out the assassination—American citizen Michel Townley and Captain Armando Fernández Larios—had traveled to the United States using assumed names and official (diplomatic) Chilean passports. A month later, and under significant pressure from the administration of President Jimmy Carter, Michel Townley was extradited from Chile to the United States. Once in custody, Townley confessed his involvement in the crime and accused retired colonel Manuel Contreras—the ex-director of the secret police, the Dirección de Inteligencia Nacional (DINA; Directorate of National Intelligence), and a declared enemy of the Chicago Boys—of masterminding Letelier's assassination.[2] After a long and convoluted legal process, in November 1979 Chile's Corte Suprema (Supreme Court) denied the US request for extraditing Contreras. By then, however, he had been forced into retirement and had lost most of his power.

The ousting of General Leigh and the firing of Colonel Contreras consolidated Pinochet's authority and control of the government apparatus. Although he still had to consult with the junta for approving major legislation, he now faced very little dissent and weak opposition within the ranks of the military. This gave the Chicago Boys additional breathing room to carry out the reforms and (as will be discussed in chapter 7) for expanding markets to areas where they had traditionally been absent, including education, health care, and pensions.

In early 1979, and despite a very high rate of unemployment (13 percent) and persistent inflation (40 percent), Sergio de Castro and his colleagues were satisfied with what they had achieved. The huge fiscal imbalance inherited from Salvador Allende's Unidad Popular government was transformed into a small surplus, and the economy was recovering from the "shock treatment" of 1975.[3] The rate of growth of gross domestic product (GDP) was 9.8 percent in 1977 and 8.5 percent in 1978. On the reform front, things were also moving along, particularly in three areas considered critical by the Chicago Boys: all prices had been freed; import licenses and quotas had been eliminated, and import tariffs reduced significantly; and interest rates were allowed to fluctuate freely, reflecting the birth of an incipient capital market. In addition, most firms nationalized by Unidad Popular had been privatized or were in the process of being sold to the public. There was also progress in many other policy areas, including taxation (a value-added tax was instituted), agriculture, deregulation, and infrastructure. (For details, see table 4.2 in chapter 4.) In what follows I summarize progress in the three most emblematic reforms that contributed to Chile's free-market revolution: trade openness, privatization, and capital markets reform.

The Opening of the Economy: Going It Alone

At the time of the coup d'état, Chile's external sector was a mess. Every import required a prior license, and duties went from 0 percent to 250 percent. There were ten official exchange rates, ranging from very low (for exports) to very high (for tourism and luxury goods). There was an active black market for US dollars, with a premium in excess of 700 percent. In addition, importers had to make a deposit equivalent to an astounding 10,000 percent of the value of the goods imported while the shipment was in transit. This wide array of import duties, licenses, multiple exchange rates, and prior deposits resulted in a structure of protection that created all sorts of perverse incentives. The agricultural sector was particularly hurt, as imported inputs, such as machinery and fertilizers, were subject to high duties, and the exchange rate was kept at an artificially low level, thus discouraging exports. At the other end of the spectrum, manufactured goods with very low value added and low tariffs on inputs had a very high level of implicit or effective protection. An example of this was the plants that assembled cars from ready-made kits imported from abroad. Their value added was almost nil, but because of the protectionist structure, the price at which automobiles were sold to the public was three or four times higher than in the international market. But this situation was not restricted to cars; it was also the case for bicycles (which were the working class's main means of transportation), refrigerators, textiles, pots and pans, and all types of manufactured goods.

The Chicago Boys' view of protectionism was simple and was based on the Chicago school's long tradition of favoring free trade, a tradition that had been started by the first chairman of the university's Department of Economics, J. Laurence Laughlin, and continued by Jacob Viner, Milton Friedman, Harry Johnson, and Robert Mundell, among others. The liberalization of trade, however, faced two obstacles. First, Chile was a member of the Andean Pact, a budding customs union that included all the countries in western South America. The architecture of the pact was based on the idea that in order to benefit from economies of scale, specific manufacturing industries had to be assigned to each country by the regional planning authority. In addition, the pact had high import tariffs with respect to the rest of the world. This, it was argued, would allow the members of the pact to benefit from the needed protection to launch and sustain a vibrant industrial sector. Both principles were contradicted by the Chicago doctrine, including Jacob Viner's work on trade creation and trade diversion in customs unions. In April 1976 Pinochet decided to withdraw Chile from the Andean Pact, giving the Chicago Boys a freer hand for liberalizing trade. Several senior military officers were unhappy with the move, as they believed that for

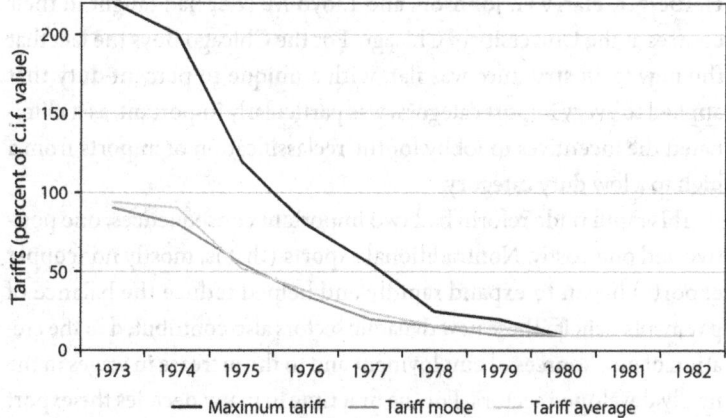

FIGURE 6.1. Import tariffs and trade liberalization, 1973–1982
Source: Edwards and Lederman (2002)

national security reasons it was essential for Chile to have a strong industrial sector. The tug of war between the reform-minded economists and the statists in the military would continue, with different levels of intensity, for the duration of Pinochet's dictatorship. Although each team scored points, at the end of the road the economists won the war, and when democratic rule was restored in 1990 the country looked remarkably different from how it had looked in 1973 when the military deposed President Salvador Allende.

Figure 6.1 presents the evolution of import tariffs between 1973 and 1982; licenses, quotas, and prior deposits were eliminated in 1974. As can be seen, the slashing of tariffs was brutal after 1976. In 1976 the highest import tariff was 65 percent, and most import duties were at the 30 percent mark, roughly corresponding to the goal set by The Brick. Encouraged by the withdrawal from the Andean Pact and by Pinochet's support, the Chicago Boys pressed on, and by 1980 they achieved their new goal of a uniform import duty of 10 percent.

This rapid and unilateral trade reform was accompanied until 1978 by a more depreciated domestic currency, just as Milton Friedman had recommended during his 1975 visit, and in line with what Arnold

Harberger, Harry G. Johnson, and Lloyd Metzler had taught in their courses at the University of Chicago. For the Chicago Boys the fact that the new tariff structure was flat, with a unique 10 percent duty that applied to every import category, was particularly important, as it eliminated the incentives to lobby for the reclassification of imports from a high to a low duty category.

This rapid trade reform had two important consequences, one positive and one costly. Nontraditional exports (that is, mostly noncopper exports) began to expand rapidly and helped reduce the balance of payments deficit. These new dynamic sectors also contributed to the creation of new sources of employment and to the increase in wages in the newly developed sectors. For the first time in many decades the export sector became the locomotive of the growth process. On the negative side, production and employment in the old protected sector declined significantly, adding to the criticisms about the "social cost" of the experiment. In July 1978 Alejandro Foxley, the economist who would become the first minister of finance after the return to democracy, wrote in the newsweekly *Hoy*, "The rapid reduction of import tariffs . . . [is one] of the factors that explain the high rate of unemployment."[4] The government dismissed these criticisms and argued that the spike in unemployment was temporary and that it was the small cost to pay for improving resource allocation and achieving a high level of efficiency. Jorge Cauas noted, "It is true that unemployment is high. . . . This is, however, by no means the results of the [program]. . . . [I]n the long run, and insofar as the process of resource allocation is consolidated and high rates of investment in highly productive sectors are achieved, the traditional problem of unemployment will be permanently solved."[5]

Financial Reform and Skyrocketing Foreign Debt

The creation of a well-functioning capital market was a priority for the Chicago Boys. It was expected that a financial liberalization reform would result in a significant increase in financial intermediation and improved credit allocation; it would also increase the ability of new and dynamic export-oriented firms to raise funds for new projects.

Banks' reserve requirements were lowered in 1974, and in May 1975 the government allowed nonbank financial intermediaries to operate. The freeing up of interest rates represented a major change in a nation where for more than three decades credit had been tightly controlled, and the real interest rate—that is, interest rates adjusted by inflation—had been negative. Following the script in The Brick, international capital movements were regulated tightly. Foreign loans with a maturity of less than twenty-four months were not allowed, and those with maturities between twenty-four and sixty-six months were subject to a reserve requirement that paid no interest. Capital outflows were only permitted under restricted circumstances, and only after a license was obtained from the Central Bank.

By the late 1970s the government claimed that the financial reform was a resounding success. Credit to the private sector increased twelve times between 1975 and 1979—from US$156 million to US$11.1 billion—and the stock market index increased by a factor of forty. But there was a dark side to these advances. Interest rates—and especially lending rates—were very high in real terms, and banks became major risk takers, borrowing internationally in foreign currency (at maturities of twenty-five months or longer) and on-lending in domestic currency. This risky behavior increased significantly in 1979 when, in an effort to reduce inflation to the one-digit level, the government fixed the exchange rate at 39 pesos per US dollar. With domestic inflation at approximately 25 percent, the interest rates' differentials were gigantic. Banks borrowed internationally at the London Inter-Bank Offered Rate plus 4 or 5 percent and lent in (fixed) pesos at rates exceeding 40 percent. As a result, a major currency mismatch developed in banks' balance sheets. Most banks' assets and revenues were in pesos, and liabilities were in US dollars. This proved to be fatal in 1982, when because of the currency crisis and the devaluation, the peso value of these loans more than doubled in a matter of weeks, and banks' clients were unable to pay them.

In 1979 Sergio de Castro dismissed concerns about the growing external debt. He pointed out that there was nothing wrong with foreign banks lending substantial amounts of money to Chilean banks. In his view, if the public sector was not involved and the transactions were between private institutions on both ends, everything was fine. A few years later, Chancellor of the Exchequer Nigel Lawson took a similar view in the United Kingdom. The notion that very large current account deficits did not matter if the government accounts were balanced became known as the Lawson Doctrine. In late 1981, when the current account deficit reached 12 percent of GDP, De Castro said, "There is no doubt that large current account deficits . . . are highly beneficial for the country and that we should make an effort to maintain them at the highest possible level and for the largest possible period of time."[6] As it turned out, he was wrong. Transactions were indeed between private parties, but when the peso was devalued by 40 percent in 1982, firms that had borrowed heavily in dollars were unable to pay back their loans and went bankrupt. This affected the banking sector, and eventually, every bank in the system was bailed out by the government at a great cost for taxpayers. (For details, see chapter 8.)

Privatization and the Battle for Codelco

In 1973, just before the coup d'état, the state owned 596 manufacturing companies and banks (see table 6.1). Most of them had been confiscated or "intervened" by the Unidad Popular government through the tender offer scheme with inflated prices that was discussed in chapter 3. By late 1974, 202 firms had been either returned to their owners or privatized, and by early 1978 all but seven "intervened" firms had been restituted to their original shareholders. Starting in 1974, commercial banks, which had been nationalized, were sold to the public with an explicit limit of how many shares individuals (3 percent) or investment companies (5 percent) could acquire. The private sector quickly found ways of getting around the regulations and, as a result, very large conglomerates—the so called *grupos* (groups), which operated in ways similar to Korean *chaebols*—were built around the newly privatized banks. These conglomerates acquired a significant amount of economic power, something that was not welcomed by the more nationalistic senior officers in the armed forces. While in power (until 1978), Colonel Manuel Contreras, the feared head of DINA, spied on the executives of the groups and built thick dossiers on their activities.[7]

TABLE 6.1. Chile: State-Owned Enterprises, 1970-2019

	1970	1973	1983	1989	1998	2019
Controlled by the state's Corporación de Fomento de la Producción (Corporation for Production Development)	46	571	24	24	22	21
Subsidiaries	(46)	(228)	(23)	24	22	21
Intervened	—	(325)	(0)	0	0	0
Banks	(0)	(18)	(1)	0	0	0
Other state-owned enterprises	20	22	21	18	13	10
Other financial institutions	2	2	2	2	2	1
Codelco	0[a]	1	1	1	1	1
Total	68	596	48	45	38	33

Sources: Constructed from data in Hachette A. de la F. (2000); Sistema de Empresas (n.d.); and Dirección de Presupuestos (n.d.).

[a] The state owned 50 percent of "large copper companies" because of the acquisition from foreign companies in 1970 during the "Chileanization process"; Codelco did not exist in 1970.

The Chicago Boys did not worry about the increasing concentration of economic power. Their views on the subject were rooted in a simple version of what they had learned in Chicago: the opening of the economy to international trade introduced foreign competition, imposing severe market-driven discipline on domestic firms, regardless of their size. Government economists repeatedly stated that according to the "law of one price," domestic prices could not exceed international prices plus transportation costs and the very low 10 percent uniform tariff. This, they affirmed, meant that barriers to entry were, de facto, very low and that every internationally tradable sector faced stiff competition from abroad. What they missed was that many of the large firms created trading subsidiaries that had exclusivity contracts with foreign brands for selling those products in Chile. As a result, the main or only producer of white goods in Chile was the main importer of refrigerators and washing machines from Asia, Europe, or the United States. A second argument used to dismiss concerns about the increasing degree of concentration was taken from George Stigler and was based on the idea that even when there was monopoly power it was not overwhelming and that, given the plausible ranges of elasticities of demand, markups would be reasonable. To this they added (also following Stigler) that regulation and control was unlikely to work, as private firms would "capture" the regulators.

In order to encourage bidders during the privatization process, the government offered loans to qualified investors. By 1982, 394 firms had been privatized. Most of them were sold at prices ranging between 35 percent and 45 percent of book value. The only exceptions were companies with great export potential, as investors understood that the new model was based on maintaining a highly competitive real exchange rate. In the years to come, critics of the model, including Gabriel Boric, the student activist who would be elected president in 2021, would argue that selling valuable assets at fire sale prices was an act of corruption that favored a group of businesspeople that were, for all practical purposes, accomplices of the armed forces.

The military supported the rapid devolution of "intervened" firms to their owners. After all, the Allende government had relied on an antiquated, and, until then, forgotten executive order to take control, without any compensation, of a number of firms, many of which were of medium size, and family owned and operated. Yet privatizing the firms that had been legitimately acquired by the state was a different story. Some officers thought that before privatizing them it was essential to analyze their role in a grand "national security" strategy. Then there were the traditional and emblematic state-owned companies created in the 1940s, 1950s, and 1960s, including the national airline, Línea Aerea Nacional; the largest steel producer, Compañía de Aceros del Pacífico (Pacific Steel Company); the national petroleum company, Empresa Nacional del Petróleo; and the national electrical company, Empresa Nacional de Electricidad S.A. Many officers thought that these firms were out of bounds and should remain in the hands of the government. The Chicago Boys understood the sentiment and decided to maintain them (for the time being) in the public sector's hands. In May 2022, I visited Sergio de Castro at his home and discussed with him many issues related to the reforms, including the privatization process and the fixed exchange rate policy that led to the currency crisis of 1982 (figure 6.2).

FIGURE 6.2. The author (*left*) with Sergio de Castro (*right*), in 2022, more than forty years after De Castro resigned from the Ministry of Finance
Source: Author's personal collection

Codelco, which was then (as it is now) the largest copper producer in the world, was in a category of its own. For the Chicago Boys Codelco was "a monster" with an enormous amount of power, and with very large and combative unions; the company epitomized everything they thought was wrong about Chile's historical economic strategy. Sergio de Castro and his colleagues decided to break the company down into smaller firms, each one owning and operating a specific mine. They thought that, eventually, it would be possible to privatize at least some of these smaller companies. The plan, however, was immediately resisted by the military. Colonel Gastón Frez, one of the ablest officers in the Chilean Army, took the lead in defending the state ownership of copper and was able to convince Pinochet of the importance of maintaining Codelco as one large company in the hands of the government. He reminded the general that every year 10 percent of Codelco's gross sales were automatically transferred to the armed forces to finance equipment purchases and argued that it would be difficult to collect the same amount if there were many smaller firms. Once Colonel Frez had persuaded Pinochet, Sergio de Castro realized that there was nothing he could do about Codelco.

———

In 1979, with the economy growing at full blast—approximately 8 percent per year—Pinochet decided to launch a new phase in his reforms program. The goal was to go beyond basic economics and to introduce deep changes in the way citizens related to each other and with the state. The new reforms, which were announced with great fanfare in a speech delivered on the sixth anniversary of the coup, were to cover labor relations and trade unions, health care, education, pensions, decentralization, property rights in the agricultural sector (including water rights), and civil service reforms. Pinochet also stated that in 1980 a referendum would be held for the approval of a new constitution. These announcements marked a turning point in Chile's history; it was at this moment that the Chicago Boys' program turned from ambitious promarkets reforms into an all-encompassing project rooted in neoliberal ideas.

7

The Birth of a Neoliberal Regime

THE SEVEN MODERNIZATIONS AND
THE NEW CONSTITUTION

IN MID-1978 the Chicago Boys' team was reinforced by thirty-year-old José Piñera, a Católica undergraduate with a doctorate from Harvard University who would become one of Pinochet's favorite civilians. The son of an ambassador who was highly respected in intellectual circles— he was a friend of the poet Pablo Neruda—Piñera saw himself as bringing some culture and sophistication to a group of technocrats whom he considered to be rather flat and gray. In conversation he was engaging and often brilliant; he quoted philosophers and writers, and dropped the names of people he had met in his different travels or through his father, the ambassador. He was an avid reader of poetry and wrote with an unusual combination of clarity and exuberance. Piñera defined himself as a humanist, and he once told me that it was a pity that I had gone to such an uninteresting school as the University of Chicago, a place that was rather strong in economics but was a wasteland when it came to culture and the arts. I should have done like him, he added, and attended an Ivy League institution. His brother Sebastián Piñera, also a Harvard graduate, was elected president twice and was in office when the October 2019 revolt erupted. After the insurgency, one of the most often found graffiti in Santiago and other cities, read Death to Piñera!

José Piñera and Chicago Boy Miguel Kast believed that in order to consolidate market orientation and ensure freedom for future generations it was necessary to move aggressively into the cultural and constitutional terrains. It was not enough to lower taxes and import tariffs, free prices and interest rates, and push for deregulation and privatize firms. In order to truly change Chile and to avoid it falling again into the hands of communists there was a need for a deep change in political institutions and in the nation's culture. According to Kast, Piñera, and their followers, Chile was not ready for a Western-style democracy; what the country needed was a long period of authoritarian rule, eventually followed by "protected democracy." These views were shared by Jaime Guzmán, a deeply conservative legal scholar and admirer of Spain's Francisco Franco, who at the time had great influence over Pinochet.

In a speech delivered on September 11, 1979—the sixth anniversary of the coup—Pinochet stated that given the success of the recovery program and of the early reforms, and given that Marxist politicians had been banned and exiled, it was time to move into the social policies arena and announced a program that he pretentiously called the Siete Modernizaciones (Seven Modernizations). These included reforms to the labor law, pensions, education, health services, agriculture (including, in particular, water rights), the judicial system, and the administrative organization of the country.[1] The speech, written by José Piñera, took its name from Mao Zedong's Four Modernizations, something that at the time neither Pinochet nor his close military advisers realized.[2] Out of the seven areas signaled in the speech, Piñera and Pinochet thought that the most important ones were labor relations (including the role of unions in the new Chile), social security, education, and health care. Although Pinochet did not mention it explicitly in the speech, behind these "modernizations" was the idea of having a referendum to approve a new constitution.

The arrival of José Piñera to the highest circles of power introduced significant tensions within the economic team. Sergio de Castro and José Piñera simply did not like each other. They disagreed on key economic issues, including whether the exchange rate should be fixed or floating, and on the merits of fully connecting wage increases to past inflation. They also had very different temperaments. De Castro was a tough, plainspoken man who often used profanity; he had been educated in Santiago's Grange School (British prep school), where he had been a varsity rugby player. Piñera, in contrast, came from a deeply Catholic background—his uncle was an archbishop—and had been educated by German priests; he used metaphors when he spoke, loved classical music, and as mentioned, was fond of poetry. In the years to come they would clash repeatedly as they positioned themselves to have Pinochet's ear.

The Seven Modernizations

The launching of the Seven Modernizations marked a turning point in Pinochet's regime. The goal was no longer to reform the economy, making it more competitive and efficient; the objective now was to expand market relations everywhere in order to change Chile's values and character. It is not an exaggeration to say that this was the moment when Chile adopted a transformational neoliberal perspective.

The new labor law, the Plan Laboral, approved in late 1979 by the junta brought revolutionary changes to labor relations. It regulated the creation of unions, established new rules for collective bargaining, and determined the legal features of labor contracts. The law greatly reduced unions' power relative to what it had been historically. Union membership became voluntary, and unions could not join forces across firms in order to negotiate at the industry or national levels. Firms could impose lockouts and temporarily lay off workers.[3] Changing this legislation became a high priority for the democratic forces and Pinochet's opponents. This was done in 1990, during the early months of the first postdictatorship democratic government led by President Patricio Aylwin.

A key aspect of Pinochet's labor law, which was the brainchild of José Piñera, was that it set a floor to wage increases during a union-company bargaining process. According to article 26 of the Plan Laboral, firms were, during a contract negotiation, obliged to offer wage increases that at least reflected accumulated past inflation. At the time, Piñera argued that this provision of the law was politically astute, as it assured the military's support, including the support of the increasingly powerful

Comité Asesor (Advisory Committee), the body that Pinochet had created to scrutinize legislation proposed by his own economic team. In his authorized biography, Sergio de Castro argued that this legislation was extremely detrimental to the functioning of the Chilean economy.[4] By impeding downward movements in negotiated inflation-adjusted wages, the new labor law made it impossible for Chile to maintain full employment when international economic conditions deteriorated and, in particular, when the price of copper and other key exports fell in global markets.

In 1979, when the law was being discussed, De Castro confronted Piñera and urged him to modify the proposal by removing the wage indexation clause. Piñera refused, asking Pinochet to make a decision on the matter. The general, in turn, asked the members of the Comité Asesor for their opinion. After some deliberation, the generals and admirals sided with Piñera, and the new labor code was approved as drafted. The episode greatly increased the bad blood between the two economists. Years later, in a candid interview, De Castro remembered the episode and insisted that he was right and Piñera wrong: "Well, as I predicted at the time, eventually, [during the 1982 crisis] shit flew all over the place."[5]

There is little doubt that the 1981 social security reform was the most important, revolutionary, and controversial policy implemented during the dictatorship. A traditional pay-as-you-go system, in which active workers' contributions were used to pay pensions for retired workers, was replaced by a system based on individual retirement accounts. Workers were required to save 10 percent of their wages in these accounts, which were managed by licensed firms (for a fee). On reaching retirement age (sixty-five years for men, and sixty for women), these funds were used to purchase an annuity.

The plan, which was described in some detail in The Brick (see chapter 4), was the brainchild of Emilio Sanfuentes and Sergio Undurraga and was implemented under José Piñera's supervision. What made this scheme unique was that the government played no role in the financing or payment of old-age pensions. As it turned out, and as I will discuss in chapter 14, the new pension system was seriously flawed; pensions rarely surpassed 25 percent of preretirement wages. Of course, given the long-term nature of the reforms, it took decades for the population to find out how low pensions were: the first cohort of retirees under the new system retired in 2010–11. Once it was apparent that the system was producing very low pensions, a massive and vocal movement protesting "miserable pensions" sprang into life. At the time of the 2019 revolt, the idea of putting an end to the private pension system—the reform that at one point was the jewel in the crown of the Chicago Boys—was supported by a large proportion of the population.

Between 1979 and 1982, vast progress was also made in the education and health care fronts. Schools were transferred to municipalities as a way of improving school administrators' accountability and weakening the national teachers' union, and a system of vouchers for primary and secondary schools was established. In 1981 a higher-education law was passed, allowing the creation of new private universities. Consistent with the proposals in The Brick, there were no subsidies to higher education, and every university or technical institute, public or private, charged a market-determined tuition.

At the heart of these policies was the "subsidiarity principle" pushed by legal scholar Jaime Guzmán and enshrined in the 1980 Chilean Constitution. According to this principle, the state should not be directly involved in the delivery of any services that could be provided efficiently and effectively by "intermediate organizations," including foundations, religious orders, not-for-profit institutions, or for-profit firms.[6] For Guzmán this meant that there was no need for the state to control, own, or run universities, colleges, or trade schools. For political reasons—including the fact that many army officers belonged to the Freemasons movement, a group traditionally involved in education—public-sector universities were allowed to continue functioning. But their budget was greatly reduced and their plans for expansion were kept in check.

There was a quirk in the higher-education reform. The military decided that while for-profit primary and secondary schools would be allowed, for-profit universities would not be permitted. It didn't take too long for the private sector to find ways of getting around that legislation, however. The university itself was a not-for-profit institution, but it was an almost empty shell, an organization that existed on paper, hired professors, charged tuition, and granted degrees. But it did not own any equipment, buildings, libraries, gyms, or any physical assets. All of these were leased or contracted from for-profit firms, which were owned by the same individuals who controlled the university or professional institutes. As I will discuss in chapter 12, this structure became extremely controversial in the early part of the new century and was at the heart of the protests that began in 2006 among university students and ended up in the uprising of October 2019.

The health reform of 1981 allowed workers to use the health tax (7 percent of wages) to finance the purchase of private insurance. This allowed the members of the professional and managerial class to get around public health provision. Therefore, a dual health care system was created. The well-to-do had health care close to that of the First World, while the poor had mediocre medical services and were subject to long waiting lists for surgeries. In chapter 11, I discuss the health reforms put together by the left-of-center governments after the return to democracy. The budget to the public health system was greatly increased, as was its coverage. But the voucher scheme that created a segregated health system was maintained. During the 2019 uprising the questionable quality of health care provision became another rallying cry for protesters.

A Neoliberal Constitution and the 1980 Referendum

The idea of writing a new constitution came up very early during the military government.[7] According to the "Secret Minutes of the Junta," currently held at the Biblioteca Nacional de Chile (National Library of Chile), the idea was first discussed on September 13, 1973, two days after the coup.[8] On December 21, 1973, a commission of four lawyers, led by legal scholar Jaime Guzmán, was appointed to draft a new constitutional text. Jaime Guzmán's political ideas were influenced by the nineteenth-century Spanish Carlist movement, and by *Rerum Novarum*, the encyclical issued by Pope Leon XIII in 1891. Although the main purpose of the papal document was to reflect on the dire conditions of the working classes, Pinochet's lawyers interpreted it narrowly and relied on it to support a natural rights constitutional perspective centered around the notion that property rights preceded the creation of the state and were thus inalienable. In addition to Jaime Guzmán, the group included Sergio Diez, a conservative and deeply religious politician who as Pinochet's ambassador to the United Nations denied that the junta had violated human rights; Enrique Ortúzar, a seasoned lawyer who had been attorney general during President Jorge Alessandri's conservative administration (1958–64); and Jorge Ovalle, a lawyer and Freemason who was an adviser to air force general Gustavo Leigh, the great adversary of the Chicago Boys during the early years of the regime.

On the basis of national security arguments, nationalist members of the military convinced Pinochet that the constitution should state that all mineral deposits belonged to the state and were inalienable.[9] Sergio de Castro lobbied strongly against the idea and asked prominent legal scholars to explain to the general the consequences of this provision for foreign investment and Chile's economic future. He pointed out that a poor country, such as Chile, would never have sufficient capital to mine its vast copper deposits. What was needed was foreign capital under appropriate conditions. If the constitution declared that all mines and all mineral reserves belonged to the state, however, no investment would come. Members of the military, on the other hand, argued that God had endowed Chile with mineral wealth and that it would be political suicide to give it away to the private sector, either domestic or foreign. They reminded Pinochet that the nationalization (without compensation) of American-owned mines was the only initiative unanimously approved by the Chilean Congress during Salvador Allende's socialist government. After an intense give-and-take, state ownership of deposits was included in the constitutional draft.

It would take more than a year for a team led by José Piñera, who by then had become the minister of mining, to write new legislation on mining concessions. The 1981 Ley Orgánica Constitucional sobre Concesiones Mineras (Organic Constitutional Law on Mining Concessions) law established that although the state owned (and was forbidden to sell) mineral deposits, it could write contracts with private companies, allowing them to mine the minerals. From a legal point of view, these contracts were protected at the same level as regular property rights, and any cancellation or expropriation required compensating the owner using market value and making a cash payment before the concession was taken away. This statute became fundamentally important during 1984–85, the years of Chile's economic takeoff, when there was a boom in mining investment on the part of multinational corporations.

On September 11, 1980, the junta held a national referendum to decide whether the new constitution would be approved. The plebiscite took place under highly questionable conditions: there were no voters' registries, opponents of the new constitution were not allowed to campaign, and ballots were printed on very thin, almost translucent, paper that allowed election officials to see how people voted. The "Yes" option received 67 percent of the votes, and the new constitution was adopted on March 11, 1981.

Constitutional scholar Frederick Schauer has argued that there are two types of constitutions: "constitutions of hope" and "constitutions of fear."[10] "Constitutions of hope" capture the belief that the legal charter should reflect society's collective aspirations and dreams and a shared vision about the future. Aspirational constitutions enshrine a number of social rights—health care, education, housing, old-age pensions, and access to culture—even when, for fiscal reasons, it is difficult for the country to provide them to everyone. "Constitutions of fear," in contrast, are rooted on the view that, if left on their own, governments (even democratically elected governments) will tend to abuse their power and restrict people's freedoms. It is precisely for this reason that constitutions should establish a well-defined list of constitutional political rights—for example, freedom of speech, habeas corpus, and freedom of assembly—that protect people from a potential power grab by the government.

Pinochet's constitution was clearly a constitution of fear and a product of the Cold War: a text written to protect the country from communism. The paradox, of course, is that it provided this protection by limiting political rights. Some members of the senate were not elected through elections; they were appointed among those who had held certain positions, including ex–commanders in chief of the armed forces and former presidents of the republic. This last provision meant that when Pinochet stepped down as president, he would automatically become a senator and, thus, would have immunity from prosecution for malfeasance, corrupt acts, or human rights violations. The 1980 constitution had several built-in provisions that made it almost impossible for a government like Salvador Allende's to get into power and attempt to move the country to the ranks of socialist nations. At the doctrinal level the 1980 constitution was based on the "principle of subsidiarity," or the notion that the state (or central authority) should give precedence to the private sector and the civil society in organizing economic and social activities, including the provision of social services. The state would fund these services, but the actual delivery of them was often left in the hands of private entities.

The restrictions imposed by Pinochet's constitution worked, at least, on two levels. First, there were specific stipulations in the text itself that protected the military's vision and sheltered the Chicago Boys' economic reforms. An example was the prohibition against public-sector workers striking. Second, several rules and regulations were written into "laws with constitutional rank," which required supermajorities from 60 percent to 66 percent to be amended. Some of the most important higher-quorum laws included the education law, which became a focal point during the 2019 revolt, and the law that granted the Central Bank independence. In addition, the electoral law—also of constitutional rank—established a system for electing members of the Chilean Congress, through which each district elected two deputies and two senators. This meant that political coalitions with one-third of the vote in a particular district had the same representation in the Congress as coalitions with two-thirds of the vote. This electoral system was known as a "binominal" regime.

In 2005, and after long and arduous political negotiations, major reforms were made to the constitution. Unelected, appointed senators—one of which had been Pinochet—were no longer permitted, and the control of the military by elected officials was reasserted. An important symbolic outcome was that, because of the number of amendments (fifty-eight in total), the constitutional text now carried the signatures of President Ricardo Lagos and his cabinet, and not that of Pinochet and his collaborators. In 2015 the electoral law was changed, and the binominal system was replaced by a regime based on districts with multiple representatives, elected through a proportional mechanism. An immediate result of this change was that several small political parties sprang to life, creating a fractured political mosaic or political archipelago.

Seeking Respectability: Hayek and the Mont Pèlerin Society

After Orlando Letelier's assassination in 1976, international sanctions against Chile became more acute. Pinochet was shunned by the heads of state of democratic nations, and Chilean officials were unwelcomed in many multilateral meetings. In early 1980, and as part of an effort to gain some international acceptance, Pinochet embarked on a trip to the Philippines, where he was to meet strongman Ferdinand Marcos to discuss possible bilateral economic and cultural agreements. When Pinochet's plane was in the middle of the Pacific Ocean, he was informed that Marcos had withdrawn the invitation; after refueling in Fiji the Chilean delegation had to turn around and return to Santiago. The general and his wife were livid. Never in Chile's almost two hundred years as an independent nation had a head of state suffered such a humiliation. Hernán Cubillos, the minister of foreign affairs, was the scapegoat and was summarily fired. At home political repression intensified, and the persecution of dissidents reached new heights.

The Chicago Boys were deeply troubled by the fact that the government was spurned internationally. Their development strategy was based on the rapid expansion of exports, and that required good diplomatic and commercial relations with as many nations as possible. They were also concerned about their personal reputations. Although sentiments varied across individuals, most of them did not want to be labeled as heartless technocrats serving a brutal dictatorship. In order to combat this reputation and to gain global respectability among classical liberal intellectuals, a group of senior Chicago Boys decided to set up an interdisciplinary think tank to support their ideas about the economy and society. After raising significant sums of monies from industrialists and bankers, in 1980 the Centro de Estudios Públicos (CEP; Center of Public Studies) was launched with a seven-member executive board that included Pablo Baraona, Jorge Cauas, and Sergio de Castro. Austrian economist and Nobel Prize winner Friedrich Hayek was named honorary president, and other superstar academics and free-market economists, including Armen Alchian, Karl Brunner, and Theodore Schultz, became members of the CEP's advisory board. Milton Friedman was invited to join by Sergio de Castro, but in a letter he declined, saying that he did not serve on councils or advisory boards if he could not devote enough time to them. He added, "I realize the very difficult circumstances under which you are operating; I have tried my best in my private capacity in this country to provide as much support as I could [to Chile's reforms and the Chicago Boys]."[11]

For years the CEP became the focal point of free-market believers. It was the host of several University of Chicago faculty who visited Chile to watch in person how the school's Department of Economics alumni had created a "miracle." The visitors included Gary Becker, James Heckman, Robert Lucas, and Deirdre McCloskey. With time, however, the CEP's executive director, Arturo Fontaine Talavera, moved the focus of the institution toward the humanities, and an increasing number of visitors were writers and philosophers, including novelist and Nobel laureate Mario Vargas Llosa, a firm supporter of free markets.

A number of ill-informed commentators on the Chilean experiment have made a big fuss out of the fact that Friedrich Hayek, the founder of the Mont Pèlerin Society (MPS) and one of the participants in the Paris meeting that launched the neoliberal movement in 1938, was the honorary president of the CEP. These analysts have even asserted that many Chicago Boys were members of the MPS and that Chile was a key link in the society's efforts to indoctrinate country after country with an extreme free-market ideology.[12] None of this is correct. In an interview in November 2021, Carlos Cáceres, who was minister of finance since February 1983 and minister of the interior at the end of the dictatorship, told me that he was the only member of Pinochet's cabinet who belonged to the MPS. Not one of the other economic leaders was a member of the society while serving in the government, a fact that is consistent with the membership lists I have been able to consult.[13] What is true, however, is that Cáceres and former Senator Pedro Ibáñez, the first Chilean member of the MPS, worked very hard to organize the society's regional meeting in Chile in 1981. The event was attended by Friedman, among others, and was a free-market jamboree of sorts. At the time, the economy was already showing signs of strain, and questions regarding the sustainability of Sergio de Castro's fixed exchange rate policy were mounting. As will be discussed in chapter 8, as soon as Milton Friedman arrived in Santiago to participate in the meeting, reporters asked him about a possible devaluation crisis. He tried to avoid making a statement, but toward the end of his stay he acknowledged that things did not look too good on the currency front.

Friedrich Hayek, one of the founders of the Mont Pèlerin Society and its president from 1947 to 1961, visited Chile twice during the Pinochet dictatorship. In November 1977 he was invited by former conservative senator Pedro Ibáñez, who at the time was the president of a promarkets foundation, Fundación Adolfo Ibañez, which sponsored one of the premier business schools in the country. During his visit, Hayek met with Pinochet—with whom he discussed the virtues of a "limited democracy"—and gave a series of lectures and interviews. As Bruce Caldwell and Leonidas Montes have convincingly argued, at the time—and although he had been awarded the Nobel Prize a few years earlier (1975)—almost no one in Chile knew about Hayek or his work. The senior Chicago Boys had not met him during their time in Hyde Park, and very few intellectuals—at most three or four—had read his books. Moreover, according to Caldwell and Montes, those who had done so had only read the popular *The Road to Serfdom*, about which George Stigler said, "I simply cannot understand why it became popular."[14]

In a 2021 interview on the Chicago school, I (SE) asked Arnold Harberger (ACH), about Hayek and the Department of Economics at Chicago:

SE: Your last year as a student was Friedrich Hayek's first year at Chicago. And he was a member of the Committee on Social Thought, so he was up there on a different floor, with [Frank] Knight, [John U.] Nef and others. And when you came back as a member of the faculty in 1953, he was still there. Hayek left Chicago in 1964, so you were colleagues for about ten years. Did you interact with Hayek?

ACH: No.

SE: Not at all? He didn't come to the workshops?

ACH: No. He had his own group, and there was almost no interaction between him and the members of the Department, as far as I remember. He never came to the regular workshops.

SE: You didn't talk to him?

ACH: Not really.[15]

The Gathering Storm

In January 1982 the *Wall Street Journal* published a front-page article in which it stated that Chile's experiment with free markets appeared to be facing some hurdles. The problem was that a highly indebted private sector had been unable to withstand the sharp decline in export prices experienced during the previous six months. The most serious impediment was exchange rate inflexibility combined with wages that increased automatically thanks to José Piñera's labor law. As the article asserted, "[Chile's] plunge into free markets is in serious trouble, the worst since the experiment began eight years ago. . . . [F]or four years inflation declined while economic growth boomed at 8% a year, the highest rate in Latin America. The fact that Chile accomplished this with balanced budgets and reduced state intervention has frequently been cited as proof that the Reagan administration's economic policies in the United States are on the right track."[16]

The article also noted that there was major infighting within the economic team, with the two bands known as the "flexibles" and the "dogmatics." It cited a former member of the cabinet—with all likelihood José Piñera, who had stepped down in December 1981—as stating that Sergio de Castro's fixed exchange rate "dogmatism could actually destroy the free market experiment."[17]

8

Milton Friedman and the Currency Crisis of 1982

IN EARLY 1978, with annual inflation running at 57 percent, Sergio de Castro and his colleagues decided to change the country's anti-inflation strategy. Instead of controlling the money supply, as Milton Friedman had insisted in his many writings, the Chicago Boys decided to adopt an exchange-rate-based stabilization program. For the next four years, the manipulation of the peso-to-dollar exchange rate was the main tool in the efforts to bring down inflation to single digits. The strategy was based on the idea that there was a close—almost a one-to-one—relation between changes in the price of the dollar and changes in domestic prices. If the Central Bank slowed down the rate of peso depreciation, inflation would decline accordingly. Initially, in February 1978, the government announced a rate of depreciation for the next four months that was deliberately set below the ongoing rate of inflation. In a speech, Sergio de Castro explained the new strategy: "The preannouncements of the rate of devaluation until the end of 1978 [21.4 percent] will rapidly generate competitive imports for those domestic products whose internal prices rise above reasonable limits. . . . This mechanism will also allow us to generate important increases in internal liquidity without risking higher inflationary pressures."[1]

In June 1979, with inflation still in the upper 30th percentile, the government doubled down on the new strategy and decided to completely fix the exchange rate at thirty-nine pesos per US dollar. The mechanism

was supposed to work in ways similar to the way it did for the gold standard, when different currencies were pegged to gold and inflation rates
were very similar across nations. In short, it was believed that a fixed
exchange rate would impose price discipline, forcing domestic inflation
to converge speedily to international levels.[2]

As it turned out, the Chicago Boys' experiment with fixed exchange
rates was a serious mistake that ended in a major and costly currency
crisis. Every month between June 1979 and June 1982, Chile's domestic
inflation exceeded international inflation by a significant margin, generating a growing overvaluation of the peso and a rapid loss in the country's degree of international competitiveness: domestic costs increased
at the rate of inflation, while prices for export goods (when expressed in
pesos) rose at the much slower rate of increase of the dollar. As a result, a
progressively large current account deficit developed; it was almost
6 percent of gross domestic product (GDP) in 1980, climbed to 8 percent
in 1981, and reached the staggering figure of 14 percent of GDP in 1982.
These deficits were financed with short-term dollar-denominated bank
loans and other forms of speculative capital. In mid-1982 the authorities
could no longer hold the line, and the peso was devalued by 13 percent.
This was only the beginning of a process of heightened instability and
recurrent devaluations; in the next thirty months the peso lost 70 percent
of its value. Figure 8.1 shows the evolution of the peso-dollar exchange
rate between 1975 and 1982.

The cost of the crisis was gigantic in terms of losses in output and in
employment. The government spent billions of dollars in taxpayers'
monies to rescue the banking sector from bankruptcy and to assist the
unemployed; open unemployment reached the astonishing level of
22 percent. Joseph Stiglitz blamed Chicago school's ideas and teachings
for the debacle and argued that the root cause of the crisis was the rapid
privatization of banks without proper supervisory and regulatory systems. In an extensive interview accompanying the PBS documentary
series *The Commanding Heights*, Stiglitz said, "When they followed
Friedman's prescription, Chile had a crisis, the free banking experiment
that was done under the intellectual leadership of that free market
hypothesis. They had the kind of bank boom and bust that we've seen

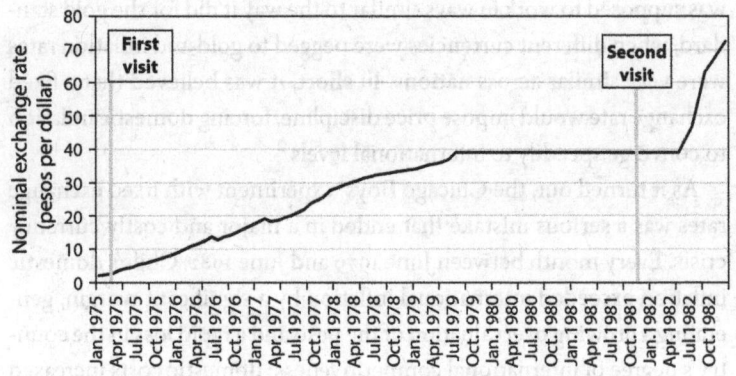

FIGURE 8.1. The nominal exchange rate between the Chilean peso and
the US dollar (pesos per dollar), 1975–1982, monthly data
Source: Edwards and Edwards (1991)

around the world." Stiglitz went on to state that the very good performance of the Chilean economy after 1985 was not "an example of the
free market; it's an example of a success of combining markets with
appropriate regulation."[3]

Things were much more complicated than what Stiglitz suggested,
however. The idea of fixing the exchange rate was not Friedman's. In
fact, he only became fully aware of the change in strategy in mid-1981,
when he was about to travel to Chile for the second time, to attend the
regional meeting of the Mont Pèlerin Society (MPS) in Viña del Mar.
After his 1975 visit, Friedman had not followed Chile's policy developments in detail. From time to time, Arnold "Al" Harberger would fill him
in regarding specific issues, but Friedman had no particular interest in
the minutiae of day-to-day decisions or in detailed policy options.
When it came to Chile, most of his energy was devoted to dealing with
demonstrators who accused him of being an accomplice in the junta's
violations of human rights and debunking the idea that he was President
Augusto Pinochet's adviser.

During his first visit to Chile, in 1975, Friedman had pointed out that
countries with high inflation could not maintain a fixed exchange rate.

As he had done in other emerging countries, he also criticized the Bretton Woods regime of a fixed but adjustable rate. For a country such as Chile, with a very high rate of inflation (360 percent) in 1975, he favored an exchange rate regime with frequent (daily) small changes in the price of foreign exchange—the so-called crawling peg system. He thought that, in the longer term, less developed countries should either opt for a flexible, market-determined exchange rate or of an irrevocably fixed rate and no Central Bank.[4]

The Costs of the Crisis

By June 1981 it became clear that the Chilean economy was not working well. Interest rates continued to climb and asset prices to fall. In July, a medium-size conglomerate, the Compañía de Refinería de Azúcar de Viña del Mar (Sugar Refinery Company of Viña del Mar), could not pay its debts and went bankrupt. Despite reassuring statements by ministers Pablo Baraona and Sergio de Castro, a number of analysts began to question whether the large external imbalance was sustainable. The newly formed conglomerates, the *grupos* (groups), faced increasing difficulties in rolling over their debts and obtaining new foreign funds. In an attempt to rescue their investment, group executives began desperately shuttling between Santiago and New York City, trying to obtain additional loans from international banks. In late 1981 the number of bankruptcies doubled, and two major banks—Banco de Talca and Banco Español— had to be rescued by the government. The CEO of Banco de Talca was a young Católica graduate with a Harvard University doctorate named Sebastián Piñera, the same man who almost thirty years later would be president during the 2019 revolt and uprising.

In late 1981—around the time Milton Friedman visited Chile for the second time—Sergio de Castro noted that in a highly competitive market economy, bankruptcies were healthy and had a cleansing effect. Although he did not make a reference to Joseph Schumpeter's "creative destruction," the idea was implicit in his different statements. "It is important not to forget that bankruptcies are the appropriate channel through which the economy gets rid of inefficient investments," De Castro wrote.

"If the government intervenes in this process the period of inefficiencies is lengthened."[5]

Conditions changed drastically in early 1982, when foreign banks suddenly decided that Chile was not a good risk any longer, and the nation became a victim of what economists call a "sudden stop." In the first half of that year net capital inflows fell by almost 60 percent with respect to the second half of 1981. Commercial banks were hit particularly hard and experienced a drop in foreign financing of 75 percent. All of a sudden, the extremely large external deficit could not be financed. Basic economic theory, including the teachings of Milton Friedman, Al Harberger, Harry Johnson, Robert Mundell, and the other University of Chicago professors, indicated that adjustment required a "real exchange rate devaluation." Under flexible exchange rates, this process takes place through a change in the nominal parity. Yet as Milton Friedman had written as early as 1953—and his University of Chicago teacher Lloyd Mints even before that time—under fixed exchange rates this was not possible. When the exchange rate was pegged, the way to achieve equilibrium was by reducing domestic wages or engineering a "domestic devaluation." But given that the labor law, the Plan Laboral, introduced major downward rigidities on wages, this channel would not work either. This meant that the only way to generate a major reduction in the external deficit was by engineering a recession and generating massive unemployment.

In a perceptive front-page story, the *Wall Street Journal* noted that the financial difficulties had led to a profound rift between the economists who worked for Pinochet.[6] The senior Chicago Boys'—Alvaro Bardón, Pablo Baraona, and Sergio de la Cuadra—coalesced around Sergio de Castro and defended the fixed exchange rates strategy; they argued that it was only a matter of time for domestic inflation to reach convergence with international levels. A younger generation, including Juan Andrés Fontaine, Cristián Larroulet, and José Piñera, believed that exchange rate flexibility was paramount, and that in order to expand exports it was essential to avoid a strong peso. Jorge Cauas, the man responsible for the "shock treatment" of 1975, was now a banker and sided with the "flexibles." According to the *Wall Street Journal* article, "The critics' main target is the reclusive finance minister, Sergio de Castro. . . . Although Mr. de Castro increasingly clashes with other free-enterprise economists in Chile, he still has the absolute backing of President Augusto Pinochet. . . . What is at issue is a policy that departs from strict free market theories: Mr. de Castro's insistence on keeping the exchange rate fixed at 39 pesos to the dollar even though Chilean prices have risen 60 percent and U.S. prices have risen less than half that since the rate was fixed 2½ years ago."

On April 22, 1982, De Castro stepped down as minister of finance. Technically, he was not fired, but everyone knew that Pinochet had had enough and wanted a new face in charge of the economic program, someone different who would shepherd the country out of a crisis that had been generated by the combination of a pegged exchange rate and declining foreign financing. De Castro was replaced by his friend and former student Sergio de la Cuadra, the Chicago Boy who had managed the trade reform and had run the Central Bank since 1981.

The Chicago Boys Are Ousted by Pinochet

In early June 1982 it became clear that foreign financing had completely dried up and that there was no alternative but to abandon the fixed exchange rate experiment. On June 14, 1982, the peso was devalued by 13 percent. It was also announced that for the next six months the peso-to-dollar rate was to increase 0.8 percent per month. Although Sergio de la Cuadra was the chief economic officer and the minister of finance, it was not he who made the announcement on June 14 that the peso was being devalued and that the fixed exchange rate policy had come to an end. Pinochet decided that it was more symbolic if the news was given by a senior army officer and asked general Luis Danús, who had just been appointed as minister of economics, to inform the country of the new peso-to-dollar exchange rate regime.

The market did not react well to the announcement. The magnitude of the adjustment was perceived as insufficient, and expectations of further exchange rate changes emerged, putting further pressure on domestic interest rates. Given the circumstances, and contrary to its previously announced policy of not favoring particular groups, the government decided to establish a dual exchange rate system, with a lower dollar price for large foreign currency debtors.

The devaluation was particularly devastating for the *grupos*. All of them had used aggressive borrowing tactics to expand and to buy some of the firms being privatized. The notion of "arms-length" relations was ignored by both the *grupos* and regulators. In June 1982 almost half of all loans by the two largest banks—Banco de Chile and Banco Santiago—went to "related firms" owned by the banks' controlling shareholders. What complicated things was that almost 40 percent of loans were in foreign currency. As soon as the peso was devalued, the domestic currency value of those loans jumped, and many of the companies and banks went bankrupt.

In August 1982, two months after the currency collapse, Sergio de la Cuadra was replaced by Rolf Lüders, the Chicago Boy who arranged Milton Friedman's visit to Chile in 1975. In February 1983 Lüders was dismissed, and the position was taken by Carlos Cáceres, who at the time was one of only two Chilean members of the MPS and a great admirer of Gary Becker, Milton Friedman, and Friedrich Hayek. Although Cáceres had not been to Chicago, he was clearly accepted by the gang as one of their own.

In April 1984, Pinochet lost patience with the Chicago Boys and decided to entrust the economy to Luis Escobar Cerda, the economist who in 1955, as dean of the faculty of economics of the Universidad de Chile, declined Albion "Pat" Patterson's invitation to launch a joint program with the University of Chicago; in an indirect way, he was responsible for the Chicago Boys' growth and prosperity at rivaling Católica. Escobar Cerda quickly tried to put into action an industrial policy aimed at fostering a domestic manufacturing sector. His first measure was to increase protection by raising import tariffs by more than three times to a 35 percent uniform level. On the macroeconomic front, an effort was made to invigorate the economy through an aggressive fiscal stimulus that resulted in a setback in the efforts for dealing with the foreign debt crisis and reestablishing external balance. Instead of declining, the external imbalance grew.

The Chicago Boys and the Exchange Rate Debacle

Why did the Chicago Boys opt for a pegged exchange rate anti-inflation strategy? Surely they knew that Friedman was very critical of that type of system.[7] The explanation is that the Chilean authorities were influenced by Robert Mundell, who for a long time had argued that fixed exchange rates were the best arrangement in (almost) every country in the world. Mundell's views were rooted in his original work on "optimal currency areas," a research program cited by the prize committee when the Nobel Prize in Economics was conferred on him. But Mundell's influence on the Chicago Boys was indirect. Sergio de Castro and the other senior Chilean economists left Hyde Park before Mundell had joined the faculty, and the younger ones typically did not take Mundell's course, nor did they work with him on research or dissertation projects.[8]

Mundell's influence came through Larry Sjaastad, a member of the faculty at the University of Chicago who was very close to Latin American students and who after the 1973 coup became an adviser to the Chilean military government. Sjaastad believed that the purchasing power parity condition—stating that price levels in two countries are intimately connected through the exchange rate—held in the short run and that a credible fixed exchange rate regime would provide almost instantaneous discipline, allowing for rapid and low-cost stabilization.[9] As he explained Chile's 1979 exchange-rate-based stabilization program, "The rationale . . . was that once economic agents understood, or inferred, that the equilibrium between the prices of tradables and nontraded (home) goods is neither random nor arbitrary, a change in the price of tradable goods will cause a revision of expectations concerning the equilibrium price of home goods. Under such circumstances, excess supply would not be required to drive down inflation; *the change can occur spontaneously*, as it were."[10]

Harry Johnson, who joined the Department of Economics at the University of Chicago in 1959 and who in the 1970s championed the "monetary approach to the balance of payments," also influenced the policy change. Johnson was close to several Chilean economists, including to Sergio de la Cuadra, who was governor of the Central Bank during the early 1980s and was named minister of finance in early 1982. Although Johnson favored floating rates for advanced nations, he thought that they would not work in poor and "narrowly specialized" countries where exports were dominated by a handful of commodities. In these cases, Johnson argued, the "advantages of rigid convertibility . . . outweigh the relatively small advantages that may be derived from exchange rate flexibility."[11] In a 1972 article Johnson wrote that the new monetary models assume that under fixed rates "a [small] country's price level is pegged to the world price level and must move rigidly in line with it."[12] And in 1977, just before Chile embarked on its exchange-rate-based stabilization program, Johnson wrote, "[Under] a fixed exchange rate system *inflation is a world monetary phenomenon*, which cannot be prevented by national monetary policy . . . or national 'wage-price policy.' . . . [Inflation is] 'world' or 'externally caused' to the extent that countries' exchange rate policies aim at maintaining some conventional [fixed] value or range of values of their currency in term of foreign currencies."[13]

Johnson, like Sjaastad, believed that in most small countries the "relative" version of the purchasing power parity theory—a proposition that said that under fixed exchange rates domestic inflation mimicked international inflation—held in the short term. This belief was based on empirical research undertaken during the first half of the 1970s at the Institut des Hautes Études Internationales (Graduate Institute of International Studies), the London School of Economics, the University of Chicago, and the University of Manchester. If the fiscal deficit was under control, and the exchange rate was credibly fixed, domestic inflation would rapidly—or "spontaneously," to use Sjaastad's terminology—converge with world inflation.[14]

In Chile, however, things worked differently. After the peso was fixed to the US dollar, inflation declined very slowly. Between June 1979 (when the exchange rate was completely fixed relative to the dollar) and June 1982, Chile's domestic inflation exceeded international inflation significantly. This was largely the result of expectations, and of the ingrained backward-looking indexation system introduced to the labor reform promoted by José Piñera (see chapter 7). Additionally, the strengthening of the US dollar in the global markets meant that the peso was appreciating relative to the relevant basket of trade partners' currencies. As will be seen, this last point was emphasized by Milton Friedman when, many years later, he compared Chile's failed experience with fixed exchange rates with Israel's successful policy based on a pegged currency value.

Friedman's 1981 Visit to Chile and the Currency Crisis

When Friedman visited Chile for the second time, in late 1981, the pegged exchange rate experiment was entering its third year. At the time the country was running an increasingly large current account deficit financed with short-term syndicated bank loans and other short-term foreign capital flows. Between the first quarter of 1978 and the second quarter of 1982, the trade-weighted real exchange rate, measured relative to a basket of ten currencies, appreciated by almost 40 percent.[15] Sergio de Castro dismissed concerns about the growing external imbalances by stating that the public finances were under control and that the current account deficit was being financed by monies that were voluntarily entering the country. In 1981 he noted, "There is no doubt that the current account deficits [financed privately] are beneficial for the country, and that we should make an effort to maintain them at the highest possible level for the longest period of time."[16]

On November 17, 1981, reporters were waiting for Milton Friedman at Santiago's Arturo Merino Benítez Airport. Friedman immediately told them that he was in the country to attend the MPS meeting and not "to give advice, neither to analyze Chile's policies."[17] The next day he was a bit more forthcoming with the press but restricted his remarks to generalities: "I believe this country has been notably successful during the last years without my advice, and I believe it will continue to be successful."[18]

Friedman's paper for the MPS meeting was titled "Monetary System for a Free Society," and focused on the post–Bretton Woods international monetary architecture. The last section dealt with alternative currency regimes for developing countries and discussed the case of Chile.

Friedman explained that while he had always supported floating and market-determined exchange rates for advanced countries, he did not think that flexibility was the best option for poorer nations. In his opinion, the preferred monetary and exchange rate system for a less developed country was abolishing the central bank and permanently fixing its exchange rate with respect to its main trading partner. He called this system a "unified currency regime" and argued that in Hong Kong it worked extremely well.[19] In earlier writings he had emphasized that the abolition (or absence) of a central bank was an essential component of the arrangement; the currency had to be irrevocably fixed, and the credibility of the system had to be (virtually) complete. In his 1972 Horowitz Lectures in Israel, Friedman said, "I conclude that the *only way* to refrain from using inflation as a method of taxation is to *avoid having a central bank*. . . . [A] unified currency assures a maximum degree of integration of the country in question with the greater world."[20]

As Friedman noted in his 1981 MPS presentation,

> Only Chile has in recent years effectively unified its currency with that of a major developed country. . . . Experience since I gave the lecture in Israel [where he suggested a "unified currency" for the first time] has not led me to alter my views on the economics of the issue [the superiority of the unified currency], though it has led me to become far more modest about judging political feasibility (in the sense of likelihood of adoption). Perhaps the example of Chile, *if its policy continues to be as successful as it has been so far*, will lead other developing countries to follow suit.[21]

Two aspects of Friedman's assertions are worth discussing. First, Friedman stated that Chile had effectively implemented a unified currency. This, however, was not the case. What Chile had done was implement a fixed but adjustable rate in the tradition of the Bretton Woods Conference, with an additional verbal commitment to maintaining parity. Yet there was no institutional or legal constraint to that effect. At any time the authorities could undertake active monetary policy and erode the credibility of the peg, or they could decide to give it up and devalue the peso. Certainly Chile had not eliminated the Central Bank and replaced it with a currency board, as Friedman had suggested in the second Horowitz Lecture in 1972 and in other writings. Friedman was aware of this, as the governor of the Central Bank was Sergio de la Cuadra, a prominent Chicago Boy.[22] Moreover, it was very unlikely that Chile's highly nationalistic military would have agreed to give up the peso and adopt a foreign currency as legal tender. It was equally unlikely that it would have favored a completely passive monetary board, as in Hong Kong. In addition, the existence of backward-looking wage indexation meant that a key adjustment mechanism under fixed rates—disinflation and the reduction of wages to achieve relative price realignment—was absent.

Second, Friedman implied that Chile's pegged rate experiment had been successful. The persistence of inflation (it was still above 10 percent per year), the large current account deficits financed by short-term speculative capital, and real exchange rate appreciation call that statement into question. As will be seen, in his unscripted remarks delivered at the MPS conference, Friedman acknowledged that things were looking rather gloomy and that there were major currency challenges ahead.

During his presentation at the MPS meeting, Friedman departed from his prepared remarks (and from the paper) in two ways. First, he talked about the relation between economic and political freedom, a subject close to his heart. He stated that economic freedom was not enough to achieve a free society, and that it was important for Chile to move toward democratic rule. Yet—and not surprisingly, given the military's severe censorship—the media did not report Friedman's remarks on the subject.[23] He became frustrated by this fact and talked about it extensively in an interview he gave in Peru immediately after his trip to Chile.[24]

Second, in his unscripted comments—which were summarized in the newspaper *La Segunda*—he expressed concerns regarding the exchange rate policy, something he had not done in the paper "Monetary System for a Free Society." He said that in the written version his remarks about Chile had been too brief and somewhat elliptic. He ended his remarks talking about the nature of the challenges ahead:

> At this moment, international institutions don't have a guarantee that Chile will stick to its policy. Chile not only faces the appreciation of the dollar and the decline in the price of copper, but also, and this is something I suspect, since I don't have all the information, it also faces a speculative attack against its currency, triggered by the expectation that Chile may devalue, departing from its original goal. If Chile reaffirms the credibility of its current policy and allows its monetary aggregates to reflect changes in the balance of payments, then in the next crisis speculative forces will help to stabilize the system.[25]

The news story ends with Friedman noting that at the time the Chilean peso seemed to be overvalued.[26] He did not, however, delve into the mechanisms through which overvaluation was corrected under a fixed rate. More specifically, he did not mention that under a unified currency the only way of addressing major overvaluation was by generating a massive disinflation, including a reduction in nominal wages. He had made this point as early as 1953 when he said that "decline of 10 percent in every internal price in Germany" was equivalent to a 10 percent devaluation of the mark relative to the dollar and had repeated it in almost every poor country he had visited during the previous twenty years.[27] Figure 8.2 captures Friedman's massive press conference in Viña del Mar in November 1981, where he publicly discussed the sustainability of Chile's fixed exchange rate stabilization program.

It is difficult to know to what extent Friedman's remarks affected market expectations of an imminent crisis and thus contributed to the decline of capital flows in the following months—and eventually to the June 1982 crisis. What is known, however, is that the probability of devaluation, as measured by interest rate differentials, almost tripled in the fourth quarter of 1981, relative to the previous quarter.[28] At the time, Chile had severe capital controls. Consequently, even in light of negative comments and a negative prognosis, there would not be a sudden spike in outflows. Changes in expectations were reflected by a significant slowdown of capital inflows, and/or by a large increase in domestic interest rates.

FIGURE 8.2. Milton Friedman gives a press conference in Viña del Mar
in November 1981
Source: La Tercera photo archive

The Morning After: Friedman's Observations
on the 1982 Crisis

Seven months after Friedman's second visit, Chile could not defend the
peg any longer, and on June 14, 1982, the peso was devalued (see figure 8.1).
The crisis that followed was one of the deepest ever faced by a Latin
American nation: real GDP collapsed by almost 15 percent, and open
unemployment surpassed the 25 percent mark. This was the crisis that
many of the Chicago Boys' critics would mention time and again in the
years to come; many of them held Friedman responsible for what had
happened.[29] It took Chile several years to recover, and once it did, policy
makers made sure not to peg the exchange rate again.

How did Friedman react to the crisis in a country where market-
oriented reform was associated with his name? What was his postmortem
on the situation? Correspondence in his Archives at the Hoover Institution sheds some light on these questions.

On July 8, 1982, three weeks after the devaluation, Friedman wrote to
Peter Whitney, the economic counselor at the US embassy in Santiago,

"I was surprised at the change [the stepwise large devaluation] since it seems to me the appropriate alternative to the [fixed rate policy] policy that Chile was following, if an alternative were to be adopted, was a fully floating exchange rate, not a prescheduled series of devaluations."[30] In a letter to journalist José Rodriguez Elizondo, written four months after the devaluation, Friedman commented on the policies that Chile's new economic team, led by his former student Rolf Lüders, was likely to undertake: "He [Lüders] may be, because of the type situation and because of a lack of previous commitments, more flexible [regarding exchange rates]. . . . Whether he can succeed in face of the tactics of the military is something else again on which I am not a competent judge."[31]

In his 1998 memoir (cowritten with his wife, Rose), Friedman is very direct, writing that it is doubtful "that there is ever a good time for a country like Chile that has a central bank to peg its currency. I have consistently taken the position that *a country like Chile with a central bank should let its currency float. The alternative is to abolish the central bank and unify its currency with that of its major trading partner*."[32] Yet this was not the message that Friedman transmitted during his two visits to Chile. To be sure, he argued that the Bretton Woods regime was unstable, but he didn't say in public that Chile faced the option of either abolishing the Central Bank or floating.

Friedman addressed Chile once again in 2001, during a debate with Robert Mundell, one of the staunchest supporters of fixed exchange rates. Friedman argued that Chile's 1979 "hard peg" policy was "disastrous" as a consequence of the strengthening of the US dollar in 1980–81.[33] He also made this point in an addendum to the paper presented to the Chile 1981 meeting of the MPS, in which he wrote, "The preceding three paragraphs, correct when written in 1981, no longer are. Chile ended the pegging of its rate to the dollar in 1982, after the sharp appreciation of the US dollar plunged Chile into a disastrous recession."[34] On August 5, 1997, Friedman wrote a long letter to Robert J. Alexander, a Rutgers University professor with whom he had had a number of exchanges regarding Chile and other Latin American countries. The purpose of the letter was to comment on the recently published book by Juan

Gabriel Valdés, *Pinochet's Economists: The Chicago Boys in Chile*. Friedman took issue with Valdés's narrative of the 1982 currency crisis, and it is worthwhile quoting him extensively:

> Valdés has no understanding of what produced the 1982 depression. What produced it was the departure from the basic Chicago School economic principles that Valdes oversimplifies. De Castro's *mistake in pegging the Chilean currency to the U.S. dollar produced the disaster*. My view has always been that a country like Chile, if it has a central bank and a separate monetary unit, should allow the exchange rate to float. That was the policy that was followed until 1979 when De Castro made the major mistake of pegging the Chilean currency to the U.S. dollar in the hope that that would impose the discipline necessary to eliminate inflation. In my opinion *that was a bad decision under any circumstances*, but it turned out to be a disastrously bad decision because of . . . the drastic appreciation of the U.S. dollar.[35]

In 1994 Friedman published a book of essays titled *Monetary Mischief: Essays in Monetary History*. The book included ten chapters and an epilogue. Six of the chapters were revised versions of previous work—including two articles that had appeared in the *Journal of Political Economy*—and one of them was based on the 1980 TV series *Free to Choose*.

One of the previously unpublished essays dealt with the experiences in Chile and Israel with pegged exchange rates during a stabilization effort and analyzed why in Chile the policy ended up in failure and a major crisis, while in Israel it succeeded.[36] Friedman begins his analysis by pointing out that in these episodes there was an element of luck: immediately after Chile fixed the exchange rate with respect to the US dollar in 1979 external conditions soured. The dollar strengthened in global markets, and the terms of trade turned against Chile. In contrast, when in 1985 Israel fixed the value of the shekel, external shocks were favorable (a drop in the price of oil and a weakening of the dollar). At the policy level, an important difference was that Israel devalued the shekel by 20 percent before fixing it relative to the dollar. By doing this, it built a "cushion" for real appreciation to take place during the transition without generating overvaluation. Chile, instead, fixed the exchange rate rigidly at a time (1979) when the peso was already overvalued. Additionally, while Israel instituted incomes policies that included a temporary wages and prices freeze, Chile put in place a backward-looking wage indexation system that, with declining inflation, resulted in automatic increases in real wages. Finally, Israel pegged the exchange rate to the dollar as a temporary measure aimed at guiding expectations in the short term. After a few months, the shekel was devalued "at irregular intervals to offset the difference between the roughly 20 percent inflation in Israel and the lower inflation in its trading partners."[37] Chile instead announced that the fixed rate would remain indefinitely, even in light of obvious overvaluation, and even if it still left the devaluation option open. By mid-1982 Chile could not defend the peg any longer, and a major currency crisis erupted. The price of the dollar doubled in twelve months, most banks went bankrupt, real GDP per capita collapsed by 20 percent, and unemployment jumped to 25 percent.[38]

During his 1981 visit, then, Friedman was not openly critical about the fixed exchange rate policy in Chile. He didn't endorse it, but he didn't disapprove it either. He covered himself by making a distinction between hard and soft pegs, and by saying that since Chile had opted for fixity, it had to make sure that its system resulted in a credible hard peg. In many ways, this ambiguity and evasiveness are surprising and are not consistent with Friedman's usual directness. At this point one can only speculate about his motives. A possible explanation is that after meeting privately with the Chicago Boy authorities—possibly with Central Bank president Sergio de la Cuadra—he realized that the government would not or could not alter its exchange rate policy; introducing flexibility was out of the question. Thus, under those circumstances it would make little sense for Friedman to criticize the exchange rate anchor openly. In fact, planting doubts about the sustainability and desirability of the fixed rate could have triggered major speculative moves and even a major currency crisis. He thus opted for circumspection and silence.

Back to Basics

Luis Escobar Cerda's efforts to take the economy out of the slump were not successful. Output and employment remained sluggish, and the external deficit continued to be a serious constraint. In October 1984 inflation surpassed the 8 percent *monthly* rate, reflecting the sensitivity of domestic prices to changes in the exchange rate. In addition, Escobar Cerda's policies placed him in the middle of a major political struggle between those who, within the military, favored a political opening and those who advocated a strong hand to dissuade opponents.

During the mid-1980s several issues dominated the political scene. There was increased international pressure on the government to allow exiles to return to the country. This effort was led by the Catholic Church and its Bishops' Conference, including Archbishop Bernardino Piñera, the uncle of José and Sebastián Piñera. At the same time, there was an effort to convince the government to allow academics and scholars to run Chilean universities. Since the coup, the military had "intervened" in every university, placing senior officers in the positions of presidents and administrators. Since his first visit, Milton Friedman was critical of this practice, and in 1986 wrote to General Roberto Soto MacKenney, the man who Pinochet had appointed rector of the Universidad de Chile, protesting the situation. Friedman noted that he had received information that "suggests that the universities in Chile are in serious danger of having their academic integrity and performance destroyed by the application of arbitrary and irresponsible force [by the military authorities]."[39]

9

The Second Round of
Reforms, 1983–1990

PRAGMATIC NEOLIBERALISM

IN EARLY 1985, and in view of Luis Escobar Cerda's failure to reignite growth and control inflation, President Augusto Pinochet decided to turn back to the Chicago Boys. He was, however, disenchanted with the senior members of the group, and turned to a younger generation to complete the revolution started in 1975 with the "shock treatment." On February 12, 1985, Hernán Büchi, a thirty-five-year-old engineer of Swiss descent with an MBA from Columbia University, was appointed minister of finance. Büchi was not an outsider; he had worked in health care reform with Chicago Boy Miguel Kast and had briefly served as minister of planning. Hernán Büchi was one of those honorary Chicago Boys who, despite never taking a class from Gary Becker, Milton Friedman, or Arnold "Al" Harberger, were entirely convinced of the merits of free markets in (almost) every sphere of society. Büchi brought with him a team of second-generation University of Chicago graduates including Juan Andrés Fontaine, María Teresa Infante, Cristián Larroulet, Joaquín Lavín, and Jorge Selume.[1] This group was made up mostly of pragmatic economists who were completely devoted to markets but were not (fully) trapped in old doctrinal fights with Keynesians and structuralists. Many of them would eventually become cabinet members in the attempts by the Chicago Boys to make a comeback during the conservative administrations of President Sebastián Piñera (2010–14 and 2018–22).

Hernán Büchi took over the Ministry of Finance at a difficult time. The currency crisis of 1982 was devastating and seriously damaged the economy. All banks were once again in the hands of the government, and many firms that had borrowed in US dollars were bankrupt. Unemployment exceeded 20 percent, the country had very limited access to foreign financing, and in order to obtain foreign exchange loans it was forced to sign a draconian agreement with the International Monetary Fund. In addition, the rift between the two factions of the original economic team—the "flexibles" and the "dogmatics," as they had been labeled by the *Wall Street Journal*—had deepened significantly. In Büchi's own words, there was "a serious fracture in the neoliberal consciousness of the economists that worked for the [military] government. . . . The climate of great unity and collaboration that had prevailed in years past was replaced by an atmosphere of fights, conflicts, and resentment."[2] But the rift within the supporters of free markets was not the main problem. After the crisis, the protests against the military government increased in frequency, and the number of demonstrators swelled by the day. The military responded with force; repression and human rights violations escalated rapidly and were denounced by the Catholic Church and by international human rights groups. In late March 1985, only six weeks after Büchi was appointed to the finance post, one of the most heinous crimes perpetrated by agents of the state took place when three opponents of the regime were kidnapped by the secret police, the Dirección Nacional de Comunicaciones de Carabineros (Dicomcar, National Directorate of Communications of Carabineros) in plain daylight. A few days later, their bodies were found on the outskirts of Santiago with their throats slit.[3]

Growth as a Priority

In 1985 Pinochet and the junta demanded quick results. If Büchi and his team failed to deliver, the statist wing of the military would gain the upper hand and the progress achieved during the first phase of the reforms would be in danger. Considering these conditions, the new economic team decided to focus narrowly on two interrelated priorities: the acceleration of growth and the recovery of employment. Controlling inflation, which was running at 25 percent per year, was, of course, important, but was not an obsession as it had been for Sergio de Castro and the older Chicago Boys in the late 1970s. The new team decided to live, at least for some time, with inflation in the mid-20th percentile.

Büchi's strategy for achieving rapid growth was based on a swift expansion of exports, sustained by a cheap and highly depreciated peso. This required going back to the crawling peg or mini-devaluations exchange rate mechanism that Milton Friedman had approved during his first visit in 1975 and that Sergio de Castro had discarded in 1978. In contrast with the 1978 anti-inflation program, the rate of mini-devaluations was not preannounced. Instead, the rhythm at which the peso-to-dollar rate was adjusted was decided on a weekly basis and depended on several variables, including past inflation, international prices and interest rates, the price of copper, and the flow of investments into the country.

But the road to higher growth was full of obstacles. First, the banking sector was in shambles. Immediately after the crisis, the government took over most financial intermediaries and closed fourteen banks that were deemed to be insolvent. Most surviving banks had huge nonperforming loans and could barely stand on their own feet. There was an urgent need to recapitalize them in a way that bailed out depositors but not shareholders. In order to deal with the problem, the Central Bank bought private banks' bad loans. The banks, in turn, paid a 5 percent interest rate (in real terms) on the bad portfolios and committed themselves to repurchase them out of retained profits. Banks could not pay dividends to original shareholders while the Central Bank held some of the bad debt. In addition, banks were forced to issue new stock, which were sold to the public in small lots, as a way of encouraging widespread ownership or "popular capitalism." Over forty thousand small investors participated in the program and purchased banks' shares, as did the newly launched Administradoras de Fondos de Pensiones (AFPs; Administrators of Pension Funds).[4] After eighteen months all financial intermediaries—banks, brokerage houses, and financial boutiques—were back in private hands and their equity base was significantly larger than before the crisis.

A second impediment for accelerated growth was the very low level of investment in equipment and machinery. After the crisis, fixed capital formation dropped to 12 percent of gross domestic product (GDP), the lowest level ever recorded and barely enough to cover the depreciation of existing capital; during the 1960–70 period, investment in GDP had averaged 20 percent. The new economic team decided to use a three-pronged approach to raise investment. First, the tax rate on retained and reinvested corporate earnings was cut from 46 percent to 10 percent. As a result, between 1985 and 1990 investment by the private sector grew in excess of 10 percent every year. The second component of the strategy was an almost 10 percent annual increase in public-sector investment, especially in infrastructure. The third and most important element in the strategy was encouraging foreign firms and multinationals to invest in Chile through a highly innovative debt-to-equity swaps program. Foreign firms bought Chilean debt at a discount in the global secondary market and exchanged it in Chile, at a favorable ratio, for equity in productive firms that were in distress. Investors committed themselves not to repatriate dividends for five years, and the principal could only be repatriated after ten years.[5] Between 1985 and 1990, debt-to-equity swaps amounted to over US$10 billion.[6] A large proportion of those investments went to mining, a sector that was now legally protected by the 1981 mining legislation. Time and again, members of the economic team told foreign firms in the mining sector that if that level of legal protection had existed during the government of President Salvador Allende, the state would have paid a just price to the expropriated American companies.

Growth, Ideas, and Human Capital

Most of the younger economists on the new team had studied at the University of Chicago in the mid- to late 1970s and early 1980s, after Milton Friedman had left for the Hoover Institution. Of course, they read most of his important papers and books (both scholarly and popular), but when it came to economic growth and economic policy, they were influenced by other faculty members, including Gary Becker and Theodore Schultz, who had pioneered work on human capital and had pointed out that its accumulation through better education was key for aggregate performance and for improving social conditions. At that time—between 1979 and 1984—Robert E. Lucas was also beginning his research on the new theories of growth, and several graduate students were trying to develop models that would explain why some countries grew faster than others. In particular, Paul Romer was launching his work on the role of ideas and innovation in economic growth process. Romer's enthusiasm in class and at workshops was legendary, and most of his classmates, including the Chileans, were impressed by his insights, with some even predicting that he would eventually win the Nobel Prize in Economics, which he did in 2018.[7]

Influenced by Becker, Lucas, Romer, and Schultz, the younger Chicago Boys went back to Santiago convinced that in order to accomplish a major and permanent acceleration in growth it was essential to encourage innovation and ideas and to improve the quality of education. At the policy level, the main mechanism was increasing competition across schools. For primary and secondary education that meant decentralization. Municipalities, and not the national Ministry of Education, would own the schools, hire teachers and administrators, and interact with parents. In theory, transferring responsibilities to municipalities would result in a healthy rivalry across districts and greater accountability. The general idea was already contained in The Brick and was consistent with Milton Friedman's belief that school vouchers were the most efficient way of organizing the educational system.[8]

There was, however, an additional and purely political objective in the reform of public education. As noted in chapter 7, decentralization meant that the powerful and left-leaning teachers' union would cease to exist at the national level. Bargaining and demands related to working conditions would have to be dealt with in local governments, greatly reducing the union's influence. Years later, when democracy was reinstated, one of the first actions of the government of President Patricio Aylwin was to put in place a national teachers' statute that unified contract conditions, promotion standards, and specialization courses for teachers in all public schools in the country.[9]

Primary and secondary education was organized in a multitier system. At the bottom tier were the purely public and free schools run by the municipalities; their funding was based on the number of students enrolled and in attendance. The voucher system meant that families could enroll their children in private schools that would receive from the government the same financing per student as the municipal schools. Most of these private schools were run by religious—almost exclusively Catholic—orders. A small number of these schools were for-profit, family-owned businesses. At the very top tier of the system were purely private schools and academies that were not eligible for vouchers.

The 1980 Chilean Constitution explicitly established that there could be no for-profit universities or trade institutes. With the acquiescence of the Chicago Boys, however, private investors quickly found a way around the constitutional provision: the institution of higher learning—the new university or professional institute—was a not-for-profit entity that did not own any assets. It hired instructors and charged tuition but did not own buildings, computers, gyms, or laboratories. Physical assets were leased from companies owned or controlled by the founders of the university; these companies could (and did) make a profit.[10] With time the higher education scheme came back to haunt the Chicago Boys and the Center-Left politicians from the Concertación coalition, as many graduates from the new universities could not find jobs in their fields of choice and ended up with huge student loan debt. Not surprisingly, most of them joined Far-Left political parties and participated in the 2019 revolt. Some were elected to the Constitutional Convention, where they supported radical proposals, including the expropriation by the state of all natural resources. (For more on this, see chapter 15.)

Reopening the Economy

According to the new theories of endogenous growth, a small developing country will benefit from the prompt adoption of technological advances in rich countries. But for this process of productivity-enhancing "imitation" to take place, the economy has to be very open to the rest of the world and be welcoming of foreign direct investment; exporters and business leaders have to be exposed to the latest techniques and imbue themselves in a "learning by looking process."

For the new economic team it was obvious that import tariffs, which had been hiked during Luis Escobar Cerda's tenure as minister of finance, had to be reduced, once again, to a uniform 10 percent. A key question was how quickly to proceed. Was the best strategy to do it gradually, or was a more rapid approach preferable? During his 1975 visit, Milton Friedman had recommended an abrupt approach, one where all the pain was felt at once and where, in theory, gains were obtained promptly. Hernán Büchi and his colleagues chose not to follow Friedman's advice; they decided that for political reasons it was better to be cautious and move slowly. The insight for moving gradually came from a different Chicago giant. In his course on the history of economic thought and doctrines, George Stigler required students to read Adam Smith's *The Wealth of Nations* cover to cover. It was there where the younger Chicago Boys had carefully read book 4, chapter 7, titled "Of Colonies," in which Smith wrote about the dynamics and political economy of trade liberalization and openness:

> To open the colony trade all at once to all nations, might not only occasion some transitory inconvenience, but a great permanent loss to the greater part of those whose industry or capital is at present engaged in it.... In what manner, therefore, the colony trade ought gradually to be open; what are the restraints which ought first, and what are those which ought to be last to be taken away; or in what manner the natural system of perfect liberty and justice ought gradually to be restored, we must leave it to the wisdom of future statesmen.[11]

Smith's reasoning was based on politics and not economics and considered the serious and costly dislocations and losses in employment generated by an abrupt trade reform. Pragmatism, then, led the new team to undo the protectionist policies of Luis Escobar Cerda one step at a time. For example, instead of reverting to the 10 percent import duties, tariffs were reduced from 35 percent to 15 percent. Ironically, perhaps, it would be the Socialist Party president Ricardo Lagos who would open the economy further in the first five years of the 2000s (see chapter 11).

A New Round of Privatization

The currency crisis gave the Chicago Boys an opportunity to push privatization further. As was noted in chapters 6 and 7, during the 1970s the military had been very reluctant to privatize those state-owned enterprises that had been created in the 1940s and 1950s, during the first push for industrialization under the import substitution strategy. These emblematic firms included the major steel maker, Compañía de Aceros del Pacífico (Pacific Steel Company); the national airline, Línea Aerea Nacional (LAN); the state-owned electrical company, Empresa Nacional de Electricidad S.A.; and the national nitrates and lithium company, Sociedad Química y Minera de Chile (SQM; Chemical and Mining Society of Chile), among others.

What was new in the mid-1980s was that privatization did not mean giving control of these companies to large conglomerates or foreign multinationals. It was possible (at least on paper) to sell shares to the general public, including small investors from the middle class through the "popular capitalism" scheme discussed earlier. Furthermore, workers were offered shares of the state-owned firms where they worked at subsidized prices and with long-term layout plans. The stock market had experienced significant growth and was now broad enough to accommodate sales of shares through auctions. Additionally, the fact that there were individual retirement accounts meant that every Chilean worker would own parts of the companies in their savings for old age.

Between 1985 and 1988 the government divested itself of twenty-seven traditional companies. In many cases, 100 percent of shares were sold to the AFPs, foreign investors, workers, and investment funds. Even so, the government kept a significant block of shares in those companies that the military considered strategic. Total revenue from these operations added up to almost US$2 billion, a figure that even then was considered to be low. In the years to come, the military, Hernán Büchi, and the rest of the economic team were accused of practically giving the companies away to relatives and friends. The most commented case was the sale of SQM, the lithium and nitrate company, which was sold to a group of investors led by Julio Ponce Lerou, Pinochet's son-in-law. Another controversial operation was the sale of the national airline LAN to a consortium of investors that included Sebastián Piñera as one of its senior partners. In the process leading up to the 2019 revolt, one of the most common complaints by demonstrators was that the military and its civilian "accomplices" had plundered Chile by selling valuable companies with very bright potentials for very little.

Pragmatism, Exchange Rates, and the Independent Central Bank

The second round of reforms was characterized by "pragmatism within neoliberal parameters." When possible, the use of markets was expanded, targeted social programs were maintained, vouchers were used for education and health care, and the state was kept away from as many activities as possible. Despite the clear market orientation (or neoliberal) character of these policies, Hernán Büchi and his colleagues maintained an important level of pragmatism. Import tariffs were lowered gradually, and no attempts were made to reform areas that would generate strong opposition from the military or would pose threats to the overall reforms process.[12] It was for that reason that controls on capital mobility were maintained; they would only be relaxed after the return to democratic rule by Center-Left governments.

It was in the area of exchange rate policy, however, that the greatest degree of pragmatism was exhibited. The goal was to avoid overvaluation and to encourage exports through a general nondiscriminatory mechanism. Instead of choosing a market-determined exchange rate system, or a truly fixed regime without a central bank—the two options recommended by Milton Friedman for emerging nations—Hernán Büchi and his colleagues resorted to the old and tried regime of mini-devaluations. As Chicago Boy Juan Andrés Fontaine, one of the brains behind the second round of reforms, wrote,

If one had to choose from the policies implemented just one as deserving credit for obtaining the results, that would be undoubtedly the exchange rate policy. Since the end of 1982, the Central Bank has applied a policy of daily mini devaluations of the peso aimed at preserving a given real exchange rate level. This level has been altered from time to time in order to set a real exchange rate deemed to be consistent with the medium-term outlook for terms of trade, interest rates and the availability of foreign financing. . . . The adjustment of relative prices induced by the devaluation of the peso has worked wonders in the promotion of exports and the substitution of imports.[13]

This pragmatic approach to exchange rates had been suggested by Al Harberger as early as 1974, when he argued that in a country like Chile, whose main export (copper) was subject to wide price fluctuations, it was very difficult and costly to have a fixed exchange rate. Harberger would go on to point out that within the Latin American context, a fixed rate would work in a country such as Panama, where foreign exchange earnings were very stable due to its canal, but would not work well in Chile, a country whose main export (copper) was subject to wide price swings in international markets.

In October 1989, a few weeks before the first presidential election since 1970, the junta passed a law granting independence to the Central Bank. The idea, which at the time was novel in Latin America, was influenced by research undertaken at the University of Chicago and elsewhere on the role of institutional constraints to achieve credibility and macroeconomic stability. David Gordon, a Chicago graduate who had been a classmate of many of the younger Chilean economists, had worked on the issue in his dissertation and had published a very influential paper coauthored with Robert Barro from Harvard University.[14] The idea was that in a strategic setting, the Central Bank would generally be tempted to go back on its promise to maintain low inflation. Once nominal wages were set through a union-employer bargaining process, it was in the Central Bank's interest to produce a higher inflation than promised and, in this way, increase aggregate demand and employment.

Unions, of course, learned that this was the bank's modus operandi and asked for higher wages than they would if the banks' promise were credible. The result was a high equilibrium rate of inflation. Under these circumstances, argued Gordon, it paid for the Central Bank to "tie its own hands," making sure that it could not act on its temptation. Since, such a restriction was not easy to achieve, an independent Central Bank run by officers who did not respond to politicians and that had a longer horizon would (almost) do the job. Once the idea of granting independence to the Central Bank was agreed on by the Right and the Left, there was a long negotiation on the composition of the five-member independent board. At the end, a compromise was reached, and Andrés Bianchi, a graduate of Yale University and a former international civil servant who was highly respected on all political sides, was appointed president of the bank for two years. Two board members from each coalition were appointed to the board. An important aspect of this legislation is that, for the first time since 1962, it liberalized the foreign exchange market. For almost thirty years those who bought or sold foreign exchange without a license could be sent to jail.

Harberger's Growing Influence

During the second half of the 1980s, Al Harberger's influence among the Chicago Boys became even greater than during the early reforms. Since his years as a student, Harberger had clearly favored markets, openness, and competition. At the same time, he thought of himself as an applied economist who took constraints—political, cultural, and others— seriously, and sought practical solutions. He prided himself in not being doctrinaire and not being a Milton Friedman clone. During the early years of the dictatorship, Harberger visited Chile once or twice a year, most of the time as the guest of the Fundación BHC, the promarkets foundation run by Rolf Lüders and associated with the Grupo BHC.

In contrast to some of the more doctrinaire members of the University of Chicago faculty, Harberger understood that in poorer countries the state played a very important role in the economy and that many times it had to shoulder the heaviest burden regarding investments. In his mind it was not enough to decry an oversized state and to recommend divestiture of public-sector enterprises. What was needed was a meticulous, well-reasoned methodology to evaluate the merits of specific investments projects supported or undertaken by the government. For years Harberger worked on developing a coherent approach to "project evaluation." The core of his methodology was presented in an elegant paper titled "Three Basic Postulates for Applied Welfare Economics." The three principles were very simple, and yet extremely powerful: demand curves provide the best estimates of the value that citizens attach to certain goods or services; supply curves provide the best estimate of the costs (in terms of resources) of producing those goods or services; and projects' net benefits should be calculated by a simple addition of dollars related to costs and benefits. This third principle implied that, when evaluating a public-sector investment project, the analyst should not use "distributional weights" that favored a particular group within the income distribution scale. Applying the methodology was not that easy, since the correct supply-and-demand curves that captured externalities, side effects, and other distortions had to be defined and constructed.[15]

In 1975, and based on Harberger's ideas, the Chicago Boys estimated "shadow" or "social" prices for the most important components of investment projects: capital, labor, and foreign exchange. These social prices considered a myriad of distortions in the Chilean economy and were used by the Office of Planning, Odeplán, to evaluate whether specific projects were worthwhile and socially beneficial. With time, as the distortions were lifted or eliminated, the need of using social prices was reduced. Harberger's role was not restricted to assisting his former students on how to evaluate a particularly complex investment project. He was consulted about a variety of issues related to both macropolicy and social policy.

Harberger: The Economist and the Man

I met Al Harberger in early 1976, when I was a junior economist in the research department of the Grupo BHC conglomerate. I had been hired by Rolf Lüders to help group executives understand the way in which the Chilean economy evolved and responded to the reforms. My undergraduate career was checkered and unconventional. After high school

I enrolled in the Facultad de Economía Política (Faculty of Political Economy) at the Universidad de Chile, where I was a student activist affiliated with Salvador Allende's Partido Socialista de Chile (Socialist Party of Chile). After the coup d'état our school was closed because, according to the military, it was a "nest of communist rats." All students were suspended, some were expelled, and a handful just disappeared into the torture chambers of the dictatorship. In 1974, after a surrealistic amount of paperwork and what seemed to be an interminable succession of meetings, I managed to transfer to Católica, from which I graduated in late 1975. To say the least, working for a conglomerate run by one of the most respected Chicago Boys was strange for a young man who had supported Allende and his Chilean path to socialism.

A month after joining the Grupo BHC, I was told by Rolf Lüders that Professor Arnold Harberger, the father of the Chicago Boys, would visit Chile for one week as a guest of the Fundación BHC. I was to assist him in anything he needed: data collection, references, and meetings. In short, I was to be his driver, valet, and research assistant. I had read many of Harberger' s articles, and had always been captivated by the elegance of his models and the clarity of his prose. I had particularly enjoyed reading "The Dynamics of Inflation in Chile," a paper in which he compared the explanatory power of the monetarist and structural views on inflation.[16] In his analysis he had been very evenhanded and had not tilted the methodology to favor his prior beliefs. This was, I thought, the way to do empirical work: use theory to formulate hypotheses, collect the data, analyze them carefully from more than one perspective, and use the evidence to support a particular conclusion. Then, submit your analysis to a battery of robustness tests.

Although Harberger was a frequent visitor to Católica, I had never met him, and I didn't know what to expect. As it turned out, he was gentle, kind, and thoughtful. When someone asked him a question, Harberger would take off his glasses and rub his eyes. He would then say, "Well," and pause. You could almost see his brain working. He would frequently pace up and down while he was thinking, often with his hands in his back pockets. He would lean slightly forward, and look at the ground, as if he was searching for something he had lost—a coin, a key, a small object. He would never rush. It was from him that I learned that one should never be an "instant expert."

Harberger was a big man with a sunny disposition. When I met him, he wore crumpled suits, which in later years he replaced by equally crumpled tropical guayaberas. When he traveled, he carried all sorts of things in his suitcase, including bags of peanuts, cans of sardines, tomato sauce, and crackers. In 1976 he was still drinking, and favored gin and tonics. Invariably his drinks—and ours, for that matter—would have a lot of gin and very little tonic water. In his briefcase there were always two or three yellow pads, and several pens of different colors. As I would find out later, when I took his courses at the University of Chicago, he needed different colors to draw his elaborate diagrams, with supply and demand curves; marginal costs and marginal revenues; triangles that measured welfare losses; and rectangles that captured the indirect welfare consequences of different distortions, such as taxes or import tariffs. But the most important item in his briefcase was a copy of the *International Financial Statistics Yearbook*, published by the International Monetary Fund. These were large format books—in quartos—with soft blue covers. Each country was given two to four pages, and the statistics, for each year since 1950, were presented line after line. I had never seen the publication until I met Harberger, but I immediately discovered its usefulness and secured my own copy of it. Harberger taught me how to unearth complete narratives from those small numbers that looked like ants on a counter where honey had been spilled. Harberger would take base money, break it down into its two main components (foreign assets and domestic credit), and construct indicators of financial fragility and impending currency crises. In those years most emerging countries, including Chile, had some variant of fixed exchange rates—purely fixed, crawling pegs, and the like—and the domestic currency would often get out of line with fundamentals. Governments went out of their way in efforts to defend the exchange rate, as Sergio de Castro did in Chile in 1982. Heads of state accused their enemies of conspiring against the currency, blamed multinationals and imperialist forces for trade imbalances, and promised to defend the currency "like a dog."[17] Harberger, however, would always take a deeper perspective; he would analyze the data, make international comparisons, look under the veneer, and examine the accounts of state-owned enterprises to find out the true forces that were destabilizing these countries. In 1976, I would never have imagined that a few years later I would travel the world with him as his assistant, always carrying a copy of the *International Financial Statistics Yearbook* and a large number of small bottles of gin in my briefcase, spending weeks at a time in foreign countries in an effort to understand the forces behind their economic problems and to determine the best path toward solving them.

I picked up Al Harberger at Arturo Merino Benítez Airport in April 1976. While we drove toward the city, he told me that he needed some data for the talk he was to deliver a few days later. This was his fourth public address in Chile in less than two years. The first two talks had been in June and December 1974 and had focused on the need to eliminate the fiscal deficit as a precondition for reducing the 700 percent inflation to manageable levels. The third talk had been in March 1975. That time Milton Friedman was with him, and they met briefly with General Pinochet. As noted in earlier chapters, this meeting created huge problems for Friedman, who since then had been accused of being an accomplice of the Chilean military and of its systematic violations of human rights.

During his 1976 visit I drove Harberger throughout Santiago in my small Fiat 600. Most of the time we would drive in silence. He would leaf through his notes, and occasionally would look at figures in the "big blue book." We went from his hotel to Católica, from Católica to the Central Bank, to the BHC Group headquarters, to the electrical company, and back to his hotel. On one occasion, while we were having a drink, I tried to engage him in conversation about politics. I pointed out that one of his former Chilean students, Ricardo Ffrench-Davis, had written a severe criticism of the government's stabilization policy and accused the Chicago Boys of neglecting the social costs of the "shock treatment." But Harberger didn't take the bait. "Well," he said, "Ricardo is a good trade economist. But monetary theory is not one of his strengths." Figure 9.1 shows Rolf Lüders, one of the first Chicago Boys, and a minister of finance and economics during the Pinochet

FIGURE 9.1. Rolf Lüders (*left*) with Arnold Harberger (*right*) in 2008
Source: Rolf Lüders's personal collection

dictatorship, and Al Harberger in 2008. Lüders organized Milton Friedman's first visit to Chile in 1975.

In 1984 Harberger left the University of Chicago for the University of California–Los Angeles, and we became colleagues. We continued to travel the world assisting governments, central banks, public companies, and private enterprises. When the assignment required deep analyses in multiple areas, Harberger assembled a group of professionals that, almost always, included a number of the Chicago Boys. Never in any of these travels did any of them—Sergio de la Cuadra, Ernesto Fontaine, Juan Andrés Fontaine, or Juan Carlos Méndez—mention the fact that in September 1973, when President Salvador Allende was deposed by the military putsch, we were on different sides. They were with the insurgents, and I was with Chile's constitutional president. In those trips the issue was never brought up; we were all members of the "Harberger Team."

On August 2, 1994, Gary Becker, who at the time was president of the Mont Pèlerin Society (MPS), wrote to Milton Friedman about Al Harberger and the society. Becker pointed out that Harberger had expressed some misgivings about joining the MPS, saying that he thought that it was excessively doctrinaire. Harberger and I had discussed the issue numerous times during many of our travels around the world. On more than one occasion he told me that it was a two-way street: he was reluctant to join the MPS, and the senior members were unsure whether to invite him to join. I remember him saying something like "They think that I am too independent-minded for their group." In his letter, which may be found in the Friedman Archives at the Hoover Institution, Becker wrote to Friedman, "I have spoken to Al Harberger about becoming a member of the Mont Pèlerin Society. He has doubts, because he believes that too many members are ideologues. I tried to point out to him that while many members are unswerving ideologues, there are many excellent members, including many new members, with views similar to his and ours."[18]

At the end, and after discussing the issue with Friedman, Harberger decided to join the MPS. The episode (and, in particular, Becker's letter) illustrates and confirms the fact that Harberger's views were always different—broader and more flexible—that those of other University of Chicago faculty. While Gary Becker, Ronald Coase, Milton Friedman, and George Stigler, among others, may be referred to as the "neoliberal section" of the university, Al Harberger and Harry Johnson were part of what I have called its "pragmatic wing." In a 2021 interview Harberger told me,

> I resist very much the idea that Chicago was basically a sounding
> board for Friedman. In point of fact, we had as many people voting
> Democratic as voting Republican. The thing is that the other leading department had mostly Democrats. It's not that we were

predominantly Republican; we had some, and they didn't have any (or had very few), so to speak. The question is: What determines the Chicago School? My belief was that the Chicago School meant believing that market forces were extremely important in determining how things worked out in the real world, and there was no one at Chicago who disagreed with that principle.[19]

Did the Chicago Boys Know about Human Rights Violations?

Throughout the years I have often been asked if the Chicago Boys knew about the human rights violations during the Pinochet regime. In the 2015 documentary *Chicago Boys*, Sergio de Castro is asked that question by journalist Carola Fuentes. The former minister, who until that moment in the interview has been jovial and forthcoming, becomes clearly rattled by the question. He states that he did not know about those episodes. The journalist is incredulous, asking, "Really?" She then tells him that he surely had friends who worked at the International Monetary Fund and the World Bank and that those friends must have told him about the stories of kidnappings, executions, and disappearances that circulated in Washington, DC. De Castro becomes more uncomfortable, and says that he had heard rumors, and that in his mind—and in the minds of other members of the economics team—they were nothing more than rumors, part of an international campaign led by the Partido Comunista de Chile (Communist Party of Chile) to attack the military regime. Fuentes does not give up easily, and asks whether any political and security issues, such as the repression of demonstrators and government opponents, were ever discussed in cabinet meetings. De Castro declares that there was a clear and firm separation between politics, on the one hand, and economics, on the other, and that he and his team dealt exclusively with the latter and did not get involved with law-and-order issues, nor were they aware of human rights violations.[20]

We will never know for sure the facts on these thorny issues. What is clear, however, is that the Chicago Boys were aware that Colonel Manuel Contreras, the head of DINA, was extremely powerful and detested them. Contreras believed that the Chicago Boys were in cahoots with the heads of large conglomerates to obtain great financial and economic benefits from privatization and the liberalization of markets. According to investigative reporters Ascanio Cavallo, Manual Salazar, and Oscar Sepúlveda, Colonel Contreras investigated the private lives of all of the Chicago Boys; by June 1975 he had amassed thick folders on each of them. In addition to suspecting the ultimate motives of the economists, Contreras was upset that they did not provide DINA with the budget that he requested.[21] And, of course, it is also indisputable that Sergio de Castro and his colleagues learned early on—certainly before the general public did—that DINA agents were involved in the assassination of a former ambassador, Orlando Letelier.

On July 2, 1976, Albert Fishlow, an economic historian at the University of California–Berkeley and a former US deputy assistant secretary of state, wrote to Milton Friedman and asked him for his "personal help in obtaining the release from prison of Fernando Flores, a Chilean economist and former Minister of economics and finance in the Allende government." Fishlow explained that Flores's political affiliation was "with the left wing separatist segment of the Christian Democrats, the MAPU [Movimiento de Acción Popular Unitaria, or Popular Unitary Action Movement], and not the extreme groups in the Unidad Popular." According to Fishlow, Flores was "being held because there is resentment in high military circles at his intimacy with Allende." Fishlow ended his letter noting that there was "reason to believe that a *personal* [from Friedman] and direct appeal on Flores's behalf to President Pinochet, whom you have met, would carry great weight, and might in the present circumstances make all the difference."[22]

Friedman did not hesitate to write to Pinochet on behalf of Flores, whom he had never met and would not meet in the years to come:

> Like many another friend of Chile, who is also a believer in human freedom and liberty, I have been greatly distressed by reports of restrictions on personal and human freedom in Chile that have been widely circulated in the West. . . . The immediate occasion for this letter is the case of a former Allende cabinet minister under detention

in Chile, Fernando Flores Labra. .... I have never met Fernando Flores personally and have had no direct contact with him. However, I have done my best to inform myself about him. As I understand it, Fernando Flores is eligible for a US visa under US immigration laws, Stanford University has offered him a position in its Computer Science Department, and Chile has not granted him permission to leave the country.

Friedman ended his letter by stating that "freedom is indivisible. Greater economic freedom promotes and facilitates greater political freedom. But equally, greater political freedom promotes economic freedom and it contributes to economic progress and development."[23]

Al Harberger was also aware of the repression and violation of human and civil rights during the Pinochet dictatorship. I remember being in his office late in the spring of 1980 when he received a call from Chile about a young economist, Guillermo Geisse, who had been detained by the military because he was the editor of a forbidden newsletter published by MAPU. He was the son of a respected urban planner who worked at Católica and had met Harberger on more than one occasion. On that day I personally heard Harberger calling his friends in Santiago and interceding on behalf of Geisse. I am not sure if his calls helped, but the fact of the matter is that instead of spending years banished in a small northern town, according to his sentence, Geisse was released after eighteen months. What makes this episode particularly ironic is that at the time of his banishment, Guillermo Geisse worked for future president Sebastián Piñera at one of the local banks, Banco de Talca.

The "Miracle" Arrives

Economic performance during the second round of reforms was impressive. In 1988 and 1989, the rate of investment in fixed capital averaged 24.5 percent, the highest it had been since 1960. This rapid accumulation of capital, coupled with a jump in total factor productivity, resulted in the longest sustained acceleration in growth in the gross domestic product in Chile's history.[24] During the second round of reforms (1984–90), average annual GDP growth was 6.4 percent. In 1985 the rate of unemployment was 12 percent; by 1989 it had declined to almost one-half, 6.8 percent. In March 1990 the democratic forces would inherit a competitive and dynamic economy advancing at full blast. They would also inherit a country traumatized by an authoritarian government that had committed thousands of human rights abuses, had tortured and murdered opponents, and exiled dissidents. One of the greatest challenges faced by the country was working on reconciliation, reparation, and, if possible, forgiveness.

PART III

Neoliberalism under Democratic Rule, 1990–2022

10

The Return of Democracy and Inclusive Neoliberalism

CHILE'S TRANSITION toward democracy began on October 5, 1988, when a national referendum was held, with a single question: Should Augusto Pinochet stay in power for another eight years? The ballots were printed on yellowish paper and read as follows:

Plebiscite—President of the Republic

Augusto Pinochet Ugarte

Yes   No

The "No" option won by a landslide, and fifteen months later, on December 14, 1989, Patricio Aylwin, a Christian Democrat and the candidate of the left-of-center Concertación por la Democracia coalition, was elected president with 56 percent of the votes. Pinochet's candidate, minister of finance Hernán Büchi, obtained a mere 29 percent of the vote; a third—conservative—candidate got 16 percent. When the Concertación took power on March 11, 1990, Chile's economy was completely changed relative to 1973, when Salvador Allende had been ousted in a coup. Markets operated freely, Chile had joined the globalized world, the vast majority of state-owned enterprises had been privatized, foreign investment was flowing in large amounts, social programs were strictly targeted to the poor, education had been partially privatized through a vouchers system, there was a two-tier health care system that operated with vouchers, there was a dynamic capital market, pensions were based on individual savings accounts, and the exchange rate was maintained at a competitive level, through mini devaluations, in order to encourage nontraditional exports.

Table 10.1 provides an economic and social scorecard for the (almost) seventeen years of the Pinochet dictatorship, a period during which most of the economic decisions were made by the Chicago Boys. In order to highlight the differences between the two phases of the reforms, which were separated by the 1982 currency crisis, I provide data for three moments in time: 1973, 1983, and 1990.

Taken as a whole, the performance for Pinochet's seventeen years is not impressive. After almost two decades in power, during which it faced no political opposition or the challenges of governing in a democratic system with an elected legislature, a free press, and an independent judiciary, the military did not have much to show in terms of traditional metrics. Between 1973 and 1990, real gross domestic product (GDP) grew at an average of only 1.7 percent per year (this was slightly below the rate of growth of the population); inflation was stuck at almost 30 percent, and at the end of the period those living below the "extreme" poverty line—also known as those living below the "destitution line"— were still 14 percent of the population. Despite the decline in poverty, during the dictatorship inequality increased significantly: while in 1971 the Gini coefficient was 0.47, it was 0.52 in 1990. Figure 10.1 displays the rate of open unemployment. If one assumes a "natural" or "normal" rate of unemployment of 6.5 percent—a rate that is, admittedly, on the high side—the average yearly rate of "excess unemployment" for the whole period of the dictatorship is 9.1 percent. That is a huge number. Taking that into consideration, it is not surprising that the regime suffered massive electoral losses, both in the 1988 referendum, when Pinochet asked the people if they wanted him to stay for another eight years, and in the 1989 presidential election.

The data in table 10.1 show a marked difference in growth after 1983. Indeed, during the second round of reforms (1984–90) the expansion of GDP per capita jumped to an average of 4.7 percent per year. This

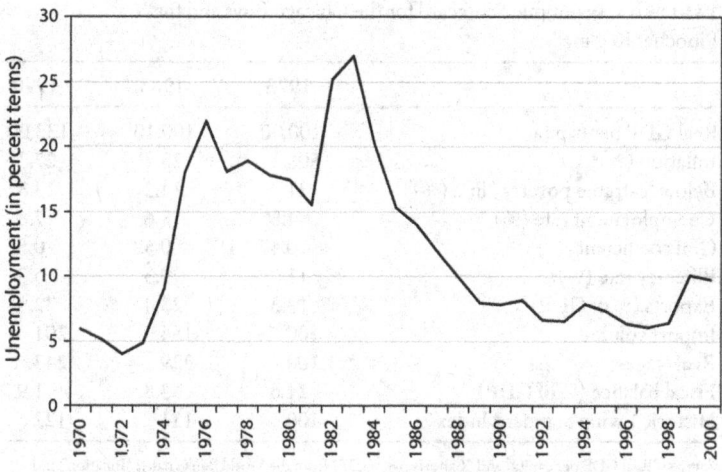

FIGURE 10.1. Unemployment, percentage by year, 1970–2000
Source: Díaz, Lüders, and Wagner (2016)

impressive performance, both from the perspective of Chile's and Latin America's history, continued during the first twenty-five years of the return to democracy, making Chile the absolute regional leader. The way in which that exactly happened is the subject of the analysis in this chapter, where I discuss what may be called the great persuasion, or the decision made by the incoming team of left-of-center politicians and economists to maintain, and even deepen, the promarkets reforms. Convincing their longtime rivals to preserve the model—albeit with some adjustments—was a major achievement of the Chicago Boys. Pinochet lost the electoral battle, but the Chicago Boys won the "war of ideas." As the 2019 revolt showed, however, that triumph was not permanent. With time, fissures appeared in the neoliberal edifice, and these cracks were ignored by the economic and political elite who continued to live in a social and cultural bubble, enjoying their wealth and perks, without making an effort to truly understand the plight of vast segments of the people.

Patricio Aylwin, a deeply religious Catholic, lawyer, and experienced politician from the Christian Democratic Party, assumed the presidency

TABLE 10.1. Economic Scorecard for the Chicago Boys and the Pinochet Regime

	1973	1983	1990
Real GDP per capita	100.00	100.10	133.00
Inflation (%)[a]	508.1	23.1	27.3
Below "extreme poverty" line (%)[b]	21	14.2	13.8
Unemployment rate (%)	4.8	18.6	7.8
Gini coefficient	0.47	0.52	0.52
Illiteracy rate (%)	11	9.3	6.3
Exports (% of GDP)	13.3	23.4	32.5
Import volume	100	154	201
Real wages	100	229	243
Fiscal balance (% of GDP)	−24.6	−3.8	1.9
Historic Living Standard Index	100	111	122

Sources: "Real GDP per capita" and "Exports over GDP" from the World Bank (n.d.); "Inflation" and "Fiscal balance / GDP" from the Banco Central de Chile (2001); "Unemployment rate" for 1973 and 1983 from Edwards and Edwards (1991), and for 1990 from the International Monetary Fund (n.d.); "Gini coefficient," "Illiteracy rate," "Import volume," and "Historic Living Standard Index" from Thorp (1998); "Real wages" from Matus and Reyes (2021).

Note: Data on social indicators in each column correspond to the closest year available. For instance, the Historic Living Standard Index for 1973 corresponds to 1970, and the index for 1983 corresponds to 1980.

[a] Diaz, Lüders, and Wagner (2016) estimate inflation in 1973 to be equal to 606 percent.

[b] The data for 1973 and 1983 correspond to the characterization following the methodology in Molina et al. (1974). The data for 1990 correspond to the methodology based on the poverty line in the Chile Encuesta de Caracterización Socioeconómica Nacional (CASEN, n.d.; Chile National Socioeconomic Characterization Survey); the previous CASEN record is 1987, and extreme poverty at that time was 16.8 percent; see Beyer (1995) and Rojas (1986).

in March 1990. During the Unidad Popular government, Aylwin, who was then a senator, had been a strong opponent of Allende and his policies. Immediately after the September 11, 1973, coup Aylwin was not particularly critical of the military; in fact, many detractors have said that he was relieved and that he supported the coup. Soon, however, as it became evident that Pinochet did not plan to restore democracy in short order, Aylwin and his Christian Democratic comrades—including former president Eduardo Frei Montalva—became severe critics of the dictatorship and worked incessantly for the return of democratic rule.

Embracing "Markets"

Alejandro Foxley, the first minister of finance upon the return of democracy in 1990, was a highly telegenic and urbane economist, with deep-sea-blue eyes and a raspy voice. He had a PhD from the University of Wisconsin and a vast network of friends and associates around the world. During the dictatorship, Foxley and his colleagues at Corporación de Estudios para Latinoamérica (CIEPLAN; Corporation of Studies for Latin America), an independent research center that was well funded by international foundations, became the most severe critics of the Chicago Boys. They condemned the stabilization program (too abrupt and too costly), the opening up of the economy (too fast and in the wrong sequence), the agricultural policy (agrarian reform should be continued), the educational program (vouchers were elitists, and university education should be free), the lack of industrial policy (efficient import substitution was of the essence), the lightly regulated capital market (free interest rates encouraged speculation), the pensions system based on individual saving accounts (intergenerational solidarity was needed), and the privatization of state-owned enterprises (firms sold too cheaply; the state should have a productive presence in strategic industries). They opposed the overall Chicago Boys' strategy, which relied on free markets, low inflation, openness, targeted social programs, and competition. Throughout the dictatorship, CIEPLAN economists argued that Chile's private sector lacked the force and innovative spirit required to move the economy forward without substantive guidance from the state. In their view, during the dictatorship the Chilean economy was dominated by monopolies that abused consumers.[1]

In 1982 Alejandro Foxley published the first comprehensive and detailed criticism of the Chicago Boys' model. The book, titled *Experimentos neoliberales en América Latina* (Neoliberal experiments in Latin America), became extremely influential and was used as a reference by development experts from around the world, and especially in the rest of Latin America. The English translation, published in 1984, had a slightly different title: *Latin American Experiments in Neoconservative Economics*. The small difference in the title—*Neoliberal* was replaced by

Neoconservative—is another reflection that the term *neoliberal* gained currency only slowly in the Anglo-Saxon world and that in the early 1980s it was not yet a commonly used term in the economic or political literature.

Given Alejandro Foxley's background and his writings during the dictatorship, everyone expected that as minister of finance under President Patricio Aylwin he would lead the dismantling of the Chicago Boys' policies. But he did not do that.[2] With a remarkable sense of opportunity and great pragmatism, and after considering the extraordinary acceleration of growth of 1985–89, Foxley convinced President Aylwin that instead of reversing the market reforms his administration should further many of them. In Foxley's view, the first democratically elected government in almost two decades had to combine a promarkets strategy with the development of a sturdy safety net to help the poor and the disadvantaged. After long discussions, Aylwin acquiesced, reluctantly. Deep inside, however, the new president never agreed with the new vision, and on occasions he let people know about his disagreement. At one point the president told reporters that "the market was very cruel." He also criticized consumerism and noted that he had never been in a shopping mall and never expected to visit one.[3]

In April 1990, one month after assuming power, the new administration decided to immediately address two critical economic reforms: it put in place a tax package aimed at funding new social programs, and it passed a reform to the military's labor law, the Plan Laboral, which had been severely criticized by union leaders and political commentators on the Left. Foxley was careful to note that these constituted the only two important modifications to the economic model. By tackling these issues early on, the government sought to minimize the possible negative effects of policy uncertainty. In a *Newsweek* interview, Foxley talked about recapturing the balance between economic conditions conducive to growth and social policies aimed at improving the standard of living of the poor. Equally central to the democratic project, he said, was making sure that macroeconomic stability was maintained; he talked about "avoiding at all costs the typical cycle of populist economic policies in Latin America."[4] Edgardo Boeninger, a leader of the opposition to

Pinochet and one of the brains behind President Aylwin's strategy, wrote in his memoirs that the new government deliberately opted for a gradual approach. One of the objectives of this tactic was to avoid opposition from those sectors that felt threatened by the new political reality—mostly the military and the business sector.[5]

Improving social conditions was, of course, one of the Concertación government's fundamental goals and the one that, in the view of its leaders, set it most clearly apart from the Chicago Boys. New programs were put in place in education, health care, housing, and old-age pensions, but the Chicago Boys' principle that government support should be strictly targeted to the poor was maintained. In order to receive government assistance, families had to register with a government agency and demonstrate that their income and assets were below a certain threshold. Once families' income exceeded a predetermined value, they stopped being eligible for support. One of the consequences of these "targeted programs" was that most students had to pay market fees for tertiary education, both university and vocational. Public universities, including the prestigious Universidad de Chile, one of the oldest schools in Latin America, charged the same tuition as private schools, such as Católica. In chapter 11, I analyze in detail the social and economic policies of the left-of-center governments, and I discuss how they propelled Chile to first place in terms of income and social conditions in the region. Figure 10.2 shows General Augusto Pinochet and newly elected president Patricio Aylwin. Pinochet retained the title of commander in chief of the army until March 1998, at which time he became senator for life.[6]

Staying the Course

The agreement reached between Pinochet and the democratic forces after the 1988 plebiscite stated that the first elected president would serve for four years. From that point onward, the presidential term would revert to six years, the historical norm since the early twentieth century. When the agreement was signed, the military had the hope that a conservative, law-and-order candidate—possibly a retired army

FIGURE 10.2. General Augusto Pinochet (*left*) stayed on as commander in chief
of the Chilean Army after Patricio Aylwin (*right*) became president in 1990
Source: La Tercera photo archive

general—would inhabit the presidential palace, La Moneda, in 1993. They
were wrong. Eduardo Frei Ruiz-Tagle, the candidate of the Concertación
and the son of former president Eduardo Frei Montalva (1964–70), was
elected by an ample majority in the first round of the election, becoming
the second Center-Left president after the return to democracy.

Once again analysts and observers asked whether the Chicago Boys'
policies would be maintained, or if President Frei would steer away from
free markets and adopt a program based on the social doctrine of the
Catholic Church. His father, a revered figure among the poor and
loathed by the conservatives because he had handed power over to Salvador Allende, was a great champion of the dispossessed, including
landless peasants. A few weeks after the election, President-Elect Frei
announced that he would appoint Juan Villarzú, a University of Chicago
graduate and one of the authors of The Brick, as the new minister of
finance. During the early years of the dictatorship Villarzú had been the
director of the budget and the author of the first tax reform of the junta.

Although Villarzú was not as doctrinaire as Sergio de Castro and Ernesto Fontaine, he was clearly a promarkets economist, and everyone expected a continuity of policy in the years to come. Villarzú's appointment was further evidence that the Chicago Boys had won the "war of ideas."

A few weeks before Frei's inauguration an investigative reporter found out that, because of some of his business associations, Juan Villarzú had a conflict of interest and could not take over the influential and powerful post of minister of finance. Frei decided to give him a different position of power and named him head of the state-owned copper company, Codelco. Frei appointed Eduardo Aninat, a graduate of Católica and of Harvard University and a former foreign debt negotiator with close ties to bankers from around the world, as the chief of the economic team. Aninat had been a colleague of Alejandro Foxley at CIEPLAN and had impeccable credentials as a promarkets economist "with a bleeding heart." In 1998 President Frei Ruiz-Tagle appointed Carlos Massad, an economist who in 1956 was one of the first Chilean students to attend the University of Chicago under the auspices of the Chile Project, as governor of the Central Bank. His professors in Chicago had considered him to be among the best in his class. Once again it was clear that there would not be major deviations from the path set by Pablo Baraona, Sergio de Castro, Sergio de la Cuadra, and the other Chicago Boys in 1975.

Capital Inflows and the Price of Success

Starting in 1990, large volumes of capital began flowing into Chile due to economic success, a peaceful transition to democratic rule, the new government's support for market reforms, and high interest rates. It rapidly became apparent that these flows were strengthening the peso and negatively affecting exports' competitiveness. In an effort to avoid currency overvaluation—the 1982 currency crisis was fresh in everyone's minds—Chile adopted the novel policy of controlling capital *inflows*. This was a radical departure from the tradition in less developed countries, where for many decades the concern was how to avoid capital *outflows* or "capital flight."

Capital controls on inflows worked in a simple way: 20 percent of financial capital entering the country had to be deposited, for one year, at the Central Bank, where it earned no interest. From a financial point of view, this unremunerated deposit worked as a tax, with a rate proportional to the interest income forgone during that year. The system was built in a way that the rate of the implicit tax was higher for short-term flows than for longer-term ones. As the authorities had anticipated, volatile and speculative capital inflows in the (very) short term declined precipitously, while longer-term capital inflows, including foreign direct investment, increased. Chile was a global leader in the adoption of controls to slow down the inflow of capital. During the late 1990s and early 2000s, similar schemes were used by other nations, including Brazil, Colombia, Malaysia, and Thailand, and were eventually endorsed by the International Monetary Fund. These policies received the support of economists with different views about government regulations. For example, in a 1998 New York Times article, Nobel laureate Joseph Stiglitz said, "You want to look for policies that discourage 'hot money' but facilitate the flow of long-term loans, and there is evidence that the Chilean approach, or some version of it, does this."[7]

In 1999, and because of the East Asian and Russian currency crises, there was a significant slowdown of capital flowing into Chile and other emerging markets. The minister of finance, Eduardo Aninat, decided that the time was ripe to open the economy fully to international capital movements. In a matter of months Chile moved into a Milton Friedman type of world: the value of the currency was freely determined by the interaction of supply and demand, with (virtually) no government intervention, and firms and individuals were allowed to move monies in and out of the country without restrictions.

Many observers argued that allowing unfettered capital movements was yet another indication that the left-of-center Concertación had been captured by neoliberal ideologues and that financial outcomes were more important than reducing inequality, industrializing the country, and protecting the environment. Critics predicted that the adoption of freely floating rates would bring speculation, instability, and misery. Nothing of that sort happened, however, and for the next twenty years the Chilean economy was one of the most stable and open among the emerging markets. The average rate of economic growth during the early years of the transition (1990–97) was an impressive 7.7 percent per annum, reflecting faster growth than that of any other Latin American country by a wide margin.

By the mid-1990s, and largely as a result of the decisively promarkets policies of the Concertación governments, the rate of investment in machinery, equipment, and infrastructure jumped to 28 percent of GDP, from 12 percent in 1984 and 24 percent in 1989. By deepening the reforms Chile was able to move to a "second phase" of a growth transition in which the most important sources of growth were a combination of productivity improvements and an increase in productive capacity through the accumulation of capital. Forty years after it was launched by Albion "Pat" Patterson and Theodore Schultz, the Chile Project was bearing full fruit.

11

Staying Neoliberal

IN 2002 CHILE became the Latin American country with the highest income per capita. Surpassing Argentina, their neighbor to the east, was particularly sweet for Chilean citizens, as for over two hundred years they had lived in Argentina's shadow. This was true with respect to economics, the arts, culture, and sports—time and again Argentina defeated Chile on the soccer field. President Ricardo Lagos, a socialist who had courageously led the opposition to Augusto Pinochet during the final years of the dictatorship, was understandably proud of the achievement. Yet as an economist and an expert in labor markets—he had a doctorate from Duke University—he understood the difference between *economic growth* and *economic development*. The latter was a multidimensional concept that included the provision of social services to the population and a reduction in inequality, an area in which Chile had traditionally done very poorly. During the electoral campaign Lagos affirmed that his administration would pursue "equitable growth." On January 16, 2000, he defeated Chicago Boy Joaquín Lavín in the second round of presidential elections and became the third president from the Concertación coalition to win the presidency and the first socialist to do so since Salvador Allende in 1970.

A Multitude of Free Trade Agreements

Ricardo Lagos was interested in consolidating Chile's move into the global economy, something that was essential in order to maintain a rapid expansion of national income through export growth. His objective was to sign free trade agreements with as many countries as possible.

In late 2002, and after two years of arduous negotiations, Chile and the United States agreed on the text of a free trade agreement. The treaty was the jewel in the crown of Lagos's efforts to modernize Chile.

On March 11, 2003, weeks before the final document was to be signed, Lagos got a call from US president George W. Bush asking him for Chile's support in the United Nations Security Council for the US invasion of Iraq; at the time, Chile was a nonpermanent member of the council. As Lagos revealed many years later, during the call he told Bush that, in his view, there was not enough evidence confirming the possible existence of weapons of mass destruction in Iraq and that, consequently, Chile could not, in good faith, support the invasion. Bush thanked him for his frankness and ended the call.

At the time there was fear among Chilean officials that Lagos's refusal to join the so-called coalition of the willing would result in the free trade agreement not being approved by the US Congress or the White House. These fears seemed to materialize when a few weeks later, it was announced that instead of voting on the free trade agreements with Chile and Singapore on the same day, Congress would only consider the Singapore deal, which was promptly approved. There was panic in Chile's Ministerio de Relaciones Exteriores (Ministry of Foreign Affairs) as officials wondered how the setback would affect the nation's overall strategy for integration into the global economic system. President Lagos, however, stayed calm and told his associates that he was willing to pay that cost for maintaining an independent foreign policy. Six weeks after the Singapore deal was passed, the Chile–United States free trade agreement was finally approved by the US Congress; the agreement came into effect in late December 2003. The effective import tariff rate in Chile dropped to a mere 3 percent, and the Chicago Boys' dream of (almost) free trade became a reality.

Economic and Social Policies after the Return to Democratic Rule

Tables 11.1 and 11.2 present a summary of the most salient policies of the Concertación governments between 1990 and 2018; in the interest of thoroughness I also include the achievements of the second government

TABLE 11.1. Major Social Policies Implemented by Left and Center-Left Democratic Governments, 1990–2018

Policy area	Policies implemented
Education and science	Poorly performing schools (mostly rural) given support (P-900 program).
	Teachers' statute implemented in order to standardize teachers' pay across the country.
	"Copayment" allowed in public schools, creating a fourth tier in the system.
	Major school building program created.
	One shift instituted in every school; twelve years of obligatory and free education.
	Significant number of private universities are licensed and new state universities created.
	Standardized tests used to rank schools.
	Elimination of the selection of students at public schools.
	Student loans system through private banks implemented via Crédito con Garantía Estatal (Credit with State Guarantee).
	Research funds for universities greatly expanded via the Fondo Nacional de Desarrollo Científico y Tecnológico (National Fund for Scientific and Technological Development).
Pensions	Administradoras de Fondos de Pensiones (AFPs; Administrators of Pension Funds) allowed to merge, reducing the number of firms.
	Each AFP is allowed to offer different funds, ranked from less risky to more risky.
	"Solidarity pillar" added to pensions' system, complementing pensions from retirees' own funds, at a declining rate.
	Measures taken to increase competition across AFPs and thus to lower fees and commissions.
Health	Dental programs enacted in poor neighborhoods.
	Shift from curative to preventive medicine system.
	AUGE program put in place; treatment of several medical conditions is guaranteed.
	New hospitals are constructed using the "concessions" model initially developed for roads.
	National drug law guarantees timely access to medicines at a fair price.
Gender	Ministerio de la Mujer y la Equidad de Género (Ministry of Women and Gender Equality) created in 2015.
	Effort to appoint more women to high-level government positions.
	Law requires that 40% of candidates to the Chilean Congress from each party are women.
Poverty	Ministerio de Desarrollo Social y Familia (Ministry of Social Development and Family) created to ensure the consistency of social benefits in the country and design and apply social development policies.
	Creation of social protection system to overcome extreme poverty.

TABLE 11.1. (*continued*)

Policy area	Policies implemented
Civil and human rights	Divorce law passed.
	Recognition of couples of the same gender through the Acuerdo de Unión Civil (Civil Union Agreement).
	Abortion legalized under some circumstances.
	Instituto Nacional de Derechos Humanos (National Institute of Human Rights) created.
	Commissions created to find and determine victims of the dictatorship and compensation from the crimes of the dictatorship.

Sources: Biblioteca del Congreso Nacional de Chile Archive; Cavallo and Montes (2022); Edwards (2010); Lagos (2020); Larraín and Vergara (2000); Ministerio de Hacienda (n.d.).

of President Michelle Bachelet, technically not a Concertación administration, as during her second campaign she added the Communist Party to form a new coalition called Nueva Mayoría (New Majority). Table 11.1 concentrates on social policies. Table 11.2, on the other hand, concentrates on economics. It was the combination of policies—both social and economic—that catapulted Chile to the forefront of the Latin American nations and transformed the country into one of the most celebrated cases of reforms and modernization.

During the Concertación era a major effort was made to improve the quality of education. President Aylwin decided to maintain Pinochet's decentralization reform, which had given municipalities control over public schools. In order to improve teachers' morale and commitment, however, he passed a law that standardized pay and work conditions across the country. Independently of where they worked and which municipality employed them, teachers had the same salary and faced the same working conditions throughout the nation. Aylwin also decided to put an end to the "two shifts" practice in public schools, where one group of students attended in the morning and a second group in the afternoon. In order to achieve this goal a major school's construction program was put in place. Hundreds of new schools were built, and a large number of old structures were refitted and upgraded. As a way of improving the conditions of the very poor, a program to support the weakest public schools, the so-called P-900 program, was launched. Most of these

TABLE 11.2. Major Economic Policies Implemented by Left and Center-Left Democratic Governments, 1990–2018

Policy area	Policies implemented
Globalization	Import tariffs reduced to a 6% uniform level.
	A number of free trade agreements signed with countries from around the world, including the United States.
	Numerous bilateral investment treaties signed.
	Controls on international capital mobility abolished.
Privatization	Remaining blocks of shares of many "emblematic" state-owned enterprises sold to the private sector.
	Water supply and sewage companies privatized.
	Concessions for exploration and exploitation of copper and other minerals granted to national and international companies.
	Some ports privatized.
	Lithium concessions given to private companies for thirty years.
Infrastructure	Concession contracts signed with a number of private companies for major highways; these became toll roads.
	Concession to build a perimeter toll road in Santiago.
	Concessions for toll roads in Santiago.
	Private-sector-built schools, hospitals, ports, airports, and jails under the concessions modality.
Macroeconomic policy	Flexible exchange rates.
	Inflation targeting monetary policy (Central Bank decision encouraged by the government).
	Fiscal rule established that the government will run a 1% of GDP structural surplus; rule later modified to structural balance and 1% structural deficit.
	Creation of Consejo Fiscal Autónomo (Autonomous Fiscal Council) to provide guidance on fiscal policy and public debt.
	Creation of sovereign wealth fund to accumulate fiscal surpluses.
Taxation	Value-added tax increased to 19%.
	Specific tax (royalty) on mining; sliding rate depending on profit margin.
	Higher corporate tax rates, a "semi-integrated" system, and reduced exemptions.
Labor	Reduced restrictions for unionization, making it easier for agricultural and temporary workers to unionize.
	Unemployment insurance scheme.
	Increased role of labor courts.
	Increased maximum allowance for being dismissed to eleven months of salary.
Culture, sports, and the arts	Fund for the arts established; grants are provided by jury.
	Ministerio de las Culturas, las Artes y el Patrimonio (Ministry of the Arts, Cultures and Heritage) created in 2018.
	Ministerio de Deporte (Ministry of Sport) created in 2015.
	Constitutional reform to eliminate censorship from cinematographic production.

TABLE 11.2. (*continued*)

Policy area	Policies implemented
First Nations	Corporation to promote, coordinate, and execute state policies for the development of Indigenous people.
	Participative program to improve capabilities and opportunities in different aspects to improve indigenous development by retaining Indigenous identity.
	Norms to protect land, and fund for land acquisition for Indigenous communities.
Environment	Ministerio del Medio Ambiente (Ministry of the Environment) to develop and apply environmental regulation and protect natural resources, among others.
	Extended network of national parks and protected marine areas.
	Integration of unconventional renewable energy sources in the energy system.
	Environmental courts to solve disputes related to the environment.
	Imposition of "green" taxes, such as a tax on carbon emissions for thermoelectric plants.
Agriculture and water	Provide and maintain strong sanitary and phytosanitary conditions.
	Improve the sustainability and the recovery of degraded soils.
	Strong promotion of agricultural exports worldwide.
	Expansion of irrigation, and a more efficient system for it.
Political system	Major amendments to the constitution eliminate many (but not all) of the authoritarian enclaves (e.g., designated senators and senators with "for life" terms).
	Transparency of public functions, and access to information of state administration.
	Creation of system of primary elections to nominate official candidates to the presidency, the Congress, and mayoralty.
	Replacement of the binominal system with new proportional electoral system.
	Foreign voting allowed.
Judiciary	Modernization to the judiciary's criminal procedure reform, with the introduction of oral trials, new courts, and the creation of the national public prosecutor, among other efforts.
	Creation of Tribunales de Familia (Family Courts) focused on matters of family law.
Transportation system	Extension of metro system in Santiago as one of the largest in Latin America.
	Modernization of the urban transportation system in the capital city, named Transantiago.
	Creation of a suburban train system, named MetroTren.

Sources: Biblioteca del Congreso Nacional de Chile Archive; Cavallo and Montes (2022); Cortazar (1997); Edwards (2010); Lagos (2020); Ministerio de Hacienda (n.d.).

establishments were in rural areas and had one or two teachers who taught all primary grades. Curricula were revised and modernized.

These educational policies were largely successful. In a few years Chile became the leader among Latin American countries in all international standardized tests, including the Programme for International Student Assessment (PISA) exam of the Organisation for Economic Co-operation and Development (OECD) and the Trends in International Mathematics and Science Study test that measures eighth graders' proficiency in those concentrations. At the political level, one of the consequences of these policies was that the national teachers' union, the Colegio de Profesores, was once again able to flex its muscles and play an important role in national politics.

Notably, two of the most important features of Pinochet's educational policies were maintained: schools continued to be administered in a decentralized way by municipalities, and vouchers could still be used by families who preferred to send their children to private (often religious) schools rather than public ones. In the mid-1990s, during Eduardo Frei Ruiz-Tagle's administration, a new type of for-profit school geared to the middle class was authorized. In addition to the funds provided through the vouchers, these schools could demand a (modest) copayment or partial tuition from parents. Years later (starting in 2006), during massive students' protests, the Concertación governments were accused by Far-Left demonstrators of entrenching a market-based educational system that helped maintain inequality and segregation.

In terms of higher education, the Concertación's objective was to expand enrollment greatly. In order to achieve that goal, several new private universities were licensed, in an expansion of the policy initiated by the Chicago Boys in 1981. The vast majority of the new schools operated under the system discussed earlier (chapters 7 and 9), in which profits were obtained indirectly through leases and the provision of services by companies owned by those who controlled the universities. In conjunction with the expansion of enrollment, a massive students' loan program was developed. Loans were provided by the banking system and guaranteed by the government. If students did not pay, the government bought the loan back from the bank at a convenient price. While many students had problems servicing the loans—their degrees did not get them the jobs of their dreams—banks made buckets of money.

In the health care arena, the vouchers system implemented by the Chicago Boys was preserved, but there was a new emphasis on preventive medicine. In 2005 a new health care program called Acceso Universal a Garantías Explícitas (AUGE; Universal Access to Explicit Guarantees) was unveiled by President Lagos that guaranteed coverage for a series of common and recurrent health conditions, including breast cancer and appendicitis. With time, additional conditions were added, and by 2020 close to one hundred conditions were included. The initial public reaction to the program was very positive, but as time went by, and as inevitable waiting lists developed, criticisms became pervasive. Opponents to the model pointed out that Chile had a segregated health system, in which the rich received First World coverage (partially) financed with taxes, via vouchers, while the poor had to wait for months to have surgery or receive other types of treatment.

Concertación leaders were also committed to introducing legal changes in the social values sphere, including those regarding divorce law and the death penalty. Pregnant girls were allowed to stay in school—previously they had been expelled and could only get an equivalence certificate by going to night school—and in 2004, and despite strong opposition by conservatives and the Catholic Church, a divorce law was passed; Chile was the last Western country to approve divorce legislation. Conversely, the Catholic Church supported the Lagos government when in 2001 it abolished the death penalty.

Around 2007, the first pensions were paid to workers enrolled in the new individual savings system. It immediately became apparent that there was a serious problem: pensions were much lower than what workers anticipated and what they thought they had been promised. On average, pensions under the new system were around 25 percent of final years' wages, significantly lower than the 75 percent retirees expected. During her first administration, President Michelle Bachelet (2006–10) decided to tackle this issue by implementing a "solidarity pillar" characterized by a government supplement that declined with the level of pensions financed with personal savings. Only those in the lower

60th percentile of the income distribution scale were eligible for the government transfer. Yet no steps were taken toward solving the fundamental flaws in the military's pensions law. It maintained a very low 10 percent rate of contribution and did not address the fact that a large portion of Chileans (approximately 50 percent) worked in the informal labor market and thus did not make any contributions to their individual savings accounts. As it turned out, the very low pensions—critics called them "miserable pensions"—became a rallying point for protesters starting in 2006; replacing the system by a government-run scheme became one of the most important demands made during the 2019 revolt. (For more detail on pensions, see chapter 14).

The left-of-center governments continued with the privatization process that was initiated in 1974 and expanded in the second phase of the Chicago Boys' reforms. During President Patricio Aylwin's administration, the government sold the remaining blocks of shares of emblematic companies kept in the hands of the government by the military. During Eduardo Frei Ruiz-Tagle's government, further privatizations took place, including the sale of government stock in the national airline, Línea Aerea Nacional, and several electrical generating companies. Under Ricardo Lagos, the remaining shares of the national electrical company, Empresa Nacional de Electricidad S.A., were sold to the private sector, as well as 100 percent of water processing and sewage companies. In contrast with the time of Pinochet's dictatorship, these sales were at relatively high prices.

The Fiscal Rule and Taxes

One of the most admired policies of the left-of-center governments was the enactment of a "fiscal rule." For a long time, most Latin American countries—including Chile—ran very damaging procyclical fiscal policies.[1] When the economy faced a boom—many times generated by high international commodity prices—fiscal expenditure increased, amplifying the expansive phase of the cycle; when international prices turned against the country and the economy slowed down, so did public-sector expenditure, making the contraction even worse. Basic economic theory indicates that the optimal fiscal policy is exactly the opposite: the public sector should build reserves during the years of economic expansions, and these should be used during recessions in order to reduce the impact on employment and consumption of the lean years.

During Ricardo Lagos's administration, finance minister Nicolás Eyzaguirre and the director of the budget, Mario Marcel (who would be appointed minister of finance by President Gabriel Boric in 2022), developed a policy that resulted in an automatic countercyclical fiscal policy. The mechanism was quite sophisticated and relied on an estimation—by an independent board of experts—of the expected "normal price of copper" in the future. This general approach was celebrated in international forums, and several countries, including New Zealand, considered adopting it.

In order to finance some of its social projects, the Lagos administration enacted a new scheme for taxing large mining companies. The new tax on mining had a sliding schedule, and it was levied on gross margins. Lagos's preference had been a straight royalty tax on the total value of sales. At the end, however, it became clear that opposition from the conservatives in the National Congress of Chile was unwavering and that the royalty tax could not be passed.

Since the return of democracy, taxes were debated time and again. The Left—including presidents Lagos and Bachelet—argued that tax revenues were too low and that they must be increased in order to finance the expansion of social programs. The Right, on the other hand, claimed that corporate and value-added tax rates were already higher than in the average OECD country, and that total tax revenues were approximately equal, when properly measured, to the revenues OECD nations had when they were at Chile's stage of development. Higher taxes, they stated, would discourage investment and reduce the rate of growth. Since the dictatorship, Chile had had an "integrated" tax system that avoided double taxation. Taxes paid at the corporate level were used as a tax credit by shareholders when they received dividends from these companies. During Michelle Bachelet's second term (2014–18), the system was partially disintegrated, meaning that only a fraction of taxes paid by corporations could be used by individuals as tax credits. Despite these efforts, by 2022, Chile's total tax revenue was approximately 21 percent of gross domestic product (GDP), while the OECD average was 31 percent. This "tax gap" became an important topic during the 2017 and 2021 presidential campaigns, with Gabriel Boric promising a major reform aimed at taxing the wealthy and increasing total tax revenues by one-third. (For details, see chapter 15.)

Latin America's Brightest Star: Accolades and Scorecards

By 2015 Chile was the undisputable economic leader of Latin America. It was the country with the highest income per capita, the lowest incidence of poverty, and the best overall social indicators.[2] Analysts talked about the "Chilean miracle," and policy makers from around the world studied the path that had taken the country from the seventh position in the region, in terms of income per person, to a clear number one. Of course, there were still critics from the international Left who continued to talk about the social and human costs incurred during the dictatorship. But most analysts considered these complaints to be overly partisan. The fact of the matter, most observers opined, was that in the mid-1980s Chile, Costa Rica, and Ecuador had an almost identical income per person, and that a generation later, Chile's income per capita was more than double that of Ecuador and 40 percent higher than that of Costa Rica (see figure 11.1). Further, according to the United Nations Human Development Index (HDI), in 2020 Chile was ranked number one in the region in terms of social conditions. In sum, it was argued in international seminars, essays in academic journals, and newspaper articles, Chile's economic and social performance had been fantastic since the return of democracy.

Accolades and admiration for Chile's market-oriented development strategy came from all over the political spectrum. In 1994 Bruce Maclaury, the president of the Brookings Institution, wrote that Chile's reforms provided a blueprint for reforms in nations from the former Soviet bloc: "Chile has emerged as the nation with the fastest growing economy in Latin America. This surge in growth followed one of the most extensive economic reform programs ever undertaken in a developing country. . . . Chilean economic policies are often held up to the countries of eastern Europe and much of the rest of Latin America as a model." [3]

In 2007 Manuel Castells, a prominent progressive academic who eventually became a cabinet member in Spain's socialist government, said that Chile's "democratic [neo]liberal inclusive model . . . [is] the only success story of Latin American development."[4] In 2012, and from the other end of the political spectrum, Daniel Mitchell and Julia Morriss from the promarkets Cato Institute argued that Chile had become the "Latin Tiger."[5] With time, a growing number of analysts referred to the strategy pursued by the leftist Concertación coalition as "neoliberalism with a human face." Harvard University professor Robert Barro noted that the policies of the new democratic administration of Patricio Aylwin reminded him of "Pinochet with a human face."[6]

In 2019, Freedom House, a nonpartisan nongovernmental organization, gave Chile the highest marks among Latin American nations in terms of "global freedom." In addition, Chile was the only South American country given, also by Freedom House, the highest marks for "global press freedom." In this arena Chile was ranked higher than the advanced Mediterranean countries Greece, Italy, and Spain. In 2020, the *Economist* classified Chile as one of three Latin American countries that were "full democracies"; the other countries were Costa Rica and Uruguay.[7] Figure 11.1 shows the evolution of income per capita (in international dollars) for Chile, Costa Rica, and Ecuador between 1980 and 2019. These data provide a stark illustration of Chile's rapid growth during the period. As noted earlier, in the early 2000s Chile became the country with the highest GDP per person in the Latin American region. It held the number one position until 2019, when it was surpassed by Panama.

Tables 11.3 and 11.4 present a series of indicators that summarize economic and social progress after the return to democratic rule in 1990. The data in table 11.3 show the rapid increase in income per capita, the convergence of inflation to advanced countries' level (around 3 percent), the rise in real wages, and the fall in interest rates toward the international benchmark. Perhaps the most impressive accomplishment is that

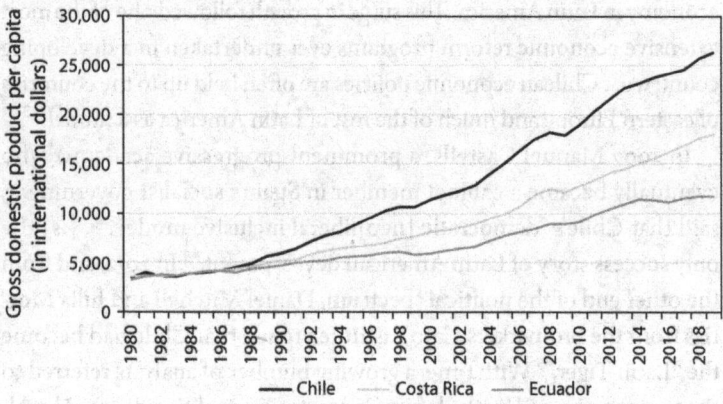

FIGURE 11.1. Chile, Ecuador, and Costa Rica: gross domestic product
per capita, 1980–2019, in international dollars (purchasing power parity)
Source: International Monetary Fund (n.d.)

income per capita tripled between 1985 and 2019. Table 11.4 includes a
battery of social indicators that also tell a story of accomplishments and
success. Extreme poverty, as measured by the World Bank metric of 3.2
dollars per person (in 2011 international dollars), all but disappeared.
And although inequality (measured by the Gini coefficient) was still
high, it declined gradually during the period. (For a discussion on the
reliability of inequality data, however, see chapter 13.) These figures indicate that starting in 2010 Chile ranked number one in the region on
quality of education (PISA test score), and in human development
(United Nations HDI metric). Moreover, life expectancy increased by
almost ten years between 1985 and 2020—from 71.7 to 80.2 years. This
simple and remarkable fact played an important role in the generalized
dissatisfaction with the pension system based on individual savings accounts. With an unchanged age of retirement (sixty years for women
and sixty-five for men), and the same rate of contributions at 10 percent
to fund an old-age piggy bank, an increase in life expectancy necessarily
meant lower pensions. (For a detailed discussion, see chapter 14.)

As may be seen in table 11.4, the total number of students in university and vocational institutes went from less than 200,000 in 1985 to

TABLE 11.3. Economic Indicators Scorecard, 1985–2020

Indicator	1985	1990	1995	2000	2010	2015	2019–20
GDP per capita, constant prices, purchasing power parity	7,544	9,592	12,841	15,118	20,551	23,625	22,150
Inflation, end-of-period consumer prices	26.8	27.2	8.3	4.6	2.9	4.4	2.9
Unemployment rate	15	7.8	7.4	9.7	8.3	6.3	10.8
Real wage	100	115.9	146.2	161.3	199.8	225.2	245.2
Tax revenue (% of GDP)	18.1	13.3	15.1	16.2	17.4	17.4	17.8
Real interest rate (%)	-1.2	21.6	5.8	10.1	-3.9	0.5	1.8
Current account balance (% of GDP)	-8.2	-1.5	-1.8	-1.1	1.4	-2.4	1.4
Exports of goods and services (% of GDP)	26.3	32.5	28.6	30.5	37.7	29.4	31.5

Sources: "GDP per capita, constant prices, purchasing power parity," "Inflation, end-of-period consumer rate," "Unemployment rate," and "Current account balance (% GDP)" from the International Monetary Fund (n.d.); "Inflation, end-of-period consumer prices," "Tax revenue (% of GDP)," "Real interest rate (%)," and "Exports of goods and services (% of GDP)" from the World Bank (n.d.); "Real wage" from the Instituto Nacional de Estadísticas (INE, n.d.; National Institute of Statistics).

TABLE 11.4. Social Indicators Scorecard, 1985–2020

Indicator	1985	1990	1995	2000	2010	2015	2019–2020
HDI world ranking—official (ranking in reports)		38/160	31/174	38/173	45/169	38/188	43/189
HDI world ranking—data (author calculations)		50/144	44/174	49/174	48/188	43/188	43/189
HDI Latin America ranking—official (ranking in reports)		4/33	3/33	3/33	3/32	1/33	1/33
HDI Latin America ranking—data (author calculations)		3/25	3/25	4/29	3/33	1/33	1/33
Gini coefficient	0.562[a]	0.572	0.564[d]	0.528	0.47[d]	0.444	0.444[c]
Income share held by highest 10%	45.4[a]	47	45.9[d]	42.6	38.2[d]	36.1	36.3[c]
Poverty head count ratio at US$3.20 a day (2011 purchasing power parity; % of population)	28.4[a]	22.2	15.2[d]	12.1	4[d]	1	0.7[c]
School enrollment, secondary	667,797	719,819	679,165	822,946	1,020,687	910,239	922,892
School enrollment, secondary (% population ages 15–18)	68.6	74.0	69.8	79.8	99.0	92.1	93.4
Higher education enrollment	196,609	245,408	337,604	435,830	940,164	1,165,906	1,151,727
Higher education enrollment (% population ages 25 and above)	3.3	3.6	4.4	5.1	9.0	10.2	9.0
PISA math—world ranking				44/53[b]	45/59[d]	50/73	60/79[d]
PISA math—Latin America ranking				2/6[b]	2/8[d]	1/10	1/10[d]
PISA reading—world ranking				36 out of 41	42 out of 59[d]	42 out of 73	44 out of 78[d]
PISA reading—Latin America ranking				3 out of 5	1 out of 8[d]	1 out of 10	1 out of 10[d]
Life expectancy at birth, total (years)	71.7	73.5	75	76.4	78.8	79.6	80.2

Sources: HDI from the UNDP (n.d.); "Gini coefficient," "Income share held by highest 10%," "Poverty head count ratio at US$3.20 a day (2011 purchasing power parity; % of population)," and "Life expectancy at birth, total (years)" from the World Bank (n.d.); "School enrollment, secondary," "School enrollment, secondary (% population ages 15–18)," "Higher education enrollment," and "Higher education enrollment (% population ages 25 and above)" from Díaz, Lüders, and Wagner (2016), Datos.gob (n.d.), Subsecretaría de Educación Superior (n.d.), and INE (n.d.); PISA from the OECD (n.d.-a).

[a] Corresponds to 1987.

[b] Corresponds to 2006.

[c] Corresponds to 2017.

[d] Corresponds to data from the previous year.

almost 1.2 million in 2019, a sixfold increase. Yet there was a dark side to this accomplishment. Student debt skyrocketed, and many graduates could not find employment in their fields of study; the number of journalists and psychologists (to mention just two professions) who were unemployed, worked as salespeople, or drove a cab or drove for Uber increased rapidly. Scores of young men and women felt cheated and began to question a system that had promised them and their families that if they worked hard and became educated—that is, if they accumulated "human capital"—they could get ahead and move decisively into the comfortable ranks of the professional and managerial classes. Most of the underemployed were first-generation university graduates who, having believed the "pull yourself up by your bootstraps" story, had gotten into debt to pay the (high) tuition bill charged by private universities that, on paper, could not make a profit. Student debts to private banks piled up at a rapid clip, adding to frustration and criticism and helping the Far Left recruit more and more followers.

Ricardo Lagos and Neoliberalism

In October 2005, at an international meeting in Salamanca, Spain, Hernán Somerville, the head of the Chilean business-sector organization—an institution like the Business Roundtable in the United States—said, "My businessmen love [president] Ricardo Lagos. . . . They really have a tremendous admiration for him."[8] Somerville was sincere and telling the truth. The business elite loved Ricardo Lagos for a very simple and powerful reason: during his presidency (2000–6) policies that propelled national growth and companies' profits were put in place. To be fair, that was also the case during the administrations of Center-Left presidents Patricio Aylwin (1990–94) and Eduardo Frei Ruiz-Tagle (1994–2000), and during the first administration of Michelle Bachelet (2006–10).

Just as the business community—and especially the major conglomerates—loved President Lagos, the incipient Far Left detested him and deemed him responsible for most of the country's ills. Far-Left leaders disregarded the courageous role Lagos played in the resistance against the dictatorship, including the time when, putting his life at risk, he openly denounced Pinochet's violations of human rights on TV. For example, on September 2, 2016, Gabriel Boric, the student activist who would be elected president in 2021, declared in an interview that the malaise and political crisis that had gripped the nation were due to the policies of Ricardo Lagos.[9]

Twenty years after he was elected to the presidency, in November 2019, Ricardo Lagos finished writing the second volume of his autobiography. The story starts with the 1988 plebiscite that put an end to Pinochet's ambitions of eight additional years in power. It continues with Lagos's role as a cabinet member during the first two democratic governments—he served as minister of education and minister of public works—and ends up with his experience as president (2000–6). Before sending the manuscript to the printer, Lagos wrote a lengthy preface in which he reflected on the 2019 insurgency and on the causes behind people's anger and dissatisfaction.

Lagos's main point was that the revolt responded to the inequities of the neoliberal system—a system that, he argued, was maintained despite his own personal efforts to introduce deep changes to Chile's economic, political, and social regimes. The problem, he observed, was that Pinochet's constitution was full of constraints and "locks" that impeded changing some of the most important legislation. In particular, he asserted, it was not possible to put in place a system with universal social services, as opposed to those targeting the poor. He went on to say that his ideal system, the one he could not enact because of the Chilean Constitution's rigidities, was one in which every citizen got a minimal level of "civilized social rights," an idea he attributed to Italian philosopher Norberto Bobbio.[10]

Lagos's argument is appealing and sounds plausible, but it is not completely correct; it is an attempt to revisit history after the facts, an effort to come out on the side of newer generations and to distance himself from the actions taken by the Concertación governments—including, paradoxically, his own. Of course, it was difficult to change the constitution—although, as I have noted, major amendments were passed in 2005 precisely during the Lagos administration—but the hurdle for constitutional change is not the complete story. As it turns out, many—if not most—of the grievances voiced by the demonstrators during the massive and violent 2019 uprising were unrelated to constitutional constraints; they were demonstrating against policies enthusiastically pushed, endorsed, and passed by successive Concertación administrations and were largely unrelated to what the constitution and existing laws said or what the Chicago Boys thought. The truth of the matter is that, in 2019, demonstrators rose up against policies that Concertación governments had voluntarily, willingly, and with gusto implemented out of their own volition. As I have noted in the preceding chapters, many of these were promarkets policies that consolidated and significantly deepened the Chicago Boys' model and contributed to Chile's remarkable economic success in the period 1990–2015.

Consider the following three policies that were at the center of demonstrators' demands during the revolt; all three were unrelated to the 1980 constitution (for a more detailed discussion of the most important criticisms of the Concertación policies by the new generation of Far-Left activists, see chapter 12):

1. Demonstrators demanded the forgiveness of students' debt and an end to the education loans system put in place by the Lagos administration. The original policy of granting, through the banking sector, loans to higher education students was the brainchild of Ricardo Lagos's minister of education, Sergio Bitar, a politician who had been one of the youngest cabinet members during Salvador Allende's presidency. This policy had no relation to mandates or restrictions in the 1980 Chilean Constitution. Notably, the idea was in The Brick, but had not been executed during the dictatorship; its implementation had to wait for a left-of-center government.

2. Protesters revolted against toll roads operated by private companies. As minister of transportation, and later as president, Ricardo Lagos executed a massive and impressive infrastructure investments plan based on concessions to the private sector. From a legal point of view, the contracts signed between the government and private operators were based on the precepts developed by

José Piñera in 1981 for the mining sector. Private firms built roads, ports, hospitals, jails, and airports and ran them for a fee during a predetermined number of years. Protesters rejected the (high) fees and the fact that investors and operators obtained high rates of return by providing social services. Again, these policies, which for many years were considered to be efficient and highly beneficial for the country, had no relation to the constitution. Charging citizens to use roads, even in major cities such as Santiago, was, purely, a Concertación idea. (To be fair, the idea was in Milton Friedman's book *Capital and Freedom*, but the Chicago Boys had never thought of implementing it in Chile.)

3. In 2019 the protesters argued that Chile had given up its sovereignty by opening unilaterally to international trade and by signing free trade agreements with a myriad of countries. They claimed that these policies had resulted in an "extractivist" development strategy through which Chile mostly exported commodities and did not manufacture sophisticated or complex products. The policies proposed by Gabriel Boric during the presidential election were aimed at reversing this situation (for details, see chapter 15). To be sure, a central goal of the Chicago Boys was liberalizing trade and establishing a very low and uniform 10 percent import tariff. But nothing in the constitution or in the legal structure created by the Chicago Boys forced the Concertación coalition to push openness further. It was under those governments—and especially during the Lagos administration—that Chile went on a binge of free trade agreements. This policy, which lowered the effective import tariff to about 3 percent and made Chile one of the most open countries in the world, helped to generate an era of exports-led growth that propelled Chile to the top of the Latin American economies. The strategy was voluntarily pushed by the Concertación and was completely unrelated to the constitution.

What is true, however, is that there was one constraint in Pinochet's constitution that could not be changed during the 2005 reforms: it continued to be difficult to raise taxes, as supermajorities in both chambers of the Congress were required. In his autobiography, Lagos points out that during his administration no effort was made to change personal or corporate taxes; the focus was on reducing tax evasion and elusion. In order to achieve that goal new powers were given to the national tax enforcer. President Michelle Bachelet, who succeeded Ricardo Lagos in 2006, did negotiate a major tax reform with the conservative opposition. Despite it, tax collections in Chile continued to be low, at approximately 21 percent of GDP, a full 10 percentage points below the OECD average.[11]

Of course, it is possible to change one's views with the passage of time, and it is understandable that in 2020 Lagos distanced himself from those policies that were labeled *neoliberal*. But, in order to have a complete historical picture it is important to go back to 2005 when the Congress passed a long list of constitutional reforms. At the time, President Ricardo Lagos said, "The new [constitutional] text, reflects today the unity of all Chileans. . . . Today we celebrate in Chile a day of joy and unity, a reunion with our history. As President of all Chileans, I thank all citizens that fought for a Constitution consistent with our spirit of freedom, [and] I thank all [political] parties."[12]

12

Grievances, Abuses, Complaints, and Protests

ON OCTOBER 18, 2019, the elite found out the hard way that everything was not well in Latin America's "oasis," as President Sebastián Piñera had referred to Chile in an interview with the *Financial Times*.[1] In the months that followed, one of the most repeated phrases by analysts and pundits of all stripes was "We didn't see it coming." As it turned out, there had been several signs and warnings that, in spite of the overall economic success of the last four decades, there was a growing *malestar* (malaise) that affected a growing segment of society.

The *malestar* hypothesis was first put forward in 1998 in a report by the United Nations Development Programme (UNDP) that emphasized the role of "human security" in determining social and political sentiments in Chile. Human security was defined as "the way people live and breathe in a society where they can exercise different life options, including having access to different markets . . . in a safe and secure way, with some confidence that existing opportunities will not disappear tomorrow."[2] The UNDP computed two human security indexes: one based on "objective" data, such as the level of income, and the availability of education, health services, and old age-pensions; and the second constructed on the bases of people's "subjective" feelings, fears, and perceptions.[3] The most important finding was that there was a significant discrepancy between the two indicators. Despite objective and real improvements in the quality of life, including the rapid increase in wages, the improvement in social conditions, the expansion of education, and the very rapid reduction in poverty, large numbers of Chileans lived in fear of retrogressing both socially and economically and rejoining the ranks of the poor. The report also noted that although the sentiment of unhappiness was, at the time (1998), only latent, there was the risk that it could eventually move from a dormant stage to a more explosive one, creating serious political upheaval and dislocations.

The political and economic establishment dismissed the UNDP report as being little more than political propaganda. For example, José Brunner, a former cabinet member during the administration of President Eduardo Frei Ruiz-Tagle (1994–2000) and a sociologist revered by the Center-Left elite, argued that fear and apprehension were not unique to Chile, nor were they the result of the economic reforms. These were common sentiments in every modernization process. The problem, Brunner posited, was not neoliberalism, but rapid change.[4] He sympathized with economist Joseph Schumpeter, whose idea of "creative destruction" in capitalistic systems masterfully encapsulated the notion that although progress has a dark side, the benefits of moving forward exceed the costs by wide margins. Brunner also pointed out that low turnout during elections—a phenomenon identified in the UNDP report as a sign of disaffection—reflected that people were satisfied with their own lives and did not see reasons to get deeply involved in politics.[5]

The first signs that people like José Brunner were mistaken and that maybe, after all, there was such a thing as a growing sense of unhappiness came in 2006, during President Michelle Bachelet's first administration. Secondary students demanded major changes in legislation, improvements in public schools infrastructure, a reduction in the cost of taking the university admissions test, and reduced fares in public transportation. At the center of their protests was the rejection of an educational system that relied strongly on for-profit schools—a system that, according to the protesters, created segregation and class division and perpetuated inequality. The government was slow to respond and argued that the demand for a reduced fare in public transportation was impossible to fulfill, as it would worsen public finances by some $US300 million a year. The students' demonstrations quickly turned violent, and the government deployed the antiriot police force. Clashes between the police and masked protesters who threw rocks and Molotov cocktails became a daily affair in downtown Santiago and in several provincial cities. In May 2006, student leaders called for a national students' strike, and several public high schools were taken over by adolescents who locked themselves in and swore not to leave until their demands were met. Soon the national teachers' union, the Colegio de Profesores, joined in the protest, as did university students who, among other things, demanded the forgiveness of their student loan debt.

As the protests grew, so did the list of demands. Demonstrators were now protesting the government's environmental policy and demanding changes in the old-age pensions system and the labor law—the Plan Laboral, as amended during the Concertación governments—that still imposed restrictions on unions' actions. By the end of May, over a hundred schools were on strike, and about thirty-five were controlled by students who erected barricades to impede teachers, administrators, and the police from entering the buildings. Demonstrations and clashes between protesters and police continued throughout the year. Thousands of adolescents were detained and taken to court, and there was millions of dollars' worth of property damage. At the end of the year, the student movement had gained significant strength and political force, while the government, led by the first Socialist Party female president, had lost credibility and support.

During the years that followed, groups of citizens organized themselves to demonstrate against the model. At first the demonstrations were small, but little by little they became massive. One of the most vocal groups protested the pension system, which, as noted, was based on individual savings accounts, and pointed out that actual pensions were much lower than what the military government had promised in 1981. They further claimed that old-age pensions were a social right and that, as such, they should not be subject to the rigors and risks of business and financial activities; they protested the fact that pension savings were run by for-profit firms that obtained returns that greatly exceeded the returns of the pension funds themselves. Increasingly, demonstrators demanded the end of the individual account and the adoption of a traditional pay-as-you-go system run by the government. (For details, see chapter 14.)

After a period of relative calm, political turmoil returned in May 2011, during conservative president Sebastián Piñera's first administration. Once again, the for-profit nature of the educational system was strongly questioned. Students pointed out that even though for-profit universities were prohibited by a law passed in 1981 by the military, the private sector continued to take advantage of the system and was making lots of money in the process. Once again demonstrations became violent, and once again other groups joined in support of the student movement. In contrast with 2006, this time the demands were broader and included nationalizing copper mines, ending gender discrimination, creating a national health system, and closing all coal-powered electric plants. The overall theme of the demonstrations was to end the neoliberal model instituted by the dictatorship. In April 2013, the minister of education, Harald Beyer—an economist close to the Chicago Boys—was accused in the Chilean Congress of dereliction of duties for not making sure that institutions of higher education did not profit either directly or indirectly from their educational mission. A month later, the Senate approved the charges, and Beyer was forced to step down. One of the most articulated, fierce, and charismatic student leaders was Gabriel Boric, a young law student born in Punta Arenas, one of the southernmost cities in the world, a city that faces the rough waters of the Strait of Magellan.

The *malestar* thesis was hotly debated among Chilean politicians and academics. On one side were progressive scholars, many of them coalescing around the UNDP and its pessimistic view of social and political conditions. On the other side were conservative, promarkets defenders of the model and of the Chicago Boys, as well as Concertación politicians. A prominent voice among this group was none other than Harald Beyer, the former minister of education, who was now the director of the think tank Centro de Estudios Públicos and who declared that there was not such a thing as *malestar*. Both sides conducted surveys and interviews, released reports, and presented their views in seminars and conferences.

In June 2017 the UNDP published a new report titled *Desiguales* (Inequalities), in which the authors argued that inequality in Chile had many dimensions. While in the previous decade income inequality had declined somewhat, other forms of inequality, including access to public goods and amenities, had remained very high. In addition, education and health services continued to be segmented, with the rich living in a completely different world from that of the average citizen. More important, perhaps, the report noted that there was a high degree of inequality in the way people interacted with each other—an inequality rooted in racism, segregation, and classism. The authors also argued that despite the emphasis that the Chicago Boys had placed on merit, education, and human capital accumulation, Chile continued to be a country where a small elite of people—mostly men—that had attended a handful of prep schools (mostly Catholic) and two universities (Católica and the Universidad de Chile), controlled political and economic power.

Around the same time, the promarkets Centro de Estudios Públicos published a book titled ¿Malestar en Chile? in which, on the basis of surveys, it was argued that despite the tensions that came with every modernization process—including some cases of abuse and collusion, which are discussed below—most Chileans were happy with the way they were living their lives and appreciated the benefits of the model. The coordinating author of the report, economist Ricardo González, went as far as to posit that what was happening in Chile had nothing to do with unhappiness or malaise; on the contrary, citizens acknowledged that, overall, they were benefiting from life's comforts. Another author of the report was Vittorio Corbo, an economist close to the Chicago Boys, who was governor of the Central Bank between 2003 and 2007 and who regularly appeared in the popular press in defense of the model.

As Ricardo González declared, "Clearly, we don't see 'malestar.'" Using the results from a survey in which a large cross-section of people was interviewed, he added, "The report shows that 82 percent of those surveyed in 2015 were satisfied with their lives in general; 20 percentage points higher than in 1995. Furthermore, satisfaction grew with respect to work and leisure activities, as well as with respect to health and financial matters." He concluded that President Michelle Bachelet had been wrong when she said that inequality was the source of unrest and unhappiness.[6]

A Chronicle of Collusion and Abuse

Starting in 2007, a succession of major collusion cases involving firms controlled by some of the wealthiest families in the country added to the notion that the "neoliberal model" was at the service of the powerful and ignored "real" people.[7]

The first major case involved three pharmacy chains that in 2007, and after a prolonged and costly price war, increased prices for two hundred prescription drugs in a coordinated way.[8] In 2011, and while the pharmacies' cases were moving through the courts, the Fiscalía Nacional Económica (National Economic Prosecutor's Office) accused the three largest producers of chicken of colluding through an agreement to restrict output and share the market. The judicial investigation unearthed a decades-old scheme, going back to at least 1994. Overall output was capped, and the largest firm, Agrosuper, was assigned 61 percent of total sales. The second largest, Ariztía, got 30 percent, and the smallest one, Don Pollo, had 9 percent. The fact that chicken was Chileans' main source of protein added to the political scandal and to the notion that by having a light regulatory system the model allowed large companies to abuse consumers. The competition court fined the three chicken producers for a total of US$60 million. The court also ruled that three of the main supermarket chains had been accessories to the collusive scheme and fined them for a total of US$12 million.

The third big collusion case erupted in October 2015, when the Fiscalía Nacional Económica charged Chile's two major toilet paper producers of illegally agreeing to fix prices. The fact that the dominant firm was part of the Matte Group, a conglomerate controlled by one of the oldest and more traditional families in the country, was particularly shocking. The scandal was such that Eliodoro Matte, the patriarch of the family, had to resign as chairman of the board of overseers of the Centro de Estudios Públicos, the institution founded by Sergio de Castro and Jorge Cauas that in 1992 had released the Chicago Boys' blueprint, The Brick, in book form.

Supporters of the Chilean model argued that the surfacing of these cases was proof that regulatory institutions were working as designed, making sure that markets remained competitive. Not surprisingly, critics of the model had a different view. They pointed out that these cases were possibly just the tip of the iceberg and conjectured that hundreds of other cases of unfair competition and abuse of consumers went undetected. But the main issue raised by the critics was that despite the investigation proving beyond any doubt that there had been collusion, not a single executive involved in planning and executing the schemes served any prison time. This, they pointed out, contrasted sharply with the type of sentencing—usually jail time—received by petty thieves and by those who broke laws that protect private property. According to the model's detractors, this showed that neoliberalism had even invaded the judicial system and mentioned Gary Becker's work on criminal justice and the "law and economics" legal doctrine developed at the University of Chicago by Ronald Coase, Aaron Director, and Richard Posner, among others.

The rapid accumulation of household debt—between 2000 and 2021, it doubled from 25 to 53 percent of gross domestic product—was another source of apprehension and concern. Critics of the model argued that a system based on the "marketization of everything"—as philosopher Michael Sandel had referred to neoliberalism—required consumers to always purchase more and more (mostly useless) goods. Furthermore, they said, consumerism was pushed by unscrupulous advertising agencies that glamorized the possession of material goods, to the detriment of culture and the high arts.

In June 2011 a major scandal involving the large retail chain La Polar exploded. The company served a middle-class segment and had many locations throughout the country. Management informed the regulator that for some years the company had been underreporting nonperforming consumer credit. There were two angles to the case, and both were damaging for the reputation of the model. On the one hand, the balance sheet showed a healthy, profitable company, while the company had struggled for years. When the news became known, the stock lost 98 percent of its value, wiping out the life savings of many small investors and affecting millions of workers who owned, through their individual retirement accounts, stock in the company. Second, customers' debts were periodically restructured under new terms without the clients being consulted or informed. Many middle-class families did not know that their debts were growing at a rapid clip—interest rates were as high as 22 percent in real terms per year. Once they found out about the scheme, they felt a combination of rage and anxiety. Once again, the Left accused the neoliberal system of abusing people and of impunity.

Little by little the cases of abuse, collusion, price rigging, use of inside information, tax evasion, artificially inflated balance sheets, bribery, and corruption added to the notion among some groups (and especially among young university students) that things were not quite right and that the narrative of transparency, competition in a leveled playing field, and meritocracy was mostly an illusion. Many suspected that the problem involved not only the business elite but also left-of-center politicians from the Concertación coalition—politicians who despite their prodistribution and equity rhetoric had been captured by the private sector and the corporate world. It is not clear whether *captured* is the right term, but what is true is that many former cabinet members and senior officials in the Aylwin, Frei, Lagos, and Bachelet administrations joined the boards of the largest corporations and conglomerates—boards with high pay from an international comparative perspective, and with numerous perks. From those positions they lobbied in favor of corporations and the large conglomerates and tended to play down the plight of consumers and workers.[9]

In the early 2000s, it became apparent that an increasingly important area of conflict was the Araucanía, the area in the south of Chile where the Mapuche people had lived since before the arrival of the Spanish conquistadores. A group of Mapuche activists demanded the creation of an autonomous region, with its own system of governance based on ancestral customs and traditions, an area where their language, Mapudungun, would be taught in schools and used in courts and other state institutions. They demanded that the state return large swaths of land and compensate them for suffering, humiliation, and discrimination. The Mapuche cause resonated with young people, and the Far-Left Frente Amplio (Broad Front) made it a central component of its political platform. During the massive protests of 2019, many demonstrators carried Mapuche flags and chanted in favor of the Indigenous cause. The November 15, 2019, concordat that resulted in the writing of a new constitution gave a special role to the Indigenous population in the drafting of the new charter. Seventeen out of the 155 seats in the body in charge of drafting the new document were reserved for members of the First Nations (see chapter 15).

In 2003 a new campaign finance law was passed. Following the example of the United States, limits were set on contributions to candidates for public office by individuals and corporations. A novel aspect of Chile's legislation was that those contributing could decide whether they wanted their contributions to be public or to keep them anonymous to everyone, including the candidate. The idea was that it was not easy to ask for favors if there was no proof that a contribution to a particular election committee had been made. In 2015 it was found out that several large firms had gone around the law and contributed massive amounts of funds to politicians on both sides of the aisle. The procedure was simple: members of a campaign were "hired" by the companies and received "professional fees" that were, in reality, campaign contributions. The company wrote off the expenses from its earnings and got a tax benefit, and the recipient paid income tax for the contribution. As it turned out, the company that provided the largest amount of illegal campaign funds was Sociedad Química y Minera de Chile (SQM; Chemical and Mining Society of Chile), a firm that dominated lithium production in the country. The fact that SQM's main shareholder was Julio Ponce Lerou, Augusto Pinochet's former son-in-law, added to the sensation that the powerful and wealthy had special access to politicians, and that after thirty years of democracy, the same groups continued to control the nations' destiny.

Chile in 2019: Two Points of View

Figure 12.1 presents data on Chile's economic growth between 1970 and 2020. Figures 12.2 and 12.3 display information on the percentage of the population living below the poverty line and on the Gini coefficient,

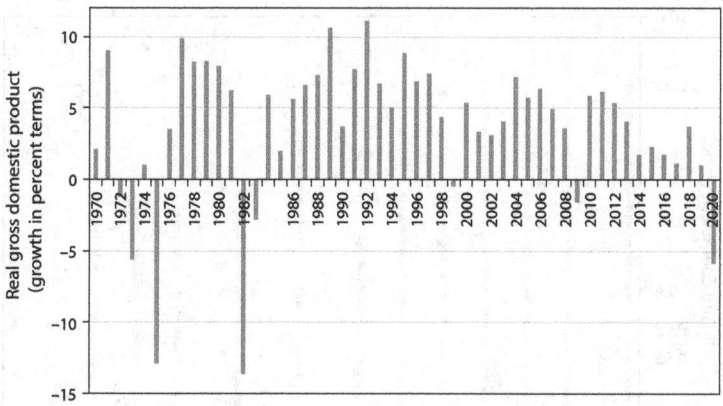

FIGURE 12.1. Annual real gross domestic product growth in Chile, 1970–2020
Sources: Banco Central de Chile (2001); International Monetary Fund (n.d.)

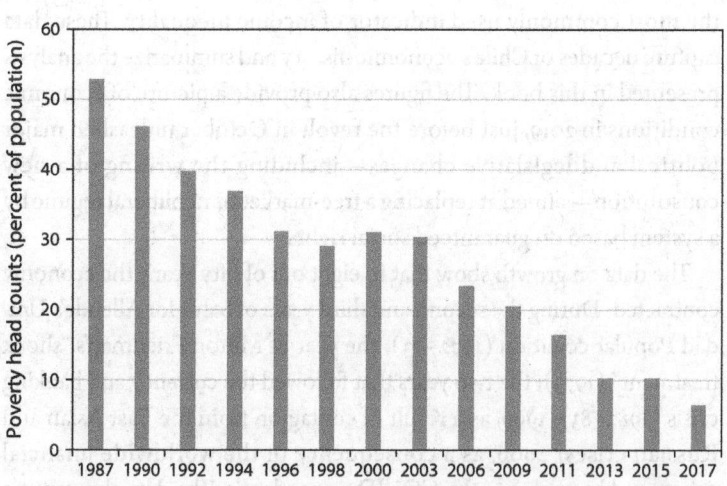

FIGURE 12.2. Percentage of the population living below the poverty line in Chile, 1987–2017, measured as anyone living with less than $5.50 a day (2011 purchasing power parity). *Source*: World Bank (n.d.)

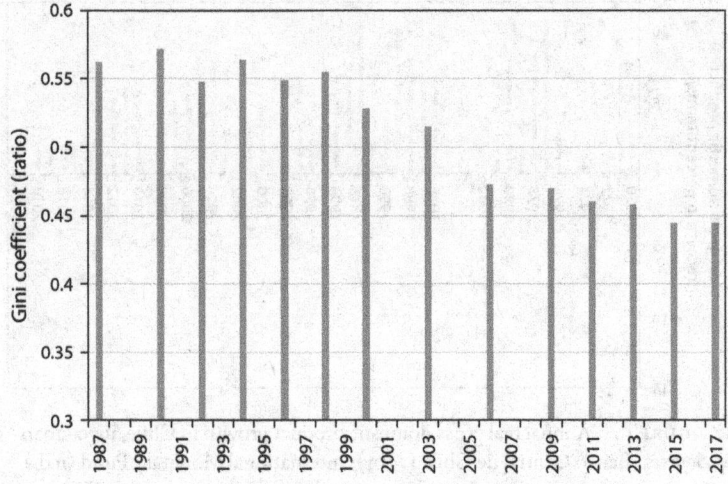

FIGURE 12.3. Chile and inequality: the Gini coefficient, 1987–2017
Source: World Bank (n.d.)

the most commonly used indicator of income inequality. These data capture decades of Chile's economic history and summarize the analysis presented in this book. The figures also provide a picture of economic conditions in 2019, just before the revolt in October unleashed major political and legislative changes—including the writing of a new constitution—aimed at replacing a free-market or neoliberal regime by a system based on guaranteed social rights.

The data on growth show that in eight out of fifty years, the economy contracted: During the second and third years of Salvador Allende's Unidad Popular coalition (1972–73); the year of Milton Friedman's "shock treatment" (1975); the two years that followed the currency and banking crisis (1982–83); 1999, as a result of contagion from the East Asian and Russian crises; 2009, as a consequence of the worldwide financial crisis; and 2020, due to the COVID-19 pandemic. The data also capture recoveries and growth accelerations, and show the rapid growth years of 1987–2010, when Chile was, by a significant margin, the best performing country in the Latin American region.

The data in figure 12.1 also demonstrate a gradual decline in the rate of expansion of the economy, suggesting that toward the end of the first decade of the twenty-first century the model entered a phase of declining returns. Average annual growth went from 7.5 percent in 1987–97, to 4.4 percent in 2000–2010, and to 3.0 percent in 2010–19. The most important factor behind this substantial deceleration was the decline in productivity growth, a problem rooted in a number of factors, including excessive centralization—almost 45 percent of the population live in the greater Santiago area—and a labor force that, in spite of several governments' efforts to improve human capital, lacked the skills required to continue expanding exports and adding value to those goods and services already exported.[10]

In mid-2019, just a few weeks before the revolt, there were two narratives about Chile: one of success and one of gloom. The first was built around the data presented in figures 12.1 and 12.2 and pointed out that Chile was the most prosperous country in Latin America. According to this story, this success was rooted in the promarkets reforms initiated by the Chicago Boys in 1974 and continued, with improvements, by the left-of-center Concertación coalition. There were, of course, some variations within this overall story: conservatives wanted more markets, fewer regulations, and lower taxes; in fact, they blamed remaining regulations for the deceleration of growth after 2010. Those on the Center Left, on the other hand, wanted to add more social democratic policies, without abandoning openness, markets, fiscal restraint, and competition.

Side by side with the "narrative of success" there was a completely different story, one pushed by progressive, Far-Left activists, most of them young politicians who had cut their teeth during the student protests of 2006 and 2011. This alternative narrative was based on the idea that the leaders of the democratic transition had sold out to big capital. This was the "narrative of gloom, malaise and inequality," the narrative that toward the end of the 2010s became dominant and allowed a Constitutional Convention dominated by gender, environment, and Indigenous activists to be held. In 2021, it was also the narrative that catapulted Gabriel Boric to the presidency. Chapters 13 and 14 analyze in detail two of the most important components of this narrative of discontent: inequality and low pensions. In chapter 15 I discuss how the Constitutional Convention overestimated the people's appetite for drastic change, and how, by going well beyond this narrative, their radical constitutional proposal was rejected in the "exit plebiscite" of September 4, 2022.

13

The Distributive Struggle

VERY FEW PEOPLE know the Chilean economy better than Arnold "Al" Harberger, the man rightly called the father of the Chicago Boys. Harberger traveled to Chile in 1955 with Theodore "Ted" Schultz and was involved in the Chile Project from day one. He often provided guidance to Chilean reformers and toured the world advising governments on how to put together economic packages that would generate results like those obtained in Chile. Yet despite his admiration for the Chicago Boys and his friendship with many of them, Harberger was always willing to acknowledge limitations, problems, and shortcomings in the policies advanced by his students. In his 2016 oral history, Harberger reflected on what he saw during his first trip to Chile in 1955 with respect to positions of influence, class origin, and inequality:

> So I go to Chile, and I'm here in the Union Club [a gentlemen's club] and in the agricultural sector they have the farm workers. They are *inquilinos*, [workers who] lived on the farm, like serfs in a way. . . . So I'm here in this Union Club and some big lunch with 10 people around the table or something like that and I innocently, truly innocently, asked how many members of this club are children of *inquilinos*. . . . They practically fell off their chairs; it was inconceivable to them that any would be. And I am sad to say that sometime after 2000 I was in the Union Club again and I asked the same question, a little bit snidely, and I had almost the same reaction. I mean in spite of the tremendous social mobility there has been in Chile, the great

advances, all these good things, it was still true in the 2000 to 2010 era that it was not really conceivable that a child of an *inquilino* would be a member of the Union Club.[1]

A few years later, Harberger came back to the subject and intimated that deep down there were racial roots to inequality.

Not an iota of difference in 50 years. And I say . . . it is an unfortunate situation that a country that is so vital and [has] so much growth and so much dynamism should be in that kind of a situation [regarding inequality]. And I think that as we proceed, more serious effort has to be made to integrate people coming from lower down in the hierarchy. Chile is wonderful at integrating immigrants from Europe. We have had Chilean presidents who were children of immigrants from Europe who came penniless. So, it isn't that Chile doesn't know how to integrate. But there is kind of a . . . perhaps racial type, perhaps traditional type distinction that really holds down people at the bottom.[2]

During the 2020 meetings of the Mont Pèlerin Society, held at the Hoover Institution, there was a session on Chile, where the causes behind the 2019 revolt were analyzed in detail. Al Harberger was a discussant in the session, and expressed his surprise at the massive demonstrations, the violence, and the destruction of public and private property. How could this happen in the fastest-growing country in Latin America? He was stunned, but he also tried to find explanations for these events. He opened his remarks by stating that in his view there was a deep-rooted "elitism" in Chilean society, something documented by Seth Zimmerman in a research paper on the links between elite schools and social mobility.[3] Harberger then talked specifically about the higher education system, and the role played by for-profit universities: "[At some point] it became easy for for-profit universities to start. And some of these for-profit universities were like our University of Phoenix and ITT. . . . [T]hese are universities that provide a D– or F+ education and charge an A– or B+ tuition, most of which is paid by the government. But people who come out of that kind of inferior educational system can't get jobs, and they have every good reason to feel they have been put upon. So, they have to be part of the story [of the revolt]." He also pointed out that for a long time it was difficult for women to move up in the corporate and professional worlds: "The average board of directors will just laugh if somebody mentions adding a woman to the board of directors, for example. They make jokes about it. So, there are that kind of problems in the situation."[4]

To be sure, Harberger never argued that Chile would have been better off if the reforms had not been put in place or if a significantly different path had been followed. Quite the contrary, in many of his writings he praised the reforms and recognized the achievements of the Chicago Boys and of the Concertación economists who oversaw policy making after 1990. And yet, this was not blind support. His search for causes of the revolt are particularly important, precisely because they come from him, and not from a rabid Far-Left critic.

Chicago in the 1970s, and Income Distribution

During the late 1970s and early 1980s, there were no formal courses at the University of Chicago that focused in-depth on issues related to inequality and income distribution. This was so even though the second course in price theory (Economics 302) in the doctoral program was titled The Theory of Income Distribution and that a number of faculty members were interested in the subject as a research topic. In 1973 Harry Johnson published a book with the notes from his Economics 302 lectures. There is an extended discussion on the "functional" distribution of income—much of it based on the geometrical tool called the Edgeworth box—between capital and labor, but very little on "personal" income distribution; there are no details on how to measure it, or on the most efficient and less costly policy options to alter it. In the last chapter of the book Johnson does tackle the poverty problem. In his opinion, this is a more difficult and important issue than inequality; it is on poverty reduction that development economists should focus their efforts.[5] This view was shared by Ted Schultz, who in 1992 wrote the foreword to Tarsicio Castañeda's book *Combating Poverty*, in which he criticized "the logic that seeks to reduce the inequality in the personal distribution of income" and praised Chile's policies of targeting social programs to the very poor, adding, "Targeting is a process designed to keep . . . income-enhancing [programs] . . . from creeping up the income ladder and thus no longer servicing the poorest of the poor. It is necessary to keep the political process from inducing and supporting such shifts away from the poorest people."[6]

Milton Friedman's famous textbook *Price Theory* has a detailed discussion on the functional distribution of income but no analysis of personal distribution. A reading list at the end of the book includes eight items on the theory of distribution, including chapter 10 of Adam Smith's *The Wealth of Nations* and chapters 1–5 of Alfred Marshall's *Principles of Economics*, but there is nothing on modern theories of inequality or on policies (including tax policies) to reduce it. George Stigler's textbook *The Theory of Price* has a chapter on personal distribution of income (chapter 15) in which the standard tools for measuring inequality are presented—the Lorenz curve and the Gini coefficient—and briefly discussed. Stigler concludes the chapter by stating that his "discussion of inequality makes clear the absurdity of a criterion of a good income distribution that ignores the complexity of the economy's structure, but it does not yield a criterion. Such a criterion depends partly upon one's ethical goals, of course. . . . Moreover, the ethical factors are complex, and only a very naïve and dogmatic set of judgments will permit one quickly to decide on the kinds and extent of inequality he likes."[7]

The closest to teaching inequality-related issues came from Al Harberger, who in his project evaluation course (Economics 364) discussed whether income distribution should be considered explicitly when evaluating the benefits of public investment projects. The question, which at the time was being hotly debated in international multilateral institutions such as the Organisation for Economic Co-operation and Development (OECD) and the World Bank, was whether projects that generated benefits to low-income people should regard that as an additional benefit. Harberger argued that using "distributional weights" would result in serious distortions and in the approval of projects that would make no contribution to national well-being. He pointed out that this did not mean that distributional considerations should be completely ruled out in project analysis, and claimed that the right way of doing it was by following a "basic needs" approach. This consisted of recognizing that most societies favor providing a minimal amount of certain goods and services to everyone, without any exclusions.[8] In many ways Harberger's views were similar to Norberto Bobbio's principle that everyone should obtain a minimal level of "civilized social rights," an idea strongly supported by President Ricardo Lagos in Chile.

With the above discussion I do not imply that at that time (the late 1970s and early 1980s) faculty members at the University of Chicago were not intellectually interested in inequality and distributional issues as research topics. Many of them did, in fact, do research on the subject—including Gary Becker and Jim Heckman—but they did not cover it in any depth in formal courses, or at least not in the courses that my friends and I took during those years.

The Chilean Reforms and Income Distribution

For the Chicago Boys, reducing inequality was not a priority. Their concern—and it was a very serious one—was with reducing poverty. In their view, if the incidence of poverty was reduced significantly, it did not matter what happened to income distribution. In the pursuit of poverty reduction their approach was to develop a very strict procedure for identifying the poor and targeting government assistance strictly to them. One of the first steps undertaken by the Chicago Boys under the leadership of Miguel Kast as Chile's minister of planning was to construct a "Map of Extreme Poverty" for the nation. The analysis identified where the poor lived, what their living conditions were, and which basic services they lacked. This analysis uncovered that until that time most of the government's assistance went to middle-income people and that very little percolated all the way down to the lowest 10 percent of the distribution. Based on this information, the Oficina de Planificación (Odeplán; Office of Planning) developed a strategy for providing social services—drinking water, sewage, nutritional support—to those below a certain threshold. In the view of the Chicago Boys, any leakage of assistance to households with higher income than those defined as "poor" was a mistake. With time, Chile developed a sophisticated "national registry of households" that included detailed data on the finances of families, their income, their level of education, the assets they owned (TV sets, cars, bicycles, and so on), and the level of assistance they got from different public-sector programs. In order to receive transfers from the government, families had to show that they had a score below what the government considered to define the deserving poor. Most transfers enacted during the Chicago Boys' tenure—and mostly maintained by the Left after 1990—were in-kind transfers. Cash transfers were avoided, as it was thought that recipients would spend the money unwisely. This strategy violated one of the basic premises in neoclassical economics. Indeed, I remember vividly when in Economics 301, Price Theory, Gary Becker showed that transfers in kind were always inferior, from a welfare point of view, to transfers in cash.[9]

The Chicago Boys' view of inequality is clearly captured by a statement made by former minister of finance and economics Rolf Lüders in the documentary Chicago Boys. Although I quoted Lüders in chapter 4, it is worth repeating his words: "I really don't care about inequality . . . the problem with income distribution is that it's an envy problem. . . . Do you understand me?"[10]

Although Concertación politicians were highly concerned with income distribution—as noted in chapter 11, the slogan of Ricardo Lagos's administration was "equitable growth"—they maintained the targeting approach developed by the Chicago Boys. During left-of-center administrations, the social registry of households became an even more important tool that guided social policy, including transfers to the elderly with low pensions financed from their accumulated personal savings.

As families left poverty and moved to the ranks of the middle class, they stopped being eligible for several social programs. Their social ascension was, however, fragile; many continued to live at the margins of poverty and were fearful that any unexpected shock, such as an illness, an accident, or losing employment, would result in them rejoining the ranks of the poor. Strict targeting of social programs was a reasonable policy during the early years of the reforms, when the extent of poverty was almost 60 percent of the population and when government revenues were very scarce. But as poverty declined toward the single digits and the coffers of the public sector became more plentiful, insisting on targeting assistance to the very poor generated a political problem that was paid for dearly during the revolt and its aftermath.

In figure 12.2 (in chapter 12), I presented data on the evolution of the percentage of the population living below the poverty line between 1987 and 2017.[11] These data show significant progress in the antipoverty fight and confirm that most of the improvement—if not all of it—took place after the return to democracy. If alternative definitions are used—say, a multidimensional and national measure—the level of poverty in the final years (2019–20) is higher (14 percent) but the improvement in social conditions is similar and still remarkable. Nothing like it had been seen in Latin America. In figure 12.3 (in chapter 12), I presented data on the Gini coefficient that measures inequality (the higher the number, the more unequal is the income distributed) for 1987–2017. These data are also from the World Bank and show progress after the return to democracy. Notably, however, although inequality declined steadily, by 2017 it was still at the level it had been in the mid-1960s.[12]

In order to put things into an international perspective, figure 13.1 presents data on the Gini coefficient for all OECD countries for 2018 (or the closest year). As may be seen, Chile is the third most unequal country; only Costa Rica and South Africa have a greater degree of inequality. While in most OECD member states taxes and public transfers reduce inequality significantly, in Chile they do not. For example, in 2017 Chile's Gini coefficient before taxes and transfers was 0.495; after taxes and transfers it was a very similar 0.460. In contrast, the numbers for Spain were 0.491 (before taxes) and 0.320 (after taxes); for the United Kingdom they were 0.508 (before) and 0.366 (after). According to a study by Rodrigo Valdés, the able minister of finance during Michelle Bachelet's second administration, this unique characteristic of the Chilean economy is due both to a tax system that lacks sufficient progressivity and to the fact that, since the mid-1970s, there have been very limited cash transfers to the middle class; most government programs are in kind.[13]

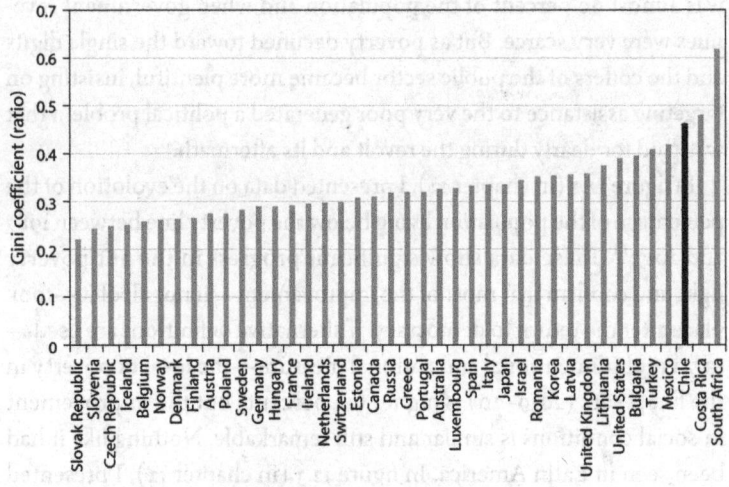

FIGURE 13.1. The Gini coefficient in Organisation for Economic Co-operation and Development member countries, 2018
Source: OECD (n.d.-c)

Chile's Paradox and Relational, Horizontal Inequality

Latin America has historically been a notoriously unequal region. For many years Brazil was the country with the highest Gini coefficient recorded. Rosemary Thorp shows that between 1938 and 1995, Uruguay was the only country in the region with a Gini coefficient below 0.40. According to Thorp, in 1970, when President Salvador Allende was toppled by the military coup, the Gini coefficient in Chile was estimated at 0.47, approximately the same level it had in 2017.[14]

Data from the Inter-American Development Bank indicates that in 2018 Chile's degree of inequality was typical of the region; at 0.482 Chile's Gini coefficient was almost the same as that of the typical Latin American nation—the average for the region was 0.480 and the median was 0.488. The same Inter-American Development Bank data set shows that during the early 2000s Chile was one of the countries in Latin America that had made the most progress in reducing inequality.[15] Despite these improvements, in 2018 Chile was one of nations where the *perception* of inequality was the highest. This was reflected in surveys conducted by the United Nation Economic Commission for Latin America, as well as in the United Nations Development Programme (UNDP) report on *malestar* (malaise) discussed in chapter 12.[16] This is "Chile's paradox": Why, in the most successful country in the region—a nation that had the best social indicators, had made significant progress in reducing inequities, and had (almost) eradicated extreme poverty— did people feel that they lived in a highly unequal society?

There are three possible, and interrelated, explanations for this "paradox."

The first is that we are talking about two different meanings of *inequality*. While most economists focus on "income inequality," there is a broader concept that includes quality of life, social interactions, access to basic services, the nature of interpersonal relations, and the degree of fairness (perceived and real) of the political and economic systems.

Second, it is possible that most Chileans did not realize that conditions greatly improved during 1985–2020. It is conceivable that the narrative about the country's social and economic trajectory had been captured by the critics of neoliberalism, by activists who resorted to the tactics of Italian Marxist thinker Antonio Gramsci about the role of *common sense* and compelling narratives in the battle for controlling power. These critics may have convinced people that, in contrast with reality, things had been going south for many years. In some ways, this is a "veil of ignorance" type of argument. Analysts who favor this interpretation argue that the massive use of social media by critics of the model help explain why people came to believe that the economic situation was extremely bad, when it was, by a wide margin, the best in Latin America.

The third possible explanation is that people recognized progress but believed that things were moving too slowly. This is an *impatience* argument that compares reality with aspirations. This disconnect between hopes and actual achievements is captured vividly by the privately run pensions system, a subject to which I will return in chapter 14. While people expected—and were implicitly promised—a high replacement rate, this has been, on average, a very low 25 percent: after a lifetime of work, their individual saving accounts allow most retirees to draw a pension of about one-fourth of their average salary during their last ten years of work.

Of course, there is some truth in every one of these explanations. Having said that, the most interesting factor behind the paradox is related to different notions of inequality. In order to fully understand Chile's revolt and explain the paradox, it is useful to distinguish between "vertical," or income, inequality and "horizontal," or social, inequality. While the former is narrowly defined and can be measured with some degree of precision with tools such as the Gini coefficient, the latter is a somewhat imprecise concept that many times depends on how people perceive their lives and social interaction with others in their communities and workplaces. What I have called "horizontal" equality is very similar to the concept of "relational" or "democratic" equality developed by philosopher Elizabeth Anderson.[17]

During the last few years, the OECD has made an effort to analyze a broad array of indicators of social conditions and quality of life, which add up to a comprehensive notion of "horizontal inequality" (see the OECD Better Life Index).[18] As it turns out, Chile does poorly in almost every one of these indicators.

Table 13.1 provides a list of the eleven components of the OECD Better Life Index. The table shows Chile's ranking within the forty-country sample (most of them OECD members), and provides information on which Latin American country is the most highly ranked nation in each category. When Chile is compared with the other Latin American countries in the OECD sample (admittedly a small sample that, besides Chile, includes Brazil, Colombia, and Mexico), the picture that emerges is checkered and ambiguous. Chile is ranked first among the Latin American countries in only four out of the eleven indicators; and in the "Civil engagement" category it is dead last within the forty countries in the complete sample. In contrast, when traditional and purely economic metrics are used, Chile is always ranked first among these Latin

TABLE 13.1. Chile and the Organisation for Economic
Co-operation and Development Better Life Index, 2019

Subindex	Chile's ranking in a sample of 40 nations	Highest ranked Latin American country in category
Housing	25/40	Chile
Income	35/40	Chile
Jobs	31/40	Mexico
Community	37/40	Brazil
Education	35/40	Chile
Environment	32/40	Brazil
Civic engagement	40/40	Brazil
Health	29/40	Brazil
Life satisfaction	21/40	Mexico
Safety	35/40	Chile
Work-life balance	34/40	Brazil

Source: OECD (n.d.-b).

American countries, often by a wide margin. Take, for instance, income per capita and the Gini coefficient: In 2018, Chile's gross domestic product per capita (purchasing power parity) stood at US$23,000, Mexico's at US$18,000, Brazil's at US$14,500, and Colombia's at US$13,600. Regarding the Gini coefficient, Chile had the lowest degree of inequality in this (small) sample; according to the United Nations Economic Commission for Latin America and the Caribbean, in 2017 the Gini coefficient was 0.43 in Chile; it was 0.54 in Brazil, 0.51 in Colombia, and 0.50 in Mexico. The above discussion shows that when one moves to broader measures of horizontal inequality, the view of Chile as Latin America's "paradise" or an "oasis" becomes blurred.

As I noted in chapter 12, several studies undertaken by the UNDP during the last decade have shown that, at least since the late 1990s, there has been a subterranean dissatisfaction among Chile's population. Many people are convinced that the playing field is not even, that the elites enjoy massive privileges, and that access to social services is profoundly skewed. There is a growing sense that private firms can collude to abuse workers and consumers without being penalized, that the segregated education system produces a network of privileged people that get all the good jobs, and that the health system is profoundly unfair and segregated by social class.

It May Be Worse Than What They Told You

In the last few years, researchers associated with Thomas Piketty's project on income and wealth distribution have argued that official data greatly underestimate the extent of inequality in Chile. According to Piketty's World Inequality Database (WID), in 2019 Chile's pretax and pretransfer Gini coefficient was 0.680, significantly higher than the 0.496 reported by the OECD. These researchers concluded that Brazil and Mexico also had a Gini of 0.680, and that these three countries were the most unequal nations in a very unequal region.[19]

The WID arrives at its estimates after making several adjustments to the raw data and after using numerous assumptions—some reasonable and some heroic—to recalculate top incomes. Instead of using survey data, the WID researchers rely on information from tax offices; the reason for this is that the wealthy seldom disclose all their income when asked about it in surveys. When this adjustment is done, the share of income going to top 1 percent increases from 7.5 percent to 16.5 percent of total income, with the concomitant increase in the estimated Gini coefficient.[20] The second adjustment has to do with the definition of income. Instead of relying—as most international studies do—on taxable or fiscal income, the WID uses an "adjusted definition" that includes companies' nondistributed profits as personal income. According to Ignacio Flores and colleagues, "the presence of tax incentives favor[s] the artificial retention of profits within corporations."[21] In order to take advantage of these tax incentives, many wealthy individuals set up holding companies into which they pay the corporate tax rate, which is much lower than the top marginal rate on the personal income tax. In addition, many top income individuals would in the past register siblings, spouses, and children as employees of the holding company and would write off many expenses—cars, trips, leases—that were not genuine business charges.[22] When data that includes nondistributed profits are used, the share of income of the top 1 percent increases further to 26 percent of total income, almost four times higher than the traditional figure of 7.5 percent. The Gini coefficient of 0.680 discussed above is obtained when this "adjusted income" is used.

The efforts by WID economists and other researchers to analyze in greater detail distributive issues are, of course, welcome. By pointing out that official data underestimate the extent of income disparities they provide additional light on the causes of the revolt and help explain, at least partially, what I have called the Chilean paradox. It is important to acknowledge, however, that due to the lack of historical and reliable data series, these analysts have been forced to make strong assumptions to allocate the nondistributed profits to individuals along the income scale. There are two areas where the assumptions are particularly debatable: What fraction of nondistributed profits should be attributed to foreign investors? And, what proportion of these profits should be allocated to the top 1 percent, 0.1 percent, and 0.01 percent? As Flores and colleagues show, most studies that use a broad "adjusted income" measure rely on figures for two years only (2005 and 2009) to make the adjustments and to allocate the retained income along the income scale.[23] This means that the WID results should be considered as preliminary and subject to possible revisions. This is, in fact, recognized by the directors of the WID team, who write that "due to lack of proper data . . . these series should be viewed as imperfect and provisional. They are based in some cases on regional and country imputations based on regions and countries with similar characteristics."[24]

An important consideration when looking at the WID's adjusted figures is that there are additional adjustments to the rough data that could provide a more precise picture of the "true" degree of inequality in Chile. A particularly important step is to allocate a monetary value to transfers in kind, adding those amounts to monetary income. One of the principles instituted by the Chicago Boys and continued by the Concertación was that social programs had to be strictly targeted. One way of making sure that that was the case was by eschewing transfers in cash. Consequently, it is very likely that the incomes of the lower deciles are underestimated by the official data. Economists Osvaldo Larrañaga

TABLE 13.2. Wealth Distribution in Selected Countries: Top 10% and
1% of Population, World Inequality Database Calculations

Country	Net personal wealth, top 10% (share, adults, 2020)	Net personal wealth, top 1% (share, adults, 2020)
Argentina	0.5755	0.2450
Brazil	0.7929	0.4758
Chile	0.7976	0.4781
Colombia	0.6346	0.3229
Costa Rica	0.6794	0.3507
Dominican Republic	0.6094	0.2774
Ecuador	0.5628	0.2304
El Salvador	0.5761	0.2432
Guatemala	0.6096	0.2775
Honduras	0.6085	0.2765
Latin America	0.7658	0.4470
Mexico	0.7871	0.4688
Panama	0.6087	0.2766
Peru	0.7636	0.4371
Uruguay	0.5727	0.2398
Venezuela	0.6103	0.2783

Sources: WID (n.d.-b, n.d.-c).

and María Eugenia Rodríguez (2014) have provided one of the few
studies that make these kinds of adjustments. In their estimates they
assign monetary values to the government programs in education,
health, and housing. Their results indicate that when that correction is
made, the "adjusted incomes" of the lower deciles increase considerably.
For 2011 their Gini coefficient estimates decline from 0.500 to 0.411. Although the reduction is significant, even after these changes the degree
of inequality continues to be very high, especially when compared with
the OECD countries.[25]

Critics of neoliberalism have argued that in addition to income it is
important to analyze distribution of wealth. In line with the results on
income, the WID adjusted figures suggest that the well-to-do control a
much higher proportion of wealth than what official sources indicate.
Table 13.2 presents data on the distribution of wealth for Chile and

selected Latin American countries. Although these numbers are not fully comparable across countries—different methodologies are used to make the adjustments, depending on data availability—the results are telling. According to this study, in Chile the richest 1 percent of the population control almost 48 percent of the nation's total net wealth. Table 13.2 shows that the only countries that are close to Chile in terms of wealth inequality are Brazil, Mexico, and Peru. It is precisely these data that prompted those on the Far Left, including president Gabriel Boric and his immediate team, to suggest, in 2022, a wealth tax that would be raised on those with net assets valued in excess of US$5 million.

14

Broken Promises

PENSIONS AND THE REVOLT

GARY BECKER, whom Michel Foucault considered to be the most prominent figure of American neoliberalism, visited Chile three times. In 1993 he gave the keynote speech at a seminar celebrating the fifth anniversary of the promarkets think tank Libertad y Desarrollo (Liberty and Development), an outfit founded by Chicago Boys Hernán Büchi, Carlos Caceres, and Cristián Larroulet. Becker traveled again to Santiago in 2000 to attend the general meeting of the Mont Pèlerin Society, where he presented a paper on addiction and drugs. His final visit was in December 2007, when he again was hosted by Libertad y Desarrollo. On each of these trips Becker met with former students and some government officials, but he did not give any advice on economic policy. He never met Augusto Pinochet or the other ex-members of the junta.

Although Becker was deeply interested in what was going on in Chile, he never did research that directly focused on the country or used Chilean data. Possibly, what interested him the most was the pensions' reform that replaced a traditional pay-as-you-go system with a regime based on individual savings accounts. He summarized his enthusiasm for Chile's new pensions scheme in some of his nontechnical writings. For example, in a 1994 *Wall Street Journal* column by Becker and Isaac Ehrlich, they note, "Chile and a few other countries have also adopted systems that mandate contributions to individual accounts. In these retirement protection systems, private funds compete for the right to manage individual accounts. Since these systems have the advantage of competition among private companies, they are superior to government-managed central provided funds systems which are in turn much better than pay-as-you-go systems."[1]

In a policy paper titled "Economic Dimensions of the Family," presented in Madrid in 1999, Becker wrote:

> Western nations have a pay-as-you-go social security system where the young are taxed to pay the support of the old. A better system, found in Chile . . . is to have each worker save for old age in individual retirement accounts that they can spend when they are older. Since these are retirement accounts, they are less affected by the growing number of elderly and declining number of young persons, a demographic problem for the social security systems in effect in western Europe. Also the present system encourages parents to have fewer children because the elderly are supported from a fund. This effect would be eliminated under my system which makes individuals responsible for their own old age support, except for the poverty-stricken.[2]

As it turned out, Becker's celebration of Chilean pension reform was premature and overlooked the need for continuous adjustments. For several reasons, including the low contribution rate and the low number of years during which the average worker added to his or her savings account, pensions paid were, on average, very low. This generated growing discontent and gave birth to the protest movement that lobbied—sometimes peacefully and sometimes violently—for returning to a pay-as-you-go regime run by the government.

In September 2021 presidential candidate Gabriel Boric unveiled an economic program that included fifty-three specific reforms. The number one priority was eliminating individual savings accounts and replacing them by a system that combined collective (as opposed to individual) savings and a pay-as-you-go component financed by additional contributions paid by employers. During the revolt, and in the months that followed, one of the most often seen graffiti in Santiago and other cities was: "NO + AFP," meaning "No more private pensions."[3]

Historical Background

Chile's first social security law was passed in 1924, and was amended several times (in 1926, 1932, 1952, and 1969) before the military introduced the individual savings accounts in 1981.[4] In the late 1970s social security was characterized by a patchwork of subsystems that covered people differently in different jobs. There was clear discrimination against blue-collar workers, who had significant hurdles to overcome to be vested and to obtain reasonable pensions. At the other end of the spectrum, politicians, members of the judiciary, and employees in the banking sector were eligible for hefty pensions after very few (fifteen to twenty) years of contributions. In some cases, the pension was indexed to the salary of the position the individual held when he or she retired. This type of perk was highly valued and was known as a *pension perseguidora* (chaser pension).[5]

The total rate of contribution for pensions—that is, the sum of contributions by employer and employee—was, on average, about 35 percent of wages. When health contributions were added, total social security taxes exceeded, in some sectors, 60 percent of wages.[6] The fragmentation of the system meant that there was an immense bureaucracy and rampant inefficiencies, and that administrative costs were huge. Many of the subsystems were literally bankrupt and had to be supported by the government through transfers financed by money creation on the part of the Central Bank. Figure 14.1 shows Carlos Cáceres, Gary Becker (Nobel laureate in economics for 1992), Hernán Büchi, and Juan Andrés Fontaine during Becker's visit to Santiago in 2007. The three Chileans played important roles during the Pinochet regime; Fontaine was a member of the cabinet in both administrations of conservative president Sebastián Piñera.

Pinochet's Reform

During the early years of the Pinochet dictatorship, pensions were not considered to be a priority; there were other urgent issues to tackle, including controlling inflation and privatizing state-owned firms.[7] In 1979

FIGURE 14.1. *From left to right:* Carlos Cáceres, Gary Becker, Hernán Büchi, and Juan Andrés Fontaine, Santiago, 2007
Source: Collection of Carlos Cáceres

a decree (Decreto Ley 2448) was passed that eliminated the differences between blue- and white-collar workers and unified the retirement age at sixty-five for men and sixty for women.[8] The pensions problem was brought to the forefront of the discussion a year later, in Pinochet's Seven Modernizations speech of 1979. José Piñera was put in charge of the pensions reform project. The young economist proceeded, with gusto and great enthusiasm, to add operational details to the general idea of replacing the pay-as-you go regime with individual savings accounts, as outlined in The Brick (and discussed in chapter 7).[9]

The government decided that the new system would apply only to workers who had formal work contracts. Their savings were managed by licensed and highly regulated firms, the Administradoras de Fondos de Pensiones (AFPs; Administrators of Pension Funds), which competed among themselves and charged a management fee. The AFPs could not engage in any other type of business. The self-employed were not required to make retirement contributions; they could do it voluntarily but were exempt from the obligation. This meant that dentists, accountants, and other independent professionals were not covered, nor were those who worked in the "informal sector": people employed in microfirms, peddlers, occasional farmhands, and others. Because of this provision of the law, only 50 percent of the workforce was part of the new pension system. Two reasons were given for this decision. First, at the time it was technically difficult to enforce contributions from millions of independent and informal workers. Second, in the old pay-as-you-go system, independent and self-employed workers were also not covered, so no one would be worse off after the reform. In fact, since even those who had sporadic formal jobs were now obliged to add to their savings accounts, it was expected that at the end of their work life they would at least collect something, which was an improvement over the previous system, through which they had not gotten any payments (remember that under the pay-as-you-go regime there were lengthy vesting periods—between ten and fifteen years).

Young workers who joined the (formal) labor market after 1981 were automatically enrolled in the new system. At the other end of the spectrum, workers about to retire were not eligible to switch systems and had to stay in the old regime. Those who lay in between could opt in or could remain under the old scheme. People who were at midcareer—say, they had already contributed for ten years—and decided to enroll in the new program received in their savings account a government bond that captured the capitalized value of their past contributions. This security was called the "recognition bond."

After some discussion, José Piñera and his advisers decided to set a contribution rate of 10 percent of wages. This was significantly lower than contributions in the old regime, which in some cases were almost 35 percent of wages. In contrast with the traditional system, and with most countries' experiences, there was no sharing of the burden; the 10 percent was paid fully by employees. At the time Piñera explained that by drastically reducing the rate of contribution to only 10 percent, take-home pay would increase substantially, making the reform popular among workers.

The retirement age was set at sixty-five for men and sixty for women; the fact that life expectancy for women was significantly higher than for men was ignored. Early retirement was allowed only if accumulated savings resulted in a pension higher than a certain threshold. Voluntary additional retirement savings were allowed, with tax benefits, up to a limit. There was also a minimum (and very low) pension guaranteed to be financed by general taxes for those with twenty or more years of contributions.

In drafting the law Piñera also decided that workers could move AFPs at will, and that these would charge a management fee on the flow of saving they received (as opposed to a fee on the stock of assets under management). Moreover, in order to avoid conflicts of interest, the AFPs had to have a unique mandate: their only business was to manage retirement funds, and they could not provide any other services. This meant that banks, insurance companies, and other entities could not participate in the business. Since these were individual savings that belonged to the worker, there was no vesting period. When the system was launched with great fanfare in late 1981, there were fifteen newly formed firms ready to collect and manage retirement funds for a fee. With time, however, there was significant consolidation of the industry, and a number of firms merged. By 2022 there were seven managers, four of which were owned by foreign multinationals, including MetLife, Prudential, and Principal.

According to the law (Decreto Ley 3500), at retirement age, workers could use the balance in their individual accounts to do one of the following:

- purchase an immediate annuity and obtain lifetime retirement benefits
- set up programmed withdrawals to provide income over the retiree's expected life span; when the retiree died, dependents would inherit the balance in the individual account (and in order to make sure that the accounts would not run out of funds, the maximum withdrawal was calculated assuming a rather long life expectancy)
- purchase a deferred annuity, which meant setting a future date for purchasing an annuity and, until that date, making programmed withdrawals from the individual account
- purchase an immediate annuity with a portion of the funds and make programmed withdrawals with the rest of the funds[10]

Since the bases of the system were lifelong savings, it was expected that the first pensions under the new regime would not be paid until 2005 or so. The first wave of retirees would be people who by the time the law was approved (in 1980) already had ten to fifteen years under the old system and thus had received a sizable "recognition bond" in their individual accounts.

In a book in which he reminiscences about the process that led to the reforms, José Piñera writes that between 1979 and 1981, the greatest opposition to the new pensions' architecture came from the military. Senior armed forces officers in Pinochet's Comité Asesor (Advisory Committee) thought that the neoliberals had gone too far. In May 1980 they persuaded Pinochet that this scheme would give the private sector excessive power, and the general canceled the reform. In September 1980, after the new Chilean Constitution was approved, José Piñera launched a new effort and was finally able to convince Pinochet to move forward with the new system. The new plan had a major difference with respect to the original proposal, however: the armed forces were not included in the new scheme and maintained their traditional pensions perks. Decreto Ley 3500 was approved by the junta on November 30, 1980, and the new system became operational in early 1981.

Promises and Flaws

For years, pensions reform was the jewel in the crown of Chile's promarkets reform. The system, which had been dreamed up by Chicago Boys Emilio Sanfuentes and Sergio Undurraga, became a reality thanks to the tenacity, creativity, and political ability of José Piñera, one of the most prominent honorary members of the Chicago Boys' tribe.

The reform was based on the notion of individual responsibility and on the idea that there had to be a close relationship between individual effort (amount saved) and individual benefits (pension received).[11] Decades later, critics of the model made the exact opposite argument. To them—including future president Gabriel Boric—it was inconceivable that a social right such as old-age pensions would be guided by individualism, egotism, and a neoliberal perspective; what was needed (and had to be introduced into the new constitution that was drafted in 2021–22), was a regime based on solidarity, a system through which those who had more and those who were fortunate shared their retirement income with the poor and with those farther down in the social scale.

The new system was a "defined contribution" system, and as such there were no explicit promises on the expected replacement rate; pensions would depend on the amount saved and on the rate of return of the funds. Yet when promoting the reform, government officials intimated that given the typical characteristics of Chilean workers and the historical yields on investments in Chile, the average replacement rate would hover around 70 percent of last wages. A pamphlet published by José Piñera in 1992, approximately ten years before the system paid its first pensions, contributed to the notion that the payout would, in fact, be around 70 percent of wages. Piñera wrote, "If everything proceeded reasonably well, our computations indicated that by saving 10 percent of wages, pensions could reach amounts equivalent to 70 percent of wages at [retirement]. . . . It is estimated that a pension of this order of magnitude allows workers to maintain a standard of living similar to the one before retirement. This is so, since a retiree has fewer expenses than an active worker (work clothes, transportation, children schooling, etc.), as long as there is health insurance."[12]

The 70 percent replacement rate became ingrained in peoples' minds and was considered an implicit promise. Years later, when the actual replacement rate turned out to be significantly lower—less than 35 percent for the median worker, as shown in table 14.1—the 70 percent figure was used by critics as "proof" that the system had failed and that the military, José Piñera, and the Chicago Boys had lied to the people.

In 1981, AFPs were permitted to invest only in low-risk domestic securities, and they could have up to 100 percent of their assets in government bonds. By 1985, when the country's capital market began to develop, the limit on government-issued instruments was lowered to 50 percent, and AFPs could invest between 10 percent and 30 percent of assets in eligible stocks. For the first nine years of operation, AFPs were prohibited from investing in foreign assets. By 1996, restrictions were eased and AFPs could invest up to 6 percent of assets in foreign securities. This limit gradually increased to 30 percent in 2004 and 45 percent in April 2008.

During the next forty years, the AFPs generated high returns for their clients—above 8 percent in real (inflation-adjusted) terms on average. Yet despite the AFPs' success in managing money, the resulting self-financed pensions tended to be, on average, very low. This was the result of several design flaws that eventually caused the demise of the system. In retrospect, some of the most egregious mistakes included the following:

- At 10 percent of wages, the rate of contribution was obviously too low. The average for the OECD countries was 19 percent. It was quite clear that if the contribution was low, the total volume of savings would also be low, and possibly not enough to finance a politically "acceptable" level of pensions.
- The system assumed a rather static labor market, where workers in the formal sector stayed for thirty to forty years. The reality was very different, with many workers moving in and out of the formal sector in a fluid way. For a few years they would work for a modern firm; then they would become self-employed and make no contributions; and a few years later they would join the public sector, where they would make contributions again. About half of workers contributed for only twenty years instead of the forty years assumed in official simulations. Not surprisingly, then, a system with about one-half the contribution used in the theoretical exercise (10 percent, instead of 19 percent) for one-half the number of years (twenty, instead of forty) generated pensions that were 25 percent of those in the benchmark nations and assumed in most official documents and simulations.
- Employers split payment to workers into two parts: a salary proper, subject to the 10 percent savings, and pay related to a freelance contract that was contribution-free. Accumulated funds were thus low, and the resulting pension was only a small fraction of total earnings, adding to criticism and frustration.

In retrospect, what is remarkable is that, as an employer, the government engaged in this practice year after year and made contributions to civil servants' accounts for less than their actual earnings. As a result, the most vocal anti-AFP groups were made of former public-sector employees with very low pensions.

- José Piñera's plan assumed that workers considered the contributions to their individual accounts as deferred compensation and not as a tax. This, however, was not the case, and for a long time, most workers were doubtful on whether they truly owned the funds or if they had just been paying a disguised tax.[13]

- Contrary to what The Brick suggested, workers' representatives were never included on AFP boards or on the boards of companies in which they invested. This meant that for many years workers did not feel that they "owned" the system. The literature (and practice in numerous countries) had emphasized repeatedly the importance of "ownership" to obtain political support for the reforms.

- Perhaps one of the most serious flaws was not including an automatic adjustment to retirement age. Between 1981 and 2021, life expectancy of Chilean citizens increased by an amazing eleven years—from seventy in 1981 to eighty-one in 2018—but the retirement age was stuck at sixty for women and sixty-five for men. If the same volume of savings were stretched over the double number of retirement years, the resulting monthly pensions would obviously decline.

- During the early years, and despite a large number of AFPs, management fees were very high. At first, this did not create a political problem, but around 2005, when it was realized that pensions were much lower than anticipated, the issue became central to the debate. The AFPs' rate of return on capital exceeded, on average, 20 percent, significantly higher than the return on the retirement funds, about 8 percent in real terms. This added to the notion that the private sector was profiting greatly by taking advantage of the poor and the elderly.

In the late 1990s there was concern about a sudden drop in the value of the pensions' portfolios. Wall Street crashed in October 1997, and a number of emerging markets collapsed during those years: those of Argentina, Brazil, the East Asian nations, Russia, and Turkey. Drastic declines in life savings—20 percent or more—were particularly traumatic to those about to retire. As a result, the government decided in 2002 to require management firms to offer alternative portfolios organized according to risk. Younger people could choose which fund to be in, but after a certain age, and to reduce the risk of sudden declines just before retirement, they had to be in the least risky portfolio, Fondo E.

Solidarity at the Base: The 2008 Reform

In 2006, on the twenty-fifth anniversary of the reforms, many workers began to retire under the new rules. To their surprise, pensions were much lower than expected. President Michelle Bachelet appointed a high-level technical and bipartisan commission, known as the Comisión Marcel, to propose improvements to the pensions system. The commissioners made a series of simple and yet powerful points. They argued that there was a large number of people who at retirement had very low savings. This was especially the case for women who had been only sporadically employed in the formal labor market. As a remedy, the commission recommended a basic pension supplement based on solidarity and financed by general taxes. The amount of these government transfers declined as the self-financed pensions increased. In addition to adding this "solidarity pillar" to the system, the presidential commission made the following recommendations:

- Management fees were too high; greater competition was needed. It recommended allocating, for three years, all new entrants to the AFPs with the lowest fees. This allocation was decided through an auction.
- A 10 percent contribution was excessively low. It had to increase by approximately 4 percentage points. This additional contribution was to be paid by employees.

- With a very rapid increase in life expectancy, the funds accumulated by workers for forty years resulted in lower pensions than what had been anticipated. It was important to provide incentives for workers to postpone retirement. That is, the commission recognized the problem created by a much higher life expectancy but stopped short of recommending a mandated increase in retirement age.
- The discrepancy in retirement age between men and women was a problem, and it was recommended that it be standardized at age sixty-five.
- The commission recognized that not requiring the self-employed to contribute was a major problem. It was fundamental to improve coverage and find a way of incorporating them into the system.

By 2014, accumulated assets in the six (and soon to be seven) pensions management firms had grown to almost 80 percent of the country's gross domestic product, or US$250 billion. To put things in perspective, in the United States that would mean around US$17 trillion in 2022 dollars. The portfolios were by now highly diversified and included domestic stocks and bonds, as well as international securities. The very large volume of assets under management had two important implications: it meant that the system provided a significant support to the local capital market, and it also meant that it was a great bounty for politicians, many of whom were dying to get their hands on (a fraction of) the funds.

A Failed Reform in 2014

Despite the adjustments introduced in 2005, 2008, and 2010, pensions continued to be a major political problem. During the students' demonstrations in 2011, those on the Far Left—including one of their leaders, future president Gabriel Boric—argued that the provision of social services could not be left to for-profit management firms; they had to be provided by the public sector or by not-for-profit institutions that operated in "the public sphere." They also questioned why, if a man and a woman had the same amount of savings, the man would receive a higher pension. The supporters of the system argued that since women lived longer, on average, it was not discrimination; it was a straightforward application of markets-based financial engineering: for a given pile of money, the longer you lived, the lower the annuity. These two views were a clear reflection of the cleavage in the country: the increasingly popular solidarity-based vision pushed by the young supporters on the Far Left and the "neoliberal" perspective of the more traditional politicians who believed that economic theorems were to be maintained under all circumstances.

President Michelle Bachelet, who was now serving her second term, was alarmed, and convened a new technical commission to look, once again, at the pensions problem. There were twenty-three commissioners, including world-renowned academics who had worked for a long time doing research on pension systems from around the world—Orazio Attanasio, Nicholas Barr, Costas Meghir, and Carmelo Mesa-Lagos. After more than a year of work, the commissioners had to decide between two proposals: Propuesta A introduced specific and significant reforms to the model, but maintained individual savings accounts managed by private firms as the base of the system. Propuesta B called for the replacement of the individual accounts with a mixed regime with a pay-as-you-go component for everyone, and obligatory savings accounts for higher-income workers; these accounts would be managed collectively, and thus financial risks would be shared by all workers. In the final vote, Propuesta A was supported by twelve commissioners and Propuesta B by eleven commissioners; a third proposal, consisting of a traditional pay-as-you-go regime without a savings component, obtained one vote.

In order to do its job, the commission gathered almost a half million data points on actual pensions being paid (as opposed to simulated pensions from a model). The data are summarized in table 14.1, which distinguishes between self-financed pension payouts and total pensions, the latter including government supplements granted to those in the 60 percent lower end of the income distribution. The data also distinguish between men and women. The information is organized

TABLE 14.1. Median Replacement Rate by Number of Months of Contributions to Pension Plan, 2007–2014

Months of contribution	Range	Self-financed pensions			Total pensions (includes subsidy)		
		Women	Men	Total	Women	Men	Total
Low contributions (≤25%)	1–35 months	4%	5%	4%	21%	128%	64%
Medium low (26–50%)	36–146 months	10%	23%	13%	15%	69%	33%
Medium high (51–75%)	147–285 months	23%	45%	33%	27%	57%	42%
High (>75%)	286–386 months	36%	55%	46%	37%	59%	48%
Total		24%	48%	34%	31%	60%	45%

Source: Comisión Asesora Presidencial sobre el Sistema de Pensiones (2015).

according to the "density," or number of months of contributions: low, medium, medium high, and high density.

The "Low contributions" row in table 14.1 refers to people who contributed to their individual savings accounts for less than thirty-five months during their work life of forty years (full contributions would be 480 months). As may be seen, the replacement rates—defined as the pension received as a percentage of the (inflation-adjusted) average salary over the last ten years—are extremely low when the government subsidy is excluded. These workers saved so little that the resulting pensions financed from their own savings hovered around 4 percent of their salaries. It was this group that benefited the most from the 2008 reform that instituted the solidarity supplement. As can be seen, once the government transfer is added, for women the replacement rate increases by five times, and for men it shoots up above 100 percent.

From a political point of view, workers with medium contribution density—between thirty-six and 285 months—were the most important. Although their savings were low, many of them did not qualify for government support because their household income and assets placed them in the higher 40 percent of the income distribution scale. As can be seen in the table, even when the subsidy was added (to those who qualified), the rates of replacement for these groups were very low: their pensions were between 15 percent and 27 percent of the final years' salaries. When it came to protesting against the privately managed pensions, it was this middle-class group that was the most vocal and articulate, and the most committed toward changing the status quo.

The new technical report from the high-level commission was released in September 2015. In addition to supporting the general principles of Propuesta A (maintaining the individual accounts), the commission made several concrete recommendations aimed at improving pensions:

- Increase contributions by 4 percentage points, 2 points of which would go directly to the individual private savings accounts. The other 2 percentage points would be used to fund a solidarity fund to provide further transfers to the poor. These additional contributions of 4 percent of wages would be paid by employers.
- Create a government-owned AFP, which would compete with the existing management firms. The idea was that by not having a 100 percent profit motive, this state-owned AFP would bring discipline into the market, helping to reduce the still very high management fees.[14]
- Given that, once joining a management firm, workers do not switch often, introduce forced turnover. The idea was that a fraction of existing contributors would be automatically reassigned to the lowest management firm every four years. Workers, however, could immediately switch back to their old management firm or to any firm they wanted to be affiliated with. It was expected that this measure would increase competition and lower management fees.

The AFPs rejected the report and argued that most of the suggestions would violate contracts and the principles of free competition. They were particularly opposed to the creation of a government-owned AFP and to the forced reallocation of contributors across managers. Their lobbying machine went into overdrive, and they managed to stall the reforms for the next six years. When the revolt erupted in 2019, and it became evident that the new political regime would eliminate (or greatly reduce) the role of the private sector in the provision of pensions, AFP executives and controlling shareholders wished that the 2015 report had been implemented. But it was too late.[15]

The COVID-19 Pandemic, Withdrawals, and Boric's Election

When the COVID-19 pandemic erupted in 2020, the Chilean government, led at the time by conservative Sebastián Piñera, was slow to respond and to provide economic assistance to families and to the unemployed. Politicians on the Left decided that, given the government's reluctance to act aggressively, they would pass legislation allowing workers to withdraw 10 percent of their pensions savings. A lively debate ensued, with supporters of markets arguing that withdrawing funds would create a terrible precedent and result in even lower pensions. On the other side of the aisle, critics of the AFPs and of the model pointed out that if the conservative and neoliberal government did not want to provide assistance, there was no other option than to use people's savings during the emergency.

Throughout 2020 and 2021, even as the government rectified its policies and put together a generous and massive assistance program for those affected by the pandemic, three withdrawals of up 10 percent of pensions' savings were allowed, and total assets under management for the system as a whole declined by US$55 billion. An indirect consequence of the withdrawals was that people now understood that the funds were there and that they truly belonged to them. All of a sudden, the issue of "ownership" was resolved.

In February 2022 legislation was passed to provide a basic universal pension. The payout was set at the poverty line, or 55 percent of the minimum wage; the only requirement for obtaining this basic pension at age 65 (for both men and women) was to be in the 90th percentile of lower income. Those who benefited the most from this legislation were middle-class people who until then had been unable to get the solidarity benefit because their income and assets indicated that they were above the

60 percent income threshold—that is, the greatest beneficiaries were those in the two medium density categories of contributions in table 14.1.

On November 1, 2021, Gabriel Boric released his platform as a presidential candidate for the Far-Left coalition Apruebo Dignidad (Approval and Dignity). The document was 229 pages long and included fifty-three specific policy initiatives—referred to as "concrete changes." The first among these policy proposals read, "We will end the AFP system, replacing the D[ecreto] L[ey] 3,500 [enacted by Pinochet] by a new social security system that assures minimal pension of 250,000 pesos [80 percent of the minimum wage] for everyone older than 65 years old, including the 2.2 million people who are currently retired. We will also substantially improve all pensions with a special emphasis on pensions received by women."[16]

During the presidential campaign Gabriel Boric pointed out that in his administration a pension system similar to the one existing in Sweden would be enacted. The bulk of contributions would go to a national savings fund, and individuals would have "notional" accounts in which their contributions would be registered. These savings would receive a notional rate of return calculated as a moving average of the actual (net) rate of return of the collective savings fund. The program also called for increasing contributions by 6 percentage points, to be paid by employers. Those monies would not go to the savings fund, but would be used directly, in a pay-as-you-go fashion, to finance inter- and intragenerational transfers benefiting women and low-income people. According to Boric, in his government the motivation behind the individual retirement accounts would finally be replaced by a solidarity-based regime that would provide decent pensions and respect old-age dignity. Putting an end to the individual retirement savings account would be the most important nail in the neoliberal coffin. As it turned out, things were significantly more complicated than candidate Boric thought. People didn't like the AFPs and wanted higher pensions, but at the same time they liked the idea that they truly owned their retirement funds and that these could be left to their heirs as inheritance. As will be discussed in chapter 15, ownership of retirement funds would become an important issue during the drafting of the new constitutional text.

15

The Constitutional Convention and the Election of Gabriel Boric

THE DAYS that followed the October 18, 2019, revolt were chaotic. Toward the end of each nonviolent demonstration, gangs of violent protesters went to work. They set churches and businesses on fire; looted supermarkets, pharmacies, and banks; attacked bystanders; and burned metro stations and buses. They built barricades and collected tolls from motorists. In some cases, people were taken out of their vehicles and forced to dance or sing before they were allowed to go on their way. "If you don't dance, you won't pass!" became an oft repeated chant at the barricades, an easy way of humiliating those who looked bourgeois or even had a remote probability of belonging to "the elite," an ill-defined category that grouped together a variety of enemies of the radical Left. During my visits to Santiago, I was not subjected to these indignities, but some of my acquaintances did suffer them. A Jewish friend could not hold back his tears when he mentioned that his grandparents had gone through a similar experience in Nazi Germany. The legendary Carabineros police force was unable to control the crowds and resorted to tactics banned in most countries: they shot antiriot ammunition over demonstrators' heads, wounded scores of protesters, and left a number of them blind. Amid this anarchy, many observers thought that the government would fall and were unsure of what could happen next.

On October 19, President Sebastián Piñera declared a state of emergency and the military was called in to patrol the streets. Most people were shocked to see soldiers in combat fatigues carrying heavy weapons. Those old enough to remember the 1973 coup d'état were particularly demoralized by what they saw. In a somber speech the president said that the "country was at war with a formidable and dangerous enemy." When the army general in charge of the patrols was asked about Piñera's statement, he said that the Chilean armed forces were not at war with anyone; their job was to safeguard critical infrastructure, as mandated by law. He added that he expected that his men and women would go back to their barracks in short order. Social media accounts repeated again and again the generals' words: "I am a happy man; I am not at war with anyone."

The fact that protesters did not have known leaders made things more difficult for Piñera; there was no one with whom the authorities could negotiate. It was not exactly clear what the demonstrators' demands were—except for Piñera's resignation—or what the government could do to appease them. At the same time, politicians from the Center Left, including virtually every one of its representatives in the Chilean Congress, refused to support the administration and to denounce and oppose the violence. Instead of rejecting anarchists and the destruction of property, they criticized the government for showing a firm hand and denounced the Carabineros for violating demonstrators' human rights. Traditional politicians were afraid of being attacked on social media by an increasingly aggressive cybermob that would "cancel" anyone suspected of supporting the neoliberal model and law and order. The political system became paralyzed, and day after day the country relived the same scene: massive pacific demonstrations followed by violent action from gangs of masked ultra-left-wing activists. It is not an exaggeration to say that by November 10 the country was going down in a spiral of chaos and destruction. An analyst paraphrased Karl Marx and said that the specter of anarchy haunted Chile.

A New Constitution as an Escape Valve

On November 12 an idea began to make the rounds in the presidential palace. What about reaching an agreement with all—or most—of the political forces, and convene a Constitutional Convention to write a new law of the land? The president's advisers thought that this would provide an escape valve for the awful political pressure accumulated during the previous weeks. For some time, a group of legal scholars led by lawyer Fernando Atria, a follower of liberation theology, had argued that the existing constitution was undemocratic and cheated the people out of their rights. Atria and his circle claimed that despite the large number of amendments passed between 1989 and 2005, including the amendments led by President Ricardo Lagos in 2005, it was still Augusto Pinochet's constitution. In order to have a true democracy it had to be replaced by a text written from scratch by a convention freely elected by the people.

In 2016, during her second term in office, President Michelle Bachelet launched a process of town hall meetings to discuss the possibility of writing a new constitutional text. People from all walks of life and ages met to talk about their aspirations, about individual and collective rights, and about the political system. All sorts of questions were addressed during the town hall meetings: Should Chile be a unified or a federal country? Should the right to abortion be protected by the constitution? Which social rights had to be guaranteed? Should the constitutional text address gender issues, as demanded by the feminist movement? Should the country continue to have a presidential political system, or should it adopt parliamentarism? Should Indigenous populations be recognized at the constitutional level? And, if so, should Chile have more than one official language? Should the legislative branch have two chambers or only one? No question was out of bounds, and those who participated in the discussions felt that for the first time in their lives they had been able to speak up and present their views to other citizens and to the organizers of the town hall meetings.

In early 2018, a few weeks before finishing her second term, President Bachelet submitted to the Chilean Congress a proposal for a new constitutional text. The draft was based on the town hall discussions and made important changes in three areas: it declared that Chile was a "social rights democracy"; it expanded social rights and stated that providing (most of) them for free was an obligation of the state; and it made it easier for the charter itself to be amended. The incoming conservative government was strongly opposed to the idea of a new constitution, and as soon as Sebastián Piñera was inaugurated in March 2018, it withdrew the reform proposal from the Congress's consideration.

The revolt, however, changed the political landscape drastically. Between November 13 and 15, 2019, and as the country was being burned down by rioters, hurried and secret meetings between the newly appointed minister of the interior, Victor Pérez, and different opposition leaders took place in rapid succession. By November 15 a deal had been reached. That night most political parties agreed on a procedure for dealing with the constitutional issue, but the extreme Left—Communist Party members and the Frente Amplio (Broad Front)—did not join in. To them such an accord would take steam off the pressure to oust Piñera. Out of the twenty-one Frente Amplio members of Congress, only one joined in the Acuerdo por la Paz Social y la Nueva Constitución (Agreement for Social Peace and a New Constitution): Gabriel Boric. The deal included the following points:

- A referendum would be called, and voters would be asked if they favored a new constitution. This was called the "entry plebiscite."
- If the answer to this first question was "yes," a second question would be asked: Should the new constitutional text be written by the Congress or by a fully elected convention?
- If the convention option was chosen, the body would have 155 members, the same number of seats in the lower house of congress. At least 50 percent of the members had to be women. After arduous negotiations it was agreed that seventeen out of the 155 seats would be set aside for Indigenous peoples. Members of Indigenous groups could decide, on election day, to use the Indigenous ballot or the Chilean ballot.[1]
- The convention would have a complete free hand to write the new constitutional text and could take up to a year to write it. There were only a handful of restrictions on what it could incorporate into the new charter: international treaties signed by Chile had to be respected; the same applied to firm rulings by the courts.

- For norms and articles to make it to the new constitutional text they had to be approved by two-thirds of the members of the convention.
- Once the draft was finished, a new national referendum would be called—this was the "exit plebiscite." Voting would be obligatory—until that time it was voluntary—and the new constitution would be approved if more than 50 percent of voters supported it.

The option that a fully elected convention would write a new consti-tution won the entry referendum by a landslide, with 78 percent of the votes. When, a few months later, the convention members were elected, conservative and promarkets forces obtained less than one-third of the seats, meaning that they would be unable to veto any of the proposed norms. That, in itself, presaged that the new constitutional text would enshrine the principles of the Left and would put an end to many of the principles that had guided the Chicago Boys and their economic revolu-tion. The Center Left—that is, the political parties from the old Con-certación coalition—also did poorly in the elections. Most of the elected members had no links to political parties and were activists who supported different niche causes related to gender, identity politics, the environment, and Indigenous peoples' demands. Many of the convention members praised the role played by the "front line" during the uprising and, paraphrasing Karl Marx, argued that violence was the midwife of deep and necessary social change. Most of its members declared that the convention's goal was "refounding" Chile as a plurinational country.

One theme united most convention members: they were committed to ending the neoliberal model, a model that in their view was based on individualism and egoism. They would replace it with a state of "social rights" rooted in solidarity. They were committed to writing a text that would help people achieve a "better life" based on the Mapuche tradi-tional cosmovision. For-profit education would come to an end, as would private health care financed by vouchers; privately managed in-dividual pension accounts, private education supported by the state through vouchers, and other for-profit activities would be forbidden. Foreign policy would be centered on the Latin American region, giving priority to links with other plurinational countries. State-owned enterprises would be promoted, and the protection of the environment would be central in the new Chile. The country's productive structure would be changed, and instead of exporting goods that relies on natural resources, Chile would become an exporter of complex and technological products with high value added. Indigenous peoples, who according to official figures represented 12 percent of the population, would have autonomy and any law that affected them would require their prior consent; property to their original lands would be restored and would be held collectively. The market for water would come to an end and existing water rights would be confiscated without compensation. Most convention members were highly optimistic and motivated, and considered the pro-Indigenous constitutions adopted by Ecuador in 2008 and Bolivia in 2009 as points of reference. The possibility that such a charter could reduce the attractiveness of Chile as an investment destination; weaken the peso; lower employment; generate instability; and reduce growth, employment, and wages did not cross their minds.

Gabriel Boric's Economic Program: Looking at the Future through a Rear-View Mirror?

The Constitutional Convention began its work on July 4, 2021, just as the campaign for the 2021 presidential elections got underway. During the next six months the convention discussed its governance rules, while, in parallel, seven candidates competed to move on to the second round of the presidential election. As the campaign proceeded, it became apparent that the two centrist candidates—one from the Center Left and the other from the Center Right—were getting very little traction. At the end, it would be a contest between the Far Right, represented by former congressman José Antonio Kast, the brother of Chicago Boy Miguel Kast, and the Far Left, represented by former student activist Gabriel Boric.

Boric—who eventually won with a massive 56 percent of the votes—offered an economic platform full of ideas; some were relatively new, and some were nostalgic. In presenting his program, Boric mentioned Aníbal Pinto, the economist who in the 1950s and 1960s was the Chicago Boys' main critic, as one of his inspirations. Following Pinto, Boric and his team thought that the government should provide substantial incentives to local industry in order to encourage a sophisticated production mix with a greater degree of "complexity" than currently prevailing exports. While the structuralists in the 1950s called for protective import tariffs, Boric and his group supported soft loans granted by a newly created development bank, tailored after Brazil's Banco Nacional de Desenvolvimento Econômico e Social (National Bank for Economic and Social Development), and a doubling of the research and development budget through fiscal incentives. They also favored some protectionist measures, but not in the scale of the import substitution era.

Boric's views on industrial policy and greater value added were also influenced by Albert Hirschman's "forward and backward" linkages theory, a model that became popular in the 1950s among some development economists. According to Hirschman, support should be provided—through protection, subsidies, or soft credit—to those industries whose expansion would, at the same time, feed into other promising industries, and demand inputs and material from deserving sectors.[2] During the 1960s and 1970s, steel was usually mentioned as an example of an industry with significant forward and backward linkages. On the one hand, steel mills required iron ore and coke coal; on the other hand, the finished product could be used in the manufacturing of white goods, automobiles, trucks, and tractors. Boric felt that lithium—of which Chile has the second largest deposits in the world—could be at the center of a remarkable industry with forward and backward linkages. On the back end, he believed that Chile could produce the kind of machinery and sophisticated equipment required to extract and process the lithium; on the front end, Chile could produce batteries and electric vehicles. Many people found the idea promising, even obvious. There were, however, two serious problems: those who supported this theory did not consider that international trade in modern times is based on global supply chains, and countries that are far away and geographically semi-isolated, such as Chile, have a serious disadvantage related to high transportation costs. They also ignored what the late Carlos Diaz-Alejandro, once a progressive economist at Columbia University, had said regarding Hirschman's approach: it was putting a complex and fragile policy tool "in the sloppy hands of mediocre followers [bureaucrats]."[3]

Gabriel Boric's program called for an increase in tax revenues of 8 percent of gross domestic product, a very significant number equal to approximately, 40 percent of tax collection in 2022. Boric's economic team recognized that such a major boost in tax collection could not happen in a short period of time, and talked about doing it over eight years, meaning that it would go past his presidential term. The sources of greater revenues were to be a significant increase in taxes on mining (royalties, mostly on copper), a tax on wealth levied yearly on wealth exceeding US$5 million, new inheritance taxes, and a very significant reduction in tax evasion and tax elusion. The tax plan was based on the analysis of inequality made by the World Inequality Database (discussed in chapter 13).

In terms of social programs, the new administration looked to undo some of the most important reforms undertaken by the Chicago Boys. The pension system, based on individual savings accounts, would be replaced by a solidarity-based regime that, as noted in chapter 14, would combine collective savings in notional (and not individual) accounts with a pay-as-you-go component.[4] The existing dual health care system, through which people could use government-issued vouchers to purchase private insurance, would be replaced by a national universal health system like the one in the United Kingdom. A massive program for mental health was also called for. The new administration would launch a "land bank" to provide inexpensive land to developers that would build social housing. Public transportation would be free, and drinking water would be provided at low cost to everyone.

There would also be major changes to labor laws. Bargaining between unions and firms could now take place at the industry level, the minimum wage would be raised by 40 percent, and the workweek would be cut from forty-five to forty hours. Regarding the environment, the program called for imposing "green taxes" to reduce emissions, signing the international environmental protection treaties that the conservative administration had not signed, and providing incentives for unconventional renewable energy. There would also be a change in the fishing law, with fishing quotas being auctioned rather than grandfathered to historical fishing companies.

Boric made a commitment that his administration would be a "feminist" one, and that in every government department there would be gender parity, with the same number of women and men in deliberative bodies. In appointing his first cabinet he went even further, naming fourteen women and ten men. Indigenous groups would be recognized by the state, and negotiations would take place to acknowledge the taking of property during the Spanish rule as well as during the first century of the Chilean Republic. Mechanisms for restitution and compensation were to be analyzed and implemented.

The Constitutional Draft, the "Plurinational" State, and the Economy

The Constitutional Convention finished its work on July 4, 2022, when the Boric administration was barely three months old. For the next two months there was an intense campaign that pitched the *apruebo* (approval) option against the *rechazo* (rejection) alternative. To everyone's surprise, on September 4 the new constitution was rejected by voters. According to a *New York Times* article published on September 6, "The transformational vision laid out by a constitutional convention of 154 elected members, many of them political outsiders, proved too drastic an overhaul."[5] In a piece published on September 5 the *Economist* wrote, "Much of the blame for the defeat lies with the convention itself. . . . More than two-thirds of those elected were outside mainstream political parties. They included many political newbies and activists from the hard left. . . . They quickly alienated the average [voter]."[6] On September 5, Michael Stott wrote in the *Financial Times* the following about the plebiscite results: "This is a setback for leftwing president Gabriel Boric, the former student protest leader who had staked much political capital on the now-rejected radical draft. Voters were, almost literally, promised the earth (the draft would have granted constitutional rights to nature). Attractive-looking carrots abounded among the 388 articles drawn up by a specially elected assembly after a year of sometimes raucous debate."[7]

The draft was, indeed, long, full of adjectives, and largely inspired by the principles of "identity politics." Its most controversial norm—and the one behind the decision by the majority of citizens to reject the proposal—was declaring that Chile was an *estado plurinacional* (plurinational state), consisting of several nations; the draft recognized eleven nations and left the door open for adding additional Indigenous peoples to the list. Each Indigenous group would have great autonomy in its region and would have its own justice system. Land restitution would be used as the main mechanism for redressing injustices committed in the past. Any political, social, or economic decision that affected the Indigenous peoples' interests would require their consent. The draft also stated that Chile was a democracy with gender parity.

The proposed text included a lengthy catalog of social rights—103 in total, more than any constitution in the world—and obligations of the state. Some were standard rights, and some were esoteric. The former included the rights to education, health care, pensions, shelter, and leisure time. The latter included the obligation of the state to promote the use of seeds historically utilized by Indigenous peoples and to encourage farmers' markets.

Gender equality in all institutions of the state was assured, and women were given control over their bodies. This last provision rattled the conservative Right, the Catholic Church, and evangelical Christians. The political system was profoundly reformed to reduce the power of the executive branch. The Senate was abolished, and in its stead a Cámara de las Regiones (Chamber of the Regions) with diminished functions was created. The lower house of Congress was given new powers, including greater control over the government's purse. Autonomous regions were allowed to issue debt and to manage their own budgets. The Sistema de Justicias (Justice System) was created to supervise the work of judges with a combination of members belonging to the judiciary and political appointees. Several seats in the Congress were reserved for the eleven officially recognized Indigenous peoples. The fact that this amounted to gerrymandering at a national scale did not bother the Far Left.

The proposed text was inspired by the new Latin American constitutionalism, a doctrine based on the notion that in Latin America true democracy can only exist if Indigenous peoples are given autonomy and if their lands and property are restituted. These ideas had been fostered for years by neo-Marxist thinker Álvaro García Linera and were the doctrinal bases for the new constitutions of Ecuador in 2008 and Bolivia in 2009.

Article 1 of the constitution, as drafted by the Constitutional Convention, stated the following:

> Chile is a social State of democratic rights. It is plurinational, intercultural, regional and ecological. It is built as a republic based on solidarity. Its democracy is inclusive and based on gender parity. It recognizes the intrinsic and inalienable values of dignity, freedom, and substantive equality of human beings and their indissoluble relation with nature. The protection and guarantee of individual and collective human rights is at the base of the State and guides all of its activities. It is the obligation of the State to generate the necessary conditions and to provide the goods and services that would assure equal rights and the integration of people in the political, economic, social and cultural life so they can achieve their full [personal] development.[8]

On the economic front, some of the most important changes introduced in the constitutional draft were geared at eliminating those norms based on the "subsidiarity principle" and replacing them with mandates that guaranteed the provision of social rights by the state. As it turned out, and as was reflected in exit polls and surveys, most people agreed with the spirit of these proposals. It was not the economic aspects of the draft that people objected to; what they disliked was the political system, including, in particular, the creation of what many considered to be an "indigenist political system," a plurinational state with autonomous groups that were granted more rights than Chileans. The most important proposed changes related to the economy were:

- The state had the obligation to provide free social services in education, pensions, and health. The private sector may offer these services, and people would be allowed to purchase them. No government vouchers would be used, however, as had been the tradition in Chile since the mid-1980s. A single payer national health service was to be created and public universities had to be given a priority in state funding. These provisions represented a major break with the philosophy promoted by the Chicago Boys and maintained by successive left-of-center governments. The proposed text also recognized the right to shelter as a constitutional right. Social rights would be satisfied in a "progressive" fashion, meaning that such satisfaction would be gradual process that could not be reverted by future legislation.
- The protection of property rights would be somewhat weakened. According to the old constitution, if someone's property was expropriated for whatever reason (building a road, for instance), compensation had to cover the actual loss in value and payment had to be in cash and made before taking the property. This provision was replaced by the requirement of compensation at a "just price," a notion that according to the critics of the convention was so vague that it would discourage investment. The requirement that payment had to be made before property was taken was maintained. Critics of the process argued that according to the new text, payment could be made using government bonds issued in nominal pesos, as had happened during the agrarian reform of the 1960s and 1970s, when inflation reduced the real value of compensation to almost nothing.
- Property rights over water usage would be eliminated. A new national council of water would be created and given the power to administratively allocate water to different users. The secondary market for water rights would be forbidden. One supporter

of the new constitutional text argued that this eliminated one of the most egregious aspects of the neoliberal order: putting a price and marketing a public good that belonged to society and was needed to satisfy a basic need. On the other hand, critics noted that if water rights could not be owned or traded, investment in mining, agriculture, and green hydrogen, among other things, would greatly decline.

- The power of unions would be greatly boosted. According to the new constitution there were no limitations on strikes, except for limited cases in which national health and safety were at risk. Unions would be free to bargain at the firm, regional, or national industry level (the old charter restricted bargaining to the firm level), and "solidarity" strikes, in which a particular union staged a stoppage in support of any cause, would now be constitutionally protected.

- The proposed new constitution included several provisions that would give special protection to property rights of Indigenous peoples. For example, Article 102 stated, "The State recognizes and warranties the right of the indigenous peoples and nations to their lands, territories and resources. Property of indigenous lands enjoys especial protection. The State will establish judicial and efficient instruments to catalog them, regularize, demarcate, provide property titles, and provide reparation and restitution. Restitution constitutes the preferred mechanism of reparation."[9]

- Article 191 established that the Indigenous population also had to give its consent for any legislative or administrative decision that affected its interests. Even before the ink was dry on this provision, a controversy erupted over its interpretation. Did it only apply to policies that affected the new Indigenous autonomous territories, or was it more general? For instance, it was not clear if the Indigenous peoples would have to give their consent to a constitutional amendment that changed or eliminated their reserved seats in the national legislature.

- The ability of Congress to spend public monies would be greatly increased. For decades, legislation had implied that new government expenditures could only be introduced to Congress for consideration by the president. The rationale of this norm, which exists in several Latin American countries, was to put a check on congressional clientelism, a practice that results in pork barrel spending and significant pressures on fiscal accounts. The new constitution, however, would allow any member of Congress to propose legislation that could result in increased expenditures. For the proposal to become law, the president would have to agree with it and support it.

• After a spirited debate, the Convention maintained the independence of the Central Bank. The number of members of the board would be increased from five to seven, and a clause was introduced establishing that the bank had to "coordinate" with the government regarding its stance in monetary policy. Additionally, the censuring and impeachment of members for "dereliction of duty" would become easier.

The New Constitution Is Rejected, but the Process Continues

As the Convention's deliberations proceeded during 2021–22, an increasing number of people became disenchanted with the constitutional process. They resented the aggressive tone used by some of the members, rejected the attacks on anyone who dissented on any topic, and were offended by the open dismissals of Chile's traditions and historical institutions. A particularly notable episode took place during the inaugural session on July 4, 2021, when the representatives of Indigenous peoples, led by member Elsa Labraña, did not allow a children's orchestra to play the national anthem. During the first few months, most members voted for not allowing Chilean flags in any of their official meetings; in contrast, Mapuche flags were permitted and fully displayed.

In March 2022, and despite the Convention's declining popularity, it appeared that the *apruebo* option was going to win the exit plebiscite and that Chile would, indeed, have a new and very progressive constitution.

However, during the second week of April the debate on the proposed political system intensified. Several Center-Left politicians, including some who were members of the Convention, argued that the elimination of the senate, coupled with the immediate reelection of the president, would weaken democracy by diminishing the system of checks and balances. Led by Senators Ximena Rincón and Matías Walker, left-of-center politicians affirmed that "plurinationality" was contrary to history. Chile, they said, was a mestizo country with a long tradition as one united nation. Yes, they affirmed, the constitution should enshrine multiculturalism and recognize the Indigenous peoples. But establishing that the country was formed by several nations, each with a great degree of autonomy, was going too far. Asking for the Indigenous peoples' consent before passing legislation was also considered to be divisive and disruptive.

Suddenly, the public began to scrutinize the proposed text in great detail, and new objections appeared. Several analysts argued that the number of guaranteed rights was excessive and that it would be impossible to deliver them. This, it was noted, would produce a great gulf between what was written and the social services that were actually provided, generating frustration and disaffection with the democratic system. As the process continued, new concerns were discussed, including the elimination of property rights for water use, a provision that would negatively affect three hundred thousand small farmers. Analysts also raised an issue with unions' increased power, including their (proposed) constitutional right to strike in solidarity with any cause, even with those unrelated to work conditions or with their industry or economic sector. Left-of-center economists, led by René Cortázar, a former cabinet member during the administrations of Patricio Aylwin and Michelle Bachelet, argued that the new constitution would create heightened uncertainty and negatively affect growth and investment. If there was no growth, the government would not be able to increase its revenue and, thus, it would be impossible to finance the provision of the 103 guaranteed rights.

Starting in late April 2022, most polls showed that the *rechazo* option had gained significant traction and was likely to receive 53 percent of the preferences. In June 2022 the *Economist* wrote, "Chile and its young left-wing president, Gabriel Boric, seemed to offer the chance of a new social contract along [progressive] lines. Instead his fledgling government is *hostage to a constitutional convention shot through with the familiar Latin American voices of Utopianism and over-regulation*."[10]

On July 5, one day after the Convention finished its work and two months before the referendum, former president Ricardo Lagos, an icon of the Center Left, released a statement that shocked the country. Although he did not say how he would vote in the plebiscite, he affirmed that he was disappointed with the Convention. The proposed constitution, he stated, was overly "partisan" and did not address the country's needs or help solve its political challenges. He further said that it was important to recognize that, independent of which option won the referendum, the constitutional process would have to continue after September 4, 2022. In particular, he noted that if the *rechazo* option won, it was necessary to try again, possibly by electing a new convention. If, on the other hand, the *apruebo* option came out on top, the brand-new text would need to be amended immediately.[11] Lagos's opinion gave significant impulse to the movement "rechazar para reformar" (reject in order to reform), which was backed by an increasingly large group of voters that went from the Center Left to the Right.

On September 4 the *rechazo* option won by a landslide: it got 62 percent of the votes, while *apruebo* garnered only 38 percent. The result shocked most observers and was a major blow to President Gabriel Boric and his supporters. During the campaign Boric had noted that it would be much easier to enact his economic and social program under the new text. After acknowledging the results, Boric said that his administration's goals had not changed: they would push for deep reforms that would end the neoliberal system; they would do it more gradually, but they would still do it, as mandated by those who voted for his ticket in the presidential election of December 2021. He repeated this during a September 20, 2022, speech delivered at the United Nations.[12]

In an article published in the *Guardian*, Chilean author and playwright Ariel Dorfman, a well-known progressive intellectual, argued that the constitutional proposal was rejected because most people "found its 388 articles—it is the longest such document in the world—confusing and even extravagant (giving legal status to glaciers and defending culturally appropriate food)." He further wrote, "A large number of my fellow countrymen and women are uneasy about the emphasis on the autonomy of Indigenous peoples, and the insistence on 'plurinationalism' in a land that prides itself on its unity."[13]

On September 14, 2022, barely ten days after the plebiscite, Chilean politicians from (almost) every ideological persuasion were on the verge of agreeing on how to continue the constitutional process: a new, smaller (one-hundred-member) convention would be elected. Gender parity would be maintained, and the number of Indigenous seats would be reduced to reflect the actual number of Indigenous voters, rather than their population. The Convention would be assisted by a Comisión de Expertos (Experts' Commission) made up of constitutional scholars. The goal was to have a new proposal in late June 2023 and an exit plebiscite in August of that year. If the timetable was maintained, Chile would have a new Magna Carta written by a democratically elected body by the fiftieth anniversary of the 1973 coup d'état and of President Salvador Allende's death. At the substance level there was agreement that the new constitution would declare that Chile was a "democratic state of social rights," a definition that moved it closer to the European social democracies and away from the principles that had guided the Chicago Boys' revolution and economic policies in place since 1973.

16

The End of Neoliberalism?

THE STORY of Chile's free-market reforms may be summarized with two words: *success* and *neglect*.

There was great success in generating very rapid growth and drastically reducing poverty. These accomplishments catapulted Chile from the middle of the Latin American peloton to the clear lead in the region. From an economic point of view the country became, within one generation, Latin America's brightest star. But side by side with these successes there was neglect. The most visible area of neglect—but not the only one—was inequality. As I discussed in chapter 13, the Chicago Boys—and many of their teachers at the University of Chicago, for that matter—believed that income distribution should not be at the center of economic policy formulations; the goal was to reduce poverty through rigorously targeted social programs. If poverty was, in fact, lowered, there was no need to be concerned about inequities. This view was perhaps best expounded by George Stigler in his famous textbook *The Theory of Price: Revised Edition*, in which he wrote that "good income distribution" was an absurd policy goal in a complex modern economy.[1]

But it turns out that income distribution is politically important, even in societies with a very low incidence of poverty. Citizens resent large income disparities and end up supporting politicians who promise to do something about them. And, in Chile, income differentials were very large and persistent, as has been shown in the preceding chapters. It is true that inequality declined somewhat during the Center-Left governments, but in 2022 Chile still had the third highest level of inequality of states in the Organisation for Economic Co-operation and Development. The perception that Chile was an unfair country was augmented by the succession of scandals and cases of collusion and corruption discussed in chapter 12, and by a profound "horizontal inequality" that included an unequal provision of amenities and public goods, the uneven quality of its schools, and urban segregation.

The Far Left, led by Gabriel Boric, offered a consistent narrative that blamed the neoliberal model for these problems and promised to reduce them rapidly through higher taxes, significant increases in spending in social programs, the recognition of Indigenous peoples and the restitution of their lands, the protection of the environment, and an industrial policy aimed at making Chile's productive structure more "complex" and with a higher value added. It was against these inequities that masses of people demonstrated during the 2019 revolt. The fact that the model was seen as Augusto Pinochet's legacy played a fundamental role in the uprising. For young people it was inconceivable that a system put together by a dictator who had abused human rights and tortured and murdered his opponents was still in place.

The election of the Constitutional Convention, with all of its excesses and radical ideas, reflected this unhappiness. The fact that the proposed constitutional text was not approved in the September 4, 2022, referendum does not contradict the notion that inequality had become an increasingly serious political issue. As argued in chapter 15, the proposal was rejected because of its "extravagance" and because, by promoting "plurinationalism," it threatened the country's unity. But people still demanded a new social pact, a new political, social, and economic system that would reduce abuses and inequities. At the time of this writing—late September 2022—all political forces agreed that despite the plebiscite's result on September 4, a new social pact was needed; it was also recognized that the new social contract had to be translated into a new constitution. It would not be as radical as the one that was rejected, and it would not seek to completely rebuild the country from scratch. But every political leader concurred that the new social agreement would be rooted in the notion that Chile was "a democratic state with social rights." This meant that, as in most European social democracies, a number of social rights would be guaranteed by the state and enforced by the judiciary. This agreement confirmed that the neoliberal model put in place by the Chicago Boys and continued by the Center-Left Concertación coalition had, for all practical purposes, run its course.

At the time of this writing the only open question was the procedure through which the new constitution would be written: the Far Right wanted to have the Congress do the job, while a vast arc of parties from the Center Right to the Far Left agreed that the only way to satisfy the people was by having a new convention. As noted, the majority was leaning toward a smaller number of delegates, a shorter timeline, and a truly representative number of Indigenous reserved seats. Gender parity—an equal number of men and women—was not disputed.

The Neglect of Doctrine

Giving low priority to inequality was not the only form of neglect during Chile's experience with free markets and capitalism.

The political and economic elites—including the elites in the economics profession—also neglected other concerns of the younger generations. Issues related to gender inequality, environmental protection, and the rights of animals and nature were not addressed with sufficient vigor and urgency. Little by little this neglect fed into a generational discontent. Young people became affiliated with new political parties whose main goal was replacing neoliberalism with a new social order based on solidarity, a strong government, environmental protection, feminist principles, gender parity at every level, and universal and free provision of social services.

Every Concertación official I have spoken with over the years—including former President Ricardo Lagos and ex–cabinet members José De Gregorio, Nicolás Eyzaguirre, Claudio Hohmann, Carlos Hurtado, Máximo Pacheco, Rodrigo Valdés, and Andrés Velasco—strongly rejected the notion that the Concertación pursued a neoliberal agenda. This, of course, is not surprising. Given the negative connotation that the term *neoliberal* attained through time, it would be very difficult for anyone involved in policy making to agree on that tag being used for themselves and on the policies they promoted and implemented. I was told by these officials things like "We never privatized the copper company Codelco," "We strengthened the financial regulatory authority," and "We increased social services." These statements are true, but do not get to the heart of the matter.[2]

Labels, of course, are important. They affect the way people perceive us and the way we perceive ourselves. But, independently of whether the policies pursued during the four Concertación administrations are called neoliberal or something else—neo-neoliberal, attenuated neoliberal, quasi-neoliberal, or inclusive neoliberal—the fact of the matter is that there was a remarkable continuity with respect to the policies of the Chicago Boys. In particular, and as noted throughout this book, the reliance on markets at every level—including in the provision of social services such as education, health care, and old-age pensions—was maintained, as was the emphasis on an economy thoroughly dominated by the private sector. It is true that during the Concertación a number of regulatory bodies were created and/or strengthened, but it is also true that—overall, and in comparison with other countries from around the globe—Chile was still characterized by a very light government touch.

At some point during the 1990s, promarket intellectuals and academics declared victory in the war on ideas and moved on to other pursuits, including making (a lot of) money. In doing so they abandoned the world of doctrine and ideas. In their minds, they had obliterated their adversaries and had shown that the market perspective was the best that could be offered in a country like Chile. For them it was self-evident that the Chicago Boys' policies had propelled Chile to the top of its league and opened the door to the possibility of joining the exclusive club of the advanced nations. In their view, the fact that their historical adversaries, including Christian Democrats and Socialists, had embraced their ideas was an unequivocal sign of their resounding triumph and justified lowering the guard on the ideas front.

But they were wrong. What they did not understand was that victory in the war of ideas is not eternal. Defeated opponents retreat, lick their wounds, and regroup. After some time, they are back in the battlefield of ideas, ready for new scrimmages, new debates, new discussions. During the wilderness years, those who lost the war send a new generation to school and develop new strategies for fighting a new war. In Chile, younger generations of Far-Left activists went to graduate school and developed new conceptual frameworks and narratives around the ideas of Judith Butler, the feminist thinker; Antonio Gramsci, the Italian Marxist intellectual who died in 1937; Jürgen Habermas, the German philosopher and member of the Frankfurt school; and Ernesto Laclau, the Argentine sociologist and defender of populism.

From Antonio Gramsci they took the idea that in order to gain power it is necessary to develop a persuasive narrative based on common sense. This job is done by the "organic intellectual." Whoever controls the narrative has the upper hand in the war of ideas and a higher chance of winning the hearts and support of the people. In Gramsci's time, pamphlets were the most important channel for spreading the revolutionary narrative; in modern times, it is social media. While Far-Left activists mastered Instagram, Twitter, and TikTok and used them brilliantly to get out their gospel, the old guard of free-market supporters stood on the sidelines, and, at most, wrote an occasional letter to the editor.

The Far Left took from Ernesto Laclau the idea that modern revolutionary action and success is not the result of class struggle. Modern political collisions are between "the people" and the "elite," broadly defined to include everyone who is "privileged": those who have good managerial and professional jobs, were educated in good schools, live in the better neighborhoods, and have solid networks and interact with decision makers. The people care about simple things that lead to a better life and a fairer society, free of abuses and corruption, and most of the time the elite, with its entrenched interests, stands in the way of achieving those goals. From Jürgen Habermas they took the importance of the "public sphere," an area of discourse and action on the opposite side of private and individual spaces supported by classical liberals and market economist. Activists took from Judith Butler terms like *gender power*, and the importance of incorporating "sexual dissidences" into the structure of power—six articles in the proposed Chilean Constitution of 2022 made reference to such dissidences.

After the 2019 revolt, the Far-Left narrative became so dominant that even seasoned politicians from the Center Left were afraid of voicing their opposition to the violence and destruction that followed the insurgency. Doing so left them open to accusations of all sorts and to—what in this time and age is much worse—being "canceled." The story told by the Far Left, time and again, was that of a country where the wealthy, in conjunction with the political elites from all sectors, had signed an implicit pact with the military to perpetuate a regime of abuse, inequities, and corruption. At the center of that narrative was the figure of Pinochet, a reviled character who had usurped power, tortured hundreds of citizens, persecuted his political enemies—some of whom, including ex-ambassador Orlando Letelier, were murdered in foreign countries—and sent a quarter of a million people into exile. In late June 2022, as the country was getting ready for the "exit plebiscite" that would decide whether the new constitution was approved, Paulina Vodanovic, the president of the Socialist Party, said that her party's goal was to "put an end to the institutions inherited from [Pinochet's] dictatorship."[3]

The retreat of promarket forces—I hesitate to write "conservatives," even though many of the supporters of capitalism were (very) conservative on social issues—took place at many levels. Few young people were involved in politics, and an increasingly small group became journalists or were interested in public debate. It is true that there were some promarkets think tanks (three or four), but they slowly veered away from defending the liberal and market principles behind the reforms. For example, the Centro de Estudios Públicos, which had been founded by Pablo Baraona, Jorge Cauas, and Sergio de Castro in the late 1970s (see chapter 7) became more interested in literature and literary theory than in economics.[4] Additionally, after the first administration of Sebastián Piñera the intensity of work in the think tank Libertad y Desarrollo—the institution that had hosted Gary Becker twice—declined significantly. Promarket economists were reluctant to adopt social media as a means of communicating their ideas, and the very few who did have Instagram and Twitter very seldom used them and almost never entered debates with critics.

But what best exemplifies this trend of becoming uninvolved in public policy discussions was Católica's almost complete disappearance from day-to-day economic policy debates. Younger faculty were now interested in being part of the global community of scholars and became victims of the "publish or perish" culture. In order to move up in the ranks it was not enough to publish in Spanish or to do research important and relevant to Chile's development challenges. Papers had to be published in international journals sanctioned by some diffuse global authority. The journal *Cuadernos de economía* (Notebooks on economy), in which so many important pieces on the Chilean economy were published in the 1960s and 1970s, ceased to exist and was not replaced by another outlet that focused on applied issues of interest to Chile and its policy makers.

Part of the explanation for this was arrogance. Since the Pinochet years, economists had become accustomed to having a substantial amount of influence and power. Politics was mostly carried out using economics terminology, and economists looked down on other professionals, including lawyers and engineers. Two of the postdictatorship presidents were professional economists with PhDs from top schools—Ricardo Lagos (Duke University) and Sebastián Piñera (Harvard University). Between the two of them they held power for fourteen out of the thirty-three postdemocracy years. Arrogance often leads to hubris and a sense of infallibility. For Chilean economists the economic point of view was king, and following Gary Becker's perspective they believed that economics could be used to analyze and address almost any problem faced by society. Many of them stopped listening to others and did not believe that a state of malaise and unhappiness was growing under a veneer of successes and accomplishments. When thinking about the role of economists, I am reminded of Daniel Halberstam's book *The Best and the Brightest*, in which he tells the story of the brilliant intellectuals who joined the administration of President John F. Kennedy in 1961. They had impeccable academic credentials—dean at Harvard University, head of the Rockefeller Foundation, graduates from the Groton School and Yale University—and wide networks of powerful friends. But they seldom listened to dissenters and did not want to see the reality as it unfolded in front of their eyes. It was this arrogance, Halberstam tells us, that led the United States to get involved in two tragic and extremely costly international adventures: the Bay of Pigs Invasion and the Vietnam War.

In the 1970s Deirdre McCloskey was a member of the faculty at the University of Chicago and taught the introductory price theory course (Economics 300) to many of the new generation of Chicago Boys. In later years she became interested in rhetoric and discourse, and she has written extensively on how economists present their data, how they speak, and how they are often unpersuasive to others. In her famed trilogy on the bourgeoisie, McCloskey argues that capitalist values were expanded thanks to literature (Jane Austen) and conversation that appreciated and celebrated attributes such as industriousness, work, punctuality, and deference to others.[5] In 2022, I interviewed her in San Antonio, Texas, about the Chilean experience. We mostly talked about different ways of defending the ideas of (classical) liberalism and markets from the renewed and persistent attacks from Far-Left activists. McCloskey did not hesitate in opining, and she said, "The answer to those attacks is, preach, preach, and preach!" That is exactly where classical liberal, neoliberal, and other supporters of markets failed in Chile. Instead of staying engaged in the never-ending confrontation and wars of ideas, and instead of preaching about the merits of markets, they chose the comfort of home and the lure of high-paying jobs as board members of Chile's major corporations, including several that had been involved in the collusion and other scandals of the 1990s and early 2000s.

The Future

In March 2022, Francis Fukuyama wrote this about neoliberalism:

> Classical liberalism was reinterpreted over the years, and evolved into tendencies that in the end proved self-undermining. . . . [T]he economic liberalism of the early postwar years morphed during the 1980s and 1990s into what is sometimes labeled "neoliberalism." Liberals understand the importance of free markets—but under the influence of economists such as Milton Friedman and the "Chicago school," the market was worshiped and the state increasingly

demonized as the enemy of economic growth and individual freedom. . . . Advanced democracies under the spell of neoliberal ideas
trimmed back welfare states and regulation, and advised developing
countries to do the same under the "Washington Consensus." Cuts
to social spending and state sectors removed the buffers that protected individuals from market vagaries, leading to big increases in
inequality over the past two generations.[6]

Fukuyama's essay was written as a reaction to the Russian invasion of
Ukraine and as a reflection of the diminished condition of classical liberalism around the world. Although the context is very different, the
core of Fukuyama's reasoning resonates in the case of Chile. It may be
argued that the neoliberal point of view and its policies went too far for
too long, and that this was self-undermining.

Fukuyama's quote also indicates that the downfall of the neoliberal
doctrine and its policies is a global phenomenon. The election of former
guerilla Gustavo Petro to the presidency in Colombia and the success of
Luiz Inácio "Lula" da Silva in Brazil are signs that the Latin American region is moving strongly to the Left. As in years past, most eyes will be on
Chile's experience and analysts and investors will follow developments
closely, trying to determine whether the new "democratic state of social
rights" is able to deliver on what Far-Left politicians have promised.

Of course, it is not possible to predict the future. In fact, in 1970,
when Salvador Allende became the first Marxist politician to be freely
elected as a head of state in any country, almost no one would have
predicted that a few years later Chile would become the poster child for
neoliberalism. But in spite of this uncertainty about what will happen
in the years to come, I believe that Chile will move away from markets
and competition. It is unlikely to become a very highly regulated economy dominated by state-owned enterprises, but it will veer away from
the model put in place by the Chicago Boys and refined by the Concertación governments. Some will remember the neoliberal era with nos-
talgia, and others will feel relieved that it ended. It is possible that in one
or two generations Chile will be where it was for most of the twentieth
century: in the middle of the Latin American peloton.

ACKNOWLEDGMENTS

AT TIMES I think that I have been working on this book for my whole professional life. Of course, that is not the case, but what is true is that for decades I have been working on Chile, on its challenges and tribulations, its hopes and frustrations, its progress and retrogressions. In many ways this book is the culmination of a very long research project. In it I distill my interpretation of one of the most interesting and deeper economic revolutions of modern times, a revolution that began in 1955 with the US State Department's Chile Project and the training of a group of Chilean economists at the University of Chicago.

In writing the book I have tried to keep a balanced view, a perspective that captures the success of the Chile Project and the Chicago Boys and that, at the same time, deconstructs the faults and shortcomings of the whole endeavor. I have made an effort to capture the oppressive atmosphere of the dictatorship of Augusto Pinochet and the role played by the Chicago Boys in it. I have also attempted to convey the hope that the return to democracy generated in millions of people, the jump in incomes and the improvement in social conditions of the postdictatorship era, and the frustrations of the last few years. I have sought to understand "Chile's paradox"—why there was a major and violent revolt in the most successful country in Latin America—and to extract useful lessons for policy makers from around the world.

I met and talked with almost every one of the main characters in this story, with the important exception of the military. I never met Pinochet or the other members of the junta or their immediate entourage. I didn't meet President Salvador Allende either, but I did become friends with several members of his cabinet.

The list of people I want to thank is long, and I apologize if I have left anyone out. I interviewed many of them formally for the book. With others, I had ongoing conversations over the years, when we met at a conference, at a dinner party, or just to have a coffee or a drink.

My greatest debts are, without any doubt, to Alejandra Cox and Al Harberger. For many years I have talked about economics with them, and every time I have done it, I have been marveled by how much I learn. The book is dedicated to Alita and Alito, and to young Adrian, who still does not know Chile.

I thank Michael Bordo, Charles Calomiris, Renato Cristi, Juan Andrés Fontaine, and Doug Irwin for reading earlier drafts of the manuscript and for making detailed suggestions. I am grateful to Eduardo Aninat, Harald Beyer, Ignacio Briones, Carlos Cáceres, René Cortázar, Sergio de Castro, José De Gregorio, Nicolás Eyzaguirre, Fernando Flores, Alejandro Foxley, Claudio Hohmann, Carlos Hurtado, Felipe Larraín, Rolf Lüders, Mario Marcel, Manuel Marfán, Carlos Massad, Máximo Pacheco, Ricardo Solari, Rodrigo Valdés, Andrés Velasco, and Rodrigo Vergara for conversations throughout the years. I also thank Sergio Baeza, Guillermo Calvo, Juan Ignacio Correa, José Luis Daza, Victoria Hurtado, Fernando Losada, Leonidas Montes, Patricio Navia, Marcelo Selowsky, George Tavlas, and Sergio Undurraga. My conversations with Juan Gabriel Valdés helped me understand some of the most difficult moments lived by many Chileans during their prolonged exile. I thank Andrea Repetto, Claudia Martínez, and Claudia Sanhueza for discussing with me the most recent developments, including many intricate issues related to income inequality and the Constitutional Convention. I thank Patricio Fernández, Felipe Gana, and Matías Rivas for not complaining when I asked a multitude of questions regarding the social and political angles of recent history. I benefited from conversations—many of them while working on economic reform in different countries—with the late Sergio de la Cuadra, Ernesto Fontaine, and Juan Carlos Méndez, three Chicago Boys of the highest caliber. I would be remiss not to mention Emilio Sanfuentes, one of Chile's brightest minds, a man with a remarkable sense of humor and the rare ability to see the future the way it actually turned out to be. For over a year, before going to

Chicago, I met with Emilio once a week. Every conversation was enlightening. He died in a tragic accident in 1982. Three reviewers for Princeton University Press made very useful comments that helped improve the presentation significantly. I thank my editors at the Press, Josh Drake and Joe Jackson, for their support throughout the process; their devotion went well beyond the call of duty. I am indebted to Luis Cabezas for wonderful research assistance. Every time I needed some obscure data or a reference, he was able to find them promptly. He read the manuscript several times and worked efficiently on the bibliography. As always, I thank Ed Leamer for endless conversations about economic policy and methodology; I always learn something new from him. I finally thank several classes of University of California–Los Angeles graduate students to whom I presented some of this material in my course on emerging markets.

Los Angeles
September 2022

The Origins of Neoliberalism and the Chile Project

DURING THE first half of 1979, French philosopher Michel Foucault gave a series of lectures on neoliberalism in which he celebrated the work of Gary Becker, the quintessential University of Chicago economist who would win the 1992 Nobel Prize in Economics for work that expanded the realm of economics to every sphere of life and society.[1] Three years earlier, Becker had published his book *The Economic Approach to Human Behavior*, in which he asserted that "the economic approach provides a valuable unified framework for understanding *all* human behavior." He then added, "All human behavior can be viewed as involving participants who maximize their utility from a stable set of preferences."[2] In the book he applied economic thinking to racial discrimination, democracy, criminal behavior, irrationality, marriage, fertility, social interactions, altruism, egoism, and genetic fitness. For many of his critics, including philosopher Michael Sandel, Becker's view that all human behavior was explained by economic circumstances was a clear reflection of the arrogance of neoliberals. For his followers, including the Chicago Boys in Chile, Becker had provided deep insights that could be used effectively in the design of economic policies, including those aimed at providing social services. Many of the second-generation Chicago Boys, who had only been exposed to the work of Milton Friedman through his price theory textbook and articles, thought that Becker was a significantly more sophisticated version of Friedman. In their minds,

Becker provided the technical underpinnings of many of the more daring policy proposals in Friedman's *Capitalism and Freedom*.

The international Left was shocked by Foucault's positive views on Gary Becker. There was talk of Foucault's betrayal and confusion, and many argued that he had misread Becker and failed to grasp how reactionary his thinking was.[3] What had happened? Why had Foucault, one of the most famous radical thinkers of his generation, developed a penchant for neoliberalism?[4] François Ewald, one of Foucault's closest disciples, argued that the philosopher was fascinated by Becker's "manner of thinking," by his construction of a fictional *homo œconomicus* who makes decisions on the bases of economic considerations and cost-benefit analyses and is not encumbered by morality or juridical questions.[5] According to Ewald, "Foucault gives economists a very specific status, they [economists] are truth producers ... [he sees Becker's] kind of analyses as creating the possibility to promote, to envision new kinds of liberty."[6]

For a long time, Becker was unaware of what Foucault had said about his work, or that he had called him "the most radical representative of American neoliberalism." And, in 2012, when he finally read two of the lectures in Foucault's *The Birth of Biopolitics*, Becker's overall reaction was, "I like most of it, and I don't disagree with much. I also cannot tell if Foucault is disagreeing with me."[7] Becker was pleased that Foucault seemed "to take seriously the so-called neoliberalism that was based upon human capital analysis, and a particular approach to understanding how individuals behave."[8]

What makes Foucault's lectures interesting is not only their content—including his comparisons of American, Austrian, French, and German neoliberalism—but also the fact that they were delivered two years *before* the ascension of Margaret Thatcher and Ronald Reagan to power. These lectures presaged how dominant so-called neoliberal ideas would become in the years to follow, and how fast aspects of the doctrine would capture the imagination of reform-minded politicians in Asia, eastern Europe, and Latin America.

In the lectures Foucault does not mention Augusto Pinochet or the Chicago Boys, despite the fact that he was perfectly aware of the ferocity of the dictatorship and of the free-market reforms pushed by Milton

Friedman's disciples. As was noted in chapter 3, when Chilean sociologist and left-wing activist Antonio Sánchez met with him in his Parisian apartment in 1975, Foucault told him, "Chile's tragedy [the coup and its aftermath] is not the result of the Chilean people's failure, but the result of the serious mistakes and the monstrous responsibility of you, Marxists."[9] In this regard, Foucault shared economist Paul Rosenstein-Rodan's harsh evaluation of the Unidad Popular coalition. In a 1974 article published in *Challenge*, Rosenstein-Rodan wrote, "Salvador Allende died not because he was a socialist, but because he was an incompetent. . . . It is not inherent in socialism to be inefficient."[10]

For Foucault neoliberalism is best understood as a doctrine defined *in opposition to* certain ideas and policy proposals: Keynesian policies, social pacts, and the growth of government. In his view, neoliberals have a phobia of the state. Foucault argues that this adversarial approach of neoliberals was very clear in Henry Simons's writings, including his famous 1934 pamphlet *A Positive Program for Laissez Faire* and in his criticism of the Beveridge Report on policies to promote employment and develop a welfare state in the United Kingdom. According to Foucault, this was also the case in France, where "neo-liberalism defined itself through opposition to the Popular Front, post-war Keynesian policies, [and] planning."[11] As the analysis in this book shows, this was also the case of the Chicago Boys in Chile. In the domestic war of ideas, they positioned themselves and their policy suggestions in opposition to structuralism (economist Aníbal Pinto was one of their bêtes noires), protectionism, Keynesianism, and Marxism. The Chicago Boys also defined their doctrine in opposition to the proclivity of local businessmen to eschew competition and seek advantages through government support for their ventures.

The Origins of Neoliberalism:
The Colloque Lippmann, 1938

On Friday, August 26, 1938, a group of twenty-six men gathered in Paris to discuss the future of capitalism and of representative democracy. The meeting was organized by French philosopher Louis Rougier, and its participants included Raymond Aron, Friedrich Hayek, Ludwig von Mises, Michael Polanyi, Wilhelm Röpke, Jacques Rueff, and other classical liberal thinkers.[12] The most important participant and the guest of honor was American journalist Walter Lippmann, whose book *The Good Society* had recently been translated into French, as *La cité libre* (The free city). As Rougier explained in his letter of invitation, the purpose of the Colloque Lippmann was to spend several days discussing, in a private setting, the messages, lessons, and implications of Lippmann's book.[13] In this work, published in the United States in 1937, Lippmann argued that in order to preserve democracy and defeat authoritarian and collectivist regimes it was necessary to rescue liberalism from the jaws of laissez-faire, a system that had created social distress and pushed workers toward totalitarian political movements (Marxism and fascism). In Lippmann's view, the only way to defeat the likes of Adolf Hitler and Joseph Stalin was by reforming capitalism deeply and by adding social concerns to the profit motive. Lippmann's perspective is clearly captured when he writes, "[A] greater equalization of incomes . . . is the necessary objective of a liberal policy. . . . The equalization must be effected by measures which promote the efficiency of the markets as regulators of the division of labor; they must strike, therefore, not at profits of successful competition but at the tolls of monopoly."[14]

The problem, as Lippmann sees it, is that liberals have grown too comfortable with Manchester-style capitalism without paying full attention to its social and political consequences and to its tendency to create very large companies with vast monopoly power. Liberals have ignored capitalism's tendency to generate substantial "maldistribution" of income. He notes that "latter-day liberals became mired in status quo which held them to the idea that nothing should be done . . . that nothing needed to be done [about social problems and monopolies]."[15]

There is vast agreement that the Colloque Lippmann, which lasted until August 30, 1938, represented the launching of "neoliberalism" as a set of ideas aimed at rethinking capitalism. Although the term *neoliberal* had been used before by authors such as Pierre-Étienne Flandin and Gaetan Pirou, it had not been used in a systematic and well-defined fashion to articulate a set of fairly specific policy propositions.

In the published version of the Colloque Lippmann's proceedings, Louis Rougier wrote that the ideas discussed in Paris "sketched the outline of a doctrine called by some 'constructor liberalism' [*libéralisme constructeur*], referred to by others as 'neo-capitalism' and for which use of the name 'neo-liberalism' seems to prevail." Rougier noted that he had organized the meeting "in a matter of days" in order to gather a number of thinkers "around a discussion table, for purpose of reviewing the trial of capitalism and to seek to define a doctrine, the conditions of creating, the new tasks of a true liberalism."[16]

During the colloquium, deep disagreements on how to save capitalism arose, and two distinct groups emerged. One, which included Walter Lippmann and Alexander Rustow, argued in favor of an increased role of the state in making sure that competition and the price system prevailed. They feared that without major reform, an economic system based on planning instead of markets would be adopted in country after country. In his inaugural speech at the colloquium Walter Lippmann said,

> I am of the opinion that we will not accomplish anything if . . . our goal is only to reaffirm and to resuscitate the formulas of nineteenth-century liberalism. . . . This old liberalism, let us not forget, has been embraced by the classes in power. . . . The first task of liberals consists today, not of creating presentations and propaganda, but of seeking and thinking. In the presence of the debacle of nineteenth-century liberalism, it would be futile for them to calmly await the resurrection of Mr. Gladstone, and to believe that their mission consists in repeating the formulas of the last century.[17]

In arguing for a complete revamp of the liberal doctrine, Lippmann found support in German sociologist and economist Alexander Rustow, a man who had sought refuge from the Nazis in Turkey, and who knew Ludwig von Mises very well. Rustow favored a confiscatory inheritance tax so that new generations would play on a leveled playing field.[18]

The second group, led by Hayek and Mises, was significantly more in favor of free markets and vehemently rejected increased state intervention. According to Mises, monopolies were the result of inadequate government actions; they were not, as many argued during the colloquium, a natural consequence of technological progress or, as Lippmann put it in his book, of the "division of labor." During the morning session of Saturday, August 27, Mises said, "It is not the free play of market forces, but the anti-liberal policies of government, that created the conditions favorable to the establishments of monopolies. . . . It is legislation, it is policy, that have created the tendency toward monopoly."[19]

Although the differences of opinion were strong, during the final session of the Colloque Lippmann it was agreed, unanimously, to create a center of studies to deal with the challenges faced by capitalism and the market system. This new institution was called the Centre International d'Études pour la Rénovation du Libéralisme (International Center for the Renovation of Liberalism). Participants agreed to reconvene in early 1939 to discuss the "forms of intervention of public powers compatible with the pricing mechanism." According to the proceedings, "the solution to this problem alone [the extent of government intervention] provides a definition of the liberal economy, which is that of the market."[20]

The Mont Pèlerin Society and the Chile Project

Because of the impending war, the 1939 meeting never took place. Nine years later, in April 1947, some of the participants of the Colloque Lippmann—those who had gravitated toward Hayek's and Mises's ideas—joined, in Switzerland, other supporters of the free market to found the Mont Pèlerin Society. Walter Lippmann, Louis Rougier, and Alexander Rustow were not among the founders of this new group, which for years was dominated by Friedrich Hayek. Only four of the twenty-six attendees to the Colloque Lippmann were among the founders: Friedrich Hayek, Ludwig von Mises, Michael Polanyi, and Wilhelm Röpke. Louis Rougier was only accepted as a member ten years later (his delayed acceptance had to do with Rougier's role in the Vichy government during World War II), and Lippmann and Rustow decided that they were uninterested in taking an active part in such a doctrinaire endeavor.[21] Without the interference of the more moderate participants of the Colloque Lippmann, Hayek and Mises, the leaders of the new group—which after a long discussion was named for the location of its first meeting—had a free hand to promote capitalism with a minimal role for the state.

There was not a single Latin American among the founding members of the Mont Pèlerin Society. There were, however, four University of Chicago faculty members: Aaron Director, Milton Friedman, Frank Knight, and George Stigler. Friedman and Stigler would become the leaders of what may be called the neoliberal wing of the second Chicago school in the 1950s through 1980s. They would have great influence over the Chicago Boys.

In 1973, when they were summoned by the military to work in the new government, the Chicago Boys had never heard the term *neoliberal*, nor did they know that there was a body of policies that had been given that name. To be sure, some of them had taken Milton Friedman's and Frank Knight's classes at the University of Chicago, but with the exception of Rolf Lüders, none of them had worked directly with them. The senior Chicago Boys returned to Chile from Hyde Park in 1958, before George Stigler joined the faculty. They did not interact with Ronald Coase, Friedrich Hayek, or Bob Mundell, and not one of them belonged to the Mont Pèlerin Society. Moreover, when the Chilean (and other Latin American) students arrived in Chicago, Henry Simons had already died, and Jacob Viner, another towering defender of free markets, had already left for Princeton University (in 1946).[22]

The Evolving Meaning of *Neoliberalism*

Foucault's lectures were published in French in 2004, twenty years after his death, and are verbatim transcriptions of what he said at the Collège de France between January and April 1979.[23] At the time, the term *neoliberalism* was only used in academia; it had not yet become an everyday term used in media stories and analyses to describe an economic doctrine based on free markets, globalization, and deregulation; *neoliberalism* had not been used in the popular media to refer to *homo œconomicus*, Gary Becker, the Mont Pèlerin Society, or the University of Chicago. The first time the *New York Times* used neoliberalism in this context was on November 20, 1988, in a story about Carlos Salinas de Gortari, the

Harvard University–educated president-elect of Mexico, who had run on a market-oriented reform platform. Until that time, *neoliberalism* had denoted, in the media, the thinking of Senator Gary Hart of Colorado, who was considering running for president, and the ideas of John Turner, the new leader of the Liberal Party in Canada.[24]

A search using the internet platform ProQuest indicates that the *New York Times* did not publish any articles that included the words *neoliberal* or *neoliberalism* between 1930 and 1970; there were three stories during the 1970s, the decade Pinochet took power and the Chicago Boys launched the Chilean reforms; another thirteen articles were published between 1980 and 1990.[25] After that time there was a significant increase in the number of stories in the popular press. Between 2000 and 2010, the *New York Times* published forty-eight stories with the word *neoliberal* in them, with titles like "Some Chinese See the Future, and It's Capitalist" (May 4, 2002), and "Still Poor, Latin Americans Protest Push for Open Markets" (July 19, 2002). Between 2010 and 2020, the number of stories catapulted to 164, including "The Neoliberal Looting of America" (July 2, 2020), and "Cornel West Doesn't Want to Be a Neoliberal Darling" (December 3, 2017). The earliest references to *neoliberalism* in the popular press within Chile's context are from late 1988, when Georgetown University professor Arturo Valenzuela penned two op-eds in the *Boston Globe*. The number of stories in leading US newspapers—the *Chicago Tribune, Los Angeles Times, New York Times,* and *Washington Post*—that included the word *neoliberal* in conjunction with Chile increased from merely two in 1980–89, to twenty-six in 2000–2009, and to fifty-three in 2010–19.

Controversies surrounding the term *neoliberal* are not new. Already in the late 1950s and early 1960s the label made some economists uncomfortable. For example, in a scholarly article on German neoliberals (or ordoliberals) published in 1960, Henry M. Oliver writes that "some of the authors included in this study have objected to the term 'neoliberal,' believing that it does not sufficiently distinguish them from defenders of lasses-faire."[26] According to Carl J. Friedrich, many thinkers in England and Germany favored other labels to describe their political views. Many of them preferred that their movement, based on ideas

"beyond Communism and Fascism," be characterized as "liberal con-
servatism."[27] During a visit to Chile in April 1981, Friedrich Hayek was
asked, within the context of the neoliberal doctrine, how his views differed from those of Karl Popper. In his reply, Hayek clearly stated that
he did not accept the tag of neoliberal: "The problem is that we are not
neo-liberals. Those who define themselves in this way are not liberals,
they are socialists."[28]

NOTES

Introduction

1. During the 1960s similar programs were launched by the State Department in other Latin American countries, including Argentina, Brazil, Colombia, and Mexico. In many cases US foundations were involved and helped fund the training of young economists in some of the best American universities. Edwards (2010) and Thorp (1998) analyze the economic history of Latin America during most of the twentieth century. J. G. Valdés (1989, 1995) discusses the State Department's efforts to influence economic thinking in the region.

2. When taken as a whole, the economic performance of the dictatorship is not impressive. However, as will be shown in the chapters that follow, looking at 1973–90 as a homogeneous period is misleading. During the early years—until the 1982 currency crisis—most of the costs of implementing a new capitalistic system were incurred, with the consequent sluggish growth and high unemployment. Starting in 1984 a new and younger team of Chicago Boys took over the ministries of finance and economics and a second round of reforms was launched. During this phase the rate of growth of GDP per capita jumped to an average of almost 5 percent per year, a figure that is impressive from a historical emerging-markets perspective. See chapter 9 for details.

3. In Chile the Socialist Party has a tradition of being to the left of the Communist Party. On the constitutional constraints to introduce changes to the political and economic systems put in place during the dictatorship, see chapter 7.

4. For social indicators, see UNDP (2019). For poverty head count, see World Bank (n.d.).

5. *Guardian* (1975), emphasis added.

6. See the data in ECLAC (n.d.), International Monetary Fund (n.d.), and World Bank (n.d.). All these data are available online. As I show in chapter 3 (table 3.1), between 1945 and 1970 Chile also underperformed the average Latin American nation. Growth was lower, inflation was higher, inequality was higher, and living standards were lower than the typical country in the region.

7. Poverty is measured as anyone living with less than $5.50 a day (2011 purchasing power parity), as a percentage of the total population; World Bank (n.d.).

8. See Sengupta (2021).

9. Nicas (2022). One of the original members of the convention resigned his post, making the active number 154 members.

10. *Economist* (2022b).

11. Anderson (1999).

12. Wallace-Wells (2021); Gerstle (2021).

13. Reinhoudt and Audier (2018, 9).

14. For an early biography of Lippmann, see Steel (1999). For a study of Lippmann as a public economist, see Goodwin (2014). The title of Lippmann's book is a tribute to Graham Wallas, the author of *The Great Society*.

15. Friedman (1951), version in MFAHI.

16. In the introduction to his 1962 book *Capitalism and Freedom*, Milton Friedman laments that with time the meaning of the term *liberal* had changed significantly in the United States. In this paragraph I paraphrase Friedman's text. Gerstle (2022) discusses the evolution of neoliberal policies in the United States and the United Kingdom. He does not cover Chile's case, arguably the most extreme of all neoliberal experiments.

17. Hayek, however, denied that he was a neoliberal. On Hayek and neoliberalism, see Caldwell (2011).

18. The expression "the marketization of everything" comes from Sandel (2012, 203).

19. Sandel (2018, 358), emphasis added.

20. Harvey (2005, 2).

21. Gertz and Kharas (2019, 8).

22. Stigler (1965, 284).

23. Harberger (2016); Friedman and Friedman (1998).

24. J. G. Valdés (1989, 1995).

25. On the literature of the Chicago school, see, for instance, Hammond (2013); Irwin (2018); Emmett (2010); Tavlas (2022); and Van Horn, Mirowski, and Stapleford (2011) and the works cited therein.

26. Lüders (2022).

27. For an analysis of US involvement in the coup, see Edwards (2010); and Select Committee to Study Governmental Operations with Respect to Intelligence Activities (1975). See also chapter 4.

28. Délano (1999).

29. Délano (2011).

Chapter 1: Exporting Capitalism

1. For the historical evolution of foreign aid policies of the United States and other advanced countries, see Edwards (2015).

2. On Schultz's views on Latin America, see Schultz (1956); on Patterson, see O'Brien (2007).

3. The ICA would eventually become the United States Agency for International Development. On other State Department Programs in Latin America see, for example, the papers collected in Montecinos, Markoff, and Alvarez-Rivadulle (2009).

4. Schultz (1964, 187).

5. Structuralism is a school of thought based on the idea that economic performance is largely determined by the country's "structure," and that this is very rigid and unresponsive to price and other incentives. The main representative of structuralism was Argentine economist Raul Prebisch.

6. More than thirty years later, in 1984, Luis Escobar Cerda was appointed minister of finance by Pinochet.

7. On January 14, 1954, a letter from Catalina Caldentey and Hernán Trucco (the president of the student body), to the rector, Monsignor Alfredo Silva Santiago, complained about the low quality of the learning experience. Among other things, they pointed out that the director of the school spent only two hours a day at the university; Catalina Caldentey and Hernán Trucco to Monsignor Alfredo Silva Santiago, January 14, 1954, HAPUC, Box 115, Folder 1, Document 2. A few months later the director, Lukas Bakovic, resigned; Lukas Bakovic to Alfredo Silva, April 6, 1954, HAPUC, Box 115, Folder 1, Document 3.

8. Julio Chaná Cariola to Albion Patterson, January 27, 1955, HAPUC, Box 115, Folder 1.

9. Agreement's modification by Alfredo Silva Santiago and Albion W. Patterson, HAPUC, Box 115, Folder 1, Document 5.

10. The June 1955 trip by Schultz and his colleagues happened after the ICA's Chile Project had been launched, and the University of Chicago was agreed upon as a partner. The contract, however, had not been signed.

11. Agreement's modification by Alfredo Silva Santiago and Albion W. Patterson, HAPUC, Box 115, Folder 1, Document 5.

12. For the correspondence between Lewis and the rector of Católica, see HAPUC, Box 115, Folders 1–2.

13. Alito is the Spanish diminutive of Al. To his Latin American students and friends, Harberger was, thus, "Little Al."

14. See Bray (1962, 1966, 1967); and T. E. Davis (1963).

15. See Harberger (1964); and Bailey (1962, 1968). During his three months' stay in Santiago during the (Chilean) winter of 1956, Harberger wrote a long memorandum to his Chicago colleagues on the Chilean economy. In the memorandum he tells a long story on how expensive—relative to prices in the United States—automobiles, durables, and other international goods were. He also discussed extensively the very high rate of inflation at the time (50 percent). The memorandum was never published in English; there is, however, a published Spanish version; see Harberger (2000).

16. George Shultz, in Shultz and Taylor (2020, 11).

17. The nine pioneer students, with the date of arrival and source of financing, were Florencio Fellay (October 1955, Institute of Inter-American Affairs); Victor Ochsenius (October 1955, Institute of Inter-American Affairs); Carlos Clavel (October 1955, Institute of Inter-American Affairs); Carlos Massad (October 1956, University of Chicago–Pontificia Universidad Católica de Chile Fellowship), Sergio de Castro (October 1956, University of Chicago–Pontificia Universidad Católica de Chile Fellowship), Ernesto Fontaine (January 1957, University of Chicago–Pontificia Universidad Católica de Chile Fellowship), Pedro Jeftanovic (January 1957, University of Chicago–Pontificia Universidad Católica de Chile Fellowship), Luis Alberto Fuenzalida (September 1956, Fulbright Program), and, the only woman in the group, Herta Castro (June 1957, Fulbright Program). Information is taken from the report prepared by Centro de Investigaciones Económicas; see Committee Members, Centro de Investigaciones Económicas, *Report Centro de Investigaciones Económicas, Facultad de Ciencias Económicas, Pontificia Universidad Católica de Chile,* June 15, 1957, HAPUC, Box 115, Folder 2, Document 2, pp. 2–3.

18. Scholarships included return tickets between Santiago and Chicago, tuition costs, and a living allowance of seven dollars per day for those who were single; married students received an eight-dollar allowance—that is, the marginal cost of a spouse was estimated to be one dollar a day. In addition, students had access to the library, the student health system, the gym, and received a lump sum for the cost of books. Registration and fees for attending the American Economic Association's annual meetings were also covered. Carlos Massad was the only married student; his wife Lily volunteered to cut the hair of the other Chileans. See Committee Members, Centro de Investigaciones Económicas, *Report Centro*, 3–4.

19. Carlos Clavel to Simon Rottenberg, June 14, 1956, HAPUC, Box 115, Folder 2, Document 7.

20. The importance of taking undergraduate courses is also mentioned by Sergio de Castro in his memoirs, as told to Arancíbia Clavel and Balart Páez (2007).

21. Marshall (1890); Viner (1932); Robinson (1933).

22. Mandatory readings in Economics 209 and Economics 302 and Final Examination in Economics 300A and Economics 300B, HAPUC, Box 115, Folder 1, Document 13. For a discussion on Frank Knight as a teacher, including details on his History of Thought course, see Patinkin (1973).

23. In a report written for the ICA in 1957, Lewis stated that "we have found that almost without exception the trainees, although clearly men of substantial promise, have had insufficient training in Chile"; Lewis, quoted in J. G. Valdés (1995, 141).

24. See Becker (1992).

25. Hachette A. de la F. (2016, 31).

26. E. R. Fontaine (2009, 55).

27. Hachette A. de la F. (2016, 36).

28. See Foucault (2008), lectures 9–11.

29. For details on these visits, see Caldwell and Montes (2015).

30. Thatcher (1982).

31. Pinto used these terms in a letter published in the November 1957 issue of *Panorama económico* (Pinto 1957, 738), in which he criticized a paper by Rottenberg on the growth process. For Rottenberg's paper, see Simon Rottenberg, Comment in Seminario de Integración Social, HAPUC, Box 115, Folder 1, Document 6.

32. Harberger and Edwards (2021, 16); Harberger and Edwards (forthcoming, 18).

33. H. Gregg Lewis, quoted in J. G. Valdés (1995, 144).

Chapter 2: The Chicago Boys in the Ivory Tower

1. Even before the students returned from Chicago, representatives of the private sector tried to influence the direction of the newly formed Center of Economic Research. Patricio Ugarte H. to Alfredo Silva Santiago, HAPUC, Box 115, Folder 1, Document 9.

2. Hachette A. de la F. (2016).

3. Fontaine told me that that student was Marcelo Selowsky, who would later go to the University of Chicago and become an assistant professor at Harvard University; Ernesto R. Fontaine, interview with the author, Sonora, Mexico, February 2010. In later years Selowsky

joined the World Bank, where he was chief economist for eastern Europe and Latin America. He was instrumental in guiding the bank's role in both regions.

4. During his 1957 visit to Chicago, Monsignor Silva Santiago attended one of the workshops. Walter Müller to Alfredo Silva Santiago, HAPUC, Box 115, Folder 3, Document 10.

5. Harberger (2016).

6. James Lothian, quoted in Clements and Tcha (2004).

7. Tax (1963).

8. Harberger (1950).

9. De Castro (1965).

10. See Arbildúa and Lüders (1968); and Harberger (1963).

11. The adjective *esoteric* was used by Aníbal Pinto in an article criticizing the Chicago Boys; see Pinto (1957).

12. One story is that the name Chicago Boys was first used by Carmen Tessada, the mythical director of studies at the Católica. Another version is that it was coined, in a demeaning way, by structuralist economist Aníbal Pinto.

13. The original contract called for two full-time professors during the first year, three during the second year, and four during the fourth year. Simon Rottenberg to Monsignor Silva Santiago, April 11, 1958, HAPUC, Box 115, Folder 2, Document 13.

14. Monsignor Silva Santiago's trip to Chicago was organized by the Foreign Leaders Program of the International Educational Exchange Service, a US government program. In addition to meeting with US State Department officials—including Roy R. Rubottom, the assistant secretary of state for the Western Hemisphere—the monsignor met with senior officials at the most important foundations, including H. Allen Moe from the Guggenheim Foundation, John F. Janney from the Rockefeller Foundation, Shepard Stone from the Ford Foundation, and J. Peter Grace from the W. R. Grace Foundation. He also spent time with New York's Cardinal Francis Spellman and other Catholic leaders. Walter Müller to Alfredo Silva Santiago, HAPUC, Box 115, Folder 3, Document 10; Vicente Tuskenis to Alfredo Silva Santiago, HAPUC, Box 115, Folder 2, Documents 10; Project Agreement, HAPUC, Box 115, Folder 2, Document 14.

15. Alessandri's stabilization program was based on fixing the exchange rate of 1.053 escudos to the dollar. Automatic wage adjustments based on past inflation were suspended, and a major effort was made to balance the fiscal accounts. In 1959, and despite the fixed value of the dollar, inflation was 33.3 percent. In 1960 it fell precipitously to 5.4 percent, and in 1961 it rebounded to 9.7 percent.

16. Corvalán (1962, 9).

17. Arancibia Clavel and Balart Páez (2007), 96–98; J. G. Valdés (1989), 171–172.

18. See Soto (2003) and Baraona (n.d.).

19. Ballesteros and Ballesteros (1965); Corbo and Yver (1967).

20. In the mid-1960s, and greatly influenced by Harry Johnson, the economists at Católica calculated effective rates of protection—that is, protection to value added, once inputs were netted out—for various crops, and concluded that the structure of import tariffs and quotas discriminated heavily against agriculture. See E. R. Fontaine (1967).

21. Lüders (1969); Morán (1969); Arbildúa and Lüders (1968); E. R. Fontaine (1967).

22. On Levine's prominence and influence, see Korry (1970). When I interviewed him in 1992 for an earlier project, Levine told me how he became a Keynesian: he won a sizable amount of money in the Chilean National Lottery and used all of it to import the most important books on economics from the United Kingdom, including John Maynard Keynes's *General Theory of Employment, Interest and Money*, a book that he devoured. For the Bailey-Levine controversy, see, for example, J. G. Valdés (1995).

23. De Castro (1965); Friedman (1953). On Friedman and exchange rates, see Dellas and Tavlas (2018), Edwards (2020), and Nelson (2020).

24. Myrdal (1968, 3:2081), emphasis in the original.

25. On the different views about the exchange rate in the 1940s, see Irwin (2019).

26. On September 15, 1970, barely ten days after the election of Salvador Allende, Agustín Edwards met with President Richard Nixon, National Security Adviser Henry Kissinger, and Central Intelligence Agency (CIA) director Richard Helms to discuss the future of Chile. According to the Church Report from the United States Senate on the U.S. role in the 1973 Pinochet coup, significant amounts of money was transferred from the CIA to Edwards's newspaper, *El Mercurio*, during Allende's thousand days in office; see Select Committee to Study Governmental Operations with Respect to Intelligence Activities (1975).

27. For a list of the 170 articles, see Soto (2003), 181–191. Free trade was advocated on July 6, 1969, and August 23, 1969. Flexible exchange rates were promoted on May 25, 1968, and June 9, 1969.

28. For Alessandri's economic program, see *Panorama económico* (1970, 13–18). The same issue contains the economic programs of the other two presidential candidates, conservative Jorge Alessandri and Christian Democrat Radomiro Tomic.

29. Fuentes and Valdeavellano (2015).

Chapter 3: Salvador Allende's Thousand Days of Socialism and the Chicago Boys, 1970–1973

1. There are a number of excellent works on the politics and economics of the Unidad Popular coalition; see, for example, Collier and Sater (1996); Fermandois (2013); Valenzuela (1978); Meller (1996); and San Francisco (2019b). See also Dornbusch and Edwards (1991).

2. De Onis (1970).

3. Navia and Osorio (2015).

4. The Chilean Constitution did not allow for immediate reelection. The gambit, however, involved a period of a few weeks when Frei would not be in office, making him eligible to run.

5. See *Washington Post* (1970).

6. Edward M. Korry, telegram, US Department of State, September 1970, NSA, https://nsarchive2.gwu.edu//NSAEBB/NSAEBB8/docs/doc18.pdf. The NSA includes a trove of documents on the Nixon administration's reaction to Allende's election and his Unidad Popular government.

7. Richard Helms, "Meeting with the President on Chile," September 15, 1970, NSA, https://nsarchive2.gwu.edu//NSAEBB/NSAEBB8/docs/doc26.pdf.

8. Central Intelligence Agency, "Classified Message: Immediate Santiago," October 16, 1970, NSA, https://nsarchive2.gwu.edu//NSAEBB/NSAEBB8/docs/doc05.pdf.

9. Novitski (1970b).

10. Novitski (1970a).

11. The first chapter of Unidad Popular's economic program was titled "Hacia una economía socialista" (Toward a socialist economy). See *Panorama económico* (1970).

12. Magasich Airola (2020, 39–40).

13. Carlos Altamirano, a senator and the secretary-general of the Socialist Party, wrote a long criticism of his party's role in unleashing the forces that led to the coup. Altamirano (1977).

14. Henry A. Kissinger, "National Security Decision Memorandum 93: Policy towards Chile," National Security Council, November 9, 1970, NSA, https://nsarchive2.gwu .edu//NSAEBB/NSAEBB8/docs/doc09.pdf.

15. In order to fully understand Chile's historical decline, it is useful to look, briefly, at what we may call its Latin American condition. Some of the most compelling explanations on why Latin America was left behind have to do with the differences between the institutions built by Spain (highly centralized and obsessed with the goals of the Counter-Reformation) and those built by England in its colonies (decentralized and flexible). This point is emphasized by Adam Smith in *The Wealth of Nations*; Smith (1776, book 4, chap. 7). Other hypotheses have focused on culture, religion, wealth distribution, and climate and factor endowments; see Edwards (2010, chap. 2). See, also, Velasco and Parrado (2012).

16. García (1972, 102–104). For very comprehensive summaries of the short-term policies of Unidad Popular, see Inostroza (1971); and Vuskovic (1973).

17. Edwards (2019).

18. Chile already owned 51 percent of some mining companies: Chuquicamata, El Salvador, and El Teniente. The state also had minority holdings in Andina and Exótica. In 1966 the administration of President Eduardo Frei Montalva acquired, at a mutually agreed-on price, a majority stake in some of the largest mines.

19. Book value was estimated at US$414 million, and "excessive profits" added up to US$774 million. See San Francisco (2019a, 311–337); and Zauschquevich and Sutulov (1975, 50).

20. Ley 16640 (1967). In 1975 the military junta decided to add a price indexation clause in order to reestablish the value of the bonds.

21. Decreto Ley 520 (1932).

22. Owners and shareholders of the firm sued the workers for invading private property, but their legal complaints had little practical effect.

23. I have not been able to find a published version of the model, but there were a few others that were floating around at the time that fit those characteristics; see, for example, Varsavsky and Calcagno (1971); and Infante and García-Huidobro (1972).

24. See Edwards (2010). On covert action in Chile, see Select Committee to Study Governmental Operations with Respect to Intelligence Activities (1975).

25. El Palacio de la Moneda (the Palace of the Mint [or Currency]) is so named because it was originally built in 1784 to house the national mint; it became the presidential palace in 1864.

26. Rosenstein-Rodan (1974, 7).

27. Paul Rosenstein-Rodan to Gerhard Tintner, MFAHI, Box 189, Folder 1.

28. Sánchez García (2014).

29. I interviewed Undurraga several times. These data come from Sergio Undurraga, interview with the author via Zoom, June 17, 2021.

30. De Castro (1972).

31. Cámara de Diputados de Chile (1973).

32. Kissinger (1979, 654). See also Nathaniel Davis's (1985) account of his years as US ambassador to Chile.

33. The memorandum commented on the congressional elections of March 1973, in which Unidad Popular got 44 percent of the vote; Central Intelligence Agency (1973).

Chapter 4: Augusto Pinochet's Coup and the Chicago Boys' Reform Program

1. Some of the best accounts of the coup are Cavallo, Salazar, and Sepúlveda (1989); and González (2000).

2. For a (very) detailed timeline, minute by minute, of what transpired on September 11, 1973, see *La Tercera* (2003).

3. The GAP was made up of young members of the Socialist Party who had received military training in Cuba. The group was formed in September 1970, immediately after the election, to protect Allende; at the time, he didn't trust the official police forces assigned to him. See Quiroga (2001).

4. Letelier was detained at 7:40 a.m.; see González (2000). See also *La Tercera* (2003).

5. See *La Tercera* (2003).

6. The proclamation was read by commander Raúl Guillard. See *El Mercurio* (1973).

7. González (2000, 350).

8. Not surprisingly, many of the stories about what actually happened in the palace on the day of the coup differ in their details. For instance, while González (2000, 189) writes that Augusto Olivares took his life with an Uzi, Quiroga (2001, 183) claims that he used a Walther submachine gun.

9. See Arancibia Clavel and Balart Páez (2007, chap. 5).

10. Arancibia Clavel and Balart Páez (2007, 128).

11. General González lasted barely a month in office. In mid-October he was replaced by Fernando Leniz, an executive in the Edwards Group. Sergio de Castro became an adviser to the new minister.

12. Before the coup, only twenty-five (numbered) copies were printed, and except for the authors, senior members of the armed forces, and a few others, no one else had even seen the document. During the first week of the new government, recently appointed minister of planning Roberto Kelly had 250 copies of the documented printed at his ministry. The account that followed is based on De Castro's introduction to the text (De Castro 1992), on his memoirs (Arancibia Clavel and Balart Páez 2007), on statements by other members of the team found in the CIDOC archives, and on Fontaine Aldunate (1988). Full disclosure: in 2010, I was appointed to the board of trustees of the Centro de Estudios Públicos.

13. Arancibia Clavel and Balart Páez (2007, 144). On "labor-managed" firms, see, for example, Vanek (1970).

14. De Castro (1992, 11).

15. Sergio de Castro, in Fuentes and Valdeavellano, (2015, at 38:17).

16. Sergio Undurraga, interview with the author via Zoom, June 17, 2021.

17. Fontaine Aldunate (1988, 19–20).

18. Emilio Sanfuentes died in a fishing accident in 1982.

19. In the mid-1970s, and before going to Chicago, I worked with Emilio Sanfuentes. He was, possibly, the smartest of the Chicago Boys. Although we did talk a few times about The Brick, I never asked him details on whether anyone knew that active navy officers were the final readers of the document.

20. De Castro (1992, 63), emphasis added. This statement has important similarities to what Walter Lippmann wrote in his 1937 book *The Good Society*, which launched the formal neoliberal movement.

21. Friedman (1951, 3).

22. In the early 1970s, effective rates of protection went from –92 percent in agriculture (rapeseed) to a whopping positive 400 percent for textiles (combed wool cloth). For detailed calculations for more than one hundred goods and sectors, see Edwards (1975).

23. Bhagwati (2002).

24. Arancibia Clavel and Balart Páez (2007, chap. 6).

25. Rolf Lüders, and Ernesto R. Fontaine, in Fuentes and Valdeavellano (2015, at 72:00 and 76:00, respectively).

26. See the first table in Hirschman (1963) for data on accumulated and average inflation decade by decade between 1880 and 1960.

27. Harberger (1963, 244).

Chapter 5: Milton Friedman's 1975 Visit and the Shock Treatment

1. Milton Friedman to General Augusto Pinochet, April 21, 1975, in Friedman and Friedman (1998, appendix A to chap. 24, 593).

2. The remarks on the inflation tax are in Milton Friedman, "Record of a Week in Chile, March 20–27, 1975," March 29, 1975, MFAHI, https://miltonfriedman.hoover.org/objects /57505/record-of-a-week-in-span-classqueryhlchilespan-marc?ctx=4a0a8d74f4e9832549b3f 8d5296ab81703486608&idx=1.

3. Milton Friedman to General Augusto Pinochet, April 21, 1975, in Friedman and Friedman (1998, appendix A, 591–594).

4. Friedman, "Record of a Week in Chile."

5. In February 2022, I interviewed Rolf Lüders about Friedman's 1975 visit. I asked him, point blank, how much had Friedman charged the BHC Group for the visit. Lüders made a big zero with his fingers, and then said, "Not a single dollar. He just asked for expenses for him and Rose [his wife]."

6. Friedman (1975, 58–59). Though Friedman's lecture was given in English, the published version of it and of the Q&A session that followed it is in Spanish; I have translated the proceedings back into English.

7. Friedman (1975, 41–70). Al Harberger was also asked, during a series of public talks, about the capital markets and interest rates behavior. In March 1975 he said that very high real interest rates—of the order of 8 percent per month—were a temporary phenomenon, and that he expected that by the end of the year 1975 they would be closer to 2 or 3 percent per month—still a very high 25–40 percent per annum); Harberger (1976, 143).

8. Friedman (1975, 29). As noted, the only available transcript of this talk is in Spanish. "Made in Chile" is in English in the original.

9. Friedman (1975, 70).

10. Friedman (1975, 29).

11. Friedman, "Record of a Week in Chile."

12. Cauas's views on economics were highly influenced by Don Patinkin, the Israeli economist who had been a PhD student at the University of Chicago and who frequently dueled with Friedman on issues of doctrine.

13. For the Harberger approach to public-sector project evaluation, see Harberger (1972).

14. Friedman, "Record of a Week in Chile."

15. The archive is not available online, but must be consulted in person at the university in Santiago. For a summary of the project, see Universidad Finis Terrae, Centro de Investigación y Documentación (n.d.).

16. Friedman and Friedman (1998, 594).

17. Caldwell and Montes (2015, 271).

18. I interviewed Sergio Undurraga, who drafted the plan, several times. A particularly important conversation took place in Los Angeles on September 12, 2021. The fact that the plan was not developed does not mean that the economic team was not worried about the course the economy was taking. Already in February 1975 they were very concerned about the persistent rate of inflation.

19. Fontaine Aldunate (1988, 89).

20. On DINA's efforts to embarrass the economic team, see the discussion in Cavallo, Salazar, and Sepúlveda (1989).

21. Hirschman (1963, 177).

22. The actual process was not exempt from drama, and generated a major spat between the Chicago Boys and the nationalist officers, who at the time were being advised by lawyer and former officer Hugo Araneda.

23. See Friedman (1953).

24. Friedman (1975, question 9).

25. Friedman (1975, question 12).

26. Friedman (1975, question 56).

27. Unemployment reached 24 percent in 1932. For historical statistics on unemployment since 1833, see Díaz, Lüders, and Wagner (2016, table 7.7).

28. *New York Times* (1975).

29. Lewis (1975).

30. Lewis (1975, 1).

31. Handler (1975).

32. Sulzberger (1975).

33. Frank was a student of Harberger's at Chicago. When giving his own oral history, this is what Harberger said about him:

> I can remember going for drinks to Andre Gunder Frank's house and him coming to my apartment, my coach-house apartment and having drinks. And I invited him to be a member of my workshop. I knew that he was left-wing and it didn't bother me at all. But he wanted to do his research on such a topic, so to speak, on a sociopolitical topic which was not in the spirit of my workshop at all. And in the end I said, "Well, you can do what you want but you're not going to be financed by me." How much of the animosity that he later showed to me would have been influenced by that event I don't know. But it's no doubt that his left-wing politics by itself could have led to many of the things that he railed against. (Harberger 2016, 197)

34. As an undergraduate, I attended one of Frank's seminars, in which he went over his theory of the lumpen bourgeoisie and the lumpen proletariat.

35. Frank (1976, 89).

36. Letelier (1976, 137).

37. In June, the International Monetary Fund had provided a US$40 million loan. A few days later, and in spite of the opposition of Senator Ted Kennedy, the US government had approved a loan for US$60 million from the US Agency for International Development; Cavallo, Salazar, and Sepúlveda (1989, 138).

38. Cavallo, Salazar, and Sepúlveda (1989).

39. Kandell (1976).

40. YouTube (2010). I thank Lars Jonung for translating the demonstrator's utterances.

41. Friedman devoted a complete chapter of his memoirs (coauthored with his wife, Rose) to explaining the context of the visit to Chile. See Friedman and Friedman (1998, chap. 24).

42. *Free to Choose* is a ten-part documentary series that aired on PBS during 1980. In it Milton Friedman explains the functioning of a market economic system. The documentary was taped in different locations around the world.

43. In a letter to Lüders, Friedman wrote, "Let me make clear that I have no personal regrets about having gone to Chile. On the contrary, both the visit and what happened subsequently have been highly educational and instructive." Milton Friedman to Rolf Lüders, May 19, 1977, MFAHI, Box 188, Folder 12.

Chapter 6: Market Reforms and the Struggle for Power, 1975–1981

1. In January 1977 Jorge Cauas was appointed ambassador to the United States and was given two tasks: dealing with the incoming Carter administration, which was particularly interested in reimposing sanctions due to human rights violations, and overseeing the Letelier assassination case, making sure that the investigation did not involve military authorities. The idea was to argue that the assassination plan was developed and executed by a fringe group of agents without the knowledge or authorization of their superiors.

2. Contreras was promoted to the rank of general in 1977.

3. The deficit declined from 10 percent of GDP in 1975 to less than 1 percent 1978, and turned into a 1.7 percent surplus in 1979.

4. Alejandro Foxley, quoted in Edwards and Lederman (2002, 358).

5. Jorge Cauas, quoted in Mendez (1979, 173).

6. De Castro (1981, 23).

7. Cavallo, Salazar, and Sepúlveda (1989, chaps. 14–19).

Chapter 7: The Birth of a Neoliberal Regime

1. See Pinochet (1979).

2. Cavallo, Salazar, and Sepúlveda (1989, 273).

3. One of the goals of this law was to appease the American Federation of Labor–Congress of Industrial Organizations, which had called an embargo on cargo shipments to and from Chile. See Cavallo, Salazar, and Sepúlveda (1989).

4. Arancibia Clavel and Balart Páez (2007, 109).

5. Sergio de Castro, quoted in *El Mercurio* (2018). The exact Spanish words in the interview are "Y quedó la cagada que yo predije."

6. Although the word *subsidiarity* is not in the 1980 constitution, the text was written with that principle in mind. See Cristi (2021).

7. As Renato Cristi (2021) notes, in conservative circles, the idea of reforming the 1925 constitution was not new. As far back as 1964 President Jorge Alessandri had considered a major reform that included, in the mode of Francisco Franco in Spain, a senate with members appointed through a corporatist mechanism. This option was introduced in the military's 1980 constitution.

8. Junta de Gobierno (1973).

9. The minister of mining at the time, Admiral Carlos Quiñones was a strong supporter of state ownership of deposits being established at the constitutional level. This was in spite of the fact that the Chilean Navy had been, from day one, on the side of the Chicago Boys.

10. Schauer (2014).

11. Milton Friedman to Sergio de Castro, December 16, 1980, MFAHI, Box 188, Folder 10.

12. For a discussion on the Mont Pèlerin Society and Chile, see, for example, K. Fischer (2009).

13. In 1980, Friedman invited Jorge Cauas, Sergio de Castro, and Ernesto Fontaine to present papers at the MPS meetings to be held at the Hoover Institution. The session was to be titled "The Chilean Economic Experiment." All three declined the invitation, greatly upsetting Friedman. The correspondence is in MFAHI, Box 200, Folder 08. Alvaro Bardón, a Chicago Boy who was president of the Central Bank, and undersecretary of economics during the dictatorship, became a member of the MPS after the return to democracy, when he was no longer in government.

14. Caldwell and Montes (2015); Stigler (1988, 140). Bruce Caldwell is the editor of Hayek's complete works, which are published by the University of Chicago Press.

15. Harberger and Edwards (2021, 7–8); Harberger and Edwards (forthcoming, 10).

16. Martin (1982).

17. Martin (1982).

Chapter 8: Milton Friedman and the Currency Crisis of 1982

1. De Castro (1978, 1677).

2. In the past Chile had unsuccessfully tried using the exchange rate to control inflation. The most recent event was in the early 1960s, during the presidency of conservative Jorge Alessandri. It was an episode that, as discussed in chapter 2, had been severely criticized by none other than Sergio de Castro.

3. Stiglitz (2002).

4. Friedman (1973).

5. De Castro (1981, 23).

6. Martin (1982).

7. Friedman thought that for a fixed rate to work, it was necessary for the country to eliminate the Central Bank. He called the regime of irrevocable fixity a "unified currency regime."

8. Arnold C. Harberger, interview with the author, Los Angeles, August 23, 2020. Mundell was a member of the faculty at the University of Chicago from 1965 to 1972.

9. This assumed that the small economy was open to international trade, with very low trade barriers, something that Chile had accomplished around the time the program was put in place. Just before the stabilization program was begun, Sjaastad and Cortés Douglas (1978) argued that after a two-month lag, the rate of devaluation of the peso would be fully reflected on inflation. If the peso-to-dollar rate was fixed, inflation in Chile would converge with US inflation within two to three months.

10. Sjaastad (1983, 12), emphasis added.

11. Johnson (1969, 16), emphasis added.

12. Johnson (1972, 1560).

13. Johnson (1977, 266), emphasis added.

14. Credibility was, of course, a key aspect of this view. Starting in the late 1990s, and to a large extent as a result of experiences in Israel and the Southern Cone, a vast literature on nominal anchors and credibility developed. See, for example, Bruno et al. (1988); Calvo and Végh (1994); and S. Fischer (2001).

15. Edwards and Edwards (1991, table 3.9).

16. De Castro (1981, 23).

17. Milton Friedman, quoted in *La Tercera* (1981).

18. *Ercilla* (1981, 21).

19. Friedman (1995). The paper wasn't published until 1995; an addendum was written after the currency crisis of 1982.

20. Friedman (1973, 47), emphasis added.

21. Friedman (1995, 7), emphasis added.

22. The previous two governors of the Central Bank were also Chicago Boys: Alvaro Bardón and Pablo Baraona.

23. For Friedman's discussions on the two aspects of freedom (political and economic) in the context of Chile, see Edwards and Montes (2020).

24. Milton Friedman to José Rodríguez Elizondo, December 18, 1981, MFAHI, Folder 188-13.

25. Milton Friedman, in *La Segunda* (1981). In retranslating this quote from Spanish back to English I have tried to maintain the punctuation as it appeared in the original article.

26. Apparently the reporter got a tape recording with Friedman's improvised remarks. Some of the terms appear in quotation marks and are supposed to be in English; they are either misspelled or the reporter didn't know what Friedman had said. Instead of a "pegged" exchange rate, the article reads "packed" rate; instead of a "unified" currency, it reads "unifright" currency.

27. Friedman (1953, 164–165).

28. Edwards and Edwards (1991, 68).

29. See, for example, Klein (2010); and Stiglitz (2002).

30. Milton Friedman to Peter D. Whitney, July 8, 1982, MFAHI, Folder 189-02.

31. Milton Friedman to José Rodriguez Elizondo, October 15, 1982, MFAHI, Folder 188-13.

32. Friedman and Friedman (1998, 405), emphasis added.

33. Friedman and Mundell (2001).

34. Friedman (1995, 7).

35. Milton Friedman to Robert J. Alexander, August 5, 1997, MFAHI, Folder 188-10, emphasis added.

36. The analysis that follows extends to Edwards and Montes (2020), which deals with the political implications of Friedman's two visits to Chile, including his meeting with General Pinochet; the analysis of the exchange rate issue is quite general, and doesn't go into the details of how Friedman reacted to the currency and banking crisis of 1982. See also Montes (2016). Friedman was not the only prominent economist who influenced Chile's policies in the 1970s and 1980s. On Friedrich Hayek's visits to Chile, see Caldwell and Montes (2015).

37. Friedman (1994, 241).

38. Edwards and Edwards (1991).

39. Milton Friedman to General Roberto Soto MacKenney, September 29, 1986, MFAHI, Box 188, Folder 13.

Chapter 9: The Second Round of Reforms, 1983–1990

1. Although at this point some women were added to the team, the Chilean press continued to refer to the tribe as the Chicago Boys.

2. Büchi Buc (1993, 170).

3. See *New York Times* (1985).

4. As a result of these operations, banks had two classes of shares.

5. For details on the investments, see Edwards and Edwards (1991); and J. A. Fontaine (1989).

6. Edwards and Edwards (1991), 220.

7. At the University of Chicago, Paul Romer and I were classmates. In the winter quarter of 1981 we were members of a group of senior PhD students who taught intermediate macroeconomics to undergraduates.

8. In Chile, however, there was a deeper ideological battle behind the way schools were organized. On the one hand, there were the Freemasons, who for a long time had controlled the

public-sector educational apparatus. On the other hand, there were Catholics who believed that the church should play a fundamental role in educating Chile's youth but that such education should be subsidized by the state.

9. Ley 19070 (1991); Lagos (2020).

10. During the second round of reforms, the state provided funding to those universities where students with the best scores on standardized admissions tests were enrolled. These applicants usually joined the best and most traditional schools—Católica and the Universidad de Chile—which got much better financing than other schools.

11. Smith (1977, 802).

12. There was also some concern about the public's reaction to certain policies. But these concerns were secondary, as the mechanisms of democratic rule were completely absent at the time.

13. J. A. Fontaine (1989, 216).

14. Barro and Gordon (1983).

15. Harberger (1971).

16. Harberger (1963).

17. In June 1981, José López Portillo, the president of Mexico, said at a press conference that he would defend the peso "like a dog." A few months later Mexico suffered one of the worst devaluation crises in modern economic history. That crisis forced the Mexican secretary of finance and credit, Jesús Silva Herzog, to travel to Washington and confer with his US counterpart, Donald Regan. López Portillo blamed the banking sector for the debacle, and in his last state of the union address he announced that he was nationalizing all Mexican banks.

18. Gary Becker to Milton Friedman, August 2, 1994, MFAHI, Box 200, Folder 5.

19. Harberger and Edwards (2021, 9); Harberger and Edwards (forthcoming, 12).

20. Sergio de Castro, in Fuentes and Valdeavellano (2015, at 57:01).

21. Cavallo, Salazar, and Sepúlveda (1989, 138–41).

22. Albert Fishlow to Milton Friedman, July 2, 1976, MFAHI, Box 188, Folder 11, emphasis in the original.

23. Milton Friedman to Augusto Pinochet, August 7, 1976, MFAHI, Box 188, Folder 13. Fernando Flores was freed in August 1976 and subsequently settled in the United States.

24. For a comparative quantitative study of the growth process in Latin America, see Loayza, Fajnzylber, and Calderón (2005).

Chapter 10: The Return of Democracy and Inclusive Neoliberalism

1. The junta allowed CIEPLAN to operate with some degree of freedom, as long as its work remained rather technical and researchers did not voice their criticisms openly in the press. In many respects CIEPLAN was the only place where opponents of the regime could gather and discuss alternative policies and models.

2. Some authors have argued that the new administration was constrained by the Pinochet constitution. For details, see chapters 7 and 15.

3. *La Tercera* (2019).

4. *Newsweek* (1990, 36).

5. Boeninger (1992); Edwards (2010).

6. In October 1998, while a member of the Senate, he traveled to London, where he was arrested and charged for his alleged involvement in the assassination of several Spanish citizens during the dictatorship. The British government released him in March 2000 for health reasons. He died on December 10, 2006.

7. Joseph Stiglitz, quoted in Uchitelle (1998). See also Edwards (2004).

Chapter 11: Staying Neoliberal

1. See the collection of essays in Kehoe and Nicolini (2022).

2. See Edwards (2010, chap. 5).

3. Maclaury (1994), in Bosworth, Dornbusch, and Labán (1994, vii).

4. Castells described Chile's strategy as based on export orientation, with extensive liberalization of external and domestic markets and an efficient modernization of the production process. See the interview in Breslin (2007).

5. Mitchell and Morriss (2012).

6. Barro (1992). See also Navia (2009); and Ortúzar (2022).

7. For Freedom House's global freedom ranking, see Freedom House (2022). For the *Economist*'s ranking, see Economist Intelligence Unit (2021). In 2022, however, and as a result of the violence associated with the revolt, the *Economist* demoted Chile by one notch in its quality of democracy ranking; Economist Intelligence Unit (2022).

8. *El Desconcierto* (2016).

9. *El Mostrador* (2016).

10. Lagos (2020).

11. Comparing Chile's and other OECD countries' tax revenue is not straightforward, since in Chile there are no social security taxes. An interesting comparison is between Chile and New Zealand, a country that also does not have social security taxes. In the early 1980s, when New Zealand had the income per capita that Chile had in 2020, New Zealand's tax revenue was around 31 percent of GDP, a full 10 percentage points higher than Chile's.

12. *Cooperativa* (2005).

Chapter 12: Grievances, Abuses, Complaints, and Protests

1. Stott and Mander (2019).

2. UNDP (1998, 58); the report is titled *Paradoxes of Modernity: Human Security*. The idea of centering development policy around the concept of human security was first put forward by the UNDP in its 1994 global development report. Notably, in the 1994 report—as in 1998, on Chile—the concept is deliberately vague: "Several analysts have attempted rigorous definitions of human security. But like other fundamental concepts, such as human freedom, human security is more easily identified through its absence than its presence"; UNDP (1994, 23).

3. A total of thirteen quantitative variables were used in the computation of the objective measure. See UNDP (1998, 84, table 9).

4. This view was shared by some of Chile's most prominent public intellectuals, including philosopher Carlos Peña. See Peña (2020).

5. Brunner (1998). For an in-depth analysis of the reaction (and dismissal) of the *malestar* hypothesis by the Center-Left elite, see chapter 3 of Cavallo and Montes (2022).

6. González T. (2017, 17, 27, 118).

7. For an extensive and detailed account of collusion cases in the 2010s, see Garín González (2019); for abuses in the financial sector, see Schiappacasse and Tromben (2021).

8. Full disclosure: I was an expert witness in this case and testified in front of the court.

9. See Schiappacasse and Tromben (2021).

10. See OECD (2019) for an analysis of Chilean workers' skill deficiencies.

Chapter 13: The Distributive Struggle

1. Harberger (2016, 82–83).

2. Harberger (2020, 410).

3. Zimmerman (2019).

4. Harberger (2020, 410).

5. Johnson (1973, chaps. 17–18).

6. Schultz (1992, vii).

7. Stigler (1965, 284).

8. For a detailed exposition of these ideas, see Harberger (1984).

9. The proof of this proposition is very simple. All that is required are "indifference curves" that are convex from the origin.

10. Rolf Lüders, in Fuentes and Valdeavellano (2015, at 72:00).

11. The World Bank uses purchasing power parity or "international" dollars to define the poverty line.

12. Thorp (1998, 352).

13. R. Valdés (2021).

14. Thorp (1998, 352).

15. There are differences in the Gini coefficients calculated by different agencies and researchers. I will return to this issue at the end of this chapter.

16. UNDP (1998).

17. Anderson (1999).

18. OECD (n.d.-b).

19. All multilateral institutions report Gini coefficient values around 0.48 for the early 2020s; see WID (n.d.-b).

20. Flores et al. (2020, 853).

21. Flores et al. (2020, 864).

22. Al Harberger has always been very critical of these practices. A tax reform during Michelle Bachelet's administration restricted the use of these tax-reducing mechanisms.

23. Flores et al. (2020, 851).

24. See the disclaimer on the "Methodology" web page of the WID; WID (n.d.-a).

25. Larrañaga and Rodríguez (2014, 24).

Chapter 14: Broken Promises

1. Becker and Ehrlich (1994).

2. Becker (1999).

3. AFP stands for Administradoras de Fondos de Pensiones (Administrators of Pension Funds); they were founded in 1981 with the Pensions Law. See chapter 7 for its origins.

4. The social security reform took place in two rounds, in 1978 and 1980.

5. Blue-collar workers could retire at age sixty-five, and their vesting period was fifteen years. Anyone who contributed for less than that did not receive a pension, except for a minimal subsistence transfer. In contrast, retirement for workers in the banking industry was at age fifty-five, and the vesting period was thirteen years; for journalists it was at age fifty-five with a vesting period of ten years.

6. The most comprehensive historical analysis of the social security system was done by the Klein-Saks Mission (1958).

7. In June 1994, US Representative Christopher Cox wrote to Milton Friedman asking him about the Chilean pensions reform. Friedman answered that he had not written anything on the subject and suggested he talk to Al Harberger. Christopher Cox to Milton Friedman, June 1, 1994, MFAHI, Box 188-8; Milton Friedman to. Christopher Cox, June 2, 1994, MFAHI, Box 188-8.

8. Decreto Ley 2448 (1979).

9. The proposed pensions reform is explained in great detail in section G of chapter 2 of The Brick. The authors of the plan were Emilio Sanfuentes and Sergio Undurraga. Miguel Kast contributed from the University of Chicago, where he was studying at the time The Brick was being written.

10. Decreto Ley 3500 (1980).

11. Piñera (1992, 8). Pinochet is not mentioned even once in Piñera's text.

12. Piñera (1992, 18). A few paragraphs earlier, Piñera pointed out that given that this was a defined contribution system, it was not possible to make any "promises." That is, the 70 percent number came out of a simulation exercise. It did, however, become ingrained in peoples' minds.

13. Edwards and Edwards (2002).

14. Management fees at the time ranged from 0.6 percent to 1.5 percent of wages every month. A conversion of these fees into a percentage of assets under management indicated that, at this point, the average fee was around seventy basis points.

15. Full disclosure: In 2021, my wife, Alejandra Cox, became the president of the AFPs' business association.

16. For Apruebo Dignidad's platform for the 2021 presidential elections and its fifty-three "concrete measures," see Boric (2021).

Chapter 15: The Constitutional Convention and the Election of Gabriel Boric

1. The number of Indigenous seats was set firmly at seventeen, independently of how many people decided to use the Indigenous ballot. As it turned out, only 4.9 percent of voters opted for using the Indigenous ballots. This meant that Indigenous people were overrepresented in a proportion of two to one in the Convention: with 4.9 percent of the vote, they elected 12 percent

of the Convention. During the campaign for *apruebo* (approval) and *rechazo* (rejection), this became an important issue.

2. Hirschman (1958).

3. See Edwards (2015); and Díaz-Alejandro (1984, 113).

4. The ownership of pension savings accounts became a hotly debated issue during the campaign for the approval (or rejection) of the new constitution. Opponents of the new charter pointed out that if the proposal were enacted, workers would not really own their savings. Exit polls, after the exit plebiscite, indicated that this was an important consideration when deciding how to vote in the referendum. Given the people's preference for "owning" their retirement funds, the Boric administration made some (rather minor) changes to its pension reform plan. As of mid-September 2022, they are still considering putting an end to the Administradoras de Fondos de Pensiones (Administrators of Pension Funds).

5. Nicas (2022). One of the original members of the Convention resigned his post, making the active number 154 members.

6. *Economist* (2022b).

7. Stott (2022).

8. See Convención Constitucional (2022).

9. Articles 34, 58, and 79 of the proposed constitution.

10. *Economist* (2022a), emphasis added.

11. See Montes R. (2022).

12. See Malinowski (2022).

13. Dorfman (2022). In this article Dorfman decried the fact that the *rechazo* option won the referendum, and argued that in his view a new progressive constitution would help close Chile's open wounds.

Chapter 16: The End of Neoliberalism?

1. Stigler (1965, 284).

2. For analyses of Chile's development strategy and challenges, see, for example, De Gregorio (2004, 2006) and the literature cited therein.

3. Paulina Vodanovic, quoted in *La Segunda* (2022).

4. Centro de Estudios Públicos directors Harald Beyer and Leonidas Montes slowly moved the center back to policy evaluation, including poverty alleviation and distributive issues.

5. McCloskey (2006, 2010, 2016).

6. Fukuyama (2022).

Appendix

1. See Foucault (2008, lectures 9–11).

2. Becker (1978, 14), emphasis in the original. The book includes a revised version of a number of scholarly articles published by Becker since 1955.

3. There is an extremely large literature on Foucault and neoliberalism. Some of the most significant contributions are Audier (2012, 2015); Newheiser (2016); Garrett (2019); and the nine essays in Zamora and Behrent (2016). See also the bibliographies in these works.

4. See Behrent (2009), which is reproduced as chapter 2 in Zamora and Behrent (2016).

5. Foucault's analysis of the role of *homo œconomicus* in Becker's work is (mostly) in lecture 11 of *The Birth of Biopolitics*. For Ewald's interpretation of Foucault, see Becker, Ewald, and Harcourt (2012).

6. Becker, Ewald, and Harcourt (2012, 4–6).

7. Foucault died in 1984, and never met Becker or corresponded with him.

8. Becker, Ewald, and Harcourt (2012, 16).

9. Sánchez García (2014).

10. Rosenstein-Rodan (1974, 7).

11. Foucault (2008, 217).

12. Those who were invited, but couldn't attend, included José Ortega y Gasset and Lionel Robbins.

13. Reinhoudt and Audier (2018, 9).

14. Lippmann (1937, 227).

15. Lippmann (1937, 207–208).

16. Louis Rougier, in Reinhoudt and Audier (2018, 93–94).

17. Walter Lippmann, in Reinhoudt and Audier (2018, 103–104).

18. Reinhoudt and Audier (2018, 77).

19. Ludwig von Mises, in Reinhoudt and Audier (2018, 121).

20. Reinhoudt and Audier (2018, 187).

21. Jackson (2010, 133).

22. Jacob Viner made important contributions to price theory, applying Marshallian price theory as a tool for understanding the market economy; see Irwin and Medema (2013); and Irwin (2018).

23. The English translation became available in 2008; see Foucault (2008).

24. The academic literature had, as I have noted in the Introduction and Appendix, used the term to refer to a particular form of capitalism since the 1930s.

25. The three articles from the 1970s refer to Constantine Mitsotakis and the Greek elections.

26. Oliver (1960, 117).

27. Friedrich (1955, 509).

28. Friedrich Hayek, quoted in *El Mercurio* (1981).

BIBLIOGRAPHY AND ARCHIVAL SOURCES

Archives

Biblioteca del Congreso Nacional de Chile Archive, Santiago, https://www.bcn.cl/portal/

Biblioteca Nacional de Chile Archive, Santiago

Collected Works of Milton Friedman, Hoover Institution Library and Archives (MFAHI), Stanford, CA. A select number of items in this archive are available online, https://miltonfriedman.hoover.org/collections_

Historical Archive, Pontificia Universidad Católica de Chile (HAPUC), Santiago

Memoria Chilena Archive, Biblioteca Nacional de Chile, Santiago, https://www.memoriachilena.cl/602/w3-channel.html

Mont Pèlerin Society Archives, Hoover Institution Library and Archives, Stanford, CA

National Security Archive (NSA), Washington, DC

Senator Pedro Ibáñez Archive, Universidad Adolfo Ibáñez, Santiago, Chile

Other Sources

Altamirano, C. 1977. *Dialéctica de una derrota*. México: Siglo Veintiuno Editores.

Anderson, E. S. 1999. "What Is the Point of Equality?" *Ethics* 109(2): 287–337.

Arancibia Clavel, P., and Balart Páez, F. 2007. *Sergio de Castro: El arquitecto del modelo económico chileno*. Santiago, Chile: Editorial Biblioteca Americana.

Arbildúa, B., and Lüders, R. 1968. "Una evaluación comparada de tres progamas anti-inflacionarios en Chile: Una década de historia monetaria: 1956–1966." *Cuadernos de economía*, no. 14: 25–105.

Audier, S. 2012. *Néo-libéralisme(s), une archéologie intellectuelle*. Paris: Grasset.

———. 2015. "Neoliberalism through Foucault's eyes." *History and Theory* 54(3): 404–418.

Bailey, M. J. 1962. "Construction and Inflation: A Critical Scrutiny." *Economic Development and Cultural Change* 10(3): 264–274.

———. 1968. "Comment: Optimum Monetary Growth." *Journal of Political Economy* 76(4), pt. 2, 874–876.

Ballesteros, M., and Ballesteros, M. 1965. "Desarrollo agricola chileno, 1910–1955." *Cuadernos de economía*, no. 5: 7–40.

Banco Central de Chile. 2001. *Indicadores económicos y sociales de Chile: 1960–2000*. Santiago, Chile: Banco Central de Chile.

Baraona, P. n.d. "Entrevistas en Archivo Universidad Finis Terra." Centro de Investigación y Documentación, Universidad Finis Terrae.

Barro, R. J. 1992. "To Avoid Repeats of Peru, Legalize Drugs." *Wall Street Journal*, April 27, 1992.

Barro, R. J., and Gordon, D. B. 1983. "Rules, Discretion and Reputation in a Model of Monetary Policy." *Journal of Monetary Economics* 12(1): 101–121.

Becker, G. S. 1976. *The Economic Approach to Human Behavior*. Chicago: University of Chicago Press.

———. 1992. "Gary Becker: Biographical." Web page, Nobel Prize. https://www.nobelprize.org/prizes/economic-sciences/1992/becker/facts/.

———. 1999. "Economic Dimensions of the Family." Presented at the Economic Dimensions of the Family conference, Madrid, September 1, 1999.

Becker, G. S., and Ehrlich, I. 1994. "Social Security: Foreign Lessons." *Wall Street Journal*, March 30, 1994.

Becker, G. S., Ewald, F., and Harcourt, B. E. 2012. "'Becker on Ewald on Foucault on Becker': American Neoliberalism and Michel Foucault's 1979 'Birth of Biopolitics' Lectures; A Conversation with Gary Becker, François Ewald, and Bernard Harcourt." University of Chicago Institute for Law and Economics Olin Research Paper No. 614 / University of Chicago Public Law Working Paper No. 401.

———. 2013. "'Becker and Foucault on Crime and Punishment': A Conversation with Gary Becker, François Ewald, and Bernard Harcourt; The Second Session." University of Chicago Public Law and Legal Theory Working Paper No. 440.

Behrent, M. C. 2009. "Liberalism without Humanism: Michel Foucault and the Free-Market Creed, 1976–1979." *Modern Intellectual History* 6(3): 539–568.

Beyer, H. 1995. "Logros en pobreza, ¿frustración en la igualdad?" *Estudios públicos*, no. 60, 15–33.

Bhagwati, J. N., ed. 2002. *Going Alone: The Case for Relaxed Reciprocity in Freeing Trade*. Cambridge, MA: MIT Press.

Boeninger, E. 1992. "Agenda programática para el segundo gobierno de la Concertación: Marco general tentativo, aporte para los partidos." Papeles de Trabajo, Programa de Estudios Prospectivos No. 1, Santiago, Chile.

Boric, G. 2021. "Programa de Gobierno Apruebo Dignidad." Boric Presidente. Apruebo Dignidad. Chile.

Bosworth, B. P., Dornbusch, R., and Labán, R. 1994. "The Chilean Economy: Policy Lessons and Challenges: Introduction." In *The Chilean Economy: Policy Lessons and Challenges*, edited by B. P. Bosworth, R. Dornbusch, and R. Labán, 1–28. Washington, DC: Brookings Institution.

Bray, J. O. 1962. "Demand, and the Supply of Food in Chile." *Journal of Farm Economics* 44(4): 1005–1020.

———. 1966. "Mechanization and the Chilean Inquilino System: The Case of Fundo 'B.'" *Land Economics* 42(1): 125–129.

———. 1967. "Profit Margins in Chilean Agriculture: A Rejoinder." *Land Economics* 43(2): 250–252.

Breslin, B. 2007. "Democracy and the Chilean Miracle." *Berkeley Review of Latin American Studies*, Fall 2007, 3–6.

Brunner, J. J. 1998. "Malestar en la sociedad chilena: ¿De qué, exactamente, estamos hablando?" *Estudios públicos*, no. 72: 173–198.

Bruno, M., Di Tella, G., Dornbusch, R., and Fischer, S., eds. 1988. *Inflation Stabilization: The Experience of Israel, Argentina, Brazil, Bolivia, and Mexico.* Cambridge, MA: MIT Press.

Büchi Buc, H. 1993. *La transformación económica de Chile: Del estatismo a la libertad económica.* Colombia: Grupo Editorial Norma.

Caldwell, B. 2011. "The Chicago School, Hayek, and Neoliberalism." In *Building Chicago Economics: New Perspectives on the History of America's Most Powerful Economics Program*, edited by R. Van Horn, P. Mirowski, and T. A. Stapleford, 301–334. New York: Cambridge University Press.

Caldwell, B., and Montes, L. 2015. "Friedrich Hayek and His Visits to Chile." *Review of Austrian Economics* 28(3): 261–309.

Calvo, G. A., and Végh, C. A. 1994. "Inflation Stabilization and Nominal Anchors." *Contemporary Economic Policy* 12(2): 35–45.

Cámara de Diputados de Chile. 1973. "Acuerdo de la Cámara de Diputados de Chile." August 22, 1973. https://www.liberalismo.org/articulo/298/60/acuerdo/camara/diputados/.

CASEN (Encuesta de Caracterización Socioeconómica Nacional). n.d. "Encuesta CASEN." Ministerio de Desarrollo Social y Familia. Web page. http://observatorio.ministeriodesarrollo social.gob.cl/encuesta-casen.

Cavallo, A., and Montes, R. 2022. *La historia oculta de la década socialista: 2000–2010.* Santiago, Chile: Uqbar Editores.

Cavallo, A., Salazar, M., and Sepúlveda, O. 1989. *La historia oculta del régimen militar: Memoria de una época, 1973–1988.* Santiago, Chile: Ediciones La Epoca.

Central Intelligence Agency. 1973. Classified message, March 14, 1973. https://foia.state.gov /documents/PCIA3/000099F6.pdf.

Clements, K. W., and Tcha, M. 2004. "The Larry Sjaastad Letters, Volume 2." Economics Discussion / Working Papers 04-16. Department of Economics, University of Western Australia, Perth.

Collier, S., and Sater, W. F. 1996. *A History of Chile, 1808–1994.* Cambridge: Cambridge University Press.

Comisión Asesora Presidencial sobre el Sistema de Pensiones. 2015. *Informe final: Comisión Asesora Presidencial sobre el Sistema de Pensiones 2015.* 1st ed. Santiago, Chile: Ministerio del Trabajo y Previsión Social.

Comisión Nacional de Verdad y Reconciliación. 1991. *Informe de la Comisión Nacional de Verdad y Reconciliación.* Santiago, Chile: Corporación Nacional de Verdad y Reconciliación.

Convención Constitucional. 2022. *Propuesta constitución política de la república de Chile.* Santiago, Chile: Convención Constitucional.

Cooperativa. 2005. "Lagos afirmó que reforma a la constitución supone 'un día de alegría.'" *Cooperativa*, August 16, 2005. https://www.cooperativa.cl/noticias/pais/politica/reformas -constitucionales/lagos-afirmo-que-reforma-a-la-constitucion-supone-un-dia-de-alegria /2005-08-16/125118.html.

Corbo, M., and Yver, R. 1967. "Estimación de la función de producción agrícola en la zona del Maule-Norte." *Cuadernos de economía*, no. 11: 48–64.

Cortazar, R. 1997. "Chile: The Evolution and Reform of the Labor Market." In *Labor Markets in Latin America: Combining Social Protection with Market Flexibility*, edited by S. Edwards and N. Lustig, pt. 2, chap. 8. Washington, DC: Brookings Institution Press.

Corvalán, R. 1962. "La UC tercia en polémica del dólar." *Ercilla*, no. 1421: 8–9.

Cristi, R. 2021. *La tiranía del mercado: El auge del neoliberalismo en Chile*. Santiago, Chile: LOM Ediciones.

Datos.gob. n.d. "Buscador de datos de matrícula (parvularia, básica y media)." Gob Digital Chile. Web page. https://datos.gob.cl/dataset/buscador-de-datos-de-matricula.

Davis, N. 1985. *The Last Two Years of Salvador Allende*. Ithaca, NY: Cornell University Press.

Davis, T. E. 1963. "Eight Decades of Inflation in Chile, 1879–1959: A Political Interpretation." *Journal of Political Economy* 71(4): 389–397.

De Castro, S. 1965. "Política cambiaria: ¿Libertad o controles?" *Cuadernos de economía*, no. 5: 53–60.

———. 1969. "Política de precios." *Cuadernos de economía*, no. 17: 34–40.

———. 1972. "Programa de Desarrollo Económico y Social." Documento de Trabajo No. 8, Instituto de Economía, Pontificia Universidad Católica de Chile, Santiago, Chile.

———. 1978. "Ministro Sergio de Castro esboza el curso de la economía chilena." *Boletín mensual Banco Central de Chile*, October 1978, 1675–1702.

———. 1981. *Exposición sobre el estado de la hacienda pública*. Santiago, Chile: Ministerio de Hacienda.

———. 1992. *El ladrillo: Bases de la política económica del gobierno militar chileno*. Santiago, Chile: Centro de Estudios Públicos.

Decreto Ley 520. 1932. Decreto Ley 520: Crea el Comisariato General de Subsistencias y Precios. Congreso Nacional de Chile, August 31, 1932.

Decreto Ley 2448. 1979. Decreto Ley 2448: Modifica regimenes de pensiones que indica. Ministerio de Hacienda de Chile, February 19, 1979.

Decreto Ley 3500. 1980. Decreto Ley 3500: Establece nuevo sistema de pensiones. Congreso Nacional de Chile, November 13, 1980.

De Gregorio, J. 2004. "Economic Growth in Chile: Evidence, Sources, and Prospects." Central Bank of Chile Working Papers No. 298, Central Bank of Chile, Santiago, Chile.

———. 2006. "Economic Growth in Latin America: From the Disappointment of the Twentieth Century to the Challenges of the Twenty-First." Central Bank of Chile Working Papers No. 377, Central Bank of Chile, Santiago, Chile.

Délano, M. 1999. "Un militar chileno revela que el piloto de Pinochet arrojó al mar a detenidos para hacerlos desaparecer." *El País*, June 25, 1999. https://elpais.com/diario/1999/06/26/internacional/930348014_850215.html.

———. 2011. "Chile reconoce a más de 40.000 víctimas de la dictadura de Pinochet." *El País*, August 20, 2011. https://elpais.com/diario/2011/08/20/internacional/1313791208_850215.html.

Dellas, H., and Tavlas, G. S. 2018. "Milton Friedman and the Case for Flexible Exchange Rates and Monetary Rules." *Cato Journal* 38(2): 361–377.

De Onis, J. 1970. "Allende, Chilean Marxist, Wins Vote for Presidency." *New York Times*, September 6, 1970.

Díaz, J., Lüders, R., and Wagner, G. 2016. *Chile 1810–2010: La república en cifras; Historical statistics.* Santiago, Chile: Ediciones Universidad Católica de Chile.

Díaz-Alejandro, C. F. 1984. "Comment." In *Pioneers in Development,* edited by G. M. Meier and D. Seers, 112–114. New York: Oxford University Press / World Bank.

Dirección de Presupuestos. n.d. "Empresas Públicas." Gobierno de Chile. Web page. http://www.dipres.gob.cl/599/w3-channel.html.

Dorfman, A. 2022. "Chileans Rejected the New Constitution, but They Still Want Progressive Reforms." *Guardian,* September 6, 2022.

Dornbusch, R., and Edwards, S., eds. 1991. *The Macroeconomics of Populism in Latin America.* Chicago: University of Chicago Press.

ECLAC (Economic Commission for Latin America and the Caribbean). n.d. "CEPALSTAT Statistical Databases and Publications." ECLAC—United Nations. Web page. https://statistics.cepal.org/portal/cepalstat/index.html?lang=en.

Economist. 2022a. "Latin America's Vicious Circle Is a Warning to the West." *Economist,* June 16, 2022. https://www.economist.com/leaders/2022/06/16/latin-americas-vicious-circle-is-a-warning-to-the-west.

————. 2022b. "Common Sense Prevails as Chileans Reject a New Constitution." *Economist,* September 5, 2022. https://www.economist.com/the-americas/2022/09/05/common-sense-prevails-as-chileans-reject-a-new-constitution.

Economist Intelligence Unit. 2021. *Democracy Index 2020: In Sickness and in Health?* London: Economist Intelligence Unit.

————. 2022. *Democracy Index 2021: The China Challenge.* London: Economist Intelligence Unit.

Edwards, S. 1975. "Tipo de cambio sombra y protección efectiva: Un cálculo basado en la metodología del tipo de cambio de equilibrio bajo libre comercio." *Cuadernos de economía,* no. 12: 127–144.

————. 2004. "Financial Openness, Sudden Stops, and Current Account Reversals." *American Economic Review* 94(2): 59–64.

————. 2010. *Left Behind: Latin America and the False Promise of Populism.* Chicago: University of Chicago Press, June 2010.

————. 2015. "Economic Development and the Effectiveness of Foreign Aid: A Historical Perspective." *Kyklos* 68(3): 277–316.

————. 2019. "On Latin American Populism, and Its Echoes around the World." *Journal of Economic Perspectives* 33(4): 76–99.

————. 2020. "Milton Friedman and Exchange Rates in Developing Countries." NBER Working Paper 27975, National Bureau of Economic Research, Cambridge, MA.

Edwards, S., and Edwards, A. C. 1991. *Monetarism and Liberalization: The Chilean Experiment.* Chicago: University of Chicago Press.

————. 2002. "Social Security Privatization and Labor Markets: The Case of Chile." *Economic Development and Cultural Change* 50(3): 465–489.

Edwards, S., and Lederman, D. 2002. "The Political Economy of Unilateral Trade Liberalization: The Case of Chile." In *Going Alone: The Case for Relaxed Reciprocity in Freeing Trade,* edited by J. Bhagwati, 337–393. Cambridge, MA: MIT Press.

Edwards, S., and Montes, L. 2020. "Milton Friedman in Chile: Shock Therapy, Economic Freedom, and Exchange Rates." *Journal of the History of Economic Thought* 42(1): 105–132.

El Desconcierto. 2016. "Los empresarios aman a Lagos: 5 millonarios que ya han manifestado su apoyo al ex presidente." *El Desconcierto,* November 10, 2016. https://www.eldesconcierto.cl /nacional/2016/11/10/los-4-millonarios-que-ya-han-manifestado-su-apoyo-a-ricardo-lagos .html.

El Mercurio. 1973. "Primer comunicado de la junta militar." *El Mercurio,* September 13, 1973.

———. 1981. "Friedrich von Hayek: De la servidumbre a la libertad." *El Mercurio,* April 19, 1981.

———. 2018. "Los efectos del dólar a 39 pesos." *El Mercurio,* September 30, 2018.

El Mostrador. 2016. "Gabriel Boric: 'Ricardo Lagos es el generador del malestar que hoy atraviesa Chile.'" *El Mostrador,* September 2, 2016. https://www.elmostrador.cl/noticias/pais/2016 /09/02/gabriel-boric-ricardo-lagos-es-el-generador-del-malestar-que-hoy-atraviesa-chile/.

Emmett, R. B., ed. 2010. *The Elgar Companion to the Chicago School of Economics.* Cheltenham, UK: Edward Elgar.

Ercilla. 1981. "Una visita oportuna." *Ercilla,* November 25, 1981.

Fermandois, J. 2013. *La revolución inconclusa: La izquierda chilena y el gobierno de la Unidad Popular.* Santiago, Chile: Centro de Estudios Públicos.

Fischer, K. 2009. "The Influence of Neoliberals in Chile before, during, and after Pinochet." In *The Road from Mont Pèlerin,* edited by P. Mirowski and D. Plehwe, 305–346. Cambridge, MA: Harvard University Press.

Fischer, S. 2001. "Exchange Rate Regimes: Is the Bipolar View Correct?" *Journal of Economic Perspectives* 15(2): 3–24.

Flores, I., Sanhueza, C., Atria, J., and Mayer, R. 2020. "Top Incomes in Chile: A Historical Perspective on Income Inequality, 1964–2017." *Review of Income and Wealth* 66(4): 850–874.

Fontaine, E. R. 1967. "Inflación, devaluación y desarrollo económico." *Cuadernos de economía,* no. 11: 75–79.

———. 2009. *Mi visión.* Santiago, Chile: Instituto Democracia y Mercado, Universidad del Desarrollo.

Fontaine, J. A. 1989. "The Chilean Economy in the Eighties: Adjustment and Recovery." In *Debt, Adjustment and Recovery: Latin America's Prospects for Growth and Development,* edited by S. Edwards and F. Larraín, chap. 8. Oxford: Basil Blackwell.

Fontaine Aldunate, A. 1988. *Los economistas y el presidente Pinochet.* Santiago, Chile: Zig-Zag.

Foucault, M. 2004. *Naissance de la biopolitique: Cours au Collège de France, 1978–1979.* Paris: Éditions du Seuil / Gallimard.

———. 2008. *The Birth of Biopolitics: Lectures at the Collège de France, 1978–1979.* Edited by M. Senellart. Translated by G. Burchell. Basingstoke, UK: Palgrave Macmillan.

Foxley, A. 1982. *Experimentos neoliberales en América Latina.* Colección Estudios CIEPLAN, Número Especial. Santiago, Chile: CIEPLAN.

———. 1984. *Latin American Experiments in Neoconservative Economics.* Berkeley: University of California Press.

Frank, A. G. 1976. "Capitalismo y genocidio económico, carta abierta a la Escuela de Economía de Chicago a propósito de su intervención en Chile." Colección Lee y Discuta, Serie V, No. 67. Bilbao, Spain: ZERO.

Freedom House. 2022. *Freedom in the World 2022: The Global Expansion of Authoritarian Rule.* Washington, DC: Freedom House.

Friedman, M. 1951. "Neo-liberalism and Its Prospects." *Farmand,* February 17, 1951, 89–93.

———. 1953. "The Case for Flexible Exchange Rates." In *Essays in Positive Economics,* 157–203. Chicago: University of Chicago Press.

———. 1973. *Money and Economic Development: The Horowitz Lectures of 1972.* New York: Praeger.

———. 1975. *Milton Friedman en Chile: Bases para un desarrollo económico.* Santiago, Chile: Fundación de Estudios Económicos BHC.

———. 1994. *Money Mischief: Episodes in Monetary History.* New York: Harcourt Brace Jovanovich.

———. 1995. "Monetary System for a Free Society." In *Monetarism and the Methodology of Economics,* edited by K. D. Hoover and S. M. Sheffrin, 167–177. Cheltenham, UK: Edward Elgar.

Friedman, M., and Friedman, R. D. 1998. *Two Lucky People: Memoirs.* Chicago: University of Chicago Press.

Friedman, M., and Mundell, R. 2001. "One World, One Money?" *Policy Options / Options Politiques* 22(4): 10–19.

Friedrich, C. J. 1955. "The Political Thought of Neo-liberalism." *American Political Science Review* 49(2): 509–525.

Fuentes, C., and Valdeavellano, R., dirs. 2015. *Chicago Boys.* Documentary. Santiago, Chile: La Ventana Cine, 2015. Video, 85:00. https://vimeo.com/ondemand/chicagoboysenglish.

Fukuyama, F. 2022. "Putin's War on the Liberal Order." *Financial Times,* March 3, 2022.

García, N. 1972. "Algunos aspectos de la política de corto plazo de 1971." In *La economía chilena en 1971,* edited by Instituto de Economía, 47–270. Santiago, Chile: Universidad de Chile.

Garín González, R. 2019. *La gran colusión: Libre mercado a la chilena.* Santiago, Chile: Catalonia.

Garrett, P. M. 2019. "Revisiting 'The Birth of Biopolitics': Foucault's Account of Neoliberalism and the Remaking of Social Policy." *Journal of Social Policy* 48(3): 469–487.

Gerstle, G. 2021. "The Age of Neoliberalism Is Ending in America. What Will Replace It?" *Guardian,* June 28, 2021.

———. 2022. *The Rise and Fall of the Neoliberal Order: America and the World in the Free Market Era.* New York: Oxford University Press.

Gertz, G., and Kharas, H. 2019. "Introduction: Beyond Neoliberalism in Emerging Markets." In *Beyond Neoliberalism: Insights from Emerging Markets,* edited by G. Gertz and H. Kharas, 7–16. Washington, DC: Brookings Institution.

González, M. 2000. *Chile, la conjura: Los mil y un días del golpe.* Santiago, Chile: Ediciones B.

González T., R., coordinator. 2017. *Informe Encuesta CEP 2016: ¿Malestar en Chile?* Santiago, Chile: Centro de Estudios Públicos.

Goodwin, C. D. 2014. *Walter Lippmann: Public Economist.* Cambridge, MA: Harvard University Press.

Guardian. 1975. "A New Twist in Chile Crisis." *Guardian,* April 16, 1975.

Hachette A. de la F., D. 2000. "Privatizaciones: Reforma estructural pero inconclusa." In *La transformación económica de Chile,* edited by F. Larraín B. and R. Vergara M., 111–153. Santiago, Chile: Centro de Estudios Públicos.

———. 2016. "La genesis de la 'Escuela de Chicago': Fines de los cincuenta y de los sesenta." In *La Escuela de Chicago*, edited by F. Rosende R., 29–65. Santiago, Chile: Ediciones UC.

Hammond, J. D. 2013. "Markets, Politics, and Democracy at Chicago: Taking Economics Seriously." In *Building Chicago Economics: New Perspectives on the History of America's Most Powerful Economics Program*, edited by R. van Horn, P. Mirowski, and T. A. Stapleford, 36–64. New York: Cambridge University Press.

Handler, B. 1975. "Conditions Still Grim for the Poor—Chile's Economy Improves." *Washington Post*, November 28, 1975.

Harberger, A. C. 1950. "Currency Depreciation, Income, and the Balance of Trade." *Journal of Political Economy* 58(1): 47–60.

———. 1963. "The Dynamics of Inflation in Chile." In *Measurement in Economics: Studies in Mathematical Economics and Econometrics in Memory of Yehuda Grunfeld*, edited by C. Christ, 219–250. Stanford, CA: Stanford University Press.

———. 1964. "The Measurement of Waste." *American Economic Review* 54(3): 58–76.

———. 1971. "Three Basic Postulates for Applied Welfare Economics: An Interpretive Essay." *Journal of Economic Literature* 9(3): 785–797.

———. 1972. "Survey of Literature on Cost-Benefit Analysis for Industrial Project Evaluation." Paper prepared for the Inter-regional Symposium in Industrial Project Evaluation, Prague, October 1965. In *Project Evaluation*, 23–69. Chicago: University of Chicago Press.

———. 1976. *Cuatro momentos de la economía chilena*. Santiago, Chile: Fundación de Estudios Económicos BHC.

———. 1984. "Basic Needs versus Distributional Weights in Social Cost-Benefit Analysis." *Economic Development and Cultural Change* 32(3): 455–474.

———. 2000. "Documento: Memorándum sobre la economía chilena." *Estudios Públicos*, no. 77: 399–418.

———. 2016. "Sense and Economics: An Oral History with Arnold Harberger." Unpublished manuscript, interviews conducted by Paul Burnett, 2015–2016. Oral History Center, Bancroft Library, University of California–Berkeley.

———. 2020. "What Happened in Chile?" In *A Special Meeting: The Mont Pelerin Society, 1980–2020; From the Past to the Future: Ideas and Actions for a Free Society*, edited by J. B. Taylor, 409–410. Stanford, CA: Hoover Institution, Stanford University.

Harberger, A. C., and Edwards, S. 2021. "The Department of Economics at the University of Chicago, 1947–1982." Documentos de Trabajo No. 788, Universidad del CEMA, Buenos Aires.

———. Forthcoming. "The Department of Economics at the University of Chicago, 1947–1982." In *The Palgrave Companion to Chicago Economics*, edited by R. A. Cord, 3–22. New York: Palgrave Macmillan.

Harvey, D. 2005. *A Brief History of Neoliberalism*. Oxford: Oxford University Press.

Hirschman, A. O. 1958. *The Strategy of Economic Development*. New Haven, CT: Yale University Press.

———. 1963. "Inflation in Chile." In *Journeys toward Progress: Studies of Economic Policy-Making in Latin America*," edited by A. Hirschman, 159–223. New York: Twentieth Century Fund.

INE (Instituto Nacional de Estadísticas). n.d. Homepage. https://www.ine.cl/.

Infante, R., and García-Huidobro, G. 1972. "Metodologías para determinar estructuras de consumo esencial y no esencial." *Nueva economía*, January–April 1972, 56–80.

Inostroza, A. 1971. "El programa monetario y la política de comercio exterior de la Unidad Popular." *Panorama económico*, February–March 1971, 8–10.

International Monetary Fund. n.d. "World Economic Outlook Database." Web page. https://www.imf.org/en/Publications/SPROLLS/world-economic-outlook-databases#sort=%40imfdate%20descending.

Irwin, D. A. 2018. "The Midway and Beyond: Recent Work on Economics at Chicago." *History of Political Economy* 50(4): 735–775.

———. 2019. "The Missing Bretton Woods Debate over Flexible Exchange Rates." In *The Bretton Woods Agreements*, edited by N. Lamoureaux and I. Shapiro, 56–74. New Haven, CT: Yale University Press.

Irwin, D. A., and Medema, S. G. 2013. "Introduction." In *Jacob Viner: Lectures in Economics 301*, edited by D. A. Irwin and S. G. Medema, 1–18. New Brunswick, NJ: Transaction.

Jackson, B. 2010. "At the Origins of Neo-liberalism: The Free Economy and the Strong State, 1930–1947." *Historical Journal* 53(1): 129–151.

Johnson, H. G. 1969. "The Case for Flexible Exchange Rates, 1969." *Review* (Federal Reserve Bank of St. Louis) 51: 12–24.

———. 1972. "The Monetary Approach to Balance-of-Payments Theory." *Journal of Financial and Quantitative Analysis* 7(2): 1555–1572.

———. 1973. *The Theory of Income Distribution*. London: Gray-Mills.

———. 1977. "The Monetary Approach to the Balance of Payments." *Journal of International Economics* 7(3): 251–268.

Junta de Gobierno. 1973. Acta Junta No. 1; Secreto. Junta de Gobierno, Republica de Chile, September 13, 1973. https://obtienearchivo.bcn.cl/obtienearchivo?id=recursoslegales/10221.3/34263/1/acta1_1973.pdf.

Kandell, J. 1976. "Chile, Lab Test for a Theorist." *New York Times*, March 21, 1976.

Kehoe, T. J., and Nicolini, J. P., eds. 2022. *A Monetary and Fiscal History of Latin America, 1960–2017*. Minneapolis: University of Minnesota Press.

Kissinger, H. A. 1979. *The White House Years*. Boston: Little, Brown.

Klein, N. 2010. "Milton Friedman Did Not Save Chile." *Guardian*, March 3, 2010.

Klein-Saks Mission. 1958. "The Chilean Stabilization Program and the Work of the Klein and Saks Economic and Financial Mission to Chile." Unpublished manuscript, Santiago, Chile.

Korry, E. M. 1970. "Backchannel Message from the Ambassador to Chile (Korry) to the Under Secretary of State for Political Affairs (Johnson), the President's Assistant for National Security Affairs (Kissinger), and the Chief of Station in Santiago." September 26, 1970. In *Foreign Relations of the United States, 1969–1976*, vol. E-16, *Documents on Chile, 1969–1973*. Washington, DC: US GPO. https://history.state.gov/historicaldocuments/frus1969-76ve16/d26.

Lagos, R. 2020. *Mi vida: Memorias II; Gobernar para la democracia*. Santiago, Chile: Debate.

Larraín, F., and Meller, P. 1991. "The Socialist-Populist Chilean Experience, 1970–1973." In *The Macroeconomics of Populism in Latin America*, edited by R. Dornbusch and S. Edwards, 175–221. Chicago: University of Chicago Press.

Larraín B., F., and Vergara M., R., eds. 2000. *La transformación económica de Chile*. Santiago, Chile: Centro de Estudios Públicos.

Larrañaga, O., and Rodríguez, M. E. 2014. "Desigualdad de ingresos y pobreza en Chile 1990." Working paper, United Nations Development Programme, New York.

La Segunda. 1981. "Friedman: Intervención 'fuera del libreto.'" *La Segunda*, November 20, 1981.

———. 2022. "Ante desfavorable escenario, Boric se abre al apruebo para reformar." *La Segunda*, June 29, 2022.

La Tercera. 1981. "Milton Friedman y la economía chilena." *La Tercera*, November 18, 1981.

———. 2003. "Las 24 horas que estremecieron a Chile." *La Tercera*, August 24, 2003.

———. 2019. "El triunfo de Patricio Aylwin 30 años después." *La Tercera*, December 14, 2019.

Letelier, O. 1976. "The 'Chicago Boys' in Chile: Economic Freedom's Awful Toll." *Nation*, August 28, 1976, 137–142.

Lewis, A. 1975. "For Which We Stand: II." *New York Times*, October 2, 1975.

Ley 16640. 1967. Ley 16640: Reforma agraria. Congreso Nacional de Chile, July 28, 1967.

Ley 19070. 1991. Ley 19070: Aprueba estatuto de los profesionales de la educación. Congreso Nacional de Chile, June 27, 1991.

Lippmann, W. 1937. *The Good Society*. Boston: Little, Brown.

Loayza, N., Fajnzylber, P., and Calderón, C. 2005. *Economic Growth in Latin America and the Caribbean: Stylized Facts, Explanations, and Forecasts*. Washington, DC: World Bank.

Lüders, R. 1969. "El sistema tributario chileno: Algunos comentarios." *Cuadernos de economía*, no. 17, 41–58.

———. 2022. "La universalización de los subsidios sociales es una quimera, si el país desea seguir creciendo y combatiendo la pobreza." Ex-Ante, January 11, 2022. https://www.ex-ante .cl/rolf-luders-la-universalizacion-de-los-subsidios-sociales-es-una-quimera-si-el-pais -desea-seguir-creciendo-y-combatiendo-la-pobreza/.

Magasich Airola, J. 2020. *Historia de la Unidad Popular: De la elección a la asunción; Los álgidos 60 días del 4 de septiembre al 3 de noviembre de 1970*. Vol. 2. Santiago, Chile: LOM Ediciones.

Malinowski, M. 2022. "At 36, World's Youngest Leader Boric Electrifies UN Assembly." *Bloomberg*, September 20, 2022.

Marshall, A. 1890. *Principles of Economics*. Vol. 1. London: Macmillan, 1890.

Martin, E. G. 1982. "Frayed Miracle." *Wall Street Journal*, January 18, 1982.

Matus G., M., and Reyes C., N. 2021. "Precios y salarios en Chile, 1886–2009." In *Historia económica de Chile desde la Independencia*, edited by M. Llorca-Jaña and R. Miller, 677–724. Santiago, Chile: Ril Editores.

McCloskey, D. N. 2006. *The Bourgeois Virtues: Ethics for an Age of Commerce*. Chicago: University of Chicago Press.

———. 2010. *Bourgeois Dignity: Why Economics Can't Explain the Modern World*. Chicago: University of Chicago Press.

———. 2016. *Bourgeois Equality: How Ideas, Not Capital or Institutions, Enriched the World*. Chicago: University of Chicago Press.

Meller, P. 1996. *Un siglo de economía política chilena (1890–1990)*. Santiago, Chile: Editorial Andres Bello.

Mendez, J. C., ed. 1979. *Chilean Economic Policy*. Santiago, Chile: Ministerio de Hacienda.

Ministerio de Hacienda. n.d. "Estado de la Hacienda Pública." Gobierno de Chile. Web page. https://www.hacienda.cl/areas-de-trabajo/presupuesto-nacional/estado-de-la-hacienda-publica.

Mitchell, D. J., and Morriss, J. 2012. "The Remarkable Story of Chile's Economic Renaissance." *Daily Caller*, July 18, 2012. https://dailycaller.com/2012/07/18/the-remarkable-story-of-chiles-economic-renaissance/.

Molina, S., Donoso, Á., Llona, A., Baeza, S., and Kast, M. 1974. "Mapa de la Extrema Pobreza en Chile." Documento de Trabajo No. 29, Instituto de Economía, Pontificia Universidad Católica de Chile, Santiago, Chile.

Montecinos, V., Markoff, J., and Alvarez-Rivadulla, M. J. 2009. "Economists in the Americas: Convergence, Divergence and Connection." In *Economists in the Americas*, edited by V. Montecinos and J. Markoff, 1–62. Cheltenham, UK: Edward Elgar.

Montes, L. 2016. "Milton Friedman y sus visitas a Chile." *Revista de Estudios Públicos*, no. 141: 121–171.

Montes R., R. 2022. "El expresidente Lagos propone que el proceso constituyente de Chile continúe tras el plebiscito." *El País*, July 5, 2022. https://elpais.com/chile/2022-07-05/el-expresidente-lagos-propone-que-el-proceso-constituyente-de-chile-continue-tras-el-plebiscito.html.

Morán, R. 1969. "Hacia una formula antiinflacionaria abrupta." *Cuadernos de economía*, no. 17: 19–33.

Myrdal, G. 1968. *Asian Drama: An Inquiry into the Poverty of Nations*. 3 vols., with continuous pagination. New York: Pantheon.

Navia, P. 2009. "The Chilean Left: Socialist and Neoliberal." In *Beyond Neoliberalism in Latin America? Societies and Politics at the Crossroads*, edited by J. Burdick, P. Oxhorn, and K. M. Roberts, 17–42. New York: Palgrave Macmillan.

Navia, P., and Osorio, R. 2015. "Las encuestas de opinión pública en Chile antes de 1973." *Latin American Research Review* 50(1): 117–139.

Nelson, E. 2020. "The Continuing Validity of Monetary Policy Autonomy under Floating Exchange Rates." *International Journal of Central Banking* 16(2): 81–123.

Newheiser, D. 2016. "Foucault, Gary Becker and the Critique of Neoliberalism." *Theory, Culture and Society* 33(5): 3–21.

Newsweek. 1990. "Interview with Alejandro Foxley." *Newsweek*, March 26, 1990.

New York Times. 1975. "Two Years of Pinochet." *New York Times*, September 22, 1975.

———. 1985. "Chilean Police Battle 300 Demonstrators." *New York Times*, April 1, 1985.

Nicas, J. 2022. "Chile Says 'No' to Left-Leaning Constitution after 3 Years of Debate." *New York Times*, September 6, 2022.

Novitski, J. 1970a. "Allende, Marxist Leader, Elected Chile's President." *New York Times*, October 25, 1970.

———. 1970b. "Military Leader Dies in Santiago." *New York Times*, October 26, 1970.

O'Brien, T. F. 2007. *The Making of the Americas: The United States and Latin America from the Age of Revolutions to the Era of Globalization*. Albuquerque: University of New Mexico Press.

OECD (Organisation for Economic Co-operation and Development). 2019. *Skills Matter: Additional Results from the Survey of Adult Skills*. Paris: OECD.

————. n.d.-a. "Program for International Student Assessment (PISA), 2000, 2003, 2006, 2009, 2015, and 2018. Reading, Mathematics and Science Assessments." Web page. https://www .oecd.org/pisa/data/.

————. n.d.-b. "OECD Better Life Index." Web page. https://www.oecdbetterlifeindex.org/# /11111111111.

————. n.d.-c. "Income Inequality." OECD Data. Web page. https://data.oecd.org/inequality /income-inequality.htm.

Oliver, H. M., Jr. 1960. "German Neoliberalism." *Quarterly Journal of Economics* 74(1): 117–149.

Ortúzar, P. 2022. "Por un octubre sin octubrismo." *La Tercera,* July 3, 2022.

Panorama económico. 1970. "Documentos." *Panorama económico,* August 1970, 13–31.

Patinkin, D. 1973. "Frank Knight as Teacher." *American Economic Review* 63(5): 787–810.

Peña, C. 2020. *Pensar el malestar: La crisis de octubre y la cuestión constitucional.* Santiago, Chile: Editorial Taurus.

Piñera, J. 1992. *El cascabel al gato.* Santiago, Chile: Zig-Zag.

Pinochet, A. 1979. "Mensaje presidencial: 11 septiembre 1978–11 septiembre 1979." Memoria Chilena, Biblioteca Nacional de Chile. http://www.memoriachilena.gob.cl/602/w3-article -82405.html.

Pinto, A. 1957. "La industrialización y el profesor Rottenberg." Editorial. Santiago, Chile: *Panorama económico,* November 1957, 734–736.

Quiroga Z., P. 2001. *Compañeros: El GAP; La escolta de Allende.* Santiago, Chile: Aguilar.

Reinhoudt, J., and Audier, S. 2018. *The Walter Lippmann Colloquium: The Birth of Neoliberalism.* New York: Palgrave Macmillan.

Robinson, J. 1933. *The Economics of Imperfect Competition.* London: Macmillan.

Rojas, A. 1986. "Extrema pobreza: Concepto, cuantificación y características." *Estudios Públicos,* no. 24, 151–161.

Rosenstein-Rodan, P. N. 1974. "Why Allende Failed." *Challenge* 17(2): 7–13.

Sánchez García, A. 2014. "Chile y el MIR: Carta abierta a Mauricio Rojas." in *El blog de Montaner,* a blog by C. A. Montaner, October 19, 2014. http://www.elblogdemontaner.com/chile -y-el-mir-carta-abierta-mauricio-rojas/.

Sandel, M. J. 2012. *What Money Can't Buy: The Moral Limits of Markets.* New York: Farrar, Straus and Giroux.

————. 2018. "Populism, Liberalism, and Democracy." *Philosophy and Social Criticism* 44(4): 353–359.

San Francisco, A., ed. 2019a. *Historia de Chile 1960–2010.* Vol. 5, *Las vías chilenas al socialismo: El gobierno de Salvador Allende (1970–1973), Primera Parte.* Santiago, Chile: CEUSS/Universidad San Sebastián.

————, ed. 2019b. *Historia de Chile 1960–2010.* Vol. 6, *Las vías chilenas al socialismo: El gobierno de Salvador Allende (1970–1973). Segunda Parte.* Santiago, Chile: CEUSS / Universidad San Sebastián.

Schauer, F. 2014. "Constitutions of Hope and Fear." *Yale Law Journal* 124(2): 528–562.

Schiappacasse, I., and Tromben, C. 2021. *Todo legal: Los grandes zarpazos de la elite financiera chilena 1973–2021.* Santiago, Chile: Planeta.

Schultz, T. W. 1956. "Latin-American Economic Policy Lessons." In "Papers and Proceedings of the Sixty-Eighth Annual Meeting of the American Economic Association," special issue, *American Economic Review* 46(2): 425–432.

———. 1964. *Transforming Traditional Agriculture*. New Haven, CT: Yale University Press.

———. 1992. "Foreword." In *Combating Poverty: Innovative Social Reforms in Chile during the 1980s*, edited by T. Castañeda, vii–viii. San Francisco: ICS Press.

Select Committee to Study Governmental Operations with Respect to Intelligence Activities. 1975. *Covert Action in Chile 1963–1973: Staff Report of the Select Committee to Study Governmental Operations with Respect to Intelligence Activities*. Washington, DC: US GPO.

Sengupta, S. 2021. "Chile Writes a New Constitution, Confronting Climate Change Head On." *New York Times*, December 29, 2021.

Shultz, G. P., and Taylor, J. B. 2020. "Why Choose Economic Freedom? An Opening Conversation." In *A Special Meeting: The Mont Pelerin Society, 1980–2020; From the Past to the Future: Ideas and Actions for a Free Society*, edited by J. B. Taylor, 6–13. Stanford, CA: Hoover Institution, Stanford University.

Sistema de Empresas. n.d. "SEP Chile." Gobierno de Chile. Web page. https://www.sepchile.cl/.

Sjaastad, L. A. 1983. "Failure of Economic Liberalism in the Cone of Latin America." *The World Economy* 6(1): 5–26.

Sjaastad, L. A., and Cortés Douglas, H. 1978. "El enfoque monetario de la balanza de pagos y las tasas de interés real en Chile." *Estudios de economía*, no. 5: 3–68.

Smith, A. 1977. *An Inquiry into the Nature and Causes of the Wealth of Nations*. Edited by E. Cannan. Chicago: University of Chicago Press.

Soto, A. 2003. *El Mercurio y la difusión del pensamiento político neoliberal 1955–1970*. Chile: Centro de Estudios Bicentenario.

Steel, R. 1999. *Walter Lippmann and the American Century*. New York: Routledge.

Stigler, G. J. 1965. *The Theory of Price: Revised Edition*. New York: Macmillan.

———. 1988. *Memoirs of an Unregulated Economist*. New York: Basic Books.

Stiglitz, J. E. 2002. "Commanding Heights: Joseph Stiglitz." Interview on PBS online. https://www.pbs.org/wgbh/commandingheights/shared/minitextlo/int_josephstiglitz.html.

Stott, M. 2022. "Chile's Rejection of Populism Is an Example for the World." *Financial Times*, September 5, 2022.

Stott, M., and Mander, B. 2019. "Chile President Sebastián Piñera: 'We Are Ready to Do Everything to Not Fall into Populism.'" *Financial Times*, October 17, 2019.

Subsecretaría de Educación Superior. n.d. "Informes de Matrícula en Educación Superior." Ministerio de Educación Superior. Web page. https://www.mifuturo.cl/informes-de-matricula/.

Sulzberger, C. L. 1975. "The Worst of Both Worlds." *New York Times*, November 26, 1975.

Tax, S. 1963. *Penny Capitalism: A Guatemalan Indian Economy*. Chicago: University of Chicago Press.

Tavlas, G. S. 2022. "'The Initiated': Aaron Director and the Chicago Monetary Tradition." *Journal of the History of Economic Thought* 44(1):1–23.

Thatcher, M. 1982. Margaret Thatcher to Friedrich Hayek, February 17, 1982. Margaret Thatcher Foundation Archive. https://c59574e9047e61130f13-3f71d0fe2b653c4f00f32175760e96e7.ssl.cf1.rackcdn.com/3D5798D9C38443C6BD10B1AB166D3CBF.pdf.

Thorp, R. 1998. *Progress, Poverty and Exclusion: An Economic History of Latin America in the 20th Century.* Washington, DC: Inter-American Development Bank, 1998.

Uchitelle, L. 1998. "Ounces of Prevention for the Next Crisis." *New York Times,* February 1, 1998.

UNDP (United Nations Development Programme). 1994. *Human Development Report 1994: New Dimensions of Human Security.* New York: United Nations Development Programme.

———. 1998. *Paradoxes of Modernity: Human Security.* New York: United Nations Development Programme.

———. 2017. *Desiguales: Orígenes, cambios y desafíos de la brecha social en Chile.* New York: United Nations Development Programme.

———. 2019. *Human Development Report 2019: Beyond Income, beyond Averages, beyond Today; Inequalities in Human Development in the 21st Century.* New York: United Nations Development Programme.

———. n.d. "UNDP: Reports and Publications." United Nations Development Programme. Web page. https://hdr.undp.org/.

Universidad Finis Terrae, Centro de Investigación y Documentación. n.d. "Archivo CIDOC." Web page. https://cidoc.uft.cl/archivo-cidoc/.

Valdés, J. G. 1989. *La escuela de Chicago: Operación Chile.* Buenos Aires: Grupo Editorial Zeta.

———. 1995. *Pinochet's Economists: The Chicago Boys in Chile.* Cambridge: Cambridge University Press.

Valdés, R. 2021. "Impuestos en Chile: Datos y comparaciones esenciales." Mimeo. Escuela de Gobierno, Pontificia Universidad Católica de Chile, Santiago, Chile.

Valenzuela, A. 1978. *The Breakdown of Democratic Regimes: Chile.* Baltimore: Johns Hopkins University Press.

Vanek, J. 1970. *The General Theory of Labor-Managed Market Economies.* Ithaca, NY: Cornell University Press.

Van Horn, R., Mirowski, P., and Stapleford, T. A., eds. 2011. *Building Chicago Economics: New Perspectives on the History of America's Most Powerful Economics Program.* New York: Cambridge University Press.

Varsavsky, O., and Calcagno, A. E., eds. 1971. *América Latina: Modelos matemáticos.* Santiago, Chile: Editorial Universitaria.

Velasco, A., and Parrado, E. 2012. "The Political Economy of Fiscal Policy: The Experience of Chile." In *The Oxford Handbook of Latin American Political Economy,* edited by Javier Santiso and Jeff Dayton-Johnson, 68–85. New York: Oxford University Press.

Viner, J. 1932. "Cost Curves and Supply Curves." *Zeitschr. f. Nationalökonomie* 3: 23–46.

Vuskovic, P. 1973. "The Economic Policy of the Popular Unity Government." In *The Chilean Road to Socialism: Proceedings of an ODEPLAN-IDS Round Table, March 1972,* edited by J. A. Zammit, 49–57. Austin: University of Texas Press.

Wallace-Wells, B. 2021. "Larry Summers versus the Stimulus." *New Yorker,* March 18, 2021.

Washington Post. 1970. "General Is Shot in Chile." *Washington Post,* October 23, 1970.

WID (World Inequality Database). n.d.-a. "Methodology." Web page. https://wid.world /methodology/.

———. n.d.-b. "Top 1% Net Personal Wealth Share." Web page. https://wid.world/world /#shweal_p99p100_z/US;FR;DE;CN;ZA;GB;WO/last/eu/k/p/yearly/s/false/13 .167999999999997/100/curve/false/country.

———. n.d.-c. "Top 10% Net Personal Wealth Share." Web page. https://wid.world/world /#shweal_p90p100_z/US;FR;DE;CN;ZA;GB;WO/last/eu/k/p/yearly/s/false/38.508 /125/curve/false/country.

World Bank. n.d. "World Development Indicators." Web page. https://datatopics.worldbank .org/world-development-indicators/.

YouTube. 2010. "Milton Friedman Interrupted by Left-Wing Activist at the Nobel Prize Ceremony." YouTube video, 0:30, September 27, 2010. https://www.youtube.com/watch?v =QwQioAwm-FI.

Zamora, D., and Behrent, M. C., eds. 2016. *Foucault and Neoliberalism.* Malden, MA: Polity Press.

Zauschquevich, A., and Sutulov, A. 1975. *El cobre chileno.* Santiago, Chile: Corporación del Cobre.

Zimmerman, S. D. 2019. "Elite Colleges and Upward Mobility to Top Jobs and Top Incomes." *American Economic Review* 109(1): 1–47.

INDEX

Acceso Universal a Garantías Explícitas
(AUGE; Universal Access to Explicit
Guarantees), 195

Adenauer, Konrad, 13, 110

Administradoras de Fondos de Pensiones
(AFPs; Administrators of Pension Funds):
Alejandra Cox and, 310n15; critics of,
251–52, 311n4; government owned AFP,
250, 310n14; pension reform and, 239–43,
246; Pensions Law, 310n3; popular
capitalism, 156, 161, 306n4; private
pensions and, 237; self-managed pensions,
244–45

agricultural economics: Allende policies, 56,
114; Chicago Boys plans, 90; economists
and, 28, 31; farmland expropriation, 57–58,
299n20; *inquilinos* and, 221; overvalued
currency and, 45; protectionism and,
297n20, 301n22; study of, 44

Ahumada, Jorge, 44

Alchian, Armen, 133

Alessandri, Jorge, 40–42, 48–51, 75, 89, 297n15,
304n7, 305n2

Alexander, Robert J., 150

Allende, Salvador, 58*fig*, 300n3; Aylwin and,
180; Constitution (1980) and, 131; criticism of, 285; deposed in coup d'état, 1–2,
32, 66, 71–73, 76, 78–79, 169, 228, 298n26;
economic program of, 56; election of,
50–54, 67, 298n6; fear of Cuba, 51; Frei
Montalva and, 184; inflation impact, 61;
land redistribution and, 89; nationalization of mines, 129; nationalization plans,
53, 57–58, 157; policies failure, 68, 108, 113;
presidency of, 48, 55, 64, 278; suicide of,
73–74, 269; unemployment and, 104.
See also Partido Socialista de Chile

Allende administration: agricultural economics and, 45; cabinet ministers of, 54,
61; education policies of, 205; El Ladrillo
and, 75; Flores and, 172; Navy officers and,
47; privatization after, 120

Allende years: economic conditions, 44,
61–65; following Cuba, 63

Altamirano, Carlos, 54, 299n13

American Economic Review, 31

Andean Pact, 86, 114–15

Anderson, Elizabeth, 11, 15, 230

Aninat, Eduardo, 185–86

Apruebo Dignidad (Approval and Dignity),
6, 252

Artigas, Alejandro, 73–74

Asian Drama (Myrdal), 46

assassinations: DINA agents, 107, 172; Letelier,
72, 106–7, 111–12, 303n1; Pinochet arrest,
308n6; Pinochet junta and, 2, 23, 101, 132;
Schneider, 67

Atria, Fernando, 255

Attanasio, Orazio, 248

Aylwin, Patricio and Aylwin administration,
184*fig*; Allende opponent, 180; cabinet
ministers of, 32, 36, 215, 267; Chicago
Boys' policies and, 16, 182–83; educational
policies, 191–94; inclusive neoliberalism
and, 22; national teachers' statute, 158;
neoliberal model, 203; Pinochet with a
human face, 199; presidency of, 125, 177,
179; privatization and, 196

A NOTE ON THE TYPE

This book has been composed in Arno, an Old-style serif typeface in the classic Venetian tradition, designed by Robert Slimbach at Adobe.